Researches on
the United States

Philip Mazzei in 1790. (Reprinted by permission
from Richard Cecil Garlick, Jr., *Philip Mazzei,
Friend of Jefferson: His Life and Letters*
[Baltimore: The Johns Hopkins Press, 1933])

*Philip Mazzei*

# Researches on
# the United States

Translated and edited by
Constance D. Sherman

University Press of Virginia
Charlottesville

Mazzei's *Researches on the United States*
is a publication of
the Thomas Jefferson Memorial Foundation.

THE UNIVERSITY PRESS OF VIRGINIA
Copyright © 1976 by the Rector and Visitors
of the University of Virginia

*First published 1976*

Library of Congress Cataloging in Publication Data

Mazzei, Filippo, 1730–1816.
    Researches on the United States.

    Translation of Recherches historiques et politiques sur les
États-Unis.
    Includes index.
    1. United States—History—Colonial period, ca. 1600–1775.
2. United States—History—Revolution, 1775–1783—Causes. 3.
United States—Politics and government—Colonial period, ca.
1600–1775. 4. Mably, Gabriel Bonnot de, 1709–1785. Observations sur le gouvernement et les loix des États-Unis de
l'Amérique. 5. Raynal, Guillaume Thomas François, 1713–1796.
Histoire philosophique et politique des établissemens et du
commerce des Européens dans les deux Indes. I. Title. E188.
M3913    1975    973.2    75-20037    ISBN 0-8139-0556-7

Printed in the United States of America

# Contents

Acknowledgments                                                    ix
Introduction                                                       xi

PART I

To the People of the United States of America                       1
Preface                                                             1
Introduction                                                        1
The Colonies Which Gave Birth to the Thirteen United
    States of America                           5
  The Founding of Virginia                                5
  The Founding of Massachusetts                          14
  The Founding of Rhode Island                           21
  The Founding of Connecticut                            24
  The Founding of New Hampshire                          25
  The Founding of Maryland                               27
  The Founding of New York                               29
  The Founding of New Jersey                             32
  The Founding of Pennsylvania and Delaware              33
  The Founding of the Two Carolinas and Georgia          43
  Conclusion                                             55
  The True Cause of the Revolution                       60
The Period between the Monarchy and the Republic                   65
  Virginia Separates from Great Britain                  72
Governments of the United States                                   78
  The Right to Vote and to Be a Representative           81
  The Legislative Power                                  86
  The Executive Power                                    89
  The Judiciary Power                                    91
  Conclusion                                             93
Notes A-C                                                          95
Observations Addressed to the Inhabitants of the United
    States                                    111

Part II   Reply to the *Observations* of Abbé Mably          115

Chapter 1   General Observations of Abbé Mably              117
Chapter 2   The Nature of the Governments and Character-
             istics of the Inhabitants of the United States    124
Chapter 3   Admission to Citizenship, Suffrage, etc.          127
Chapter 4   Constitutional and Common Legislative Power      130
Chapter 5   Liberty of the Press                             132
Chapter 6   The Rights of the Citizen in the Republic        135
Chapter 7   The Aristocratic Principles of Abbé Mably        139
Chapter 8   Administration and Education                     143
Chapter 9   Salaries, Entails, etc.                          146
Chapter 10  Justices of the Supreme Courts                   148
Chapter 11  Written Law and the Equity Tribunal             151
Chapter 12  Religious Liberty                                156
Chapter 13  The Revolutionary Period                         167
Chapter 14  The Confederation                                168
Chapter 15  The Dire Prognostications of Abbé Mably          172
Conclusion                                                   177
Notes D-I                                                    180


Part III   Observations on the *Philosophical History of the
            Two Indies* Relative to the United States of America   205

Chapter 1   Founding Period of the First Colonies            207
Chapter 2   New England                                      209
Chapter 3   New Jersey                                       216
Chapter 4   Pennsylvania                                     218
Chapter 5   William Penn                                     224
Chapter 6   The Quakers                                      230
Chapter 7   Maryland, Virginia, etc.                         235
Chapter 8   Climate, Soil, etc. of the United States         240
Chapter 9   The Behavior of France                           247
Chapter 10  American Behavior                                258
Chapter 11  Abbé Raynal's Counsel to France, Spain, and the
             United States                                     276
Chapter 12  Abbé Raynal's Contradictions                     279
Conclusion                                                   282
Notes K-M                                                    288

Part IV  Continuation of the Political Researches  295

Chapter 1  The So-Called Anarchy of the United States  297
Chapter 2  The So-Called Disagreement about the Division
of the States  300
Chapter 3  Paper Money  306
Chapter 4  The National Debt before and after the Revolu-
tion  312
Chapter 5  Private Debts and Commercial Credit  315
Chapter 6  Reasons for the Slow Development of Commerce
between France and the United States  318
Chapter 7  Immigration  325
Chapter 8  The Society of the Cincinnati  336
Chapter 9  General Washington and the Marquis de Lafay-
ette and the Society of the Cincinnati  340
Chapter 10  Slavery  344
Chapter 11  Savages  348
Chapter 12  Some Recent Books about the United States of
America and Maps of This Country  365
Notes N-R  376

Supplement  383

Index  405

# Acknowledgments

I am grateful to all those who assisted me in the preparation of this translation, particularly:

John Alden, Keeper of Rare Books, Boston Public Library
Whitfield J. Bell, Jr., Librarian, American Philosophical Society
Glenn H. Borders, Rare Book Division, Library of Congress
Maud Cole, Rare Book Division, New York Public Library
Elizabeth Cometti, West Virginia University
James Gregory, The New-York Historical Society
Jacob M. Price, Department of History, University of Michigan
Public Record Office, Chancery Lane, London
William M. E. Rachal, Editor of Publications, Virginia Historical Society
Robert A. Rutland, Papers of James Madison, University of Virginia
Hester Rich, Maryland Historical Society
Rutherford D. Rogers, University Librarian, Yale University
Dorothy Scutt
Nicholas B. Wainwright, Director, Pennsylvania Historical Society
Harold Whitmarsh
Shirley E. Welch, Reference Librarian, Maine Historical Society
Linda S. Winters, Connecticut State Library
Elaine Johnson Wyckoff
Sara C. Hixson and Kenneth Scott, who read the manuscript.

# Introduction

The Italian diplomat, philosopher, and critic Philip Mazzei was born in Tuscany on Christmas Day, 1730. Son of a lumberman, he was to become the friend of six rulers and to have a bowing acquaintance with six others. During the course of his adventurous career he lived in twenty cities and became a naturalized citizen of two countries, the United States of America and Poland. He wrote about the leaders of three revolutions, American, French, and Polish. Mazzei knew them all, for he hobnobbed with many of the most distinguished politicians and writers of his era.

The youngest of four children, Filippo did well in school, where he developed the habits of rising early and of drinking nothing but water. He also acquired a permanent distaste for cooked vegetables, a foible which did not prevent him from living to the ripe old age of eighty-six.

During Filippo's boyhood his favorite brother, Giuseppe, yielded to religious pressure and entered a Capuchin monastery. Shortly afterwards Giuseppe's fiancée became a nun, and they both died at an early age. This tragedy doubtless explains why Filippo became a champion of religious tolerance and, years later, with Jefferson in Virginia was to advocate separation of church and state.

For a time Filippo studied medicine in Florence at the Hospital of Santa Maria Nuova, but his elder brother, Jacopo, inherited the property upon the father's death and was loath to part with any of it. Filippo, realizing he could do nothing without money, went to Leghorn, practiced medicine for a time, and then was invited by a Jewish physician, Dr. Salinas, to go to Smyrna. He spent three years there (1752–55) and enjoyed "the undeserved reputation of being a great doctor." [1]

Although Dr. Salinas offered to renew the contract, Mazzei wanted a broader horizon, so in December 1755 he embarked for London as a ship's doctor on an English vessel sailing under letters

[1] Philip Mazzei, *Memoirs of the Life and Peregrinations of the Florentine Philip Mazzei, 1730–1816*, trans. Howard R. Marraro (New York: Columbia University Press, 1942), p. 79.

of marque. He took along supplies of opium, dried figs, and raisins, sold them at twice their cost, then ordered silks, cheeses, wine, and olive oil from Leghorn to establish a business in London.

As the venture prospered, Mazzei purchased a three-story house; he dwelt on the first floor and rented the other two. A paper-hanger named Joseph Martin occupied the top floor. Martin and his wife had one child; then another, very beautiful, baby girl was born. She died before she was a year old, and her father's death followed in several months. Mazzei, who had promised the dying man to care for the widow and the little girl, took a larger place in New Bond Street, with rooms for Mrs. Martin and her daughter. This shop was named for his brother-in-law, Martini, because Philip did not want his own name to be associated with trade; he was something of a snob.

In 1765 Mazzei went to Italy to purchase fine pearls for a Jewish firm in Mantua. Here, to his amazement, he was accused of having shipped from England a collection of banned books; the list in-cluded several by Voltaire and Rousseau, as well as a number of purely imaginary volumes. Mazzei was eventually exonerated, and this false charge was among the factors that led to the abolishment of the Inquisition in Tuscany. He wrote: "I became convinced, as I still am, that persecution will always be advantageous to a gentle-man if he has any knowledge of mankind and if he has the courage to defend himself." [2]

Shortly after Mazzei's return to London in 1767 he met Dr. Franklin, Thomas Adams of Virginia,[3] and other members of the American colony. They urged him to go to America to plant Italian grapes, and Adams wrote Thomas Jefferson, seeking to arouse his interest in the project. Since Mazzei had grown weary of the hypocrisy masked as democracy in His Majesty's government, he sailed for America from Leghorn on 2 September 1773. He took ten winegrowers and Mrs. Martin because Adams thought her little girl would have a better opportunity to find a husband in Virginia than in London.

Less than twenty-four hours after their arrival in Virginia, Jef-ferson provided Mazzei with two thousand acres adjoining Monti-

---

[2] Ibid. p. 147 and passim.

[3] Thomas Adams, born in New Kent County in 1730, moved to Augusta County in 1780 and died there in 1788. He signed the Virginia Association and represented Virginia in the Continental Congress 1777–80.

cello. Mazzei bought about seven hundred more, a hilltop, on which Jefferson's slaves built his estate, Colle, while he, Mrs. Martin, now Mrs. Mazzei, and her daughter stayed at Jefferson's home. This marriage, to which Philip had reluctantly agreed at the urging of Thomas Adams, was a mistake, for Mrs. Mazzei dedicated herself to making her husband completely miserable; she finally died in January 1788.

From the moment of his arrival in America, Mazzei was keenly interested in politics. He worked with Jefferson to gain liberty for the colonies, gave speeches, and wrote for the press. Mazzei says their articles were responsible for the establishment of the independent companies of volunteers in each county and, later, for the election of representatives to a colonywide convention.

Throughout the Revolution there was a desperate shortage of money, and in June 1779 Mazzei was dispatched as an envoy to seek funds from Grand Duke Leopold of Tuscany and other sources. On 19 October 1778 Jefferson wrote John Hancock: "Mr. Mazzei . . . possesses firstrate abilities [and] is pretty well acquainted with the European courts. . . . He is a native of Tuscany with good connections and I have seen certain proofs of the Grand Duke's personal regard for him. He has been a zealous whig from the beginning and I think may be relied on perfectly in point of integrity." [4] Unfortunately, Mazzei's ship, the *Johnston,* was captured by a British privateer before it got outside the Virginia capes; he was forced to throw his credentials overboard, and the duplicate copies, sent to Dr. Franklin in Paris, were not delivered to him for twenty months, because Franklin believed that the Confederation alone should have the prerogative of dealing with a foreign power. During the twenty-seven months Mazzei spent in Europe he did not receive a penny from the Virginia assembly; yet he did not want to borrow because he felt this would jeopardize American credit.

Although Mazzei had no official status in Europe, he wrote constantly for papers in both Italy and Holland; he also cultivated influential men, using every device he could invent to inculcate the idea that the American cause was just and that the colonies would be victorious in their struggle for independence.

A number of Mazzei's remarks on the political situation were

---

[4] Jefferson, *Papers of Thomas Jefferson,* ed. Julian P. Boyd et al. (Princeton, N.J. Princeton University Press, 1950—), 2:225.

extremely astute. On 19 April 1780, for example, he wrote Jefferson that the English seemed to be disregarding the Russian empress's dictum that the whole world should enjoy freedom of the seas: "I long to see how she will relish it. She certainly is not a lady to triffle with." [5] A month later, on May 20, he declared it would be impossible to conquer the British without superiority on the seas, and he devised a plan for bottling up the British fleet.

In June, when Mazzei learned of the surrender of Charleston, he commented: "Bad news has long legs," and it was he, without money, without status, who tried to console his friends. The Virginia assembly never took the trouble to notify him that Jefferson was no longer governor; so Mazzei continued writing to inform his friend of what was being said in Europe. Upon his return to Virginia, in November 1783, without having fulfilled his mission, he found at Monticello his letters and copies of some from Jefferson he had never received. He also discovered that Baron von Riedesel, a German prisoner of war who had been permitted to stay at Colle, had pastured his horses in the vineyards. In less than a week they had ruined the patient labor of five years, and Mazzei must have thought sadly of the horticultural plans he and Jefferson had formulated a decade before.

Mazzei hoped to be appointed a consul, but Congress wanted native Americans. Since Jefferson had gone to Paris as minister plenipotentiary, Mazzei went to France to be with him. He owned Colle and other property in Virginia and doubtless intended to return to America, but he never did so.

In Paris people were talking about Abbé Mably's book on the United States. Jefferson and Mazzei read it, and both were indignant that a man of his eminence should write a volume containing so many errors. After Mazzei wrote a humorous rebuttal for a dozen of his friends, the author Marmontel urged him to write a serious refutation because the French believed Mably. The other principal source of information about America at the time was a volume by the historian and philosopher Guillaume-Thomas François Raynal. That Jefferson did not admire Raynal either is apparent from a letter he sent M. Van Hogendorp on 25 August 1783: "With respect to the article 'Etats-Unis' of the 'Encyclopédie' now enclosed, I am far from making myself responsible for

---

[5] Howard R. Marraro, "Virginia's Agent in Europe," *Bulletin of the New York Public Library*, 38, no. 3 (Mar. 1934):263.

the whole of the article. The first two sections are taken chiefly from the Abbé Raynal, and they are therefore wrong in the same proportions. The other sections are generally right." He continued: "There will be another good work, a very good one, published here soon, by a Mr. Mazzei, who has been many years a resident of Virginia, is well informed, and possesses a masculine understanding."[6]

Mazzei wrote his book in Italian. It was then translated into French by a Norman deputy in Parliament, a young man named Faure, who asked if he might undertake it as a means of improving his Italian. Everyone was satisfied with his translation except the marquise de Condorcet, who translated the chapter on the Society of the Cincinnati, and her husband, who did the one on Washington and Lafayette in relation to the society. Jefferson supplied materials, including those he had used for his *Notes on Virginia*.

The *Researches* was hastily written, nearly a quarter of it blocked out in a month. There are, therefore, errors in the names of people and places which have been corrected in this edition as necessary. It must be stated, however, that Mazzei had no notion of writing a book when he left the United States, so he was forced to rely on his excellent memory and on the materials he could obtain in France or, to a limited extent, in England. The style is frequently careless, but Mazzei was thinking about the idea he wished to convey, not the form. Some passages are repetitive, moralizing, and full of digressions. In the present edition they have been abbreviated or, in several instances, such as the dedication, summarized. Notes by Mazzei are indicated in the text with asterisks; those by the translator are numbered. When Mazzei quotes a document, the original text has been used whenever possible.

Mazzei hoped to correct the false impressions caused by the two abbés and to make some money, for he could get nothing from his property in Virginia. Although the book helped disseminate democratic ideas in France on the eve of the Revolution, it was not popular because of what Bernard Fay has called its "lack of extravagance."[7] The *Dictionary of American Biography* says it is the most accurate work on America that had appeared in France,[8] but the French continued to read Raynal. Financially, the *Researches*

[6] Jefferson, *Papers of Jefferson*, ed. Boyd, 10:299.
[7] Fay, *L'Esprit révolutionnaire en France et aux Etats-Unis* (Paris: E. Champion, 1925), p. 136.
[8] S.v. "Mazzei, Philip."

was a fiasco, although the *Mercure de France* gave it an excellent review on 23 February 1788.[9]

The American Revolution had ruined Mazzei's horticultural achievements; the French Revolution forced him to leave France. In 1792 he went to Poland, where he served as adviser to King Stanislas and became a Polish citizen. When the second division of Poland brought an end to this period in his career, Mazzei returned to Italy, married Antonia Antoni, age twenty-two, and had a daughter, Elisabetta, in 1798. The baby was named for Mazzei's mother.

On 12 April 1802 Mazzei, at the age of seventy-two, set out on the long trip by stagecoach to Russia in order to collect from the czar the pension granted him by the Polish government. He wanted the money for his wife and little girl. Mazzei was also generous to his stepdaughter, the Martins' child, and her husband; he left them his estate, Colle.

An article in the *Richmond Enquirer* on Wednesday, 26 June 1816, tells of the death of Philip Mazzei in Pisa on 19 March 1816. The writer commented that Mazzei was a distinguished politician, an enemy of all tyrants, and a good judge of human nature. Completely devoted to the United States, he was proud to be an American citizen. Several weeks later Jefferson wrote Thomas Appleton and Giovanni Carmigniani stressing Mazzei's gift for loyal friendship.[10] Mazzei and Jefferson were friends for four decades, and Jefferson served as his executor.

That Philip Mazzei was a man of intelligence, tact, and charm is evident from his career. He began life as a physician, became a successful importer, a competent horticulturalist, and a good diplomat. A true cosmopolitan, he was at home in every country and every stratum of society. He turned a shrewd but benevolent gaze on the world of his day and depicted human frailties with both wit and candor. We see tolerance in such observations as: "No one has

---

[9] (Paris), pp. 149–65. The review stated that most writers on the American Revolution had been biased or had not known the true facts, but this U.S. citizen was well equipped to combat errors. A writer accustomed to studying men and full of respect for the rights of man, he was zealous for the progress of reason and general happiness. He witnessed many of the events he described and told the inhabitants of the Old World about his fears and hopes for his country. His object was to give as precise as possible a description of conditions in the United States, especially their governments.

[10] Jefferson, *The Writings of Thomas Jefferson*, ed. Paul L. Ford, 10 vols. (New York, 1892–99), 10:46, 49.

the right to criticize another country for its customs." There is pithy wisdom in "Foreign wars are the best remedy for domestic troubles," and "A population cannot increase if the citizens are unhappy." And this remark about criminals could have been penned yesterday: "The purpose of punishment is to correct men, not to exterminate them."

Mazzei was so deeply imbued with the spirit of democracy that he translated the Declaration of Independence into Italian and sent a copy to Grand Duke Leopold. His whole book, a hymn to freedom, expresses his conviction that the democratic ideal would triumph in the United States. He had tremendous faith in the future of his adopted country and believed that the United States, although not perfect, was closer to perfection than any government of the past. The future was bright.

# Historical and Political Researches
## on the
# United States of North America

In which there is a discussion of the establishment of the thirteen colonies, their relations to and quarrels with Great Britain, their governments before and after the Revolution, etc.

## By a Citizen of Virginia

With four letters on the unity of legislation by a native of New Heaven

Colle [Paris]
For sale in Paris
At Froullé's bookstore,
Quai des Augustins, on the corner of Rue Pavée
1788

# RECHERCHES

## HISTORIQUES ET POLITIQUES

# SUR LES ÉTATS-UNIS

### DE

## L'AMÉRIQUE SEPTENTRIONALE;

Où l'on traite des établiffemens des treize Colonies, de leurs rapports & de leurs diffentions avec la Grande-Bretagne, de leurs gouvernemens avant & après la révolution, &c.

## PAR UN CITOYEN DE VIRGINIE.

*Avec quatre Lettres d'un Bourgeois de New-Heaven fur l'unité de la légiflation.*

## A COLLE;

*Et fe trouve A PARIS,*

Chez FROULLÉ, libraire, quai des Auguftins, au coin de la rue Pavée.

### 1788.

# PART I

## To the People of the United States of America

[Summary] This book was written "to refute European prejudices about our governments and the present state of the union." The author's [1] observations about the state governments are based on the constitutions. In controversial matters he expresses his own opinion "as befits a citizen of a free country," and the volume closes with reflections dictated by his hope of seeing the governments improve.

## Preface

As most of this work was written, and some of it printed, in 1786, a supplement was necessary to acquaint the reader with some recent events of importance. This will make it apparent that the author's chief aim is to provide exact information about everything pertaining to the United States of America. The reader will thus be in a position to consider these states intelligently, to correct the infinite errors propagated through ignorance or a misunderstanding of policy, and to form reasonable opinions.

It should be observed that I use the word *people* in the sense of the whole nation, except in certain instances where I am distinguishing from the entire body of the citizenry that small number elected to conduct national affairs. Whenever I speak of the relationship between the nation and its administrators, the latter are not included in the word *people*. But where I speak of the people of Virginia, the people of Pennsylvania, etc., I refer to all the inhabitants of the state; hence it is possible to speak of the citizens, the inhabitants, or the people of the United States.

## Introduction

Since European attention was focused on the American Revolution, a number of writers hastened to treat such an interesting subject, and as each was eager to be first, he published his book before he could obtain adequate information.

[1] Mazzei does not use his name in the book.

Several turned the history of the Revolution into a novel. It has already been said that if the English general in M. d'Auberteuil's book had been called Hector and the American general Achilles, it would be the history of the Trojan War.[2]

Not long ago a three-volume work appeared pompously titled *Impartial History of the Military and Political Events of the Last War in the Four Areas of the World.*[3] It is a mass of inaccurate statements and geographical errors, but as I should have a lengthy list if I mentioned all those who have written with equal disregard of the facts, I shall confine my attention to those writers whose fame lends credence to their mistakes.

In describing us, Abbé Raynal does not seem to have displayed the accuracy upon which he prides himself.[4] We must assume he was too prone to believe anything that gave him an opportunity to be eloquent, and a well-informed reader, while admiring the warm and energetic tone with which the abbé frequently refers to truth, will wish that he had stuck to it.

Although Abbé Mably was, as he says, eager to be useful, he wrote his observations on the government and laws of the United States at a time of life ill suited for a careful study of new material.[5] It is not surprising, therefore, that his remarks are generally based on poor premises. If ignorance is preferable to error, we must admit that the current state of European opinion about America has deteriorated since the Revolution. And Abbé Mably's observations have contributed in large measure to consecrating the innumerable phantasies circulating throughout the continent to discredit the United States.

His reputation was established by a large number of books, all of which purported to be useful to mankind. At the very beginning of the American Revolution he spoke enthusiastically in favor of the United States and made the acquaintance of some of our

[2] Michel René Hilliard d'Auberteuil wrote two books on this period, *Essais historiques sur la révolution de l'Amérique septentrionale* (Brussels, 1782) and *Histoire de l'administration de Lord North et de la guerre de l'Amérique septentrionale jusqu'à la paix* (1784).

[3] [Pierre de Longchamps], *Histoire impartiale des événemens militaires et politiques de la dernière guerre dans les quatre parties du monde,* 3 vols. (Paris, 1785).

[4] Guillaume-Thomas François Raynal, *Histoire philosophique et politique des établissements et du commerce des Européens dans les deux Indes* (1770; later ed., 10 vols., Geneva, 1780).

[5] Gabriel Bonnot de Mably, *Observations sur le gouvernement et les loix des Etats-Unis d'Amérique* (Amsterdam, 1784).

most illustrious citizens in Paris. This is not all. Several months
before the publication of his observations, various gazettes stated
that Congress had requested Abbé Mably to propose a form of
government for the country. A letter from one of the most famous
writers of our day convinced me that this ridiculous story was
gaining ground.[6] The letter, dated 3 June 1783, begins: "People
are asking, sir, and they are important men in a distant land,
whether there is any truth in the rumor that the greatest republic
in the world, the United States of North America, has asked Abbé
Mably for his advice about the constitutive laws it should adopt.
If I considered only the laws of probability and my own opinion,
I should reply without hesitation that a country which has already
provided itself with a model government and with laws whose
wisdom and equity put to shame even the most enlightened nations does not need to seek aid elsewhere, etc." After telling me
what he thinks of the works of this same author, he closes, saying:
"I beg you, sir, to tell me what can have occasioned this boast and
what vague, inconsequential remark can Abbé Mably have taken
as a request from your republic to enlighten it about its laws."

I replied that by the year 1776 the states had formed their respective governments, that Congress was concerned only with matters
pertaining to the Confederation, and that it had no authority to
pass laws. It never occurred to one of the thirteen states to ask for
help from foreigners, even from its absent citizens, or to consult
them about the formation or revision of its government or the
preparation of a code of laws. I added that this rumor was false
but that I had been unable to persuade the abbé to disabuse the
public by writing to the gazetteer who had invented the story. His
silence lent credence to the assumption that he was not averse to
having people believe such a canard.

On my second trip from America to France, I saw Abbé Mably's
book. After announcing that he had read "with all possible attention the different constitutions of the United States of America,"
he referred to them as if he had seen an untrustworthy and confused account. Since his theories of government often are opposed
to true republican principles, he censures us in areas where we
have ensured a solid basis for liberty, while elsewhere he approves
the very acts wherein we have failed to guarantee it. In his first
letter he attributes to us merits we do not possess, and since he

---

[6] The translator has been unable to identify the author of this letter.

always professes enthusiastic support for our glory and prosperity, it was thought that he was prejudiced in our favor. This led readers to believe his unfavorable assertions about our present state and the future.

If his book had not appeared, it is probable that the pretended disorder, the pretended anarchy of the United States, and all the other lies printed in the English press would not have been believed, as they emanated from a country whose inhabitants are distorting every statement to malign the United States. But how can one doubt a writer who seems to take the greatest possible interest in us.* This is why his errors have had a greater impact than those of Abbé Raynal and why they require a more formal and detailed refutation. I shall not comment on books by less famous authors, especially those motivated by politics or vengeance.

My principal object is to give a precise and accurate account of the situation in the thirteen United States, especially with regard to their governments, and I shall refer to those historic events which may shed light on the subject.

I shall begin with a short description of the founding of the colonies in order to show their relations with Great Britain and to point out the real cause of the Revolution. There follows a brief discussion of the behavior of the colonies at a very interesting and highly critical period, the interval of about two years between the suspension of the royal government and the creation of the Republic. In describing the formation of the different governments, I shall try to give an adequate idea of their nature, and after commenting on the errors which escaped several famous writers in their books on our republics, I shall close with some observations of my own.

I hope that my reflections about the state governments will not offend. Every man should be interested in a good government, in whatever part of the world it may be, and he should do what he can to help create it.

The reader will not be surprised at the length of the two refutations when he sees that I took advantage of the opportunity afforded for discussion to make the subjects more interesting. Furthermore, these discussions may serve to correct the mistakes of other writers.

* The translator of Mably's remarks calls us "Abbé Mably's favorites."

# The Colonies Which Gave Birth to
# the Thirteen United States of America

Since a complete history of the founding of the colonies would have little interest for those who have no reason to examine all the details, a brief description of the beginnings and progress of these settlements will be sufficient. The most important criteria are the character of the original settlers and their relations with Great Britain. Among the founders we must not confuse fortune seekers with those who thought solely of liberty. A knowledge of the true character of the first immigrants will enable the reader to understand the conduct of their successors, and the facts will convince him that in recent times Europe has drawn its information about the United States and its inhabitants from novelists and gazetteers.

We shall not take into consideration the famous discovery made by Columbus, the voyages of Amerigo Vespucci, those of the Venetian Cabots based in Bristol, or various others made by English and French explorers who made no attempt at settlement. This book deals only with the colonies.

## The Founding of Virginia

As the English who established the colonies in North America were simple adventurers traveling at their own expense, the land they obtained by purchase or by conquest from the Indians should rightfully have been theirs. But Sir Walter Raleigh, who led the first expedition, obtained a charter from Queen Elizabeth on 25 March 1584 to forestall any claims that might be raised about his rights or those of his successors. This charter guaranteed Sir Walter and his heirs permanent sovereignty over the country he would occupy, together with the right to establish a legislative body and to form a government which, insofar as possible, was to resemble the government of England. And this country was to be united to England "in more perfect league and amitie." [7] These words give

---

[7] Rev. Increase Tarbox, *Sir Walter Raleigh and His Colony in America* (Boston, 1884), p. 99.

no implication of sovereignty on one side or subjection on the other.

Sir Walter immediately sailed with two vessels, took possession of all the land between lat. 25° and the Gulf of St. Lawrence and, since the queen was averse to marriage, named the country Virginia in her honor. He visited Roanoke Island, about lat. 36° between sandbanks and that body of water which, a century later, was named Albemarle Sound. But there is no evidence that he left anyone either on the island or on the continent. The following year he dispatched several vessels under command of Sir Richard Grenville,[8] who left 108 settlers on the island under the care of a certain Ralph Lane. Many of them perished through foolhardiness, and the following year the rest returned to England with the famous Admiral [Francis] Drake, who stopped at Roanoke after his expedition to the Spanish islands.

About this time Sir Walter Raleigh had left England with one vessel, and two weeks later Grenville set sail with three others on the same course. On the former's arrival at Cape Hatteras, he was unable to obtain any information about the 108 colonists; he then returned to England. Grenville found the island but could not learn what had happened to the settlers. He left fifty more, with provisions for two years, but all of them were murdered by the Indians.[9]

Some people claim that Raleigh never made the trip in person.[10] Whether this is true or not does not affect the basic facts.

In the summer of 1587 three other vessels arrived with several families and provisions. Raleigh appointed John White governor, gave him twelve assistants, and ordered him to settle on Chesapeake Bay, which he was probably unable to enter. This group was entitled The Governor and His Assistants in the City of Raleigh, Virginia.

The next year White returned to England to get recruits and supplies for the new colony. Raleigh equipped a fleet, which was about to set sail when the queen ordered it to join the vessels of the Royal Navy to do battle with the enormous Spanish Armada. Most

---

[8] Grenville, a relative of Sir Walter Raleigh, remained near Roanoke until 25 Aug. and returned to Plymouth 18 Oct. 1585.

[9] The next expedition, under John White, found no trace of the 15 (not 50) colonists who had remained at Roanoke in the summer of 1586.

[10] *Dictionary of National Biography*, s.v. "Raleigh, Walter," states that Elizabeth never permitted Raleigh to leave England, but that he led the way to the founding of the first English colony.

of the Spanish ships foundered on the English coast. White finally left two years later. The crossing was long and hard, and when he reached Cape Hatteras in August 1590, a violent gust of wind forced him to cut the cables and go out to the open sea. He was obliged to return to England without seeing the 115 settlers he had left on the island. The poor people were never heard from again.

White's departure from England was also delayed by Sir Walter's financial difficulties. In 1587 Raleigh already was feeling the effects of the large sums he had expended on these expeditions, and the queen's refusal to let his fleet sail was the last straw. He had spent more than £40,000 without receiving any assistance from the government, which at various times had placed a number of obstacles in his way. On 7 March 1589 * Raleigh granted Thomas Smith and others, in consideration of the sums they had supplied for the enterprise, "free trade and traffick for all manner of merchandize to and from Virginia, or any other part of America . . . free from all rents, customs and overcharges, except the fifth part of the oare of gold and silver, which he reserves to himself and his heirs." [11] He further stipulated with them and the other assistants that he would confirm the act of incorporation he had given them in 1587 with all the prerogatives, jurisdictions, rights, and privileges which the queen had granted him.†

As clarity and precision are not often characteristic of documents at this period, this concession has occasioned a great diversity of opinion among writers. In Raleigh's charter the queen had reserved one-fifth of the gold and silver, the amount Raleigh reserved in the pact he made with Smith and his associates. It would seem therefore that this one-fifth should be the queen's and not Raleigh's. The act of incorporation which he promises to confirm with the prerogatives, jurisdictions, etc. seems to indicate that he is renouncing all his rights. On the other hand, when Raleigh speaks of freedom of commerce in his new country, he appears to

* Several writers and printers have followed the old style in listing dates which precede the reform of the calendar; others have changed them, and several have not been accurate. It is probable therefore that there is an error of a year in any date between 1 January and 25 March. If this is the case, we beg the reader to excuse it for these reasons. [The date of this indenture is correct as given.]

† Abbé Raynal says, and this is highly inaccurate, "In 1584 the company formed on the basis of his magnificent promises obtained absolute rights over any future discoveries" (8:309, Geneva ed., *in*-8°).

[11] William Oldys, "The Life of Sir Walter Raleigh," in *The History of the World by Sir Walter Raleigh, Kt.* (London, 1786), 1:49.

set aside a large part for himself, although the only share specified is that of the queen. Colonel Richard Bland, in a sensible and scholarly paper on the rights of the colonies published in Virginia in 1766, says that Raleigh renounced his rights, and he makes no exception.[12] Several authors state that Raleigh made five other expeditions between 1590 and 1602. In any case, as Raleigh was put in jail at the beginning of the reign of James I, we know that he had nothing further to do with this enterprise.* It is also certain that if these five expeditions really set out, the men who took part must have met the same fate as those White left behind, for they vanished without a trace. James I, who cared very little about the rights of his subjects and much more about himself, gave Virginia to two companies in a new charter dated 10 April 1606.

It is claimed that Raleigh lost his rights in 1603 when he was sentenced, as if an English tribunal could exercise authority outside the jurisdiction of England. Furthermore, the cession made to Smith and his associates dates from 1589, and how could a sentence rendered fourteen years later affect them, even if the lands were in the same kingdom?

Some writers regard the 1606 charter as James I's confirmation of the company which had signed the contract with Raleigh. Others think he granted it to a group of new adventurers. The most likely assumption is that Thomas Smith and his associates, or his successors, joined forces with some other influential men and did not even attempt to dispute the satisfaction which a vain and capricious monarch, drunk with power, derived from trampling on Raleigh's prerogatives.

The charter was granted to two companies. The first, known as

---

* Raleigh was accused of having conspired against the king and was put in the Tower of London under a death sentence, although there was no proof of his crime. The king suspended execution but without pardoning him. In 1618, after Raleigh had spent 15 years in prison, he was permitted to leave the Tower but still was not acquitted. The king ordered him to command 12 vessels being sent to Guiana to seize what was said to be a fabulous gold mine. Upon his return from this fruitless expedition, Raleigh was decapitated on the old charge. Hume states in the sixth volume of his history that he was sacrificed to Spanish resentment. The king wanted to please the Spaniards because he was very anxious to obtain a Spanish princess for his elder son.

[12] "An Inquiry by Colonel Richard Bland, circa 14 March 1766," in William J. Van Schreeven, comp., and Robert L. Scribner, ed., *Revolutionary Virginia: The Road to Independence* (Charlottesville: University Press of Virginia, 1973–), 1:27–44.

the London Company, was ceded territory extending from lat. 34°
to lat. 41°. We shall discuss the Plymouth Company later.

The London Company made great efforts to establish a colony.
It sent Captain Newport[13] with a number of emigrants, including
several Poles and Hollanders. Newport arrived in early May 1607
between the capes through which Chesapeake Bay is entered.
Leaving the bay on his right, he continued inland about fifty miles
along the Powhatan River. He landed on a peninsula where, on his
return to England, he left some two hundred men.

Captain John Smith, called the Voyager, sailed for Roanoke,
where White had left 115 settlers. Finding himself between two
capes, he called the northern one Cape Charles and the southern
one Cape Henry, in honor of the king's sons. The Powhatan was
named the James River for the king, and the peninsula on which
the new inhabitants established their colony was called Jamestown
for the same reason.*

Colonel Bland reports that the company was eventually discouraged by the costs, as Sir Walter Raleigh had been, but new
associates contributed needed funds and it obtained a new charter.
That of 1606, in which Sir Thomas Gates and Sir George Somers[14]
head the list, was replaced by another dated 23 May 1609, in which
the earl of Salisbury[15] is named first. The title the Company had
given way to the Treasurer and the Company. James reserved for
himself one-fifth of the gold and silver, as Queen Elizabeth had
done, and almost all their successors followed suit.

According to the history of John Smith, who remained for
nineteen years in America and was for a time president of Virginia,
nine vessels with five hundred men were sent out in 1609 under
the command of Gates, Somers, and Captain Newport. The fleet

---

* A hundred and seventy-four years later, on 2 August 1781, French troops
under command of the marquis de Saint Simon landed on this same spot which
had become an island two or three years before. They were transported in a
large flotilla, thanks to which the Americans defeated the British army under
Cornwallis and restored calm in Virginia. I do not mean to imply that the flotilla
took part in the attack, for the location rendered any action impossible, but it
did prevent Cornwallis from escaping or receiving any reinforcements.

[13] Captain Christopher Newport made several voyages to Virginia and in 1609
brought out Sir Thomas Gates and Sir George Somers.

[14] Gates became governor of Virginia in 1611. Somers was elected admiral when
James I granted the charter to the London Company in 1609; he remained a member of the company.

[15] Robert Cecil, first earl of Salisbury.

was scattered by a gust of wind. Gates and Somers, who sought refuge in Bermuda with 150 of the shipwrecked men, constructed two small ships of cedar in which they set sail for Virginia 10 May 1610. They arrived on the twentieth. Sometime later they all re-embarked and would have abandoned the country entirely had they not met Lord Delaware [16] with three vessels containing everything they needed. I am omitting a whole series of anecdotes—I can only say that Smith's tale is so full of perilous adventures that one marvels at the fortitude of these early travelers.

For some time the company had been content to ship to Virginia administrators and destitute people to serve them. Had this system continued, a colony might never have been founded. Speculators had an erroneous concept of the country; instead of envisaging it as a sanctuary for liberty, they hoped it would be a source of great wealth, with mines of precious metals. Possibly they feared competition and wished to preserve a monopoly. As the savages had nothing to barter except furs, and as all the Europeans were working for the same company, commerce could compensate for only a very small fraction of the expenses. Fortunately for us, precious metals have never been found, and every loyal American must hope that nature did not poison this happy soil with them.

The members of the company finally realized that inasmuch as they were not going to settle in America, the only way to realize any profit would be to sell and rent land. In order to encourage immigrants, they rented it for a small portion of the yield. In 1617, according to the company registers, only fifty-four persons remained in its service; those who rented land carried to the warehouses four hundred bushels of Indian corn as their earnings for the year, and the price for tobacco was eighteen pence to three shillings a pound.

Because of this change in the system many partisans of liberty decided to go to the colonies. The arbitrary principles of James I also influenced their decision. In 1619 eleven vessels brought 1,216 men, women, and children to new homes along the banks of the James and York rivers.

The company government was neither stable nor suited to the ideas and the temperament of the immigrants. At times the head of the Virginia government was a president, then a treasurer, then a governor; power depended less on certain definitive laws than on

[16] Thomas West, third Baron De la Warr.

the character of the man at the helm. Among the associates were a number of noblemen, listed in a book published in 1620 by order of the treasurer and the council, when the treasurer was the earl of Southampton.[17] A society of nobles, knights, and merchants, interested only in profit, could not govern in a manner pleasing to those who had come solely to seek liberty. The lords regarded themselves as absolute masters and would acknowledge no restraints. The immigrants, therefore, began to assemble and deliberate as soon as they were sufficiently numerous. They named representatives to defend their rights and stated that all landowners had a right to vote.

On 24 July 1621 the company decreed that Virginia should have a legislative body, the General Assembly, consisting of a governor, twelve councillors, and the representatives of the people. The councillors and representatives were to make the laws, which the governor would have the power to approve or reject. These laws would not take effect until ratified by the company, but as soon as the colonial government was well established, company orders would no longer affect the colony without the consent of the General Assembly. The governor and councillors were appointed by the company, which could remove them at will.

This prompt change in the attitude of the company is not surprising in view of the fact that the people's representatives had met several months before and had determined to act. The immigrants were beginning to make serious distinctions between the rights of the natives and European claims. Most of the lands that the company ceded under certain conditions to immigrants had been purchased from the savages, while others had been obtained by peace treaties following various wars, or rather skirmishes, between the two parties. But the immigrants believed that they could purchase lands directly from their legitimate owners and that this method was both fairer and more profitable. The company therefore prudently granted what it could no longer hold, and a voluntary act preserved its sovereignty. If George III's ministers had been equally moderate, there would be no American liberty.

The company's sovereignty was of short duration. James I, who never lacked pretexts to support his claims, used force and legal tricks to deprive it of all the rights over the colony it had obtained by an expenditure of £100,000. The members of the company,

---

[17] Henry Wriothesley, third earl of Southampton. The book was *A Declaration of the State of the Colonie and Affaires in Virginia* (London, 1620).

who had never received any support whatsoever from the crown, were forced to yield. This did not affect the colonists, who were only concerned about their own rights and who, moreover, were not very happy about the company's rule. James took advantage of this attitude and used it as an excuse to take over the government. The new form of rule proposed by the king did not please the colonists either, and they protested until they were assured of all the rights they had held before the company's demise.[18]

James I thus became king of Virginia, as he was of England, although the two countries were quite different. The colonists liked their royal government so much that when, during the troubles between Parliament and the king, it was proposed to re-establish the company's charter with the authority of Parliament, the General Assembly opposed the idea in a solemn protest on 1 April 1642. It declared that anyone who tried to change the government would be considered an enemy of the country and that his property would be confiscated. Charles I therefore assured the colony that he would initiate no changes. The company's sovereignty wounded the colonists' pride, and recognition of parliamentary authority would have destroyed their liberty.

After Charles I was beheaded, Cromwell, who became a tyrant under the impressive title Protector of the Republic, was obliged to send a squadron of war vessels against the colony, which wanted to be ruled by the elder son of the late king. The colony was finally forced to yield but not until it had determined the articles of capitulation. The most important of these are:

FIRST, It is agreed and cons'ted that the plantation of Virginia, and all the inhabitants thereof, shall be and remaine in due obedience and subjection to the common wealth of England, . . . And that this submission and subscription bee acknowledged a voluntary act not forced nor constrained by a conquest upon the countrey, And that they shall have and enjoy such freedomes and priviledges as belong to the free borne people of England. . . .

2dly. Secondly, that the Grand Assembly as formerly shall convene and transact the affairs of Virginia. . . .

4thly. That Virginia shall have and enjoy the antient bounds and lymitts granted by the charters of the former Kings. . . .

7thly. That the people of Virginia have free trade as the people of England do enjoy to all places and with all nations. . . .

8thly. That Virginia shall be free from all taxes, customes and im-

---

[18] From 1624 to 1639 the General Assembly met almost every year, although there is no indication that the king approved these assemblies.

positions whatsoever, and none to be imposed on them without consent of the Grand Assembly, And soe that neither fortes nor castles bee erected or garrisons maintained without their consent.[19]

The commissioners of Parliament signed Virginia's capitulation on 12 March 1651, and it was then confirmed by Cromwell in England. On the return of Charles II, Parliament annulled everything Cromwell had done. If a solemn pact could be annulled by one of the two parties involved, Virginia should have remained absolutely independent of England. If, on the other hand, the capitulation remained valid, the dependency expressed in the first article was preserved, but under the conditions stipulated.

In January 1659 the Virginians unanimously proclaimed Charles II, then a refugee in Holland, as king of England, Scotland, France, Ireland, and Virginia, and they recalled Sir William Berkeley, who had been governor during the reign of Charles I.[20] This act of sovereignty is noteworthy because Charles II thus became king of Virginia some time before he was assured of the throne of England.

During his reign England tried to monopolize colonial commerce * on the basis of a parliamentary act of 1650. There was a great deal of oratory, and writers strove to demonstrate that the advantages would be reciprocal, especially because of the protection afforded by the British navy to colonial commerce.

Despite protests from the colony, Parliament exercised control over commerce and promulgated various acts, one of which imposed a tax on commodities transported from one colony to another. The Virginians sent deputies to England to point out that only the General Assembly could levy taxes. They returned with a statute signed by Charles II 19 April 1676 declaring that the inhabitants and proprietors of the colony could be taxed only with the consent of the General Assembly, except in the case of taxes levied by Parliament on commodities brought from the colony to England.

The General Assembly was in Virginia what Parliament is in Great Britain, and legally the colony was no more dependent on England than Hanover is today. All laws were promulgated in the

---

* By this time several other colonies had been established.

[19] "Articles at the Surrender of the Countrie," 12 March 1651, in William Hening, *The Statutes at Large . . . of Virginia* (1819–23; rept. Charlottesville, University Press of Virginia, 1969), 1: 363–64.

[20] Berkeley went to Virginia as governor in 1642; violently opposed to the Commonwealth, he remained on his plantation until the Restoration.

name of the king and the colonial assembly with the formula: "It is ordered by His Excellent Majesty the King, and with the consent of the General Assembly, etc."

## The Founding of Massachusetts

According to the charter of 1606, the territory of the second or Plymouth Company extended from lat. 38° to lat. 45°. The 39th, 40th, and 41st degrees therefore could belong to either company. The charter granted possession to the first occupant but stated that there should be a hundred-mile strip between the two plantations. Documents of the period are generally couched in terms that give lawyers something to debate.

Among the most zealous members of this company were the governor of Plymouth, Sir Ferdinando Gorges, and Sir John Popham, the chief judge.[21] In 1607 several of the associates founded a colony about lat. 44° at a place called Sagadahoc[22] and formulated plans for a large state. During the hard winter several of the men, including their president, George Popham, died.[23] Meanwhile, in England some of the leading promoters of the enterprise, among them Sir John Popham, the president's brother [uncle], and Sir John Gilbert, the admiral's brother, had died;[24] so the colonists returned home the next year and the settlement was abandoned.

This project had been inspired by a glowing description of the region from the pen of Captain Bartholomew Gosnold, one of Raleigh's associates.[25] In 1602, while looking for a more direct route to Virginia, he happened to land on a promontory near a spot where he had caught a huge number of codfish. He named the place Cape Cod. Although he constructed a small fort on one of the adjacent islands, he was unable to persuade any of his men to remain there. He named the islands Elizabeth, in honor of the

[21] Gorges became interested in America when three Indians were brought to England in 1605; in 1620 he founded the Council for the Planting of New England in America, and in 1639 he became lord proprietary of the province of Maine. Sir John Popham was chief justice of the King's Bench.

[22] Sagadahoc was on the western side of the mouth of the Kennebec River.

[23] George Popham was named in the Virginia Company patent of 10 April 1606 as president of the council of seven to govern the colony in "Northern Virginia."

[24] Gilbert was the older half brother of Raleigh.

[25] Gosnold was vice admiral of the fleet which landed at Cape Henry 26 April 1607. He did not approve the selection of an island on the James River for the settlement, but his objections were overruled; the next year he died of malaria.

queen, and as one of them grew, and still grows, a large quantity of wild grapes, he called it Martha's Vineyard.

Gosnold was followed by other adventurers, especially from Bristol; they made good profits from the large quantities of fish and from the fine furs which the savages sold them in exchange for articles of very little value. A certain unscrupulous Captain Hunt lured some twenty savages on board his vessel and then sold them to Spaniards at Malaga as African Moors.* This treachery doubtless explains why the Indians of this region have preserved a bitter hatred for the English and their descendants and have usually preferred to join forces with the French.

In 1603 the king of France, Henry IV, granted a certain [Pierre du Guast, sieur] de Monts letters patent in which he ceded to him all the land between lat. 40° and 46°, known as Acadia.

After the members of the Plymouth Company had made various expensive and futile attempts at settlement, they and the French continued to visit these shores to fish and barter with the savages. But neither nation appeared inclined to establish a colony, for that required a large initial investment and it seemed certain that no financial reward would be reaped for a long period of time. Some historians claim that Ferdinando Gorges, whom we have already mentioned, and Captain Mason[26] each lost £20,000 in these ventures. It is possible that no settlement would have become permanent, at least for a long time, if religious persecutions had not given a number of Englishmen a desire to seek new homes.

The Anglican church, which had inherited religious intolerance along with its episcopal pomp, persecuted the Puritans, Presbyterians, and all those who, by refusing to conform to its rules, were branded as nonconformists. Some of the persecuted, who had sought refuge in Holland in 1606, decided in 1617 to go to America to preserve the purity of their doctrine. The Dutch tried in vain to persuade them to settle along the Hudson River, where Captain Hudson had established their sovereignty in accordance with the common practice of going ashore, naming the country, and declaring oneself master of it. These religious bigots felt, however, that the Dutch were not sufficiently straitlaced; furthermore,

* [William] Douglass, [*A Summary, Historical and Political, of the First Planting, Progressive Improvements, and Present State of the British Settlements in North-America*, 2 vols. (Boston, 1749–52),] 1:[190].

[26] John Mason became governor of Newfoundland and received a grant with Gorges in 1622; in 1631 they were among the grantees for a tract on the Piscataqua River which was named New Hampshire.

they still had a feeling of kinship for their old compatriots. They therefore asked the London Company for a tract of land. The request was favorably received, and several of the most influential members of the company begged James I to grant them religious liberty. Douglass, (1:369) says that he consented, but this is wrong. The king's conscience permitted him to promise only that they would not be annoyed.

As an assurance of this kind did not seem a very safe guarantee, the Puritans were reluctant to emigrate. Two years later, however, they came back to their original idea with the hope that distance would deliver them from persecution by episcopal courts of justice. About half of the companions of the famous Robinson[27] went to Southampton, where they embarked on two vessels, which were forced by bad weather to return to port several times. One remained in England with some of the emigrants, but the other went back to sea and reached Cape Cod 11 November 1620.

Hutchinson (2:455) says that Robinson's companions did not "carry other powers or authority with them than what each of them brought into the world."[28] Before embarking, the emigrants learned that the lands ceded to them by the London Company were within the confines of the Plymouth Company. This group had gradually declined, as some associates had died and others lost interest. The new emigration revived hope, especially among those who had incurred considerable losses. Sir Ferdinando Gorges and Captain Mason were among those who helped procure the charter which was granted 3 November 1620,[29] but meanwhile, Robinson's companions were about to land on the American coast. During the crossing several were heard to say that as soon as they went ashore everyone would be equal and could do as he pleased. In order to forestall anarchy, the more prudent prepared the following act so that it could be ratified before they left the vessel.

In the name of God, Amen. We, whose names are underwritten, the Loyal Subjects of our dread Sovereign Lord King James, by the Grace of God, of Great Britain, France and Ireland, King, Defender of the Faith, etc. Having undertaken for the Glory of God, and Advancement

[27] John Robinson, the pastor of the Pilgrim Fathers, was forced to remain in Holland because the pilgrims did not have sufficient funds to pay his passage; he died in Leyden.

[28] Thomas Hutchinson, *The History of the Province of Massachusetts Bay*, 3 vols. (Boston, 1764–1828).

[29] The charter granted to the Council for New England all land lying between lat. 40° and lat. 48°.

of the Christian Faith, and the Honour of our King and Country, a Voyage to plant the first colony in the northern Parts of Virginia; Do by these Presents, solemnly and mutually in the Presence of God and one another, covenant and combine ourselves together into a civil Body Politick, for our better Ordering and Preservation, and Furtherance of the Ends aforesaid; And by Virtue hereof do enact, constitute, and frame, such just and equal Laws, Ordinances, Acts, Constitutions, and Offices, from time to time, as shall be thought most meet and convenient for the general Good of the Colony; unto which we promise all due Submission and Obedience. In Witness whereof we have hereunto subscribed our names at Cape Cod the eleventh of November, in the Reign of our Sovereign Lord King James of England, France, and Ireland, the eighteenth, and of Scotland, the fifty-fourth, Anno Domini, 1620.

Signed, John Carver, William Bradford, Edward Winslow . . .[30]

This act was probably signed on board by all old enough to do so. I have named the first three of the forty-one who signed and omitted the others as superfluous. The soil on which they landed was so sandy and sterile that they were forced to sail along the coast until they found a more fertile region. There they stopped and called the place New Plymouth. Some historians claim that this name had already been chosen by Captain Smith, who had landed at the same spot on one of his many voyages. The territorial rights of the immigrants were very indefinite until they obtained the patent of the new Plymouth Company in 1624. They had, it is true, purchased the land from Indian tribes who owned it,* but this afforded no protection from men armed with patents. As the Indians sold large tracts of land at a very modest price, Europeans, who based their rights on discoveries, charts, or patents, arrogated for themselves the exclusive right to make the purchases in order to have a monopoly. As the 1624 patent was very obscure, they obtained another in 1629, but the latter, according to Douglass (1:395), was no better, and when in 1641 the English commissioners were ordered by the court to settle a boundary dispute with the colony of Rhode Island, they could not understand it.

The New Plymouth Colony did not grow very rapidly. In 1624 its population numbered only 180 men, women, and children. It

---

* Douglass (1:370) says they bought it from Massasoit, sachem of the Pokanoket; since he was at war with the large tribe of Narragansetts, he was delighted to have them as allies.

[30] The Mayflower Compact, in Henry Steele Commager, *Documents of American History* (8th ed., New York: Appleton-Century-Crofts, 1968), p. 15.

continued, however, to govern itself until 1692 [1691], when it was incorporated into Massachusetts.

The charter of 3 November 1620, to which we have already referred, was granted to forty people. Among the best-known associates were Ferdinando Gorges, Captain John Mason, the duke of Lennox, the duke of Buckingham, the marquis of Hamilton, the earls of Arundel and Warwick, and Sir Francis George.[31] The new company was called the Plymouth Council for the Affairs of New England. The name New England had been given to the northern part of Virginia by Captain Smith.

Lack of a system in handling business and ignorance of geographical matters were responsible for the fact that the Plymouth Council often sold or gave the same lands to several people, and it was common for lands granted by one patent to include those granted by another. This caused a number of lawsuits more than fifty years later, suits which would have been brought at the time if the number of inhabitants had been larger or the acquisition of property had presented a greater problem. In the early years there was almost no emigration. Several colonies were established in different places, but all were small until 1628. During that year certain members of Parliament were sent to the Tower of London and other prisons for protesting openly against the abuses of the Anglican church, and this caused the nonconformists to abandon any hope of reform. A large number, especially among the Puritans, resolved to serve God in America. Ferdinando Gorges relates in his history of New England that the number of emigrants rose so rapidly that the king issued a special act forbidding anyone to leave the country without permission. The same historian adds: "So that what I long before prophesied, when I could hardly get any for money to reside there, was now brought to pass in a high measure." [32]

The charter of the Plymouth Council contained the right to cede

---

[31] The associates included Ludovick Stuart, second duke of Lennox; George Villiers, first duke of Buckingham; James, second marquis of Hamilton, who became a member of the Council for the Plantation of New England on 3 Nov. 1620; Thomas Howard, second earl of Arundel, who signed the royal charter for the company in New England on 23 July 1620; Sir Robert Dudley, earl of Warwick. The original records of the Council of New England are not extant; however, the list of forty men in Ebenezer Hazard, *Historical Collections*, 2 vols. (Philadelphia, 1792–94), 1:106, includes no Sir Francis George but does name Edward, Lord Gorges, brother of Sir Ferdinando.

[32] Gorges, *A Briefe Narration of the Originall Undertakings of the Advancement of Plantations into the Parts of America, Especially, Shewing the Begining, Progress and Continuance of That of New England*, (London, 1659).

lands but not to govern. In the same year, 1628, the members obtained another for this purpose, and the company of proprietors elected a governor (Matthew Cradock), a deputy governor (Thomas Goffe), eighteen assistants, and a secretary. A certain Mr. [John] Endecott was elected to be governor in America—with the stipulation that he was to be under orders from the governing body in England. These companies existed for only one purpose, to make a profit. Since the hope of finding mines with precious metals had dimmed, they regarded the sale of land and commerce as their chief, if not their only, objectives.

The following year a number of wealthy people, including several members of the nobility, consented to go to America on condition that the charter would follow. The company, which had not made any profits and saw no prospect of making any, agreed to this proposal. It was stipulated that during the first seven years the owners in England would share in profits derived from land and commerce. Management would be entrusted to ten persons, five in England and five in America. Furthermore, they would deal only with financial matters, for the colonists had the right to self-government and all other privileges. The five who remained in England were M[atthew] Cradock, N[athaniel] Wright, J. [Theophilus] Eaton, J. [Thomas] Goffe, and J. Young. Those who journeyed to America in protest against the arbitrary government in England were John Winthrop, Sir Richard Saltonstall,[33] J. [Isaac] Johnson, J. [Thomas] Dudley, and J[ohn] Revel.

Although many were eager to leave England, emigration presented so many difficulties that even some of the most enthusiastic became discouraged. The majority did not arrive in America until 1630, a year memorable for misfortunes.

At this time nothing was grown except a few vegetables and a small amount of Indian corn. There were few farmers among the first immigrants, and the land was heavily forested. The first task was to construct dwellings and provide shelter against the cold and Indians. A little Indian corn was brought from Virginia, but most foodstuffs came from England, and as communication was quite irregular, there were frequent famines. Whatever the cause, the 1630 famine was so severe that there were many deaths from diseases that occur when food is insufficient, unfamiliar, and of poor quality. A large number of the recent immigrants were accustomed to living well, even luxuriously, and they were less able

---

[33] Saltonstall sailed with John Winthrop in the *Arabella* in 1630, taking his five children to America.

to cope with hardship. It was hard to survive on a diet of snails, mollusks, and other shellfish, and to substitute peanuts or even acorns for bread and potatoes. Hutchinson relates that one man, who went to the governor to complain, came back with the news that the last loaf of bread had gone into the governor's oven. Hubbard mentions Lady Arabella Johnson, daughter of the earl of Lincoln, as one of the victims of the 1630 famine. He tells the story of her death in a very touching way.[34] Her husband, a highly respected man, died of sorrow about two months later.

These misfortunes did not quench the enthusiasm for emigration. The flame died down for a time but was rekindled by the arbitrary government of both church and state. Although all the plantations grew rapidly, the largest were on Massachusetts Bay, for which the colony was named.

During the early years the governor and his assistants exercised legislative and executive power. But the people, who wished to have civil, as well as religious, liberty, began to assemble in various districts to deliberate. In 1634 deputies were elected. Up to that time the colonists had enjoyed the right to elect those who governed but had no representatives. To the great surprise of the magistrates, twenty-four representatives of the freemen of the colony appeared at the General Assembly, and the people resolved: "That none but the general court * had power to make and establish laws, or to elect and appoint officers, as governor, deputy governor, assistants, treasurer, secretary, captains, lieutenants, ensigns, or any of like moment, or to remove such upon misdemeanour, or to set out the duties and powers of these officers . . . That none but the general court hath power to raise monies and taxes, and to dispose of lands . . . viz. to give and confirm proprieties." [35]

After these resolutions, they proceeded to the election of magistrates. Then they further determined:

That there shall be four general courts held yearly, to be summoned by the governor for the time being, and not to be dissolved without the consent of the major part of the court . . . That it shall be lawful for

---

* The legislative body of the commonwealth of Massachusetts is still called the General Court.

[34] Lady Arabella Johnson, wife of Isaac Johnson, had the largest estate of any of the associates. Hutchinson (1:20) quotes William Hubbard's manuscript "General History of New England from the Discovery to 1680": "She came from a paradise of plenty and pleasure . . . into a wilderness of wants, and . . . about a month after her arrival she ended her days in Salem." Hubbard's history was later published in 1815 in the *Collections of the Massachusetts Historical Society*.

[35] Hutchinson, 1:36.

the freemen of each plantation to chuse two or three before every general court, to confer of and prepare such business as by them shall be thought fit to consider of at the next court; and that such persons, as shall be hereafter so deputed by the freemen of the several plantations to deal in their behalf in the affairs of the commonwealth, shall have the full power and voices of all the said freemen derived to them for the making and establishing of laws, granting of lands, etc. and to deal in all other affairs of the commonwealth, wherein the freemen have to do, the matter of election of magistrates and other officers only excepted, wherein every freeman is to give his own voice.[36]

This was the second constitution of the American people. The colonies of Rhode Island, Connecticut, and New Hampshire followed the example of the colony of Massachusetts.

Emigration continued to increase. In 1633 the council debated the matter, and in 1637 emigration was forbidden by royal degree. This had the usual result: more and more people flocked to America. There are only two ways to keep men in a country: either you make them happy or you put them in chains. Several writers state that before 1640, 298 vessels sailed to New England with some 4,000 families, making a total of 21,200 men, women, and children. Hutchinson [1:92] says that in 1639 fishing began to flourish, and that the country already produced more foodstuffs than were needed. The colonists made large shipments to the islands, for which they received local products, as well as gold and silver, of which part was shipped to England to pay for manufactured goods.

The laws of the early immigrants reflected the austerity of their religion and customs. While a few were far too rigorous, they have been exaggerated by writers who failed to do justice to those deserving of praise. Pursuant to a law on the subject of slavery, which was rejected by the first legislators as contrary to the natural rights of man and prejudicial to society, a Negro who was brought from Africa in 1645 and sold in the colony of Massachusetts was taken away from his owner and returned to his homeland by special order of the General Court.*

## The Founding of Rhode Island

The colony of Rhode Island owed its origin to the commonwealth of Massachusetts, or rather to the religious intolerance of its inhabitants. The persecutions they had suffered in England seemed to

*Statutes of the General Court [in *The Charters and General Laws of the Colony and Province of Massachusetts Bay* (Boston, 1814), chap. 12, sec. 3, p. 53.]
[36] Ibid.

inspire the colonists with a desire for vengeance rather than with any conciliatory feelings. New sects appeared daily. The very arguments used to uphold one fantastic theory caused new ones to blossom. The Puritan sect was divided and then subdivided over and over again. Brownists, Independents, Antinomians, Muggletonians, Separatists, and numerous others were all schismatics from the same sect. Even those who professed the dominant religion did not agree on all points of dogma. Each church, or congregation as it was called, differed from the others in some way.

In order to preserve union and even uniformity (insofar as the particular bigotry of each congregation permitted), the colonists began to hold synods in Presbyterian fashion, although they selected a different name, Congregationalists. In the early years there is no reference to Presbyterians, and Anglicans did not come until about the end of the reign of Charles II. Anabaptists appeared after 1640, bringing the same fanaticism that had got them into trouble in Germany. Their conduct was such that in 1644 and 1646 laws were passed to deal with these "Incendiaries of the Common Wealths," ordering "that if any person or persons within this Jurisdiction shall either openly condemn or oppose the baptising of infants or go about secretly to seduce others from the approbation or use thereof, or shall purposely depart the Congregation at the Ministration of the Ordinance, or shall deny the Ordinance of Magistracy, or their lawfull Right and Authority to make War, or to punish the outward Breakers of the first Table and shall appear to the Court wilfully and obstinately to continue therein after due Time and Means of Conviction, every such Person or Persons shall be sentenced to banishment." [37] The Quakers arrived in 1654. They were more violent and fanatical than the Anabaptists, and the colonists were obliged to enact even more severe laws against them. Catholics did not have the courage to appear until our glorious Revolution, which changed the way of thinking about this and other points essential to human happiness.

In 1635, two years before the synods were started, Roger Williams, minister of the church in Salem and a fine man according to the historians, was excommunicated because of his Antinomian, Brownistic, and other fanatic principles. He was banished from the Massachusetts Colony as a disturber of the peace, the church, and the community.[38] Williams settled in Seekonk, after getting some

[37] Hazard, 1: 538.

[38] *Records of the Court of Assistants of the Colony of the Massachusetts Bay,* 3 vols. (Boston, 1901–28), 1: 160, 3 Sept. 1635.

land from the sachem Massasoit. The magistrates of the small New Plymouth Colony made him leave, however, because Seekonk was within the limits of their patent. Although they did not deny Massasoit's right to sell, they regarded Williams as a heretic. Furthermore, the colonial governments forbade private citizens from purchasing land from the Indians without permission. This regulation was intended to prevent fraudulent contracts, to keep any individual from acquiring holdings sufficiently large to be prejudicial to the community, and, finally, to give as much publicity as possible to the sale. This was important, since more than one tribe often laid claim to the same land. The motives of the colonies differed from those of the companies, or rather of the possessors of patents, who claimed the exclusive right of purchasing lands from the savages in order to have a monopoly. Williams crossed the Pawtucket River with his small group of followers, procured various tracts of land from the Narragansett sachem, and called the place Providence.

In the first synod, held in Newtown on Massachusetts Bay in 1637, religious opinions of various sects were condemned. The Congregationalists seem to have adopted the term employed by Anglicans, sectaries, to designate all those whose religious principles differed from their own. As these non-Congregationalists were subsequently mistreated, they withdrew with their friends and partisans to Aquidneck Island, now called Rhode Island, which they purchased from the Indians 24 March 1638. Eighteen men were selected to set up a form of government. During the next two years this was changed several times, but in 1640 they decided it should consist of a governor, deputy governor, and four assistants, and this system prevailed until 1662.

In 1642 eleven men bought from the Indians a place called Shawomet and named it Warwick in honor of the earl of Warwick, who had a patent for a very considerable piece of land in the area. A patent belonging to the marquis of Hamilton included all the land now in the state of Rhode Island, as well as parts of Massachusetts and Connecticut. As the marquis neglected his rights, the inhabitants later denied his descendants the privilege of claiming them. Almost all the members of the Plymouth Company, who held patents for whole provinces, had similar experiences. An objection to Hamilton's patent was that the lands had not been purchased from the Indians, for the colonists felt property rights should be based on a cession of land by the natives.

In 1643 Williams went to England as deputy for the colony he

had established. He obtained a kind of charter from the earl of
Warwick, who was governor and admiral of all the English
plantations * for Parliament. This grants to the "Inhabitants of the
Towns of Providence, Portsmouth, and Newport, a free and absolute Charter of Incorporation . . . Together with full Power and
Authority to rule themselves . . . by such a Form of Civil Government as . . . they shall find most suitable." [39]

These little colonies, which now form the state of Rhode Island,
were incorporated into the colony of Rhode Island and Providence
Plantations by virtue of a charter of Charles II dated 8 July 1662.
The first assembly, which met in Newport 1 March 1663, decreed
that all Christians except Catholics should enjoy the same advantages as citizens and that any purchases of land from the savages
made without the consent of the assembly would be nullified and
the purchasers subject to fines.


## The Founding of Connecticut

Like Rhode Island, the colony of Connecticut owed its origin to
Massachusetts and was established at the same time. During the
summer of 1636 a rather large group, discontented for religious
reasons, left Newtown, Dorchester, Watertown, and Roxbury
with their ministers and settled on the banks of the Connecticut,
where they founded Hartford, Wethersfield, Windsor, Springfield,
etc. Those outside the Massachusetts limit met in Hartford, decided how they should be governed, and elected magistrates. The
following year some English immigrants followed suit in New
Haven, which they had just settled on the riverbank across from
Long Island. The two small colonies, Hartford and New Haven,
continued to govern themselves separately until they were united
as the colony of Connecticut by virtue of the charter of Charles
II dated 23 April 1662.

---

* In the early days the colonies were often called plantations, and Providence
continued to bear this name even after it was incorporated with Rhode Island.
It is not surprising that Williams addressed the earl of Warwick, rather than the
king, although the war between king and Parliament had just begun. The New
England colonies were in the parliamentary party for religious reasons, just as
Virginia and Maryland were on the king's side.

[39] *Rhode Island Charter* ([London], 1643), granted by Robert Rich, second
earl of Warwick, rpt. in John R. Bartlett, ed., *Records of the Colony of Rhode
Island and Providence Plantations in New England*, 1 (1856).

## The Founding of New Hampshire

Among the large number of patents which Captain Mason obtained at different times from the Plymouth Council, and which were the source of constant litigation, that of 1629 granted him the entire state of New Hampshire, as it is now, and part of the adjacent colonies. Another, in his name and that of Ferdinando Gorges, covered a section granted by the preceding patent. On 19 August 1635 Charles I gave Mason a charter for the territory described in the 1627 patent and also bestowed upon him the right to govern and confer honors (the Mason family was always in high favor with the Stuarts). In 1639 Gorges got from the same king another charter, which gave him jurisdictional rights and included part of the area granted to Mason four years earlier. Furthermore, this jurisdictional right already had been granted to the Plymouth Council in the 1628 charter, which was carried to America by the settlers of the Massachusetts Colony.

In 1629 several inhabitants of the Massachusetts Bay Colony wanted to move to what is now the state of New Hampshire. Following the example of the founders of New Plymouth, they called a meeting of the Indian owners and made the purchase, which was notable both for the solemn ceremonies observed on both sides and for the lawsuits extending over nearly a century between the purchasers, their heirs, and the heirs of Gorges and Mason.

The Indians sold the country to John Wheelwright, Augustine Story or Storer, Thomas Wight, William Wentworth, and Thomas Leavit. They reserved hunting and fishing rights for their own use and required the purchasers to supply them with a cloth suit every year and to establish a colony within ten years.[40] This was called the Wheelwright Deed, probably because he had more to do with it than the others and was named first in the agreement. There is a difference between the rights of those who purchased land from the legitimate owners and Mason's claims, but it should also be noted that the 1629 patent, in which the Plymouth Council ceded the territory to Mason, followed the Wheelwright purchase.

[40] Jeremy Belknap, *The History of New Hampshire*, 3 vols. (Philadelphia, 1784–92), 1:10–11, says that on 17 May 1629 the planters in Massachusetts Bay named in the text procured a general meeting of the Indians and obtained a deed to settle near Piscataqua, "for what they deemed a valuable consideration in coats, shirts, and kettles."

In 1638 Wheelwright, who was a zealous minister of the gospel and brother[-in-law] of the famous Anne Hutchinson, was exiled with his partisans by the Massachusetts government following a dispute concerning Antinomian principles. As the ten-year deadline for establishing a colony in New Hampshire was approaching, they went to the territory he and his company had purchased, set up a government, and were for a time quite independent. Soon there were four settlements, each governed according to different laws.

Mason had died in 1635 and Francis Norton, who was directing the business because Mason's heir was a minor, had very different ideas from those of his predecessor. The widow, either because she lacked funds or was afraid that she and her child would be ruined, wrote Norton that she could not pay the people her husband had hired, to whom she owed a great deal of money; she therefore gave them full power to arrange matters as best they could. The furniture was sold and divided among the creditors. Among the items Belknap, who compiled the history of New Hampshire, listed a hundred large oxen and cows, for which Norton received £25 apiece in Boston. This shows the scarcity of cattle at the time. They belonged to a very large breed Mason had imported from Denmark. Rhode Island cattle, the largest I have seen in any part of the world, are doubtless related to them.

The inhabitants of these small settlements did not feel capable of protecting themselves should an invasion occur. They were, moreover, still fond of the Massachusetts government; so they asked if they might be placed under its protection and jurisdiction. When this act was signed 14 April 1741 [1641], a considerable tract of land was set aside for owners of patents. This indicates that the inhabitants recognized the validity of one of Gorges's and Mason's patents or at least appreciated the sums of money these men had spent in the colony. In considering the tangle of lawsuits caused by the patents, it should be noted that during Cromwell's time the Masons obtained only what seemed fair to the colonists, but after the restoration of the Stuarts they became powerful enough to make the settlers very unhappy.

In 1679 Charles II used specious pretexts to separate the government of New Hampshire from that of Massachusetts and then appropriated it for himself. His excuse was that he wanted to deliver from oppression the inhabitants who begged to be left under the Massachusetts government. The governors and other royal ministers were ordered to protect the Masons, and this gave the latter an opportunity to extort money and perpetrate other injustices, for the assembly was not strong enough to protect the rights of the colonists.

## The Founding of Maryland

Lord Baltimore and William Penn, who founded the colonies of Maryland and Pennsylvania, were the first to take advantage of charters granted by English kings. Among those who emigrated to America for religious reasons was Sir George Calvert, secretary of state, who later became famous as Lord Baltimore.[41] Toward the close of James I's reign he went to Virginia with a group of men belonging to various sects who also sought religious freedom. A devout Catholic, Calvert was coolly received by the Virginians, who were equally zealous as Anglicans. He then returned to England to ask Charles I for a charter which would give him land north of the Potomac that the Virginians had not included in their colony. This was promised to him, but as he died shortly thereafter, it was given to his son. In this charter, dated 10 June 1632, the territorial limits, in accordance with the superficial knowledge the English had of the area, were described in such terms that long afterward there were interminable lawsuits between Baltimore's heirs and the Penn family.

The Virginians protested against the dismemberment of what they called their territory but could do nothing about it. Lord Baltimore called his province Maryland, in honor of Mary, wife of Charles I. He sent his brother, Leonard Calvert, to govern it with Jerome Hawley and Thomas Cornwallis, Esquires, as assistants, and apparently gave them equal administrative power. They sailed from Cowes on the Isle of Wight 22 November 1632, stopped at Barbados and Saint Christopher, landed in Virginia on 24 February 1633, and reached the Potomac River on 3 March. About two hundred in number, most of them belonged to rather distinguished Catholic families, and they brought everything they needed to become well established. Writers say, however, that Lord Baltimore spent about £40,000 during the first two years. Wealthy and devout, he probably gave liberally to Catholics who asked for

[41] As Mazzei points out below, George Calvert died before his patent was granted. It was his son Cecilius, the second Lord Baltimore, who was the famous first proprietor of the colony, and who appointed his brother Leonard to be the resident governor.

help. After exploring the land near the river, they settled, with the Indians' consent, in a village called Yoacomaco, which they re-named St. Mary's.

During the civil wars in England, Cromwell deprived Lord Baltimore of his jurisdiction, but Charles II restored it on his ac-cession to the throne. James II, who succeeded his brother Charles, was an advocate of the divine right of kings. He therefore deprived Baltimore for the second time of his jurisdiction, despite the fact that the Baltimore family was devoutly Catholic. Finally Baltimore recovered his rights under William, on condition that he appoint a Protestant governor. The kings were always careful to put into the charters a clause indicating that they reserved the right of sover-eignty. Baltimore's charter stated that he was to pay a tribute of two Indian arrows to Windsor Castle every year as long as re-quired.

The population in Maryland grew rapidly. Virginia supplied foodstuffs to the new immigrants until they could get what they needed from the soil. As the frontiers adjoining the Indian territory were very narrow, it was not difficult for the inhabitants to main-tain a peaceful relationship with them. Other European colonies were at some distance, with the exception of a small group of Swedes on Delaware Bay, and they were too few in number to cause any disturbance. All Christian sects enjoyed religious free-dom. Catholics could not be persecuted, as the proprietor and most of the inhabitants belonged to this religion; yet they could not be intolerant themselves.

The greatest benefit the possessors of charters received from their lands was a very small tax known as a quitrent levied on sales and gifts. In Maryland the proprietor fixed the sum at twopence sterling for a hundred acres.* Later this went up to four pence. About 1740 he tried to raise it to ten pence but without success. If the kings had speculated more wisely, they could have obtained a considerable revenue from the quitrent. They kept it in Virginia, although Charles II transferred part of the privilege when he granted some noblemen a patent for land between the Rappa-hannock and Potomac rivers. The Virginia deputies in London were opposed to this, but the patent owners made some con-cessions to the colony and thus obtained the quitrent.†

* *Acre* is an English word, or rather a term taken to England by the Saxons or Normans and still used in Normandy. It contains 43,560 English square feet.

† The Virginia quitrent belonged to the Prince of Wales. During the early part of the Revolution this caused two members of the assembly to display their

## The Founding of New York

Before describing the founding of Pennsylvania, I shall discuss the colonies of New York and New Jersey, which were settled earlier.

The area between the plantations of the London and Plymouth companies, which the 1606 charter had granted to both, was neglected by them. A few Swedes and Finns were the first colonists on Delaware Bay. Shortly thereafter some Dutch settled near the mouth of the Hudson River, to which the English captain Henry Hudson, who discovered it in 1608 [1609], had given his name.

The story of these beginnings is more confused and obscure than that of any of the other colonies. Little information is available, and the memoirs remaining were written long afterward by poorly educated men who perhaps were not altogether impartial. From all one can gather, it appears that some English were in the vicinity of the Hudson River before 1618, that there were constant squabbles between this handful of Dutch and English settlers, and that first one side and then the other had the upper hand. The Dutch finally set up a form of government. When James I complained, he was informed that the whole business was in the hands of an Amsterdam company. After Sir Samuel Argall,[42] governor of Virginia for the London Company, defeated the Dutch in 1618, James sent a certain Edward Langdon to serve as governor.[43] He named the place New Albion, and the Dutch immigrants placed themselves under his jurisdiction. In 1620 James permitted Dutch captains to land vessels en route to Brazil so that crews could rest and obtain a supply of wood.

Some writers say that during the English civil wars the Dutch took possession of the territory that now forms a considerable part of the states of New York, New Jersey, and Delaware and a small portion of Pennsylvania. They called it New Netherlands or New

ignorance of common law. When the matter of suspending payments came under consideration, these men, who were loyal patriots but wanted to be scrupulously fair, protested vigorously, and one of them stated, "We are at war with the father, and not with a poor little boy." The Northern Neck, the territory between the Rappahannock and Potomac, belonged to several men before it came into the hands of Lord Fairfax [Thomas Fairfax, sixth Baron Fairfax], who died there at a very advanced age, in 1781. He had nothing to do with the Revolution, and the quitrent was paid to him as long as he lived.

[42] Captain Argall, navigator, was deputy governor of Virginia 1617–19.

[43] Douglass, 2:222.

Belgium, established several plantations, built a city, which they called New Amsterdam, on the tip end of the mainland between Long Island and the Hudson River, and named the Hudson the North River (it is still known by both names). Along the Delaware River they built Fort Casimir, now New Castle in the state of Delaware. They called it the South River, but it and Delaware Bay have kept the name given them in 1610 in honor of Lord Delaware, who landed there by mistake when he was looking for Virginia, of which the company had appointed him governor or president.

Other historians claim that as early as 1623 the Dutch had established a settlement in New York whose governor bore the title Director General of New Belgium. This is not without foundation, because English immigrants at this time used to go to Virginia and New England. The Dutch landing there on their way to Brazil could easily have founded a colony, and James I was not in a mood to test his strength outside his domain. He was too busy with personal vanity, royal prerogatives, and theology.

Because the Swedes and Finns inhabiting what is today the state of Delaware were simple farmers, they sought the protection of the more wealthy and numerous Dutch, according to several writers. In 1655 John Kizeing, the Swedish governor, formally ceded the land to Peter Stuyvesant, the Dutch governor. Smith, in his history of New York, says that the Dutch overran the area.[44]

When Charles II decided to conquer the colony, he began by ceding the sovereignty to his brother, the duke of York, who later became James II. On 12 March 1664 the king granted him a charter. A fleet carrying ground forces compelled New Amsterdam to surrender, and all the other plantations followed suit. The name New Amsterdam was replaced by New York, which was given to the whole territory as well. As boundaries were uncertain, the new owner endeavored to extend them as far as he could. On 24 June he gave Lord Berkeley of Stratton and Sir George Carteret the area which now forms the state of New Jersey.[45]

[44] William Smith wrote the *History of the Province of New York* (London, 1776) to call attention to all the abuses perpetrated by the British.

[45] John Berkeley, first Baron Berkeley of Stratton, sold his interest to two English Quakers; they got into debt and had to turn their lands over to three trustees, one of whom was William Penn. Sir George Carteret, former governor of the island of Jersey, was one of the eight men to whom Charles II granted the Carolinas. New Jersey was named in his honor, but it is doubtful whether he ever visited the colony.

The Dutch ceded to Charles II all of New Belgium by the Treaty of Breda in 1667; they took it back during the war Charles declared on them in 1672, ceded it again by the Treaty of Westminster in 1674, and never recovered it. On 29 June of that same year Charles gave his brother a new charter to prevent any difficulties which might arise, since the country had changed rulers since the first charter was bestowed.

Although New York was administered by appointees of a prince who favored despotism, the government was characterized by a civil and religious liberty which probably owed its existence to the fact that the inhabitants were a mixture of various nations, but chiefly Dutch. The Episcopalians, who in general favored the monarchy, did not form a congregation for a long time, and the first Anglican church, Trinity, was not constructed until 1696. There were very few Catholics, although the proprietor, and in consequence the governors, were devout; Catholicism was forbidden after James's abdication. This appears in one of the basic laws of the colony, antedating the code which they began to formulate in April 1691. I shall list seven of the laws to give the reader an idea of the colony's relationship to Great Britain and the prevailing ideas of that period.

1. There can be no Power and Authority held and exercised over their Majesties Subjects in this Their Province and Dominion, but what must be derived from their Majesties, Their Heirs and Successors.

2. The Supreme Legislative Power and Authority, under their Majesties . . . shall for ever be and reside in a Governor in Chief and Council appointed by Their Majesties.

3. That all Bills agreed upon by the said Representatives, or the major part of them, shall be presented unto the Governor and Council for their Approbation and Consent. All and every which said Bills, so approved of and consented to . . . shall be esteemed and accounted the Laws of this Province. Which said Laws shall continue and remain in Force until they be disallowed by Their Majesties.

4. No Free-Man shall be Taken or Imprisoned, or be deprived of his Freehold or Liberty, or free Customs, or Out-lawed . . . or Adjudged or Condemned, but by the lawful judgment of his Peers, and by the Law of this Province.

5. That no member of the General Assembly, or their Servants, during the time of their Sessions, and whilst they are going to and returning from the said Assembly, shall be Arrested, Sued, Imprisoned, or any way Molested or Troubled.

6. No Aid, Tax . . . Duty or Imposition whatsoever shall be Laid, Assessed, Imposed, Levied or Required . . . but by the Act and Con-

sent of the Governor and Council; and Representatives of the People in General Assembly met and convened.

7. That no Person or Persons which profess Faith in God by Jesus Christ his only Son, shall at any time be any way molested . . . *Always Provided,* That nothing herein mentioned or contained shall extend to give Liberty to any Persons of the Romish Religion to exercise their manner of Worship, contrary to the Laws and Statutes of Their Majesties Kingdom of England.[46]

Finally I should note that the people's assembly was not convoked under the duke of York until 1683. It might never have been convoked if the experience of nine years had not revealed the absurdity of trying to establish an absolute government. Some of the inhabitants had already left, and it was feared that the territory might be depopulated or that the settlers would appoint their own representatives, as the Virginia and New England colonists had done.

### The Founding of New Jersey

It has already been said that on 24 June 1664 the duke of York ceded part of the land given him by his brother to Lord Berkeley of Stratton and Sir George Carteret. [Captain] Philip Carteret, George's brother [cousin], governed this area, called New Jersey, until 1672 and established a quitrent. The inhabitants, who had purchased their lands directly from the Indians, refused to pay it. In 1672 they rebelled and appointed another governor. Philip Carteret went to England, where he was detained by the war with the Dutch until 1674. He then returned to Jersey, and everything was peaceful again.

As Lord Berkeley had yielded his rights, his property was divided between the new proprietors and Lord Carteret. That same year George Carteret received a new charter from the duke of York. He obtained a cession of the eastern portion from the successors of Lord Berkeley, who secured the western portion from him. This division, which was confirmed by an act of the General Assembly, caused the country to be known for a time as the two Jerseys.

Sir Edmund Andros was vice-governor of the province of New York, of which the duke retained the title of governor until he

[46] *Acts of Assembly Passed in the Province of New York from 1691 to 1718* (London, 1719), pp. 1–3.

ascended the throne. Andros took possession of the government of West Jersey without regard to Lord Berkeley's successors. In 1680 he seized East Jersey and put Carteret into a New York prison. Shortly afterward the eastern part was restored to Carteret, the western division to Lord Berkeley's heirs, and Andros was dismissed.

These restitutions and this dismissal have led some writers to consider Andros responsible for the seizures, but anyone who knows the deceitful and arbitrary character of James II will judge differently. When he became king he appointed Andros governor of New England and put him in charge of New York and the two Jerseys, after appropriating them as if they had been part of his own patrimony.

Upon the abdication of James, King William restored the properties to their rightful owners. The various sales, divisions, and subdivisions, the rights claimed by people who said they had bought their land from Indians, and the weakness of the government, whose leaders could not agree, led the owners to yield all right of jurisdiction to the crown in 1702. They received, in exchange, a charter specifying that all future governors should observe certain rules; they were forbidden, for example, to authorize any tax the assembly might wish to levy on vacant lands or to permit the purchase of land from Indians without consent of the owners. They were also urged to see that the owners cultivated the soil. In 1683 the assemblies of both the Jerseys had forbidden any purchase of land without consent of the owners and had set a rather severe penalty for infringement of the rule. So they merely had to ensure that the governors could not permit any revocation of these laws. In 1703 [1702] the two Jerseys were united under a single government, presided over by the governor of New York, and thirty-three [thirty-six] years later the government of New Jersey was entirely separated from that of New York.


### The Founding of Pennsylvania and Delaware

On 4 March 1681 William Penn, founder of the colony of Pennsylvania, obtained from Charles II a charter in which His Majesty reserved for himself a fifth of the gold and silver taken from the mines, as was customary, and a yearly tribute of two deerskins, to be delivered to Windsor Castle. I regard the following provisions as the most important in this very long charter.

We doe hereby erect the . . . country . . . into a province and doe call it Pensilvania.

[William Penn and his heirs may] publish any Lawes whatsoever . . . by and with the advice . . . of the freemen. [They may] appoint and establish any judges . . . provided that the said Lawes bee consonant to reason and bee not repugnant to . . . the Lawes of England, and . . . reserving to us . . . the hearing of Appeals.

Lawes . . . shall be and continue the same as . . . in England, untill . . . altered by the said William Penn.

A transcript . . . of all lawes . . . made and published within the said province shall within five yeares . . . be transmitted to the privy Councell . . . and if any of the said Lawes within the space of six months . . . be declared inconsistent with the sovereignty . . . they shall bee . . . declared . . . void.

[William Penn and his heirs may] enjoy the customs and Subsidies [within the province] as assessed by the assembly.

[He shall] appoint an attorney or Agent to reside in or neare our City of London . . . and shall be ready . . . to answer for any misdeameanors . . . or any wilfull default or neglect against our Lawes of Trade. The said William Penn. his heirs shall pay the same within one years. [If payment is not made] it shall be lawfull for us to seize and resume the government [but without molesting the other inhabitants of the province.]

[William Penn may transfer lands.]

[Christians who already occupy land may keep the property.]

[The king will not tax the inhabitants of the province] unless the same be with the Consent of the Proprietary, or chief Governor, or Assembly, or by Act of Parliament in England.[47]

It appears from the last article that the king could burden the country with taxes and assessments without the assembly's permission, provided the owner agreed or was authorized by act of Parliament. But this peculiar clause, which could destroy the colony's liberty, is contradicted several times in the same charter. Even if we accept it as binding, it could involve only the two parties, that is, the king and Penn. It had nothing to do with the other colonies and did not even bind the inhabitants of Pennsylvania, whose predecessors had made their own agreements with Penn both before and after their departure from England.

On 11 July of that same year the proprietor and those who had resolved to emigrate with him agreed:

[47] *The Charter of Charles the Second of England, Scotland, France, and Ireland, unto William Penn,* in *A Collection of Charters and Other Publick Acts Relating to the Province of Pennsylvania* (Philadelphia, 1740), p. 8.

Great roads from city to city not to contain less than *forty* foot in breadth shall be first laid out and declared to be for high-ways, before the dividend of acres be laid out for the purchaser.

There shall be no buying or selling, be it with an Indian, or one among another . . . but what shall be performed in public market.

All differences between the Planters and the natives shall be ended by six Planters and Six Natives.

That in clearing the ground, care be taken to leave *one* acre of trees for every *five* acres cleared, especially to preserve oak and mulberries, for silk and shipping.

That no Person leave the Province, without Publication being made thereof, in the Market Place, *Three* Weeks before.[48]

On 25 April 1682 a very comprehensive new act was promulgated to ensure the liberty and privileges of the people. This act, called William Penn's charter, states in part:

The government shall . . . consist of the Governor and freemen of the said province, in form of a Provincial Council and General Assembly, by whom all laws shall be made, officers chosen and publick affairs transacted.

The said freemen shall yearly choose members to serve in General Assembly, as their representatives, not exceeding two hundred persons . . . which number shall be enlarged as the country shall increase . . . so as it do not exceed five hundred.

The Provincial Council shall consist of 72 men. The Governor and Provincial Council shall prepare and propose to the General Assembly . . . all bills . . . they shall take care that all laws be duly executed . . . and shall have the care of the peace and safety of the said province. They shall also have power to inspect the management of the publick treasury.[49]

Penn determined the method of electing representatives of the people and councillors, the times of assemblies, the elections of magistrates, the procedure for administering justice, etc. He stated that during the first year the assembly should consist entirely of freemen and, later, of their representatives. Finally he declared that no article could be changed without consent of the governor and six-sevenths of the freemen united in the Provincial Council and in a General Assembly.

[48] *A Collection of Charters and Other Publick Acts Relating to the Province of Pennsylvania*, pp. 22–25.

[49] *The Frame of the Government of the Province of Pennsilvania in America*, in *A Collection of Charters and Other Publick Acts Relating to the Province of Pennsylvania*, pp. 12–17.

On 5 May of that year a certain number of articles were added, three of which are noteworthy:

Every inhabitant . . . in the province that pays scot and lot to the government, shall be deemed and accounted a freeman of the said province; and every such person shall and may be capable of electing or being elected a representative of the people in Provincial Council or General Assembly.

All persons living in this province who confess and acknowledge the one almighty and eternal God . . . shall in no ways be molested or prejudiced for their religious persuasion . . . nor shall they be compelled . . . to frequent or maintain any religious ministry.

That as often as any Days of the Month mentioned in any Article of this Charter, shall fall upon the *First* Day of the Week, commonly called the *Lord's Day*, the Business appointed for that Day, shall be deferred until the next Day, unless in Cases of Emergency.* [50]

These contracts between Penn and the emigrants were signed before they sailed. Upon their arrival in America, Penn's first project was to draw up a plan for Philadelphia, and then he proceeded to change the articles in the charter to his own advantage as much as he could. As we are dealing with a man whom several writers have celebrated and whose character has been falsely interpreted, it is good to let the reader make up his own mind on the basis of fact.

It is remarkable, or rather incomprehensible, that the London court should have given a charter to William Penn at the very time when it was considering taking back all the charters from established colonies and communities in its own kingdom, but let us examine the circumstances. The duke of York was very eager to reestablish Catholicism. Penn was his intimate confidant and continued in this role after the duke ascended the throne. Well-informed men believe that Penn suggested the idea of universal tolerance as the easiest means of reaching his goal. There is a great diversity of opinion about Penn's religious beliefs. Some say he was a Quaker; others call him a Jesuit. His conduct was certainly that of a Jesuit, and it resembled Quaker behavior only in those areas where Quakers are like Jesuits.

Before leaving London, Penn determined to set up a government favorable to the colonists with the hope of increasing the number

---

* This agreement between the Quakers and Penn, who, according to Abbé Raynal, was a Quaker, should be compared with the abbé's statement (9:12) that this day of rest was a time of "useless idleness."

[50] Ibid., pp. 32–33.

of his proselytes. He therefore published a broadside entitled, *The Frame of the Government of the Province of Pensilvania in America, Together with Certain Laws Agreed Upon in England by the Governour and Divers Free-men of the Aforesaid Province. To be Farther Explained and Confirmed There by the First Provincial Council, If They See Meet.*

The author of some historic research on the Pennsylvania constitution says (p. 12), "At the Head of this Frame or System, is a short preliminary Discourse, Part of which serves to give us a more lively Idea of Mr. Penn preaching in Grace Church Street than we derive from Raphael's Cartoon of Paul preaching in Athens; As a Man of Conscience he sets out; as a Man of Reason he proceeds: and as a Man of the World he offers the most plausible Conditions to all, to the End that he might gain some." *

The troubles between Penn and his followers began when he demanded a quitrent. They opposed it, as they thought a permanent tax on land they had purchased was both harsh and unjust. Penn was insinuating. He played two distinct roles, proprietor and governor. The proprietor sold the parcels of land, and the governor was supported by the community. The author of the book I have just quoted says that Penn combined the wiliness of a serpent with the innocence of a turtledove. The governor claimed he needed representation and made the colonists believe that by paying quitrents, they would be exempt from taxes. These arguments, coupled with his way of always adapting himself to circumstances, persuaded them to agree to the quitrent. This did not prevent the levying of taxes, but the proprietor was never willing to pay his share. This so-called father of his people, whose humanity, justice, and generosity have been widely extolled, this man who was so wonderful that Abbé Raynal asked permission to use the "language of fables" to describe his sublime character, spent his whole life fighting his own colonists to protect his property from being taxed. He transmitted this arbitrary claim to his heirs, who also refused to pay taxes, even in times of great calamity.

The concessions which Penn felt obliged to grant before leaving England had their effect; he attracted as many people as he could,†

* This book [(Richard Jackson), *An Historical Review of the Constitution and Government of Pennsylvania . . .*], printed in London in 1759 under the eyes of Dr. Franklin, contains a complete collection of facts taken from authentic reports.

† Abbé Raynal writes (9:15) that all the Quakers wanted to follow him but that "with judicious foresight he consented to bring only two thousand at the beginning."

but as soon as he arrived in America he sought a pretext to change the system of government.

In the article on New York it has been stated that New Belgium contained a small part of Pennsylvania. To prevent any difficulties, the duke of York, who was proprietor of New Belgium, ceded Penn all the land west of New Jersey. This included the three counties, known as the territory, which now form the little state of Delaware and which had been settled some time before by Europeans. Penn claimed that the king had also given him a charter with jurisdiction over this area, but no one ever saw the document, and in 1704 the representatives of Pennsylvania told him, among other things, that they doubted its existence. The author of the historic research on the Pennsylvania constitution tells about the establishment of quitrent and then adds (p. [14]), "Having in this Instance experienced the Weight of his Credit and the Power of his Persuasion, he was no sooner landed, than he formed a double Scheme for uniting the Province with the Territory, tho' it does not appear he was properly authorized so to do, and to substitute another Frame of Government in Lieu of the Former, which having answered the great Purpose of Inducement here at Home, for collecting of Subjects, he was now inclined to render somewhat more favorable to himself in Point of Government."

If the new province and the territory were to be united under a single government, some of the treaties signed in London had to be changed. In December 1682 Penn convoked the freemen of both areas in Chester to propose the union. The province was opposed to any change in its charter. The proprietor, with his customary skill, tried to prove that the union would have great advantages, while the proposed changes in the charter would do no harm. He finally succeeded in obtaining the union and a new form of government without fulfilling the conditions required by law. This made it easier for him to make further changes later, and we shall see that this was his intention from the beginning.

At the second assembly, held in Philadelphia in the spring of 1683, Penn proposed a third frame of government more in line with his opinions, and it too was adopted. This system retained a little of the first and the second, but in certain matters it was basically unlike either.

About two years later he had a quarrel about boundaries with Lord Baltimore. Penn seized this as a pretext to go to London, leaving the colony where he had promised to spend the rest of his life. James had ascended the throne and was already mounting his batteries. It was natural for Penn to want to be with him, and as a matter of fact, he served the king with considerable zeal though little integrity in various circumstances, particularly in the dispute between the monarchy and the fellows of Magdalen College.

Penn left conditions in America in a complete turmoil, and the instructions he sent to his lieutenants fostered more trouble. One factor contributing to this was the right he reserved to approve or reject any laws promulgated in his absence. This amounted to saying that a decision made by his commissioners and the deputy governor was invalid without his confirmation. He had left the government in the hands of five commissioners, but in 1686 he ordered another change in the administration. As the five had encountered strong opposition, he decided to replace them with one representative and sent a certain John Blackwell to be deputy governor. This individual undertook to cause dissension between the representatives and the councillors.[51] In May 1689, when he neglected to attend the assembly meeting, public affairs reached a stalemate. The representatives grew tired of waiting; so they made two declarations, one of which exposed Blackwell's conduct while the other forbade the payment of certain taxes he usually received.

Finally the deputy governor appeared and said some strange things, including the following:

The honourable Proprietary, for Reasons known to himself, hath given positive Directions for letting all the Laws drop or fall, except the Fundamentals, and afterwards for calling together the Legislative Authority, to pass such of them, or others, as they should see fit for the Future; which is my full Intention to do.

The honourable Proprietary, being, by his Patent from the King, authorized by himself, his Heirs, etc. with Consent of the Freemen, to make, and under his Seal to publish, necessary Laws for the Good of the People; which had never been done with all requisite Circumstances, whilst himself was here; and without which, I much doubt, whether what were passed, or should hereafter be passed, have that due Sanction or Establishment which Laws require." [52]

His last words showed that he was not disposed to do anything.

The reasons known to the proprietor, which he did not deign to communicate to us, are somewhat similar to those of Asiatic sovereigns. If the laws were not enacted according to the required form

[51] Blackwell submitted no new laws to the assembly and suspended those enacted during Penn's absence pending the proprietor's approval; he was recalled at his own request after 13 months.

[52] [Jackson], p. 21.

while the proprietor was on the spot, and if this was sufficient to render any subsequent legislation null and void, what can one think of such a legislator? This is the most favorable induction, for there could be no other reason for the mistake, if we suppose the speech to be sincere. Furthermore, how can we reconcile this mistake, which the proprietor's lieutenant believed would nullify any later act, with his resolution to establish some laws that had been abandoned or any others judged suitable?

The speech is a very long one. If the reader finds any ambiguity in the passages he has just seen, let him read the entire text and he will find that these excerpts are crystal clear in comparison. The representatives replied in a reasonable and amazingly moderate tone. Blackwell then devised other expedients as miserable and fully as inefficacious as the first. This went on for a long time, with the councillors displaying moderation and firmness and the proprietor duplicity and knavery. If similarity attracts, there is no reason for surprise that the friendship of James II and William Penn was lifelong.

Finally James abdicated. The new sovereigns were not friendly toward Penn; in 1693 they seized the government of Pennsylvania, but three years later it was restored to him for reasons unknown. At the first session of the assembly after the reinstatement of the proprietor, the representatives complained to the deputy governor because they had not been convoked according to the statutes and they thought this boded ill. In order to give the government more stability and a less complex system, the representatives proposed what was essentially a new constitution. The deputy governor agreed to this in 1697, but the proprietor did not see fit to ratify it.

At the close of 1699 the proprietor went to America for the second time, and at the assembly, in the spring of 1700, he demanded a return to the mode of government in force in 1683; this was duly granted, and in turn, he promised a system more suitable for both sides. For a long time, however, he thought only of his own interests. He occasionally convoked assemblies in New Castle, the capital of the territory; at intervals they met in Philadelphia, and he pulled every string to win the endorsement of the inhabitants of both colonies.

The last assembly he himself convoked was held in September 1701. At its opening he apologized for having called it a month before the set time, but he claimed that because enemies of the colony in England had taken advantage of his absence, he was forced to return at once. His speech was filled with expressions of affection. He implied that he deeply regretted being obliged to leave his people. He spoke of his fondness for a peaceful and quiet life and said that nothing (save his obedience to God's providence) could lessen his fondness for the country or change his resolution to return with his family to settle there. "Think, therefore (continued he in the most captivating stile and manner that ever was made use of) since all men are mortal, of some suitable Expedient and Provision for your Safety as well as your . . . Property, and you will find me ready to comply with whatsoever may render us happy by a nearer Union of our Interests. Review again your Laws! Propose new ones that may better your circumstances, and what you do, do it quickly! Remembering that the Parliament sits the End of the next month, and that the sooner I am there, the safer I hope we shall all be here." [53]

He then advised them to stay closely united, to expedite their affairs promptly, and to pay the subsidies exactly. The representatives replied in an affectionate and respectful fashion, but their message, a short one, was accompanied by a request containing twenty-one articles which indicated they felt too many precautions could not be taken when dealing with him. Events proved that his speech had not reflected his thought, for things remained in their customary uncertainty.

Penn finally presented the new system of government on 28 October, as he was about to leave, although the date showed it was ready on the eighth. One of the two most significant changes was that the right to propose laws was taken from the council and given to the representatives; the other stated that the proprietor was taking over the election of councillors, which had been in the hands of the people. A considerable change in religious liberty appears in the article: "All persons professing to believe in Jesus Christ should be capable to serve the government either legislatively or executively." Before this time belief in God had been considered sufficient for citizenship. The representatives of the territory refused to adopt this new system; they walked out of the assembly in disgust and never met with it again.

Penn left the colonies torn asunder and could not foresee what the results would be. That is one reason why the author of the historic researches thinks it very strange that Montesquieu called him

[53] Ibid., p. 40.

a new Lycurgus. His conduct toward the colonists was always the same. He never kept agreements, spared neither tricks nor evasions to get money, and occasionally even resorted to threats.

In 1704 his deputy governor, [John] Evans, went so far that the representatives resolved unanimously to request the proprietor that he be told to change his practices. On 10 June 1707 the assembly wrote Penn again to complain, but it was completely useless. These remonstrances reproached Penn for the tricks he had played to curry favor with them before and after the immigration, his methods of extorting money, his shameless injustice in appointing himself judge for his own case, etc.

Anyone who would like more details about these remonstrances will find them at the end of this work, together with the 1701 system of government, which lasted in Pennsylvania until the Revolution.*

Penn had crazy, capricious ideas that kept him continually short of money; he was therefore forced to have recourse to extraordinary devices, and his deputies had to make every effort to please him in order to keep their jobs. He died, heavily in debt, in London in 1718, after pledging his property to a certain Gee [54] and several other men, and after agreeing to yield all his rights to the crown for £10,000, £2,000 of which he had already received on account. He was on the point of signing the contract when he suffered an attack of apoplexy, so Pennsylvania remained in his family.

If William Penn had been the kind of man described in some books, the colony of Pennsylvania would have been much more prosperous. Writers have exaggerated in saying that it was never at war with the savages and in propounding other false claims. But despite the proprietor's unscrupulous disregard for covenants and his continual disputes with the colonists, Pennsylvania grew more rapidly than the other settlements. This was doubtless because the older colonies set an example, provided foodstuffs, and sent help when the frontiers were attacked. Furthermore, the system of government Penn had promised, and which he was clever enough to have published in London, attracted immigrants from all directions.

Finally, the effects of religious liberty were felt even after 1701, when citizenship was restricted to Christians. As all immigrants

---

* See Note A [pp. 97–105 below].

[54] Joshua Gee, a Quaker and silkman, was one of nine men listed as holders of the mortgage on the province to pay the debt owed by Penn to the Ford family.

were Christians, no one suffered from injustice and everyone enjoyed the advantage of having no dominant religion. At the beginning Quakers had been as fanatic as Anabaptists, although they became much more moderate later. They were not tolerated in Virginia or in any New England colony, with the exception of Rhode Island, and there were very few in Maryland and New York.

Rhode Island was too small to attract European emigrants, and it is quite possible that few people knew the difference which existed with regard to religious liberty between this colony and the others in New England. Massachusetts, Connecticut, and New Hampshire were arbitrarily governed by Congregationalists, Virginia by Anglicans. Maryland is small, and as the Catholics were in a dominant position both numerically and because of the proprietor, Protestants did not like to go there.

As the New York government was subject to James II, it did not offer much security. Protestants who settled in this colony were not very happy, and the few Catholics who arrived under the indirect protection of James were received coldly. They were banned by law in 1691 after James's abdication.

Pennsylvania was therefore preferred by immigrants of all religions, especially by Quakers. The latter included many wealthy people. As they were both economical and good businessmen, their example was useful during the early years of the colony, and its effects are still felt. The first seeds make deep roots. Plants become vigorous, and their shade stunts the growth of other species in the neighborhood.

### The Founding of the Two Carolinas and Georgia

Although the first settlement of the area which now forms the two Carolinas and Georgia preceded by a few years that of Pennsylvania, we could not discuss it earlier, because Carolina was not divided into two provinces for forty-six years, and Georgia was not founded until four years later. To give a clear picture, we must group the three colonies together.

On 24 March 1662 Charles II gave a charter for the land between lat. 31° and lat. 36° to eight people: the earl of Clarendon, the duke of Albemarle, the earl of Craven, Lord Berkeley, Lord Ashley, Sir George Carteret, Sir William Berkeley, and Sir John

Colleton.[55] The country was called Carolina by order of and in honor of the king. Hewatt, author of the history of South Carolina and Georgia, claims it had been named Carolina long before by Jean Ribaut, who was sent to this region by Admiral Coligny during the French civil wars with two vessels and a rather large number of settlers.[56] Coligny may have intended to prepare an asylum for himself and his partisans in the event that he was forced to leave France.

Hewatt says the Indians gave Ribaut a warm welcome when he told them that he was an enemy of the Spaniards. After the strife subsided in France, Coligny, who up to that time had been unable to assist the new colony, sent René de Laudonnière to America with three vessels and a large number of men. Before they arrived, Ribaut and his followers abandoned the settlement, as they lacked supplies. When Laudonnière was on the point of leaving, for the same reason, Ribaut returned from France with seven vessels. Just as the colony was beginning to prosper, a Spaniard, Pedro Menéndez de Avilés, killed Ribaut with seven hundred of his men and forced the rest to return to France. Hewatt adds that M. de Gourgues of Gascony avenged his compatriots some time later and drove Menéndez out, but neither he nor any other French immigrants tried again to establish a colony there.* [57]

Charles II's charter declared the eight associates masters and absolute proprietors of the area, with all rights of jurisdiction, royal privileges, etc. The only restriction was that any laws promulgated

---

* The Spaniards hanged the French prisoners with a sign "Not as Frenchmen but as heretics." De Gourgues had the Spaniards hanged with another sign: "Not as Spaniards, but as assassins."

[55] The Carolina proprietors were Edward Hyde, first earl of Clarendon; George Monck, first duke of Albemarle; William Craven, the earl of Craven; Anthony Ashley Cooper, first earl of Shaftesbury; the two Berkeley brothers, Carteret, and Colleton.

[56] Alexander Hewatt, *An Historical Account of the Rise and Progress of the Colonies of South Carolina and Georgia*, 2 vols. (London, 1779). Captain Ribaut established a garrison at Port Royal in 1562. On his return to France, he left 30 men who abandoned the post soon afterward. Admiral Gaspard de Coligny, a leader in the Huguenot forces, was later killed in the Massacre of Saint Bartholomew.

[57] Laudonnière, another Huguenot, had accompanied Ribaut in 1562. Two years later he led another expedition, which was reinforced by Ribaut in the spring of 1565. That fall the Spaniards under Menéndez expelled the Protestant French settlers, claiming the land as Spanish by right of discovery. Dominique de Gourgues, a Gascon, equipped three vessels at his own expense and attacked the Spanish fort in 1567.

should require the consent of the freemen. In the same charter, after these ample concessions, the king reserved for himself and his heirs absolute sovereignty over the whole country. Whether these ambiguities were accidental or intended, they were very fashionable at the time. Two years later a new charter, dated 30 June, extended the territory from lat. 29° to lat. 36½° and declared it should be separated from Virginia by a straight line running from east to west.

We now come to the period of Locke's system of legislation, a system more famous for its author than for any intrinsic merit. It is said that the proprietors gave Locke the basic principles on which it was to be established. If this is true, it seems to me that Locke should not have risked his own reputation by accepting such a commission. If we examine attentively all the parts of this machine, which is extremely complicated, we are led to believe that the architect would not have put so much work into it unless he had believed the basis to be stable and just.

As a token of respect to the author, we would have inserted the whole system at the end of this book were it not so long. It contains 120 articles, most of them lengthy, in addition to a supplement which prescribes the Rules of Precedence. It is impossible to give a résumé that will convey the whole idea, for the style is extremely concise. We thus have to limit ourselves to the most important articles, which seem to be the following:

The eldest of the *Lords Proprietors* shall be *Pallatine*, and upon the decrease of the *Pallatine*, the eldest of those who were *Proprietors* the first of *March* One thousand six hundred sixty and Nine shall succeed him . . . And when none of them are living, he that hath been longest a *Proprietor* shall succeed. . . .

There shall be *seven* other *chief Officers* erected, viz. The *Admirals, Chamberlains, Chancellors, Constables, Chief Justices, High Stewards,* and *Treasurers;* which places shall be enjoyed by none but the *Lords Proprietors;* to be assigned at first by Lott, and upon the Vacancy of any one of the *seven* great *Offices,* by death or otherwise, the eldest of those who were *Proprietors* the first of *March* One thousand six hundred sixth and Nine shall have his choyce. . . .

The whole Province shall be *divided* into *Counties;* each *County* shall consist of eight *Signiories,* eight *Baronies,* and four *Precincts;* each *Precinct* shall consist of six *Colonies.*

Each *Signiory, Barony,* and *Colony* shall consist of twelve thousand Acres, the eight *Signiories* being the Share of the eight *Proprietors,* and the eight *Baronies* of the *Nobility,* both which Shares being each of them one fifth part of the whole, are to be perpetually annexed, the one to the *Proprietors*, the other to the hereditary *Nobility*, leaving the Colonies being three Fifths, amongst the People. . . .

At any time before the Year One thousand seven hundred and one, any of the *Lords Proprietors* shall have power to *Relinquish, Alienate,* and *Dispose* to any other Person, his *Proprietorship*, and all the Signiories, Powers, and Interest thereunto belonging, wholly and intirely together, and not otherwise. But after the year One thousand seven hundred those who are then *Lords Proprietors*, shall not have power to *Alienate* or *Make over* their *Proprietorship*, with the Signiories and Priviledges thereunto belonging, or any part thereof, to any person whatsoever. . . .

For want of *Heirs Male* . . . the remaining seven *Proprietors* shall upon the Vacancy, chuse a *Landgrave* to succeed the deceased *Proprietor*, who being chosen by the majority of the seven surviving *proprietors*, he and his Heirs successively shall be *Proprietors*. . . .

That the number of eight proprietors may be constantly kept; if upon the vacancy of any *proprietorship*, the seven surviving *proprietors* shall not chuse a *Landgrave* to be a *Proprietor*, before the second biennial *Parliament* after the Vacancy; then the next biennial *Parliament* but one after such Vacancy, shall have power to chuse any *Landgrave* to be *Proprietor*. . . .

There shall be just as many *Landgraves* as there are *Counties*, and twice as many *Cassiques*, and no more. These shall be the hereditary *Nobility* of the Province. . . . Each *Landgrave* shall have four *Baronies*, and each *Cassique* two *Baronies*. . . .

That the *due number* of *Landgraves* and *Cassiques* may be always kept up, if upon the *Devolution* of any *Landgraveship* or *Cassiqueship*, the *Pallatines Court* shall not settle the *devolved Dignity*, with the *Baronies* thereunto annexed, before the second biennial *Parliament* after such Devolution, the next biennial *Parliament* but one after such Devolution shall have power to *make* any one *Landgrave* or *Cassique* in the room of him, who dying without *Heirs*, his *dignity* and *Baronies* devolved. . . .

In every *Signiory, Barony,* and *Mannor*, the respective Lord shall have power in his own Name to hold *Court-Leet* there, for Trying of all Causes both Civil and Criminal. . . .

Every Mannor shall consist of not less than *three thousand Acres*, and not above *Twelve thousand Acres* in one entire Piece and Colony; but any three thousand Acres or more in one Piece, and the Possession of one Man, shall not be a *Mannor*, unless it be Constituted a *Mannor* by the Grant of the *Palatines Court*.

Every Lord of a *Mannor*, within his *Mannor*, shall have all the Powers, Jurisdictions, and Priviledges, which a *Landgrave* or *Cassique* hath in his *Baronies* . . .

No *Landgrave* or *Cassique* shall be Tried for any Criminal Cause, in any but the *Chief Justice's* Court, and that by a jury of his *Peers*.

There shall be *eight Supream Courts*. The first called *The Palatine's Court*, consisting of the *Palatine*, and the other seven *Proprietors*. The other seven Courts of the other seven great Officers, shall consist each of them of a *proprietor*, and six *Councellors* added to him. Under each of these latter seven *Courts* shall be a *Colledge* of twelve *Assistants*. . . .

Out of these *Colledges* shall be chosen at first by the *Palatine's Court*, six *Councellors*, to be joyned with each *proprietor* in his Court. . . . No Place shall be Vacant in any of the proprietors *Courts* or *Colledges*, longer than the next *Session of Parliament*. . . .

The *Palatine's Court* shall consist of the *Palatine*, and seven *proprietors*, wherein nothing shall be acted without the Presence and Consent of the *Palatine* or his *Deputy*, and three others of the *proprietors* or their *Deputies*. This Court shall have power to call Parliaments, to make Elections of all *Officers* in the *proprietors* dispose, to nominate and appoint *Port-Towns:* And also shall have power by their Order to the *Treasurer*, to dispose of all *publick Treasure*, excepting Money granted by the *Parliament*, and by them directed to some partitcular publick use; And also shall have a *Negative* upon all Acts, Orders, Votes of the Grand Council and the *Parliament*. . . .

The *Palatine* himself or his deputy when he in person shall be either in the *Army*, or in any of the *proprietors Courts*, shall then have the power of *General*, or of that *proprietor* in whose Court he is then present, and the *proprietor* in whose Court the *Palatine* or his deputy then presides shall during his presence there be but as one of the *Council*. . . .

The Grand Council shall consist of the *Palatine* and seven *Proprietors*, and the forty two *Councellors* of the several *Proprietors Courts*, who shall have power to Determine any Controversies that may arise between any of the *Proprietors Courts*, about their respective Jurisdictions, or between the Members of the same Court, about their *Manner* and *Methods* of *Proceeding:* To make *Peace* and *War, Leagues, Treaties*, etc. . . .

The *Grand Council* shall always be Judges of all Causes and Appeals that concern the *Palatine*, or any of the *Lords proprietors*, or any *Councellor* of any *proprietors Court*, in any Cause which otherwise should have been Tried in the Court in which the said *Councellor* is Judge himself.

The *Quorum* of the *Grand Council* shall be thirteen, where of a *proprietor* or his *Deputy* shall be always one. . . .

In every County there shall be a *Court*. . . . For any *personal Causes* exceeding the value of two hundred Pounds *Sterling*, or in Title of *Land*, or in any *Criminal Cause*, either Party upon paying twenty pounds *Sterling* to the *Lords proprietors* use, shall have liberty of *Appeal* from the *County Court* unto the respective *Proprietors Court*.

In every *Precinct* there shall be a *Court*, consisting of a *Steward* and four *Justices* of the *Precinct* . . . who shall judge all *Civil Causes* whatsoever, and in all personal Actions, not exceeding fifty Pounds *Sterling*, without *Appeal;* But where the Cause shall exceed that value, or concern a Title of *Land*, and in all *Criminal Causes*, there either Party, upon paying five Pounds *Sterling* to the *Lords proprietors* use, shall have liberty of *Appeal* to the *County Court*.

There shall be a *Parliament*, consisting of the *Proprietors* or their *Deputies*, the *Landgraves* and *Cassiques*, and one *Freeholder* out of every *Precinct*, to be chosen by the *Freeholders* of the said *Precinct* respectively. They shall sit altogether in one Room, and have every Member one Vote.

No Man shall be chosen a *Member* of *Parliament*, who hath less than five hundred Acres of Freehold within the *Precinct* for which he is chosen; nor shall any have a vote in chusing the said *Member* that hath less than fifty Acres of Freehold within the said *Precinct*.

A new *Parliament* shall be Assembled the first *Monday* of the month of November every second Year. . . .

No Act or Order of *Parliament* shall be of any force, unless it be *Ratified* in open *Parliament* during the same Session by the *Palatine* or his *Deputy*, and three more of the *Lords Proprietors* or their *Deputies* and then not to continue longer in force but untill the next *Biennial Parliament*, unless in the mean time it be *Ratified* under the Hands and Seals of the *Palatine* himself, and three more of the *Lords Proprietors* themselves, and by their Order publish'd at the next *Biennial Parliament*.

Any Proprietor or his Deputy may enter his *Protestation* against any Act of the *Parliament*. . . . In such case after a full and free Debate, the several *Estates* shall retire into four several *Chambers*, the *Palatine* and *Proprietors* into one, the *Landgraves* into another, the *Cassiques* into another, and those chosen by the *Precinct* into a fourth, and if the major part of any of the four *Estates* shall Vote that the Law is not agreeable to this *Establishment*, and these *Fundamental Constitutions* of the Government, then it shall pass no farther.[58]

Article 96 declares the Anglican religion to be the only orthodox one and states that it shall be maintained by the government. People say, however, that Locke had placed all religions on the same footing and that he told a friend, to whom he gave a copy of the constitutions, that Article 96 had been inserted by one of the proprietors.

These are the essential points which must be understood before we examine the quarrels that arose between the colonists and the proprietors, whom we may call the sovereigns.

The country measures over five hundred miles along the coast

[58] John Locke, *The Fundamental Constitutions of Carolina* ([London], 1682).

and is about six hundred miles in depth. It is no less fertile than other sections. According to Locke's system, the proprietors were to own one-fifth of the territory in perpetuity, without being able to alienate any part of it. This means that each one would have had about eight million acres. As soon as the area was settled, each proprietor's income from real estate alone would have been worthy of a king. The other four-fifths were also to belong to the proprietors, who could dispose of them as they wished, selling or giving baronies, selling, giving, or ceding the territory for quitrents. I am not even considering other taxes, as that would take me too far.

The proprietors had full authority over public funds without being obliged to give any accounting; they presided in all high offices, such as the Grand Council, which proposed laws; they had absolute and exclusive power to approve them and to suspend them after they were approved; in short, they had every efficacious method of corrupting people and getting their votes. We should add that the nobles upheld the proprietors, as every landgrave could become a proprietor and every cacique a landgrave. The more we examine Locke's system, the more we see that it tended to form as extraordinary and tyrannical an oligarchy as the human mind can conceive; let anyone who doubts this read the whole document.

In 1667 the proprietors sent William Sayle to survey the region. When he returned, the king granted the proprietors all the islands between lat. 22° and lat. 27°,[59] and in 1669 they sent Sayle back with a number of immigrants. Their primary task was to work out a plan for constructing a city to be named Charleston in the king's honor.

The first settlers were very discouraged because they found nothing but vast uncultivated plains nearly covered with stagnant water. Insects were numerous and annoying, as one would expect in warm countries. The colonists' theories about agriculture were useless in this totally different climate, and Indians often made surprise forays during which they tormented the settlers with their arrows. This was not without cause, for the proprietors did not even think of purchasing the land. Their ideas were grandiose and as extraordinary as they were unjust.

When the duke of York became master of New Belgium, his methods inspired many colonists to move. A group of Hollanders proposed to go to Carolina, and the proprietors sent two vessels to

[59] These islands are the Bahamas, extending north from Great Inagua to Nassau.

get them. Their arrival revived the courage of the settlers; others came from Europe, and by 1674 there were enough inhabitants to elect their first representatives.

The rules prescribed by Locke were not uniformly obeyed. Their complexity, which would have made them difficult to observe at best, made them impossible in a new colony. Furthermore, the government did not suit the temperament of the people, and the proprietors relied on deputies, who are rarely respected. Dissensions and disorders of various types soon erupted. Religion, as usual, played a large part in this. Although Anglicans were numerically in the minority, they tried several times to disparage other sects. The constant partiality shown by the proprietors and their party to the Anglican church augmented jealousy, envy, and hatred.

About this time Charles II knighted Henry Morgan of Wales, the famous sea rover who had pillaged Portobelo and Panama. The king's example led both Europeans and the colonists to extend a warm welcome to pirates. Carolina was their favorite haven in America because of its proximity to the Spanish possessions. As they squandered the money they obtained so easily, they had no trouble making the acquaintance of settlers, who reaped very little profit from poorly cultivated land. This led to an infamous traffic. The proprietors had made no treaties with the Indians; so wars, or rather skirmishes, were of frequent occurrence. The pirates bought the Indian prisoners and sold them in the islands. This abominable traffic lasted a long time and was difficult to abolish.

James II's bad government and the revocation of the Edict of Nantes finally came to the aid of the new colony. A large number of respectable families, fleeing from persecution in both France and England, brought new life to the settlement. It is obvious that men who left their homeland in search of liberty were quite different from those sent out by companies of adventurers.

The new immigrants soon saw that the people's interests could not be reconciled with those of the proprietors. Their observations about the government began to circulate and made a deep impression. If the proprietors had been present, they might have changed their absurd system. But they resided in England and sent sovereign orders from their Palatine Court. Their deputies, acting from prudence or perhaps from necessity, occasionally disobeyed instructions to please the inhabitants. This, however, was no remedy, for the proprietors did not approve any deviation from their plan.

Governor [Joseph] Morton, a fine man in every way, lost the love of the people without keeping the proprietors' favor, for the duties of his post were such that he could not satisfy either side. In 1687 he was succeeded by James Colleton (the proprietor's brother), who to increase his prestige was given the title of landgrave by the Palatine Court. Although Colleton wanted to follow the instructions of his superiors, he understood the necessity of adhering to some new laws that disregarded them. The Palatine Court ordered him to follow instructions. The people, however, abided by the new laws and did not obey the governor. In the midst of this anarchy the secretary, Paul Grimball, annoyed the inhabitants by displaying too much zeal for the proprietors' side. In 1690 they put him in prison, took possession of the archives, refused to pay quitrents for land they could not cultivate, and convoked an assembly.

Colleton assembled the militia and proclaimed martial law. As soon as the colonists were assured this was merely a pretext devised to intimidate them, they convoked the assembly. It proclaimed Landgrave Colleton incapable of holding any civil or military office in the province and ordered him to leave on a certain date. The proprietors next appointed Philip Ludwell of Virginia, who succeeded in maintaining some order, and they set up a system of government which granted the representatives the right to propose laws.

The Anglicans, who were always trying to impose their religion, praised the new plan because they could not have succeeded in gaining their objective if the proprietors' government had been destroyed. The nonconformists included many French Protestants. The Anglicans now began training their batteries on them to try to deprive them of their citizenship, and they invoked English laws whenever municipal ones were inapplicable. As tempers waxed hotter, they began to say French Protestants had no right to own land and that their marriages were illegal. The proprietors had different opinions on these last two points but did not dare oppose the Anglicans, who were the sole support of their government.

Several French refugees had purchased vast tracts of land at £20 per thousand acres, with an annual fee of one shilling quitrent for every hundred. They had cultivated the land so that they could live comfortably and expected to leave a good inheritance to their children. Ludwell's good behavior made a number hope things would take a better turn. A few, however, who could not tolerate the insolence of the Anglicans or cope with the fear that their children might one day be called bastards and deprived of their property, went to Pennsylvania, and they were followed by some Dutch and English nonconformists.

Governmental weakness led to a return of the pirates and restoration of the practice of selling Indians. Ludwell, who despaired of
restoring order, wrote the proprietors to send another governor
and returned to Virginia. Hewatt says the proprietors deprived him
of his post because he did not defend their prerogatives. He was
succeeded by Landgrave Thomas Smith; it was at this time that the
first grains of rice were brought to Carolina by a captain of a brigantine who stopped there on his way from Madagascar to England.
Two years later Smith resigned, being unable to keep order, and he
advised the proprietors to send one of their own number. The following year John Archdale, a Quaker, was appointed. He stopped
some abuses but was unable to drive out all the pirates or to abolish
the custom of selling Indians, and he did not succeed in granting
French refugees the right to elect representatives or to vote.

Upon his return to London, Archdale told the proprietors they
would have to delete a number of articles in their system of government. They sent a new plan to Carolina, but the assembly rejected it so calmly it was clear they felt quite capable of governing
themselves. As religious disputes had more or less subsided, the proprietors no longer had any hold on the Anglicans.

After the assembly was firmly established, the French refugees
were advised to request that they be treated on a par with other
citizens. They had made many friends, thanks to their good behavior; hatred had died out with the religious quarrels; and most
citizens felt more generous since their rights were restored. Hence
these demands were granted.

While things were looking brighter, Lord Granville, one of the
greatest fanatics the Anglican sect ever had, became palatine.[60] He
was bigoted to the point of believing that anything was permissible
for his church. It would take too long to narrate all his illegal acts,
but in 1702 he ordered an election of representatives which was
held under governmental protection but without fulfilling the legal
requirements. It is easy to imagine the results of this tumultuous
gathering. An assembly which had not been elected by the free
vote of the people passed a law establishing the preeminence of the
Anglican religion; the whole country was in an uproar. The English peers disapproved of their colleague's conduct and drew up a
statement to Queen Anne in favor of the nonconformists. She replied: "I thank the house for laying these matters so plainly before
me: I am sensible of what great consequence the plantations are to

---

[60] John Carteret, first earl of Granville.

England, and will do all in my power to relieve my subjects in Carolina, and protect them in their just rights." [61]

Steps were taken, and the oppressed would probably have triumphed, if the government had not been distracted by the war about to break out with France. Foreign wars are the best remedy for domestic troubles. There was a great deal of dissatisfaction in Carolina, where nonconformists made up about three-quarters of the population; some left, and their departure increased the resentment of the others. But a threatened invasion by the French and Spaniards united the two parties and there was no more religious bickering.

In 1708 a number of people in the Palatinate decided to emigrate to Carolina. They appealed to the proprietors, who sent ships and granted them a hundred acres per person on condition that after a decade they should make an annual payment of a penny sterling per acre. This group settled on and near the Roanoke River just a short distance from the Virginia boundary and included some of the most industrious settlers of North Carolina. A short time later 130 of these valuable men were attacked one night without warning and massacred with a number of other people by Indians of several tribes. These savages had banded together to avenge old injuries and may have confused the innocent and the guilty.

The proprietors' government continued to vacillate. Their intervals in power were short, but their determination to keep control increased the colonists' disgust. In 1719 the people finally resolved to rid themselves completely of this government. The assembly notified Governor Robert Johnson that the colonists were determined to end the arbitrary and oppressive rule of the proprietors but that they would be happy to have him as governor, provided he would recognize no superior other than the king. Johnson, a fine man, not only refused but did all he could to maintain the proprietors' rights.

The assembly then elected James Moore governor pro tempore and sent an agent to the king to uphold their rights. When he arrived in London, George I was in Hanover. The regency espoused the cause of the inhabitants of Carolina; early in 1721 it appointed General Nicholson to serve as governor, and he was received with great enthusiasm. [62]

[61] Hewatt, 1:177.

[62] Sir Francis Nicholson, governor of South Carolina 1721–29, had previously served as governor of the colonies of New York, Maryland, and Virginia. He was a captain, not a general.

Seven proprietors had sold their rights to the king, but Lord
Granville retained the land assigned to him in the most northerly
region by a charter granted in 1720. As a fairly sizable colony had
already been established in the vicinity of Roanoke, a long distance
from the one in Charleston, the country was divided into two provinces with separate governments called, as they are today, South
Carolina and North Carolina.

Johnson had remained in Carolina after Moore's election and
never ceased to uphold the claims of the proprietors. Despite this
loyalty, they gave him a very poor reception on his return to London, but he was consoled for their ingratitude in 1731 when the
king sent him to South Carolina as governor. The people of
Charleston, remembering his ability, were indignant at the way he
had been treated and received him as the Romans welcomed Cicero
on his return from exile.

When the proprietors relinquished their rights, Carolina had
only fourteen thousand inhabitants, despite all the immigrants. A
population cannot increase if the citizens are unhappy. After the
change in government the settlement began to prosper.

In 1732 a large tract of South Carolina was set aside for a third
colony, named Georgia in the king's honor. The charter, dated 9
June, was granted to a company of twenty-one men who were
anxious to establish an asylum for the unfortunate. They contributed money to set up a fund, and this was increased by a number
of gifts.

One of the founders, James Oglethorpe, brought 116 poor people to this country. They landed in Charleston, where the inhabitants vied with each other in showering kindnesses on them. They
contributed food, pigs, cows, and other animals, and some even
accompanied the new arrivals to the Savannah River, on the banks
of which Oglethorpe began to build the city bearing its name. The
second leader was a Swiss, Jean Pierre Purry. He arrived in Georgia with 170 of his compatriots, built Purrysburg, [South Carolina,] and was followed by 200 other emigrants.

These founders were wealthy men with good intentions, and
their zeal inspired Parliament to encourage the enterprise. Hewatt
says they received £36,000; others claim it was £10,000. In any
event, this contribution may be responsible for the widespread belief in Europe that the colonies were founded at the expense of the
nation. The Americans knew nothing about this, and the English
did not take the trouble to correct the error.

Abbé Raynal states (9:114): "In a very short time this establishment had received five thousand inhabitants and had cost the treasury £1,485,000." This is wholly inaccurate, for the contribution from Parliament was a gift of charity, and it gave England no more sovereignty over Georgia than the money sent to Lisbon after the earthquake gave England sovereignty over Portugal.

The owners of the charter were protectors rather than masters or proprietors, but their regulations provided new proof of the difficulty involved in governing distant countries. Despite the good intentions, which were backed by numerous gifts, and despite the good will of the industrious Scottish and German immigrants, the colony did not thrive. The troubles occasioned by well-intentioned laws forced a large number of settlers to leave. The majority did not go far; they crossed the river, settled in Carolina, and began to prosper as soon as they were under a different government. Finally these worthy benefactors of humanity, who had learned from experience that assistance does not make men happy, abandoned their protectorship altogether. In 1752 they returned the charter to the king, and the government of Georgia was henceforth very similar to that of the other colonies.*

## Conclusion

This is enough to give an idea of the founding of the thirteen colonies, the character of their inhabitants, and their relationship with Great Britain; it will now be easy to understand the true cause of the Revolution. Wars between the colonies and their European neighbors, wars with the Indians, and other political and economic problems lie within the province of any writer who wants to write a complete history, but this could not be instructive without being voluminous.

The character of the founders, the motives that led most of them to leave Europe, and their behavior make any reflections on my part superfluous; it is not difficult to conceive what ideas they must have transmitted to their descendants. Europeans have believed that the colonies were largely populated by criminals transported from England. If that were the case, their descendants would be all the

---

* Abbé Raynal says (9:115): "Jurisdiction had been given to private citizens in Georgia, together with the property." Later, alluding to the vices of the government, he writes: "The British ministry thus abandoned public welfare to the selfish greed of certain individuals." Such respectable men did not deserve this kind of treatment.

more estimable, unless one credits climate and soil with the ability to improve mankind. Whatever conclusion you draw, it is contrary to those spread by rumormongers to discredit the country. But let us examine the facts, without paying attention to lies invented by politicians and accepted by the ignorant.

In 1666 England approved the first law condemning anyone found guilty of plundering in Northumberland County to be transported to the colonies. This county, as everyone knows, borders Scotland; old hatreds still persisted between the two nations, and frequent lootings in Northumberland gave rise to the law. Four years later the decree was broadened to include thieves who stole sheets spread out at night in the country to be whitened or who removed royal garments entrusted to them. Toward the close of this same year it was applied to anyone who set fire to stacks of grain or slaughtered cattle.

Before 1717 only those who had perpetrated these particular crimes could be transported to America, and the general belief is that not a single criminal was taken. During that year a judge was permitted, in certain cases, to commute the death penalty into banishment to the colonies. At this period the population of the colonies was about eight hundred thousand. It is improbable that more than a hundred criminals were ever transported in a single year. Some returned to England before their time was up, but they were chiefly vagabonds who could not make up their minds to do any work. Others, who had been led into evildoing through poverty, became good citizens on finding themselves in a country where work was well paid. As public opinion was against them, few were able to marry. The reader can now judge the accuracy of Abbé Raynal's statement (8:176): "A second class of colonists was formerly composed of criminals whom the capital condemned to be transported to America and who owed seven or fourteen years of hard labor to planters who had purchased them from the law courts. Everyone was disgusted with these corrupt men, who were always ready to commit new crimes."

Abbé Raynal would let the uninformed reader conclude that these evildoers contributed to a large degree in populating the country. The author erred in accepting the assertions of several writers who, through ignorance or Anglomania, have claimed that Parliament made this law to populate the colonies; it would be like pouring a few buckets of water in the Potomac and Delaware rivers to widen them for navigation.

The abbé is also mistaken in saying the tribunals sold criminal labor; the fact is that it cost the government £2 to transport every criminal. It is also wrong to say that the service was seven or fourteen years. At first the law restricted it to seven, but it was prolonged to fourteen, twenty-one, and even to a life sentence, depending on the crime. Again it is a mistake to say that the colonists became disgusted with the evildoers; they complained as soon as the law was enacted. Some colonies refused to receive them at all; others took them to avoid trouble with England, as one often submits to something disagreeable in order to avoid a worse alternative.

About 1766 a stowaway was arrested in New York, tried, and condemned to be taken back to England. He was put on board ship and sent back. When he landed, he was taken to prison, then into court, and the judge asked why he had returned. "I was transported," he replied. "But did you not know that it is a hanging offense to come back before your time has expired?" "I knew it, milord." "Then why did you return?" "Milord, because I was transported." The judge, who could not conceive anyone being sentenced to be transported from America to England, did not understand what the man was saying. The misunderstanding, as a friend of mine who witnessed the scene told me that very day, caused a curious dialogue between the accused and the judge and aroused the interest of all the spectators. Finally, when the judge told the prisoner he would be hanged, the latter drew from his pocket an authentic copy of the sentence of the New York tribunal. Everyone laughed when he read it, and the man was set free.

The law dealing with the transportation of evildoers tended to discredit the colonists, to give a dreadful impression of the country, and thus to discourage immigration. When the House of Commons decided to use criminals in the arsenals, the House of Lords opposed the plan, saying it tended to discredit the royal arsenals.

Parliamentary politics has not changed. In various parts of Europe the gazettes spread everything the imagination can devise to injure the United States. This policy is useless, since the Europeans who need to emigrate to America and who can find happiness there, in a word the only Europeans who would suit us, are those who either cannot read or who do not have time to do so.

Abbé Raynal is no closer to the truth when he speaks of the progress of the population. After establishing that the rapid growth of the thirteen colonies "must have two sources" (p. 90), he adds: "The first is this throng of Irish, Jews, French, Waldensians, Palatines, Moravians, Salzburgers, who, weary of the political and religious vexations they found in Europe, sought tranquillity in these remote lands." The inhabitants of Great Britain, whom he does not mention, may well have contributed more colonists than all the other nations combined, including the Irish. As for the French, no emigrations are known, except those caused by the revocation of the Edict of Nantes. A few settlers also went to America when France ceded Acadia to Great Britain. The Jewish population before the Revolution is believed to have numbered less than a hundred and even today there are fewer than a thousand. "The second source of this astonishing multiplication," continues the author, "is in the climate of the colonies." The increase, which greatly overshadowed immigration, was caused by the abundance of land and its low price. The author admits this himself (pp. 191 and 192), and we fail to see how he can attribute this growth to the climate, which he describes very unfavorably elsewhere.

Let us now examine the relationship between the colonies, the kings of England, and Parliament.

We know that the colonies were founded at private expense, for the history of each one proves it. The following document, pertaining to the New England colonies, is in a resolution of the House of Commons, addressed by the secretary to the governor of Massachusetts: "Whereas the plantations in New England have, by the blessing of the Almighty, had good and prosperous success, without any public charge to this state." * Actually the nation did not become involved with colonial affairs until very late, when it saw

---

\* In speaking of the first two companies, Abbé Raynal says (8:313): "Although they were given the proceeds from the first lottery drawn in England, their development was so slow that in 1614 only 400 people were in the two colonies." At this date there was only one colony. The first attempt to settle New England ended in 1608 and the second began in 1620. This lottery concession must be one more story in the long list Abbé Raynal accepted in his haste. We see in the *Foedera* (19:242) that in 1630 Charles I gave a charter to a certain David Ramsey to convey to London and Westminster water from some springs a mile and a half from Hodsdon in Hertfordshire, and the king authorized a lottery to raise money for this task. Anderson, in his commercial history, says this lottery is the first to be mentioned either in the *Foedera* or in the books of statutes [Adam Anderson, *Historical and Chronological Deduction of the Origin of Commerce* (London, 1764)].

The *Foedera* is a collection of public acts and historical documents compiled by Mr. Thomas Rymer under the title *Foedera, Conventiones, litterae, etc.* [20 vols. (London, 1704–32)], containing the leagues, deeds, letters, and all the other public records entered into by English kings and all the emperors, kings, popes, princes, or republics from the reign of Henry I through that of Charles I. Mr. Anderson's commercial history is fairly well known.

that there were advantages to be gained, after expenses were met and the difficulties surmounted.

Without examining how little claim English kings had to the right of sovereignty in America, and without delving into the political reasons which led the founders to accept their charters, we must admit that the colonists recognized the kings as their sovereigns as soon as the charters were accepted and that the two parties were bound to each other by mutual obligations. The colonies made their contracts with the king, not with the country, and England never had the right to make any laws for them. Each one adopted the parliamentary laws it liked, just as it could have adopted the laws of the Koran, provided they were not at variance with English law—this was one of the clauses in the charters. The mistaken assumption prevalent in Europe, that England founded the colonies and had the right of sovereignty over them, may have come from different causes, but England was happy to let it remain. It furthered a monopoly of commerce by discouraging dealings with other European nations, and before the Revolution, the latter did not consider the colonies of sufficient interest to study their history.

In accordance with the law of the jungle, the kings often violated their treaties with the colonies. Although the latter remonstrated, they let themselves be dominated through weakness or to avoid disputes, and this encouraged the desire to browbeat them still more. It is like the patient man who submits to a blow, only to have the court decree that the bully can hit him as much as he wishes. Acts of oppression were so numerous that I could not list them all without extending the length of my book. The reader will find a number in the Declaration of Independence.* Charles II and James II, his brother and successor, resolved to take back all the charters. They arbitrarily revoked the one granted to the colony of Massachusetts, and the death of Charles, followed by James's abdication, came in the nick of time for the colonists. William and Mary, who succeeded James, felt that the colony of Massachusetts should have a charter, though they made certain it was not so favorable to the people as the previous one had been. But even when revised, the charters proved that the only connection was with the king and that the British government had no sovereignty over the colonies. Bernard, the next to the last royal governor of Massachu-

* See Note B [omitted].

setts, was one of the greatest enemies of colonial liberty.[63] Seeking to prove that the English government should reduce the colonies to slavery, he stated in a letter published in England: "If the charters can be pleaded against the authority of parliament, they amount to an alienation of the dominions of Great Britain and are, in effect, acts of dismembering the British Empire and will operate as such, if care is not taken to prevent it."

## The True Cause of the Revolution

After Charles I was beheaded, Parliament seized the royal power and claimed sovereignty over the colonies. It then passed an act prohibiting them to engage in commerce with other nations. These parliamentary claims seem incredible when the facts are recalled. According to the English constitution, parliamentary deliberations must be approved by the king before becoming law. When Charles II was restored, it was assumed that his reign had begun at the time of his father's death, so that year is called the twelfth, rather than the first, of his reign. The year 1650 was therefore the second, and as he was an exile at the time, he could not sign the act I have just mentioned. Parliament nullified everything that had been done under Cromwell; yet it was this act that paved the way for the parliamentary pretensions; to revive them, Charles approved an act identical with the one passed in 1650.

We have seen that when Virginia yielded to Cromwell in 1651, it was agreed the colony should continue to enjoy freedom of commerce with all nations. Yet Charles made no distinction between it and the other colonies. If the capitulation to Cromwell is listed in the number of nullified acts, how can one envisage a parliamentary pretension founded on the claim he had abrogated royal prerogatives? The kings never had the right to submit the colonies to Parliament or to any other legislative body in Europe.

By exerting pressure the ministers exercised the right to regulate commerce, and some colonies, which were persuaded that it was, as claimed, a pact for mutual convenience, consented to it. But if all the colonies had signed this pact, would Parliament have acquired the right of sovereignty? If I let you take some of my clothing because I am afraid or because I believe that we are making an exchange, does this give you a legal right to everything I have in the world?

[63] Sir Francis Bernard, governor of Massachusetts 1760–69.

As long as these unjust pretensions were restricted to private matters, people protested, but they preferred to suffer rather than to risk a rupture. It is difficult to imagine what would have happened if the English ministers had continued to advance step by step. Luckily for the colonies, stubbornness prevailed over astuteness. The ministers declared openly that they had the right to make us obey all their laws; so we had to choose between separation and a shameful yoke. It would have been a waste of time and money to convoke our assemblies when a foreign legislative body could annul every act. We should have been better off under an absolute monarch since the sovereign of two nations has no immediate interest in ruining one to spare the other. It is a different story when one nation rules the other, so that every burden laid on the dependent country is a relief for itself. The greatest misfortune which may befall a nation is to become subject to a republic.*

The generous assistance furnished to the mother country during the war of 1756 made the ministers hope, after the peace of 1763, that they could increase public revenues by levying new taxes on the colonies. They also thought this would increase their own influence, for there would be new positions to fill. Although British subjects were heavily burdened with taxes, the colonies actually contributed more than their quota, since their commerce was shackled. Whether the ministers did not know this, or feigned not to know it, they invoked the famous Stamp Act, the taxes on paper, glass, dye, and tea. Everyone knows how energetically Americans opposed these measures. This is not the place to relate events which followed this opposition, such as the adventure of the stamped paper which was ignominiously tossed into the fire as soon as it was unloaded at Hampton, Virginia.

The ministers then changed their system. Parliament revoked the acts dealing with paper, dye, and glass and contented itself with a miserable tax of threepence on a pound of tea. This was designed to preserve a previous act in which it claimed the right to make the colonies obey every law.

If the British government had asked the colonies to impose a much heavier tax on themselves, no one would have refused. Dur-

---

* This is well known in America. Politicians who prophesy future conquests by our states either ignore what constitutes a nation's true happiness or think we do not know it ourselves. Someday the inhabitants of the United States might help their neighbors to become free, but it is improbable that they would be so imprudent and unjust as to have any subjects.

ing the war of 1756 they went into debt £10 million to help the
mother country and won a parliamentary reward of £300,000.
The colonists regarded this sum as a magnificent testimonial to
their devotion to the land of their ancestors; actually it was negli-
gible in view of their sacrifices, and thanks chiefly to the embezzle-
ment of Governor [Robert] Dinwiddie of Virginia, only part of
the amount was finally paid, but the assembly closed its eyes to
this skulduggery.

The small tax imposed on tea helped convince the Americans
that the ministers had conceived the plan of basing their pretended
claim on usage. They also learned that the ministers had talked to
the directors of the India Company. Several people think they
know what was secretly agreed, but I shall stick to the established
facts.

The company's charter only permitted it to sell at public auction
and under certain conditions. In 1773 it shipped to America a large
quantity of tea on its own account but with the government's assurance that it would make Parliament pay an act of indemnity. A
minister can disregard the laws, provided he has a majority of the
votes. It is a mistake to believe that the British prime minister is
obliged to act according to the people's wishes. He is less subject
to their resentment than the minister of an absolute monarch since
the sanction of Parliament serves as a shield, just as the sanction of
the Roman Senate protected the ministers of the first Caesars.

The oversupply of tea available at this time was an asset to the
ministers, who, to dazzle the Americans, wanted to sell it to them
at a lower price than they would have paid elsewhere, on the black
market. In Boston the tea was dumped into the harbor, while in
New York and Philadelphia the ships that had brought it were not
even permitted to dock. When the news reached London, shipments to the other colonies were canceled, for the ministers
thought, and rightly, that the tea would meet the same reception
everywhere.

Circumstances were responsible for the difference in treatment
between Boston and the other cities. In Boston the vessels were in
the harbor and the tea was consigned to merchants, who had agreed
with the governor to accept it and pay the tax. The inhabitants
prevented the crew from unloading the tea and urged that the
vessels return to England. The governor, however, refused to let
them sail. After seven or eight days of useless debate, the inhabitants, who were afraid that some English or Scottish merchant
might find a means of unloading the tea and paying the tax, went

on board and threw the whole cargo into the sea. They did this with extreme care so that no disorder would ensue. In Philadelphia and New York the merchants promised not to receive the tea. They offered the captains water and supplies for the return voyage and ordered them to leave without unloading anything. The opposition of the colonies was directed at the new system devised to force their submission, and it is clear that the financial assistance they had supplied made the ministers realize they were rapidly increasing in strength and vigor. One of them,* whose opinion carried weight, said that the colonies were already too powerful and that it was time to restrain them. It is thought the ministers intended to force them to rebel in order to have a pretext to deprive them of their charters and treat them like conquered countries. A well-informed historian will be able to demonstrate the probability, and possibly the certainty, of this opinion. He could even trace the real motive behind this plan and show that its authors hoped to make use of a subjugated America to extinguish liberty in England.

As the English ministers wanted to justify their conduct in the eyes of the nation, they sought to persuade their compatriots that Americans had been planning the Revolution for a long time. Nothing could have been more false. They knew, of course, that they and their ancestors had lost many of their rights, but they were not even thinking about recovering them. The nature of the yoke was so revolting that it seems incredible that an enlightened population could have allowed itself to be treated in this way. It would have been impossible if Americans had not felt for their ancestral country the kind of affection which blinds one to all else.

The colonists were forbidden to make certain items so that they would have to purchase them, at a high price, from English manufacturers.† They bore this burden, however, as patiently as the others and would not have revolted if the English ministers, taking their good nature for cowardice, had not tightened the bonds until they broke.

We could give several proofs that Americans did not think of revolting, but it suffices to say that the colonies sent a second re-

---

* Lord Hillsborough [Wills Hill, first earl of Hillsborough], who was in His Majesty's Council late in 1771 or early in 1772.

† The earl of Chatham, better known as William Pitt, was one of America's most zealous defenders in England. Speaking one day in the House of Lords on the subject of these taxes, he said: "But if America tried to produce a stocking or a nail for a horseshoe, I should be inclined to make it feel the entire weight of this country's power." We shall let the reader imagine the consequences.

quest to the king asking that conditions be restored to those prevailing immediately after the peace of 1763. This request, like the
first, was not acknowledged, but it shows that though Americans
were not complaining about the heavy charges they had borne,
they did not want any new ones.

# The Period between
# the Monarchy and the Republic

The royal governors gradually began to neglect their duties or to abuse their authority. In late 1773 and early 1774 some were forced to leave and others voluntarily abandoned their administrations. Still, the Americans did not think of separating from Great Britain and did not conceive of being forced to such a fatal step. Their desire to remain united made them hope the ministers would relinquish their pretensions and that things would take a better turn. The colonies had to defend their rights, but this was impossible under the existing constitutions and no one thought of writing new ones. It was therefore necessary to use an expedient which, without destroying the suspended government, would maintain law and order by making all the inhabitants responsible for what was done during this kind of interregnum. Because the colonies adopted the same system, with very slight differences, a description of one will serve for all.

The various governments were composites of monarchy, aristocracy, and democracy, with the exception of Pennsylvania and Delaware, where there was no aristocracy. Both had the same governor, a member of the Penn family, which owned both. This governor and the governor of Maryland, who was named by the proprietary heirs of Lord Baltimore, had to be approved by the king, but he never refused his sanction. Those of Connecticut and Rhode Island were elected by the people and the others, who represented the monarchy, were named by the king. He also appointed the members of the upper houses, except in New England. In Rhode Island and Connecticut the colonists controlled the election,* while in Massachusetts and New Hampshire the upper house

* Connecticut and Rhode Island were quite independent even before the Revolution, since the king could not annul their laws. Originally the Massachusetts charter was the same as that of Connecticut, but Charles II abolished it in 1684. The colony continued to use it, however, until 1686, when James II took it away to govern arbitrarily. About this same time Sir Edmund Andros tried similar tactics in Connecticut, but one evening, when the matter was being discussed in Hartford, a spectator extinguished the lights, carried the charter away, and hid it. That is how it was preserved and why it still exists.

was chosen by representatives. The people elected the lower house everywhere.

Each colony was divided into districts, generally called counties. Virginia had about sixty, very unequal in size. Each county sent two representatives to form the democratic body in the assembly, which was and is still called the General Assembly.*

The British government, which wished to retain as many representatives as possible in areas accessible to the warships, was responsible for the inequalities in the size of the counties. Frontier colonies extended to the borders, but when the population increased to such an extent that the inhabitants could no longer assemble conveniently, a county was split in two. As the number of representatives in areas far from the sea and navigable rivers would eventually have become a majority, the last English governor of Virginia (the earl of Dunmore) [64] was ordered not to permit any more divisions unless the new counties forfeited their right to send representatives. Governors of other colonies received the same order, and this is mentioned in the Declaration of Independence.

In addition to the two representatives for each county, there were four others in Virginia: one was appointed by the city of Norfolk; a second by Williamsburg, then capital of the province; a third by the college in Williamsburg; and the last by Jamestown, which had been the previous capital and where only two or three families still resided.†

The governor, like the English king, had the right to dissolve the lower house ‡ and did not fail to use it when the representa-

---

* The word *assembly* has always been considered less expressive than *parliament;* for this reason some men proposed to change it when the new government was established. After thorough consideration, however, they decided to leave it, since names are passive at best. The word *emperor,* for example, was less significant than *king* before the time of Julius Caesar, but it later meant far more when it was used to designate the master of nearly two-thirds of the known world.

† The present government has not permitted either Jamestown or the college in Williamsburg to send representatives, for unjust privileges encourage corruption. It is not astonishing that friends of liberty in England protest against the right enjoyed by abandoned towns to appoint representatives.

‡ As it was impossible to hold a new election without his permission, he had the power to keep the colony without representatives, as Lord Dunmore did on one occasion for nearly a year. He could also keep his favorites in their posts as long as he governed, for if he did not order a new election, the colonists had to wait for the arrival of a new governor or the king's death. Time was of no importance.

[64] John Murray, fourth earl of Dunmore.

tives, at the news of the blockade of Boston, announced in May 1774 that they disapproved the behavior of the English ministers and that Virginians had no intention of watching idly while their brothers were being persecuted.

Frequent violations of colonial rights by the British government, especially after the peace of 1763, various attempts to foment quarrels between the plantations, and the well-arranged British plan to attack them separately led the colonial representatives on 12 March 1773 to set up a committee of seven to correspond with those in other colonies so that everything of interest in one colony could be communicated immediately to all the others.* America owes its liberty to this institution, and it seems that the English ministers foresaw the consequences, because the governor of Virginia was severely reprimanded for not having dissolved the lower house as soon as the idea was suggested.

The British ministers flattered themselves that other ports, jealous of Boston, especially Salem, which they had favored, would take advantage of Boston's plight and that the other colonies would consider this a favorable time to obtain favors from the mother country in return for their obedience. But the inhabitants of every township in the colony and in all neighboring colonies took up arms and flew to the aid of Boston. They were so eager that many horses arrived bearing two, sometimes even three, men. More remote colonies hastened to inform Massachusetts that they intended to aid it in every possible way. Massachusetts replied it needed not men but foodstuffs, because the fields were not being cultivated.

As this help consisted of private gifts, it is impossible to determine the exact amount, but soon there was food in abundance. South Carolina sent a prodigious quantity of rice, and in Virginia I frequently witnessed men vying to get space on a vessel so that they could ship wheat or Indian corn. Several people would decide to make up a cargo, and there were so many applicants it was considered a privilege to be admitted into the group. Some men who had already loaded merchandise to be sold in the islands ordered the captains to go to Boston instead. Others, who had small vessels of which they were sole owners, wanted the cargo to go in their

---

* This idea was devised by Dabney Carr, Esquire, of Goochland County, a most remarkable man. One of his devoted relatives wrote an inscription for his tombstone to deplore the loss of this very worthy citizen 16 May 1773 at the age of thirty. [Carr was the brother-in-law of Jefferson, who wrote the epitaph from "Thomas Jefferson, who of all men living, loved him most." Carr is buried at Monticello (Jefferson, *Papers of Jefferson*, ed. Boyd, 1:98)].

own names and refused to accept any associates. Although ostentation doubtless played a role in this, it was pardonable under the circumstances.

After the governor dissolved the lower house, the representatives went home and warned their constituents of the dangers threatening the country. All the inhabitants believed it their duty to watch over the public safety and deemed it their privilege to find means of maintaining it. Everywhere representatives were elected, as in ordinary times. Only the college professors, who were English, with one exception, abstained from holding an election. In this emergency the voice of the people summoned several elderly citizens who had retired from public life. When times are critical, people select their outstanding citizens, and public welfare is more important than any other consideration.

The assembly of representatives was called a convention to show that it was a temporary group, and no one wanted to offend the suspended administration by calling it an assembly.*

The only instruction was to provide for public safety in the best way possible by joining with other colonies. At a meeting 4 August 1774 in Williamsburg twelve persons were chosen to form a Committee of Safety. The functions of this committee were: (1) to execute the decisions of the convention, (2) to correspond with the committees of safety of other colonies or with any other persons to whom the conduct of affairs might be entrusted, (3) to do anything it considered necessary during the intervals between meetings of the convention.

It was decided that the inhabitants of each county should select twelve people to form a county committee. It was to maintain order, to correspond and cooperate with committees of other counties, and to follow instructions from the Committee of Safety. As it was very important to be ready to march wherever needed and as the power to command the militia was in the hands of the English governor, citizens were advised to arm and form volunteer companies, to be called independent companies. Each volunteer agreed in writing that when the number of volunteers reached eighty, they would form a company, select a captain, two lieutenants, and an ensign, and let the captain appoint sergeants and corporals; that they would march and obey all the captain's orders,

---

* In Connecticut, Rhode Island, Pennsylvania, and Delaware it was not necessary to have recourse to a convention because the constitutions permitted the election and holding of assemblies without the consent of the crown.

provided the marching order came from the county committee; *
that when there were several companies, the county committee
would appoint the colonels, lieutenant colonels, and majors; that
when there were several regiments, the Committee of Safety would
appoint the generals.

After electing seven persons to represent Virginia in a congress
of all the colonies and decreeing that the Committee of Safety
should inform each colony about its decisions, the convention
broke up; it was decided that the second meeting should be held
20 March 1775 in Richmond. As the other colonies had made the
same resolutions, a number of couriers crossed on the road, and
they were unanimous in their choice of Philadelphia, since it was
the best-located city. Congress met for the first time 5 September
1774, with deputies from eleven colonies; those from South Carolina did not arrive until the fourteenth of the month, and Georgia
was unable to send any at the time. They came the following July;
so they were present for the opening of the third session, 5 September 1775. Congress was in charge of all matters pertaining to the
war, but its power did not extend much beyond that. Its acts were
usually recommendations which the colonies always respected and
followed as closely as possible.

Each colony appointed the officers of its regiments, and Congress named the generals. George Washington, a deputy from
Virginia, was unanimously elected commander-in-chief of the
troops of the United Colonies on 17 June 1775. At least seven
among the deputies of the Deep South knew of his prudence,
virtues, and the military ability he had displayed during the war of
1756. Men from the other colonies may have been familiar with
his record, or felt it wise to agree with their colleagues in order to
stay together; in any event, they raised no objections. The reader
may be interested in seeing the commission given to him on this
occasion.

To George Washington, Esquire
from the Delegates of the United Colonies
We, reposing special trust and confidence in your patriotism, conduct, and fidelity, do by these presents constitute and appoint you to
be General and Commander-in-Chief of the army of the United
Colonies, and of all the forces raised or to be raised by them, and of all
others who shall voluntarily offer their service and join the said army

* At this time every good citizen was a soldier; so it was scarcely necessary to
think of preparations for war. Nevertheless, Americans never lost sight of the
obedience owed to civil authority.

for the defence of American liberty, and for repelling every hostile invasion thereof. And you are hereby vested with full power and authority to act as you shall think for the good and welfare of the service.

And we do hereby strictly charge and require all officers and soldiers under your command to be obedient to your orders, and diligent to the exercise of their several duties.

And we do also enjoin and require you to be careful in executing the great trust reposed in you, by causing strict discipline and order to be observed in the army, and that the soldiers are duly exercised and provided with all convenient necessaries.

And you are to regulate your conduct in every respect by the rules and discipline of war (as herewith given you), and punctually to observe and follow such directions from time to time, as you shall receive from this or a future Congress of the said United Colonies, or a Committee of Congress for that purpose appointed.

This commission to continue in force till revoked by this or a future Congress.

[Signed John Hancock, President] [65]

Eighteen months later, when the commander needed broader powers, Congress granted him those of a virtual dictator, but he used them in such a way that most inhabitants of the United States are still unaware he had such authority.

The power of Congress, the assemblies, conventions, and committees was unbounded, and this kind of government * prevailed until the republic was created. Internal affairs were conducted with remarkable calm. Debtors paid before being harassed. Honor did more than the courts had ever accomplished. Debts were settled more promptly, and tribunals were not needed. We should be wrong in assuming that debtors were spurred by local considerations, for those who owed money in Europe paid it as soon as money could be sent abroad.

British merchants have testified to this publicly. In the Petition of the Merchants, Traders, Manufacturers, and Other Citizens of Bristol presented to His Majesty on Wednesday, 11 September

---

* Power was used in a paternal fashion. Those to whom authority was entrusted never needed it because everyone obeyed a recommendation. Although no one commanded, only a very small group failed to do their duty. Their penalty was publication of their misdeeds, and they were practically ostracized afterwards.

[65] *Journals of the Continental Congress, 1774-89,* ed. W. C. Ford et al., 34 vols. (Washington, D.C., 1904-37), 2:96.

1775, Mr. [Edmund] Burke, one of the representatives of that city, said:

We owe a testimony of justice to your Colonies, which is, that in the midst of the present distractions, we have received many unequivocal proofs, that our fellow subjects in that part of the world are very far from having lost their ancient affection and regard to their mother country, or departed from principles of commercial honor and private justice. Notwithstanding the cessation of the powers of government throughout that vast continent, we have reason to think, judging by the imports into our city, and by our extensive correspondencies, that the commodities of American growth . . . have been as regularly brought to Great Britain, as in the most quiet times. We assure your majesty that the trade of this port, and the subsistence of a great part of your kingdom, have depended very much on the honourable and, in this instance, amicable behaviour of your American subjects. We have in this single year received, within one year, from the first of September 1774, more than one million bushels of wheat, to say nothing of the great quantity of other valuable commodities essential to our navigation and commerce.[66]

The petition of the London merchants was more detailed. It stated, for example, that Americans had made larger payments since their ports were closed to British merchandise than they had ever made before. In spite of all my efforts I have been unable to obtain this document or several others. It is very difficult to procure those showing that British feeling about America differed from what it is today.

All operations this year consisted of paying debts, for it was no longer possible to import English goods. When it was proposed to permit exports as a means of helping debtors to settle their accounts, more than one politician was opposed on the grounds that such conduct would weaken our forces while giving strength to the enemy. Fortunately, nobler sentiments prevailed. Sometime later General [Charles] Lee halted a vessel on the James River because it contained a considerable amount of money destined for England, but the owners ordered the captain to set sail. Such anecdotes, which should occupy a historian quite as much as a description of battles, often pass unnoticed.

Although this book is only intended to describe the behavior of Americans at this critical period, it will not be out of place to observe that we were preparing to defend ourselves before the last

[66] *The Remembrancer: or, Impartial Repository of Public Events for the Year 1775* (London [1776?]), p. 309.

English governor departed; no one protested when he invoked his right to command the militia, because the colonists still hoped that the problems could be resolved. He was leading three thousand men in an unjust war against the Shawnee Indians, but before leaving on the expedition, he learned the convention was to meet in Williamsburg. He was kept informed about developments and told that the members were to assemble for the second session in Richmond the following March. During the interval he ordered an election of representatives for the assembly, and the people were wise enough to choose the men they had elected for the convention. After the assembly met at his order on 1 June 1775, he retired to a frigate on the pretext he did not feel safe on shore; a short time later he began open hostilities against the country.*

As my book does not claim to be a complete history, this account is sufficient to give a fair idea of the conduct of the colonies during the interval between the governments.

## Virginia Separates from Great Britain

On 15 May 1776 the Virginia Convention, acting in accordance with the wishes of its members and empowered by them, resolved to separate from Great Britain and declared:

Forasmuch as all the endeavours of the United Colonies by the most decent representations and petitions to the king and parliament of Great Britain to restore peace and security to America under the British government and a re-union with that people upon just and liberal terms instead of a redress of grievances have produced from an imperious and vindictive administration increased insult, oppression and a vigorous attempt to effect our total destruction. By a late act, all these colonies are declared to be in rebellion, and out of the protection of the British crown our properties subjected to confiscation, our people, when captivated, compelled to join in the murder and plunder of their relations and countrymen, and all former rapine and oppression of Americans declared legal and just. Fleets and armies are raised, and the aid of foreign troops engaged to assist these destructive purposes: The king's representative in this colony hath not only withheld all the powers of government from operating for our safety, but, having retired on board an armed ship, is carrying on a piratical and savage war

---

* See Note C, containing the terms on which he agreed to return to his government and the final resolution of the General Assembly, which had already sent one deputation on board the frigate.

against us tempting our slaves by every artifice to resort to him, and training and employing them against their masters. In this state of extreme danger, we have no alternative left but an abject submission to the will of those over-bearing tyrants, or a total separation from the crown and government of Great Britain, uniting and exerting the strength of all America for defence, and forming alliances with foreign powers for commerce and aid in war; Wherefore, appealing to the Searcher of Hearts for the sincerity of former declarations, expressing our desire to preserve the connection with that nation, and that we are driven from that inclination by their wicked councils, and the eternal laws of self-preservation.

Resolved unanimously, that the delegates appointed to represent this colony in General Congress be instructed to propose to that respectable body to declare the United Colonies free and independent states, absolved from all allegiance to, or dependence upon, the crown or parliament of Great Britain; * and that they give the assent of this colony to such declaration, and to whatever measures may be thought proper and necessary by the Congress for forming foreign alliances and a confederation of the colonies, at such time, and in the manner, as to them shall seem best: Provided, that the power of forming government for, and the regulations of the internal concerns of each colony, be left to the respective colonial legislatures.

Resolved unanimously, that a committee be appointed to prepare a Declaration of Rights, and such a plan of government as will be most likely to maintain peace and order in this colony, and secure substantial and equal liberty to the people.[67]

The declaration prepared by the committee in accord with this resolution underwent several minor changes when it was examined by the convention. It was approved by a unanimous vote on 1 [12] June and became the cornerstone of the new government. It reads as follows:

A Declaration of Rights made by the Representatives of the good People of Virginia, assembled in full and free Convention; which Rights do pertain to them, and their Posterity, as the Basis and Foundation of Government.

## I.

That all Men are by Nature equally free and independent, and have certain inherent Rights, of which, when they enter into a State of

---

* As Parliament had exercised the right to regulate commerce, despite the protests of the colonies, it was thought advisable to remove any doubt about the matter.

[67] Jefferson, *Papers of Jefferson*, ed. Boyd, 1:290–91.

Society, they cannot, by any Compact, deprive or divest their Posterity; namely, the Enjoyment of Life and Liberty, with the Means of acquiring and possessing Property, and pursuing and obtaining Happiness and Safety.

## II.

That all Power is vested in, and consequently derived from, the People; that Magistrates are their Trustees and Servants, and at all Times amenable to them.

## III.

That Government is, or ought to be, instituted for the common Benefit, Protection, and Security, of the People, Nation, or Community; of all the various Modes and Forms of Government that is best, which is capable of producing the greatest Degree of Happiness and Safety, and is most effectually secured against the Danger of Mal-administration; and that, whenever any Government shall be found inadequate or contrary to these Purposes, a Majority of the Community hath an indubitable, unalienable, and indefeasible Right, to reform, alter, or abolish it, in such Manner as shall be judged most conducive to the public Weal.

## IV.

That no Man, or Set of Men, are entitled to exclusive or separate Emoluments or Privileges from the Community, but in Consideration of public Services; which, not being descendible, neither ought the Offices of Magistrate, Legislator, or Judge, to be hereditary.

## V.

That the legislative and executive Powers of the State should be separate and distinct from the Judicative; and, that the Members of the two first may be restrained from Oppression, by feeling and participating the Burthens of the People, they should, at fixed Periods, be reduced to a private Station, return into that Body from which they were originally taken, and the Vacancies be supplied by frequent, certain, and regular Elections, in which all, or any Part of the former Members, to be again eligible, or ineligible, as the Laws shall direct.

## VI.

That Elections of Members to serve as Representatives of the People, in Assembly, ought to be free; and that all Men, having sufficient Evidence of permanent common Interest with, and Attachment to, the

Community, have the Right of Suffrage, and cannot be taxed or deprived of their Property for public Uses without their own Consent or that of their Representatives so elected, nor bound by any Law to which they have not, in like Manner, assented, for the public Good.*

## VII.

That all Power of suspending Laws, or the Execution of Laws, by any Authority without Consent of the Representatives of the People, is injurious to their Rights, and ought not to be exercised.

## VIII.

That in all capital or criminal Prosecutions a Man hath a Right to demand the Cause and Nature of his Accusation, to be confronted with the Accusers and Witnesses, to call for Evidence in his Favour, and to a speedy Trial by an impartial Jury of his Vicinage, without whose unanimous Consent he cannot be found guilty, nor can he be compelled to give Evidence against himself; that no Man be deprived of his Liberty except by the Law of the Land, or the Judgment of his Peers.

## IX.

That excessive Bail ought not to be required, nor excessive Fines imposed; nor cruel and unusual Punishments inflicted.

## X.

That general Warrants, whereby any Officer or Messenger may be commanded to search suspected Places without Evidence of a Fact committed, or to seize any Person or Persons not named, or whose Offence is not particularly described and supported by Evidence, are grievous and oppressive, and ought not to be granted.

## XI.

That in Controversies respecting Property, and in Suits between Man and Man, the ancient Trial by Jury is preferable to any other, and ought to be held sacred.

## XII.

That the Freedom of the Press is one of the greatest Bulwarks of Liberty, and can never be restrained but by despotic Governments.

## XIII.

That a well regulated Militia, composed of the Body of the People, trained to Arms, is the proper, natural, and safe Defence of a free

* In Virginia the right of suffrage has always included the right of being a representative.

State; that standing Armies, in Time of Peace, should be avoided, as dangerous to Liberty; and that, in all Cases, the Military should be under strict Subordination to, and governed by, the civil Power.

## XIV.

That the People have a Right to uniform Government; and therefore, that no Government separate from, or independent of, the Government of *Virginia,* ought to be erected or established within the Limits thereof.

## XV.

That no free Government, or the Blessing of Liberty, can be preserved to any People but by a firm Adherence to Justice, Moderation, Temperance, Frugality, and virtue, and by frequent Recurrence to fundamental Principles.

## XVI.

That Religion, or the Duty which we owe to our Creator, and the Manner of discharging it, can be directed only by Reason and Conviction, not by Force or Violence; and therefore, all Men are equally entitled to the free Exercise of Religion, according to the Dictates of Conscience; and that it is the mutual Duty of all to practise Christian Forbearance, Love, and Charity, towards each other.[68]

The preamble lists the reasons which led us to separate from Great Britain; I have omitted it because the diction is almost the same as that of the Declaration of Independence, since the same author was charged with writing both documents. The latter, however, contains some additional material, for certain colonies suffered from grievances not shared by all.

Five of the best-qualified men were asked to examine the code of laws and to make whatever additions or deletions they deemed necessary to make it as perfect as possible in accordance with the principles of the new government. But, as that was a task for several years,* they decided to keep the old laws in force for the time being, with the exception of those which needed immediate correction.

* This was a prodigious task for these enlightened men, who believed that every code might contain something good; so they examined all the ancient and modern ones they could obtain, including the Koran; one of their principal objectives was to make this great document as short and comprehensible as possible.

[68] Broadside, Rare Book Division, New York Public Library, adopted 12 June 1776.

I said that all the states adopted similar laws during the period between the two governments and that any differences were too slight to be significant. The Declaration of Rights also served as a basis for the other new governments. The spirit was the same everywhere, but as the methods differed in every state, each one will have a basis for comparison. They will continue to adopt what they think best until they reach the highest possible degree of perfection, and then they will all be alike.

We should recall that on 4 July 1776 the United Colonies unanimously declared their independence and took the name United States of America.

# Governments of the United States

Anyone who examines attentively and impartially the nature and spirit of our governments will realize that the least perfect is closer to the principles of liberty than any ancient or modern republic. We have not as yet achieved a state satisfactory to a philosopher or legislator, and we have no reason to be proud of having done better than other countries because, despite the problems of war, we were in a much better position than other nations (if we can believe history) when they were establishing their governments.

The fundamental sovereignty, on which the liberty of our republic is based, resides in the inhabitants, who confide responsibility to a number small enough to permit discussion, but not so small as to give too much influence to any one person. Everywhere legislators are selected so that no dangerous preponderance may exist, even if the proportion is not always as fair as it should be. The term is short and the salary just enough to cover their expenses. They have the power to make laws and some important appointments. None of them can accept one of these appointments and retain his rank as a member of the legislative body. Their power can never endanger liberty; not only is it brief, but the people have the right to abolish it by electing other representatives and authorizing them to reform or reestablish the constitution if it has been abused.

Each member of the legislative body votes as he wishes, without having to obtain the consent of his constituents. He is, however, obliged to follow any specific instructions he may receive in advance.*

The right of suffrage and the privilege of being a representative belong to all residents of the state. Anyone can hope to be chosen on the basis of his industry and thrift, just as he may be elected to any office in the republic. There is no partiality on the basis of birth, although some states require that a man have property, especially real estate. There is only one class of citizen. Titles of new

* The vote would be valid even if it were contrary to the instructions of the constituents, but this is unlikely, for the legislator would arouse the ire of the inhabitants of his district.

inhabitants have no influence, and the Georgia constitution has wisely decreed that such distinctions must be renounced before a man may hold public office.

Government representatives may not have any other position; furthermore, all important posts are so separate and distinct that the same person may not occupy more than one at a time. Several states have already decreed that no man can have two paid positions of any kind whatsoever.

Soldiers * and clergymen are not permitted to serve in any one of the three departments, legislative, executive, and judiciary.

All appointments which could influence the government are temporary. Salaries are not large enough to tempt greed, and there is just enough power to maintain order.

Liberty of the press is unrestricted so long as it is not libelous.

Freedom of religion is not fettered by any odious or childish distinctions.

No one is forced to make a contribution for the support of ministers of a religion he does not profess; no state has a dominant religion; no one is deprived of the right to vote for religious reasons. In several states, however, one must be a Christian, and in others a Protestant, to be a member of the legislative body and to hold certain offices. In some states, including Virginia, contributions are voluntary, even for the support of the religion you profess, and the only requirement for a position is an oath to be faithful to the republic.

The power of Congress is not shackled. It needs consent from the states only to regulate matters which were not foreseen in the Articles of Confederation. Each state has its vote and deliberates in the name of its representatives. If the questions under discussion are unimportant, a plurality of votes is sufficient, but if it is a matter of declaring war or spending large sums, a majority vote is required. Since the population in each state is different, there is a possibility that there might be a plurality of states but not of delegates. It has therefore been decided that nine votes are necessary for a decision. Accordingly there are cases where seven votes are enough and others where nine are required.

Unanimous approval of the states in Congress is necessary only on matters with which the Articles of Confederation do not deal. The same applies to approval by each separate state.

---

* This applies only to the armed forces. Every citizen, as soon as he is of age, belongs to the militia.

Fortunately for us, the Revolution arrived before the English ministers thought we were worthy of their titles and decorations. Pride had kept them from injecting us with the aristocratic poison, the only one which could have turned the heads of vain men and prevented the union to which we are responsible for our liberty.

As we did not have before our eyes any of the things which blind men so easily, it is not surprising that when a new government was being established, the right of suffrage was recognized. But as people realized it would be both absurd and impossible to exercise this prerogative personally, they selected a small group of competent citizens and gave them the task of laying the foundations for a just and solid government. The right of suffrage for the election was exercised only by those who enjoyed it under the former governments.

Some people may believe the moderation which prevailed was due, at least partly, to circumstances. But the American people have a high veneration for law and order, and they are convinced that abuses are not rectified in the midst of turmoil.

The deputies outlined in precise terms the natural and inalienable rights of man, as we saw in the Declaration of Rights, and protected them by establishing certain rules which future delegates would be required to follow. We must distinguish between the purpose of this assembly, called the convention, which wrote the constitution, and later assemblies that were charged with ordinary legislative power and could not depart from the principles laid down in this document.*

When you realize that our century is philosophical, at least in comparison to the others we know, that the rights of man are much better understood than they have ever been, that we have had the priceless advantage of being able to observe the mistakes of ancient and modern republics, that we did not have to combat the distinction of rank, which is the most terrible obstacle that can be opposed to the establishment of a free and just government, it seems that our governments should be better than they are. It is true that our attention was diverted by troubles, but it is no less true that a

---

* In almost every state constitution it is decreed that legislative power cannot derogate the constitution and that whenever something needs to be changed, the people will have to elect a special commission. This clause does not exist in the constitution of Virginia because the convention which determined the form of the government had not received special authorization from the people for this purpose. In New Hampshire, the last state to remodel its constitution, the clause was added.

common peril brings men together and inclines them to sacrifice their private desires to a common weal. We must also remember that the American people are very docile, with the utmost confidence in those to whom they confide the conduct of their affairs. I do not therefore criticize my compatriots when I complain because our governments have not attained the degree of perfection I should like them to have. I hope they will reach it someday, and here I rely on the free and sensible youth of our land. Anyone who has known the actors and heard their discussions cannot doubt their sincerity. Unfortunately, the majority of these men, who are elderly, could not persuade themselves that certain maxims which they had always considered excellent could be unjust. Moreover, their own peace of mind under the former government had kept them from thinking so.

## The Right to Vote and to Be a Representative

The deputies charged with the task of writing the new constitutions declared unanimously in every state that all men are born equally free and independent. Prejudice could make no headway against this truth, but when they came to the right to vote and to be a representative, which is the first step in establishing a free government and the cornerstone of liberty, they did not always respect this principle. Abuses were corrected to a certain degree, but no state abolished them completely.

Virginia, Connecticut, and Rhode Island are the only states where the right to vote is not separated from the privilege of being a representative, and where anyone with this prerogative is eligible for election to any position in the republic. But in Connecticut, and I believe in Rhode Island as well, you must have real estate valued at £2 or £40 of personal property,* and in Virginia you must have 100 acres of uncultivated land, or 25 acres containing a house, or a lot,† or a town house. In Georgia the only requirement for the franchise is a job. To be a representative a man must have 250 acres of land or property worth £250. To vote in Pennsylvania it is sufficient to have had a residence for two years and to have paid taxes; to enjoy both rights, you must be the son of a

---

* The old law still exists. When it was written, one could obtain for £2 more land than a family requires.

† Towns are divided into lots, which usually cover half an acre.

real estate owner. In Pennsylvania and Georgia the right to be a representative carries the privilege of holding any public office. In the eight other states requirements vary. Some demand more money to be a member of one legislative body than of the other, and even more to have certain positions in the executive branch. Massachusetts, for example, requires an income of £3 from real estate or a capital of £60 for the franchise; to be a member of the House of Representatives one must have a £100 in real estate or £200 of personal property. If you wish to be a member of the Senate or the Council of State, you need £300 in real estate or £600 of personal property. And it takes a £1,000 to be a governor or lieutenant governor. In New York, the difference extends to the right of suffrage in the various elections. To vote for a representative, a man has to have £20 in real estate or he must pay £2 annually in rent; to vote for members of the Senate, governor, or lieutenant governor, he needs £100.

All states were unanimous in determining their rights and expressed themselves in approximately the same terms. Reason was not blinded by prejudice in examining important truths, but the old doctrines reappeared in a discussion of specific cases, and on more than one occasion reason was obliged to yield. The worst offense was in the distinction between casting a ballot and being a representative. Preference in favor of wealth has no base other than injustice, like that which prevails in other circumstances in favor of the stronger sex.

But, someone asks, isn't money necessary to administer a state? And should the wealthy not participate to a greater degree, as they provide the public with larger sums? I deny that the possessor of wealth, as an individual, really pays more than anyone else. All that he pays is the tax on his property, which is protected from invasion by the army and from sedition by laws. In this instance the owner is like the farmer of his possessions, which would yield the same amount to any owner to whom they happened to belong. As property cannot render the public any personal service, money must substitute; the Quaker, who is forbidden to bear arms, has to pay someone to do his military service.

I pass to another opinion, which is only too widespread. It is said that men will be interested in the state's prosperity only to the extent that they have wealth invested in it. My reply is very simple. If a millionaire could step for a moment into the shoes of a man who has only ten crowns, he would discover that this small sum is as precious as all his treasures.

Another objection is that those who own nothing are not interested in the state's prosperity. I reply that, if they are regarded as indifferent in this respect, the state has no right to order them to parade, to bear arms, or to fight. The same advantages, as dear to their hearts as wealth, attach them to their country and should make all their rights as citizens sacred. It is unjust to deprive them of these privileges, unless they have committed a crime, and it should inspire horror in anyone who believes that all men are born equally free and independent.*

Every citizen has an equal right to the advantages and honors of his country; he can be deprived of this only if he has committed a crime and been judged by his peers. The sole exceptions are recipients of public welfare who do not contribute to the expenses of the state.

The arguments advanced to deprive the poor of their rights as citizens are: (1) that they have no means of becoming educated and acquiring the skill to fill certain functions; (2) that the rich could corrupt them easily. This second reason is also given as an excuse to deprive them of the right of suffrage. But is it unusual to find good parents who, although poor, have obtained by hard work and thrift the means to educate their children and make them worthy to fill the highest posts? Is it not unjust and absurd to exclude such men? If these fathers had purchased property, instead of using their money for such a laudable purpose, ignorance could not prevent their sons from rising to positions of leadership.

It is claimed that a wealthy man without ability will have difficulty getting a majority of the votes, but experience has proved the contrary. Wealth dazzles and blinds people to the faults of those who have it, whereas the poor are always neglected unless they have outstanding attributes.

---

* The Declaration of Rights begins with this great truth. The foundation of American liberty, it contains all the principles necessary to preserve it. My hopes rest on this declaration, for these maxims are in the mouths and in the hearts of all Americans who have a religious respect for liberty. As the clouds of old prejudices dissipate, the pen of one elderly and zealous citizen may perhaps provide an efficacious remedy for the greatest disorders. The people in the thirteen states read and are eager to learn. When they realize that their representatives have transgressed, they will order them to fulfil their obligations. If these principles were not expressed with a clarity that puts them within the grasp of everyone, quarrels fomented with all the arts of bad faith on one side and with patriotic fervor on the other could have made the people uncertain and restrained them from action; but the Declaration of Rights will serve as a rule and a buttress for the zealous citizen and erase all doubts.

It is also said that the poor would be apt to vote for other poor men. Anyone who harbors this opinion does not know the human heart. A poor man always looks up, unless oppression binds him to those who are suffering as he is. During the whole era when the Roman patricians insisted on governing the republic, it was thought plebeians would elect men of their class if they had the franchise. When they were admitted, they mocked commoners who presented themselves as candidates for the military tribunals, and several years elapsed before the people found anyone worthy in their own class. The poor censure the poor far more rigidly than the rich. If a biased law were compatible with liberty, you would have to discourage the influence of the wealthy. Poverty obscures merit quite enough; it should not be vilified by unjust and barbaric laws.

Our governments do not tempt the ambitious to spend their fortunes on an election. There is no question of lending money so you can pillage conquered provinces or of becoming a member of Parliament and obtaining a post paying £5,000 or £6,000. The man elected is the agent of his peers for a year; he has the right to express his opinion in a large assembly, the duty to express the feeling of his constituents on public matters and to vote for or against laws to which he will be subject like every other citizen. He will receive a set sum sufficient to repay his traveling and living expenses, if he is economical. In states where the people reserved the right to other elections, independent of the legislative body, there can be few temptations, for none of the thirteen states provides an office to satisfy greed.

I consider the difference between the ownership of real estate and personal property and the assumption that real estate ownership makes people more interested in the prosperity of others a false opinion which has become axiomatic. When errors are repeated often enough, they make a deep impression, and if they are stated by men with a reputation for wisdom, they are not questioned.

The attraction of property is derived from the means it supplies to satisfy our tastes. Personal property has the same effect as real estate, but the latter is considered more attractive. This is probably childish prejudice, for it is one of many false maxims taught to us at a tender age. It is said that he who has no real estate has no country; a man and his personal property can move easily. Yet few pieces of furniture can be transported without a loss, and you usually sell them if you wish to go abroad. In case of war, the enemy who merely wishes to dominate will treat furniture like property. If he is a brigand, he will confiscate everything. If he pillages, furniture will be more exposed than property, although it is probable that some pieces can be saved.

It is claimed that property is so easily acquired in America that those without it are scarcely worthy of attention. But we should think of our grandchildren. In time many fine people will be unable to acquire real estate, while others will be obliged to sell it in order to learn a useful profession.

Love of country in every individual is proportionate to the advantages he receives from it. No fair individual can believe the owner of real estate is more attached to his country than a man with personal property or a profession. Is it probable that a doctor, lawyer, or manufacturer who was forced to leave the United States would not suffer as much as the owner of a field, house, or farm? Why should artisans, workmen, or stevedores not be anxious to defend the country where they earn their daily bread more easily than elsewhere? Why should they not love their country as much as a wealthy real estate owner? The latter knows that if he moves, the sale of his possessions will provide a good income. Are workmen not aware that as immigrants, they might die of hunger before getting a job? The only misfortune which could cool their enthusiasm is being deprived of the rights of citizenship, and the only people who are really without a country are those deprived of those rights. Nothing could be more unjust than to make them bear arms and expose their lives to defend a country where they are regarded as foreigners.

Despite the distinctions in the right to elect and to be elected a representative, distinctions which I hope will one day be abolished, there is not a single one of the thirteen states where these rights are not more liberal than they have ever been in any other republic.* Furthermore, we can find consolation in the fact that no individual is actually excluded from any position, since anyone can, through industry and thrift, attain every office.

* In order to equalize the right to be a representative, all citizens, without exception, should have the privilege of serving and the number of those elected should be proportioned, insofar as possible, to the number of the electors. Some states, like Massachusetts, New Hampshire, and South Carolina, have already done this and have taken the precautionary measure of requiring that at certain intervals the electors be counted and the number of representatives determined accordingly. In the other southern states there is still a great deal of inequity, though it has been reduced by dividing counties when they were too large.

## The Legislative Power *

The more complicated the machine, the more easily it can get out of order. That is probably why many people think the best government is that of one person. It is true that if a prince were just, wise, and attentive to his duty and if one could be assured his heirs would be like him, no one could ask for a better government. Acting on this principle, Pennsylvania entrusted the legislative body to a single group of men. Georgia followed suit, although it took the precaution of stating that no resolutions of the legislative assembly could become laws before being examined by all the members of the executive body, except the governor.

The other states felt that any assembly could act as capriciously as an individual; so they set up restraints. A Virginian suggested that each chamber have a representative of every county, so that one chamber would approve the resolutions of the other. This would have simplified the system and avoided any slight distinction which could sow the seeds of an aristocracy.

Another method would have the electors of each county pick fifteen, twenty, or more men, who should elect the representatives. But people were afraid that intellect would take precedence over character, and it was felt that a legislative assembly—if lacking in virtue—could easily become dangerous.

After considering the advantages of each method, the eleven states decided to divide the legislative power into two bodies. The larger one, called in Virginia and Maryland the House of Delegates, is known as the House of Representatives in the other states. Almost all of them call the other body the Senate, although in New Jersey it bears the title Legislative Council. In Connecticut the House of Representatives is known as the Lower House, while the Upper House consists of the governor, lieutenant governor, and twelve assistants. It was decided in Virginia that the Senate should consist of twenty-four members. One very sensible citizen, the one who wrote the first and best model of the Declaration of Rights,[69] proposed a system of electing senators similar to the one

---

* This is called by different names: General Assembly or General Court. In New Hampshire it was known as Congress until the constitution adopted 31 October 1783 decided to call it General Court.

[69] George Mason.

suggested to keep the system simple. The counties, which now number about eighty, were to be divided into twenty-four districts; he suggested that the people elect two representatives from each one; then they should elect twelve men to meet with the twelve from each of the other counties in the same district to elect one man. He and the other twenty-three chosen by this method would form the other branch of the legislative body. This plan was not adopted; the election is handled like the one for the House of Representatives, and as there is no opportunity for a second choice, the state has lost the opportunity to form a truly superior body. Furthermore, as it is unlikely that the general public would know the outstanding men in other counties, it is probable that the one with the largest group of electors will win. This is not the only drawback which will have to be remedied when the constitution is formulated on a permanent basis.

The present government was hastily drawn up without a special delegation to perform the task. As it seemed that the slightest delay could be dangerous, delegates relied on the confidence of their constituents instead of going home to wait for a new election. Moreover, since our government was the first to be formed, other states learned from our mistakes as they did from our Declaration of Rights. The present constitution therefore must be considered temporary, and the leading citizens of Virginia always have regarded it in that light. One citizen wrote a paper to point out its mistakes, and this was signed by the inhabitants of his county. People are thinking today about how best to change it, and this will give us an opportunity to take advantage of the constitutions of the other twelve states.

There is no doubt that the same power concentrated in a small group will be more forceful than in a large one. This fear may explain why the Senate in Virginia cannot propose, but only adopt or reject, resolutions passed by the other house.* For this reason a great many useful subjects are never even considered in this body. To prevent any possibility of an aristocracy, the Senate should be deprived of all external pomp and simply called the second branch of the legislative power. Just the opposite was done. This may be because men are hard to convince that these formalities exert real influence, or it may be due to old prejudices.

---

* If the members wish to correct something, the resolution must go back to the other house for further discussion, since no resolution becomes law until it is approved by the Senate without change.

The latter are doubtless responsible for the decision not to permit the Senate to alter any decisions of the other house about financial matters. In England, where the members of one house transmit their rights by succession, there are good reasons for making such a distinction, but here both bodies are representatives of the people. Nevertheless, this distinction was adopted in every state where the legislative body is divided into two branches. No state permits the Senate to propose laws on these matters, although in every one save Virginia the Senate can change them. The other states were wise enough not to follow Virginia's decision that the Senate cannot propose any laws.

The state of Maryland is the only one which adopted Virginia's method of electing the Senate, and it has already profited from this on several occasions. The interval between elections for this body varies. In Maryland elections are held every five years, in South Carolina, every two years, in other states every year, but in several states only a certain number are chosen at a time. In Virginia, as six are elected each year, it takes four years to have a completely new slate.

I believe the election of the other house is annual except in South Carolina, where it is held every two years, and in Connecticut, where it is every six months.

In Pennsylvania no one can be a member of the legislative body for more than four out of seven years. Elsewhere the people can always elect the same representatives. Many reasons for changing men in other governmental positions do not apply to the legislative body; after weighing the matter, however, I prefer the Pennsylvania system.

Meetings of the legislative body can be held whenever the members wish. According to the constitution, the body must meet once a year and, in Connecticut, every six months. If there is an urgent matter to discuss, members of the executive branch must convoke the legislature.

Some states require a plurality of votes in both houses for a quorum; others have set a figure that is less than half; in several, such as Massachusetts and New Hampshire, no one can be elected without a majority of all qualified voters; in others, as in England, a candidate can win by a majority, even if only one vote is cast. It seems to me that the people could refuse to obey laws passed without the consent of the majority of its representatives. The same reflection applies to elections.

## The Executive Power *

Each of the thirteen states has confided the executive power to a magistrate assisted by a group of from five to twelve councillors. Ten states have given this magistrate the name governor: Pennsylvania, Delaware, and New Hampshire alone have abolished the title, which is a ridiculous carry-over from monarchy.

The title Excellency, perhaps the most out of place ever invented by human vanity, is given to the chief magistrate in almost all states, and in some it is part of the constitution.† People thought they were adorning the person, whereas it is the position which is honorable. Aside from the fact that any title is ridiculous, it should be noted that Excellency is so common in Europe that it tends to vilify the chief magistrate of a free people.

In some states, like Massachusetts and New Jersey, this magistrate enjoys prerogatives he should not possess. In Virginia he is almost powerless and completely subordinate to his advisers. Elsewhere, especially in New York, he seems to have the right amount of influence. The trouble here, however, is that he can keep the post for an indefinite period. The triennial election adopted by New York and Delaware may be preferable to an annual one, but it paves the way to the dangerous practice of keeping the same men in office.‡

The greatest problem faced by Virginia and several other states is that the chief magistrate is under the influence of the legislative body. It determines his salary, elects him annually, and may keep him in office for three consecutive years. In Massachusetts and several other states he is elected annually by the people. In New York he is elected for three years by the people, but it is unlikely that they are as well qualified to judge a candidate's merits as their representatives.

---

* This is also called *government*, an improper term. Its functions are about the same as those of European governments, except that it has nothing to do with the legislative and judiciary branches. It supervises foreign affairs, finances, war, and the navy.

† The Georgia constitution prescribes that he be called Honorable. Massachusetts and New Hampshire require Excellency.

‡ Some constitutions state that after his term has expired, the chief magistrate cannot be elected for a similar period of time. Others require a longer interval.

The influence of the legislative body in Virginia extends to all members of the executive branch because two of the eight councillors who leave their posts after three years are dropped following a vote in the General Assembly. Although this system was designed to exclude the least worthy, it is vicious, since those who wish to retain their positions work for the powerful members of the assembly. The chief magistrate and his advisers should be elected for their term of office; furthermore, their salaries should be fixed not by the legislative body but by constitutional law and revised from time to time on the basis of some essential commodity.

The New York constitution states that the governor, chancellor, and at least two judges of the Supreme Court must meet to examine the resolutions of the legislative body before they can become law. Objections of the committee to the proposed law, or to any part of it, must be sent to the legislative body in writing; if it refuses to change its opinion, a two-thirds vote in both houses is required to overrule the veto. Massachusetts entrusted the same power to the governor; so this magistrate can make it possible for fifty votes in one house to override ninety-nine in that house and a unanimous vote in the other.

It is easy to see which system is better, although the New York plan could be improved by substituting several men for the governor. It is always a grave mistake to give anyone too much authority. Furthermore, a candidate may possess all the necessary qualifications to be a chief magistrate, without knowing how to revise laws. One advantage of the New York system is that it makes the passage and revocation of laws more difficult. Minor inconveniences are less dangerous than unstable laws, and when these inconveniences are serious, no one need fear opposition to a remedy.

Certain superfluous formalities, which are relics of monarchy, prevail in the Massachusetts constitution to a greater extent than elsewhere. The General Court, for example, is dissolved by proclamation of the governor on the day preceding an election; in Virginia and in some other states dissolution is mandated by law. As there is probably no state with a deeper republican spirit than Massachusetts, I am inclined to believe their regulation comes from an excess of security. The strong feeling of equality may have given rise to a belief such formalities were necessary as tokens of respect to the chief magistrate. These should be changed as soon as possible.

In Virginia we have the opposite extreme, for the magistrate is completely subordinate to his advisers. This is equally unfortunate, since it restricts his authority and might prove dangerous in an emergency. The legislative department is characterized by lethargy and an inability to preserve secrecy. A magistrate who has no part in legislation and must give an account of his operations needs freedom to act quickly. How can he justify his decisions when he is obliged to follow the advice of others? Since he merely has to show the resolutions of his advisers and the law which requires him to execute them, a wily man could maneuver his councillors. It is true that members of the executive body can be required to explain their conduct, but if the number accused is large, condemnation is difficult.

In New Jersey the executive power can pardon any condemned criminal. Elsewhere it can suspend execution in certain cases and grant pardon in others. The legislative branch always has the power to absolve delinquents. As long as we retain any vestige of our barbaric laws, the power to abrogate a sentence will be useful, but I hope that in the near future the legislator will be indulgent and humane, following Beccaria's advice, and that the executive power will be inexorable.*

## The Judiciary Power

In every state judiciary power is conferred on justices of the peace and judges of the supreme court. There is no limit to the number of the former. It varies according to the size and population of the county, city, or district which forms the territory of their jurisdiction, and they deal with both criminal and civil cases. They are chosen among citizens outstanding for morality and intelligence, and they are distributed so that every citizen can have easy access to one. In Virginia, and in several other states, they serve without salary. I believe they were formerly appointed by the people and that the people also named them under the new constitutions. In several states, including Virginia, vacancies are filled by the men remaining. I consider this method potentially dangerous, as it tends

---

* All punishments should be proportionate to the offense. When no distinction is made between crimes, men are inclined to commit murder as quickly as to steal. For this reason cruel laws are contrary to justice, as the purpose of punishment is to correct men, not to exterminate them (Article 18 of the Declaration of Rights of New Hampshire, 31 October 1783). The Revolution is responsible for these just and humane reforms.

to create small oligarchies. The method adopted by Pennsylvania and several other states is infinitely better.

Every justice of the peace can settle small matters without appeal. In Virginia, if the sum involved amounts to 4⅙ dollars, the case must be taken to the county seat and tried before at least four justices. No civil case can be brought before a supreme court if the matter in litigation is worth less than £10; if it is worth more, or if the case involves deeds or territorial boundaries, one can appeal immediately to the higher court.

Justices of the peace do not have authority to condemn a man to death. If they believe the accused guilty of a capital offense, they refer his case to the supreme court. If the matter is purely legal, the justices decide the case themselves; if it involves factual matters, the jury decides; if the case is complicated, the jurors render their decision and are usually instructed on matters of law. If public liberty is at stake, or if there is any reason to suppose that the judges might be partial, the case may be given to the jurors to decide.

Every state has four supreme courts. The admiralty court deals only with maritime affairs. The court known in Virginia as the General Court and in other states by different titles has jurisdiction over civil cases pertaining to common law and all criminal cases.* All persons charged with a crime must be judged by twelve jurors, and there is no appeal from their verdict in criminal cases.

The court of chancery handles matters pertaining to minors and cases of equity.

In Virginia the fourth and highest court is known as the Court of Appeal. It is composed of all the judges of the other three supreme courts. The Court of Appeal meets to decide cases from which an appeal has been taken from one of the other three supreme courts, and occasionally judges themselves refer a case to this court.

There are five judges in the tribunal of common law in Virginia,

---

* The code of common law originated in England at the time of the heptarchy and was so called because its laws were common to the seven kingdoms. It was lost before the thirteenth century, but men remembered it in substance, and the same laws were found from time to time in legal decisions. After the barons obtained the Magna Carta from King John at the beginning of the thirteenth century, a second code of parliamentary laws was formed. The original was called common law, the later one statutory law, but both are included in the term *common law* when it is a question of distinguishing this tribunal from the court of chancery.

three in the other two. I hope that when the constitution is revised, there will be four in each of them. In cases where there is little doubt, three should be on the right side, and if the matter is doubtful, it would be better to have a retrial than to deprive a man of his possessions on the basis of a single vote. I should also like to see the Court of Appeal organized so that the judges of the tribunal appealing the case should not have a vote unless the judges themselves are consulting the higher court.

In several states the constitution requires the judge's salaries to be high enough so that outstanding men will accept the posts; salaries should be determined by the constitution so that the legislative body, which changes yearly, could not influence such an important department.

Our governments are very different from the picture painted by Abbé Raynal (9:304): "Each province had an assembly formed by representatives of the various districts and constituting the legislative body. Its president had the executive power. His rights and responsibilities were to listen to all citizens, to call them together in case of need, to take care of arms and troops, and to plan operations with military leaders. He was at the head of a secret committee which was supposed to maintain liaison with Congress. His appointment was fixed for two years but could be prolonged."

If the author had read our constitutions, or at least the Declaration of Rights, he would not have confused the legislative power with the executive. The other privileges and responsibilities which he attributes to the man he calls the president of the legislative power are likewise products of his imagination. Yet at the time the abbé was writing he knew Americans living in Paris, and it would have been easy for him to learn the facts.

## Conclusion

In Virginia the people retained only the right to elect the legislative body. They were convinced, and I believe rightly so, that the population of a large state cannot know the men best qualified to fill the various posts. The legislative body elects the members of the executive and judiciary bodies, the state representatives in Congress, the treasurer, attorney general, auditors, and, in a word, all the men who have to perform the most important duties in the state.

Elsewhere customs vary to such an extent that it would be

tedious to enumerate them; there are, however, no states where judges are not chosen by the legislative or the executive body, or by the two together. The same applies to the numerous other posts dependent on the legislative or executive power, with the exception of the secretary and treasurer in Connecticut, who are elected by the people. The present secretary and the former governor, [Jonathan] Trumbull, are proof that satisfied citizens are not so inconstant as some writers claim. Trumbull, who died last year, had returned to private life of his own volition two years before. He was elected governor eighteen years consecutively; the current secretary [70] has occupied his post for forty years, and the secretary-ship has been in his family for three generations.

I have described the foundations of the thirteen states. This is not the place to discuss useful reforms in the various constitutional laws, such as the abolition of the barbarous law against the heirs in a suicide case, a law which no longer exists in any state. Anyone who wishes to ascertain some particular detail will find the consti-tutions translated into French and published in Paris with excellent notes. I should warn you, however, that you need to consult a well-informed inhabitant of each state, for the constitutions were writ-ten for the citizenry and many items were omitted.

The following passages, the first from the constitution of Vir-ginia, the second from that of New Jersey, make this clear. "The right of suffrage shall remain as exercised at present."

"All the laws of this province . . . lately published by Mr. Al-linson shall be and remain in full force, until . . ." [71] Very little is clear in the Connecticut and Rhode Island constitutions.

We have said that since the New Hampshire constitution was re-vised late in 1783, it could not be translated and published with the others.

Later we shall deal with observations about American govern-ment and laws which could arouse the curiosity of a foreigner. A refutation of Abbé Mably's numerous mistakes about these will require so much discussion that if we took them separately, there would be a great deal of repetition.

[70] George Wyllys.
[71] *New Jersey Constitution* (Burlington, 1776).

# Notes A-C

## Note A (see pages 41–42)

### The Charter of Privileges Granted by William Penn, Esq., to the Inhabitants of Pennsylvania and Territories
### 28 October 1701

Here are the essential articles it contains:

Because no People can be truly happy, tho' under the greatest Enjoyment of civil Liberties, if abridged of the Freedom of their Consciences as to their religious Profession and Worship . . . No Person or Persons inhabiting in this Province or Territories who shall confess and acknowledge one Almighty God, and profess him, or themselves obliged to live quietly under the civil Government, shall be in any Case molested or prejudiced in his or their Person or Estate. . . .

And that all Persons who also profess to believe in Jesus Christ the Saviour of the World, shall be capable . . . to serve this Government in any Capacity both legislatively and executively, he or they solemnly promising when lawfully required, Allegiance to the King as Soverign.

For the well governing of this Province and Territories, there shall be an Assembly, yearly chosen by the Freemen thereof, to consist of Four Persons out of each County, of most Note for Vertue, Wisdom and Ability, (or of a greater Number at any Time as the Governor and Assembly shall agree) upon the first Day of October Forever; and shall sit on the Fourteenth [15th] Day of the same Month at Philadelphia. . . . Which Assembly shall have Power to chuse a Speaker and other their officers; and shall be Judges of the Qualifications and Elections of their own Members, sit upon their own Adjournments, appoint Committees, prepare Bills, impeach Criminals, redress Grievances; and shall have all other Powers and Privileges of an Assembly, according to the Rights of the Freeborn Subjects of England, and as is usual in any of the King's Plantations in America. . . .

That the Freemen in each respective County at the Time and Place of meeting for electing their Representatives may Chuse a double Number of Persons to present to the Governor for Sheriffs and Coroners, to serve for Three Years, if so long they behave themselves well; out of which respective Elections and Presentments, the Governor shall nominate and commissionate one for each of the said Offices, the Third Day after such Presentment, or else the first named in such Presentment for each Office as aforesaid, shall stand and serve in that

Office for the Time before respectively limited; And in case of Death and Default, such Vacancies shall be supplied by the Governor to serve to the End of the said Term. . . .

And that the Justices of the respective Counties shall or may nominate and present to the Governor Three Persons, to serve for Clerk of the Peace for the said County when there is a Vacancy, one of which the Governor shall commissionate within Ten Days after such Presentment, or else the first nominated shall serve in the said Office during good Behaviour.

That the Laws of this Government shall be in this Stile, viz. [By the Governor, with the Consent and Approbation of the Freemen in General Assembly met]. . . .

That all Criminals shall have the same Privileges of Witness and Council as their Prosecutors.

That no Person or Persons shall or may, at any Time hereafter, be obliged to answer any Complaint, Matter or Thing whatsoever relating to Property, before the Governor and Council, or in any other Place, but in the ordinary Course of Justice, unless Appeals thereunto shall be hereafter by Law appointed. . . .

If any Person thro' Temptation, or Melancholy, shall destroy himself, his Estate real and personal, shall notwithstanding, descend to his Wife and Children, or Relations, as if he had died a natural Death. . . .

And no Act, Law or Ordinance whatsoever shall, at any Time hereafter, be made or done, to alter, change or diminish the Form or Effect of this Charter, or of any part or Clause therein, contrary to the true Intent and Meaning thereof, without the Consent of the Governor for the Time being, and Six Parts of Seven of the Assembly met. . . .

The First Article of this Charter relating to Liberty of Conscience, shall be kept and remain without any Alteration, inviolably for ever.

I the said William Penn, Proprietary and Governor of the Province of Pennsylvania, and Territories thereunto belonging, for myself, my Heirs, and Assigns, have Solemnly declared, granted and confirmed; and do hereby solemnly declare, grant, and confirm, That neither I, my Heirs or Assigns, shall procure or do any Thing or Things, whereby the Liberties in this Charter contained and expressed, nor any Part thereof, shall be infringed or broken. And if any Thing shall be procured or done, by any Person or Persons, contrary to these Presents, It shall be held of no Force or Effect.

William Penn [72]

[72] *Votes and Proceedings of the House of Representatives of the Province of Pennsylvania, December 4, 1682–June 11, 1707* (Philadelphia, 1752), 1:1–3.

Fragments of the Remonstrance Which the Pennsylvania
Assembly Addressed to William Penn in 1704

THAT we find by the Minutes of Assembly and other papers as well as
living witnesses that soon after thy first arrival here, thou having obtained the Duke's grants for the three lower counties, prevailed with
the people of the province to unite in legislation and government with
them of the lower counties and then by a subtle contrivance and artifice
laid deeper than the capacities of some could fathom or the circumstances of many could admit them time then to consider of, a way was
found out to lay aside that and introduce another Charter which thou
completed in the year 1683. . . .

And as to the conveniency of the union of the province and lower
counties, we cannot gainsay it, if the King had granted thee the government as the Duke had done the soil, but to our great grief and
trouble we cannot find that thou had any such grant, and if thou had,
thou would not produce it though often requested so to do, therefore
we take it the harder that thou, who knew how precarious thy power
was to govern the lower counties, should bring thy province into such
a state and condition that whenever the Crown had assumed that
government or the people there revolted or refused to act with us in
legislation, as they often did, that then the said second Charter should
become impracticable and the privileges thereby granted of no effect to
the province because the representatives of the lower counties were
equal in number with those of the province and the Charter required a
greater number than the province had or by Charter could elect for
members of the Council and Assembly, and our numbers by that
Charter could not be increased without the revolter's consent. . . .

The motives which we find upon record inducing the people to accept of that second Charter were chiefly two, viz. that the number of
representatives would prove burdensome to the country, and the other
was that in regard thou had but a treble vote. The people through their
unskillfulness in the laws of trade and navigation might make some laws
over thy head repugnant thereunto which might occasion the forfeiture
of the King's Letters Patent by which this country was granted thee,
and wherein is a clause for that purpose, which we find very much
relied upon and frequently read or urged in the Assemblies of that
time, and security demanded by thee from the people on that account.
As to the first motive, we know that the number of representatives
might well have been reduced without a new Charter. And as to the
laws of trade we cannot conceive that a people so fond of thyself for
Governor, and who saw much with thy eyes in those affairs should,
against thy advice and cautions make laws repugnant to those of trade
and so bring trouble and disappointment upon themselves by being a

means of suspending thy administration, the influence whereof and hopes of thy continuance therein induced them (as we charitably conclude) to imbark with those in that great and weighty affair more than the honour due to persons in those stations, or any sinister ends destructive to the Constitution they acted by, therefore we see no just cause thou had to insist upon such security or to have a negative upon bills to be passed into laws in General Assemblies since thou had by the said Charter (pursuant [73] to the authority and direction of the King's Letters Patent aforesaid) formed those Assemblies and reserved but a treble vote in the Provincial Council, which could not be more injurious to thee than to the people for the reasons aforesaid.

Thus was the first Charter laid aside, contrary to the tenor thereof and true intent of the first adventurers, and the second Charter introduced and accepted by the General Assembly held at Philadelphia in the first and second months 1683 where thou solemnly testified that what was inserted in the Charter "was solely by thee intended for the good and benefit of the freemen of the province, and prosecuted with much earnestness in thy spirit towards God at the time of its composure." . . .

That upon thy being restored to the government, thou required thy Lieutenant to govern us according to Charter, which, by reason of Fletcher's interruption became impossible before thy orders reached us, and so the government fell under great confusion again; nor was the administration of thy propriety much better managed, because thou put some in that commission with whom the rest would not act, and at last the office of property and surveyor general came to be shut up, and thou kept them so whiles thou sold lands to the value of about 3,000 pounds sterling and gave thy warrants in England for surveying the said land, and also got great tracts of land laid out or secured for thyself and relations besides several valuable parcels which should have been laid out for the purchaser, but were reserved by thy surveyors whether for thee or themselves, we know not. However thou appropriated those lands to thyself by the name of *concealed lands* whereas in truth they were concealed from the purchasers, who were to have their lands laid out contiguous one to another and no vacancies left between them, and thou wast to have only thy tenth as it fell according to the concessions thou made with thy first adventurers. And if thou took it not up so, 'twas thy own (not their) fault; but the other was a manifest injury to many of them as above declared.

That upon thy last arrival here, after all the hardships and disappointments we had laboured under, we hoped to enjoy the fruits of thy former promises and engagements, but instead of that, we found thee very full of resentment, and many of our applications and addresses about our just rights and properties were answered by recriminations

---

[73] Mazzei says "are not pursuant."

or bitter invectives, and we found that the false insinuations and re-proaches that our adversaries had cast upon the province with respect to false trade and harbouring pirates, had made so great an impression upon thee that thou rather believed them than thy honest friends. And when thou entered upon legislation, thou wast pleased to repeal all the laws that were made in Col. Fletcher's time which were approved by the King or Queen, as we were informed, and as some of us gathered by the account thou gave of them, viz. that Chancellor Somers had sent for thee to know what thou had to object against any of those laws, and if it hast not been for thee none of them had passed, or words to that effect. And not only so, but the people being minded to sur-render the said second Charter, upon thy promise to give them a better in lieu of it, and under pretence of passing an act for confirming and securing their lands etc., thou obtained liberty to resurvey all the lands in the province and to bring the people to terms for the overplus, so that by this stratagem, the warrants, surveys and new patents cost the people as much, and to some more, than the first purchase of their lands, besides their long attendance upon thy secretary and surveyors to have their business done, but before thou would pass that act, it must be accompanied with an impost or excise, and a two thousand bill besides.

And all this thou esteemed but inconsiderable, when thou compared it with the vast charge thou had been at in the administration and de-fence of this government since the year 1682, though we know thy stay here at first coming was not above two years, but went home about the difference between thee and Baltimore concerning the bounds of the lower counties, and did not return till the year 1699, excusing thy stay by thy service to the nation of England in general and to thy friends there in particular (as it appears by thy letters from time to time) whilst the interest of this province was sinking, which might have been upheld by many wealthy persons that were inclined to transport themselves here after the rout of Monmouth. If thou had then come over according to thy repeated promises, and how far thy stay has either effected what thou went about, or contributed to the establishment of the inhabitants here in their just rights, liberties and properties, we leave thee to demonstrate and the world to judge. In the meantime we desire thee to consider what a burden thou art placing on this province, and not to forget that no part of thy pretended charges was expended in paying some of those who acted under thee in the administration here, one of whom, to witt, Thomas Lloyd, served thee in that station about nine years of thy absence, which thou leaves, it seems, for the country to discharge.

That after thou had managed these points and was sent for to England, thou granted the third Charter * of privileges, by which we

---

* This remonstrance does not mention the second charter adopted in Chester in December 1682. It is possible that the changes it contained were not considered of

are now convened; as also a Charter to incorporate the City of Philadelphia and signed a Charter of property but refused to order thy seal to be affixed thereunto till thou had advised upon it in England, nevertheless thou promised under thy hand that thou would confirm the first part of it relating to titles of land but thou sent thy order, under hand and seal, dated, within six months after, to countermand the sealing thereof.

That after the laws were completed for raising all the said taxes and imposts, thou proposed that if thy friends would give thee a sum of money, thou promised to negotiate their affairs at home to the best advantage; and endeavour to procure the approbation of our laws and a general exemption from oaths; we find that considerable sums have been raised by way of subscription and benevolence for that service; part thou received before thou went and more has been received since by thy secretary; but we had no account that our laws are approved, nor had we as much as a letter from thee, nor any other intimation but by thy secretary's letters, which he thought fit to communicate by piecemeals, whereby we understand, thou hast been making terms for thyself and family. And by what we gather, thou hast been upon surrendering the government. Nor are thy friends here eased of oaths, but on the contrary, an order from the Queen required oaths to be administered to all persons who are willing, to take them in all judicatures, whereby the people called Quakers are disabled to sit in courts.

That, by the last Charter of privileges, thou established an annual election of representatives for Assembly, and that they should continue and sit upon their own adjournments; yet by thy commission to thy present deputy, John Evans, thou did in a direct opposition to the said Charter give him power not only to call Assemblies by his writs, but to prorogue and dissolve them as he should see cause, and also reserved to thyself (tho' in England) thy final assent to all bills passed here by thy deputy; we suppose thou hast not forgot that what rendered the former Charter inconvenient, if not impracticable, was chiefly that Col. Fletcher's interruption had extinguished the rotation of the Council, and next to that the proposals of laws by the Council in presence of the Governor, as also the instability of the lower counties which we had before experience of, and whose result was then doubted as hath since happened; but that annual standing Assemblies, liable only to the dismission and call of the governor as occasion required, was never found an inconvenience, nor assigned as a reason for changing the said former for the present Charter; and should that of dissolution be introduced it would frustrate the Constitution because if a dissolution should happen, the province might be a great part of the year without an Assembly, and the governor without power to call one,

---

sufficient importance to have it termed a second charter. This explains why the third charter is called the second, and the fourth the third.

whatever commands from the Crown, or other occasions may happen; for that the election being fixed by Charter, which is in nature of a perpetual Writ, and has the authority of a law; if it could be superseded by the governor's writ, which is but an Act of State and merely temporary, it would be of pernicious consequence to the province, as well as thyself, and of this thou seemed very sensible when being desired by the Assembly, upon the close of the session in the year 1701, to dissolve them (being then called by Writs) thou told them thou wouldst not do it for that thou couldst not answer to the Crown to leave the province without a standing Assembly.

That as the exemption from any dissolution or prorogation seems to be an inseparable consequent of thy grant, as well as our constant practice based upon the former Charter, which this was by thy promise to exceed, so upon an attempt made by the Council to prorogue us in October last, we have thought it our duty to prepare a bill for ascertaining, explaining and settling our present Constitution; which we having presented to thy deputy for his assent, he finding that the power of dissolution and prorogation is not in express words granted away by Charter as also the inconsistency thereof with his said commission, after several conferences thereupon, had with him and his Council, he thought fit to advise us to forbear the farther, pressing it till we should hear from thee. Therefore he being unwilling to pass the said bill by us judged so necessary, and the very foundation of our present Constitution, we could not think it proper to proceed to perfect any other business whilst that remained unsettled; nor do we suppose anything will be done in legislation either by the present or succeeding Assemblies till the difficulties we labour under herein be removed, either by thy speedy order or by thy deputy without it; seeing to proceed upon other matters would be to raise a superstructure before the foundation were well laid; nor do we look upon it very advisable for us to proceed far in legislation until thou repeals those parts of thy Lieutenant's commission relating to prorogation and dissolution of Assemblies for the reasons before given; as also concerning thy final assent to laws; which we conceive to be very unreasonable in itself, and a great abuse and violation of our Constitution that thou should offer to put three negatives upon our Acts, whereas by our first Charter we had none but that of the Crown, and how thou gained another to thyself we have before shewed thee, but now to bring us under three, seems a contrivance to provoke us to complain to the Queen, that thou art not effectually represented here, and make that a motive for her to take us under her immediate care and protection, which would make thy surrender in some measure our act, which if thou should do without the consent of the proprietors and inhabitants of this province first obtained would look too much like treachery.

That it appears by several petitions now before us, that very great abuses have been and are put upon the inhabitants, and extortions used by thy secretary, surveyors and other officers concerned in property as well as courts, which might have been prevented or sooner remedied, had thou been pleased to pass the bill proposed by the Assembly in the year 1701 to regulate fees—as also the want of a surveyor general which is a great injury and dissatisfaction to the people; as is likewise the want of an established judicature for trials between thee and the people, for if we exhibit our complaints against thee, or those who represent thee in state or property, they must be determined by or before justices of thy own appointment; by which means thou becomes in a legal sense judge in thy own cause, which is against natural equity. Therefore we propose that a man learned in the laws of England may be commissioned by the Queen to determine all matters, wherein thy tenants have just cause to complain against thee, thy deputies or commissioners; or else restore the people to the privilege of electing judges, justices and other officers, according to the direction of the first Charter, and intent of the first adventurers, and as the people of New England have by King William's Charter.

That thy commissioners of property are very unwilling to make good the deficencies of those lands thou hast been many years ago paid for (though thou gave them power so to do) and so great is the difficulty and trouble to get satisfaction in this particular that 'tis better for one to forego his right than wait on and attend the commissioners about it, unless the quantity wanting be very great.

We have many other things to represent to thee as grievances, as thy unheard of abuses to thy purchasers etc. in pretending to give them a town, and then by imposing unconscionable quit-rents makes it worse by ten fold than a purchase would have been; also the abuse about the bank, and want of common to the town; and not only so but the very land the town stands on is not cleared of the Swedes' claims.

These are the Chief heads which we thought fit at this time to lay before thee, earnestly entreating thy serious consideration of them, and that thou wilt now at last (after we have thus long endured and groaned under these hardships which of late seem to be multiplied upon us) endeavour as far as in thee lies to retrieve thy credit with us thy poor tenants and fellow subjects by redressing these aggrievances, especially in getting our laws confirmed, and also to be eased of oaths, and giving positive orders to thy deputy to unite heartily with us upon our Constitution, and that the Charters thou granted us for city and country may be explained, settled and confirmed by Law;

And we farther entreat that effectual care be taken for the suppressing of vice which, to our great trouble, we have to acquaint thee is more rife and common amongst us since the arrival of thy deputy and son,* especially of late, than was ever known before, nor are we capable to suppress it while it is connived at, if not encouraged by au-

---

* Penn had sent his son to serve as deputy.

thority, the mouths of the more sober magistrates being stopt by the said late order about oaths, and the Governor's licensing ordinaries not approved by the magistrates of the City of Philadelphia, and the roost chiefly ruled by such as are none of the most exemplary for virtuous conversation. Thy positive orders in the premises will be absolutely necessary to thy deputy, who thinks it unreasonable and a great hardship upon him to give sanction to laws explanatory of thy grants or to do anything by way of enlargement or confirmation of ought save what is particularly and expressly granted by thee, it being by some of his Council urged as an absurdity in us to expect, and we desire that thou would order the licensing of ordinaries and taverns to be by the justices, according to thy letter dated in September 1697. And we hope we need not be more express in charging thee as thou tenders thy own honour and honesty, or the obligations thou art under to thy friends, and particularly thy first purchasers and adventurers into this province, that thou do not surrender the government to the crown, whatsoever terms thou may, by so doing, make for thyself and family, which we shall deem no less than a betraying us, and at least will look like first fleecing then selling but rather use thy utmost interest with the Queen to ease us in the premises; and if after thy endeavours used to keep the government, it be by force taken from thee, thou will be the clearer in the sight of God and us the representatives of the people of this thy province, who are thy real friends and well-wishers, as we hope is evident in that we have dealt thus plainly with thee.[74]

Fragments of Another Remonstrance
10 June 1707

To WILLIAM PENN, Proprietary and Governor in Chief of the Province, of Pennsylvania:

The REMONSTRANCE of the Representatives of all the Freemen of the said Province, in a GENERAL ASSEMBLY met, the tenth Day of the Month called June, Anno Domini 1707.

May it please the Governor,

We, and the People we represent, being still grieved and oppressed with the male Administration and Practices of thy Deputy, and the ill Carriage, unwarrantable Proceedings, and great Exactions of thy Secretary . . . are like to be destroyed by the great Injustice, and arbitrary Oppressions of thy evil Ministers, who abuse the Powers given thee, by the Crown, and, we suppose, have too much prevailed upon thee, to leave us hitherto without Relief.

The Assembly which sat here on the Twenty-sixth of the Sixth

---

[74] Historical Society of Pennsylvania.

Month, 1704, agreed upon certain Heads or Particulars, which, according to the Order of that Day, were drawn up in a Representation, and was signed by the Speaker, and sent thee by a Passenger in John Guy's Brigantine, who was taken into France, from whence the same Representation was conveyed to thy Hands; whereby thou art put in Mind, upon what Score the Purchasers and first Adventurers embarked with thee to plant this Colony; and what Grants and Promises thou made, and the Assurance and Expectations thou gave them and the rest of the Settlers and Inhabitants of this Province, to enjoy the Privileges derived from they [sic] own Grants and Concessions, besides the Rights and Freedoms of England; but how they were diappointed [sic] in several respects, appears in Part by the said Representation, to which we refer; and become Supplicants for Relief, not only in Matters there complained of, which are not yet redressed, but also in Things then omitted, as well as what have been lately transacted, to the grievous Oppression of the Queen's Subjects, and publick Scandal of this Government.

We are much concerned, that thou conceived such Displeasure as thou did against that Assembly, and not in all this Time vouchsafe to shew thy Readiness to rectify those Things which they made appear was amiss; nor hast thou shewed they particular Objections to the Bills, which with great Care and Charge were then prepared, for confirming thy Charters to this City and Country, respecting both Privileges and Property, and for settling the Affirmation instead of Oaths; But, on the other Hand, we find, to our great Disappointment, that thou gave Credit to wrong Insinuations against them, as appears by thy Letter from Hyde-Park, dated the Twenty-sixth of the Twelfth Month, 1704–5, wherein thou treated some Particulars very unfriendly, and, without any just Grounds, blamed the People's Representatives, who, we perceive by their Proceedings, were ready to support the Government under thy Administration and desired nothing but to have their just Rights, Privileges and Properties, confirmed; the Judicatories regularly established; the Magistracy supplied with Men of Virtue and Probity, and the whole Constitution so framed, that the People called Quakers, might have a share with other Christian People in the Government, which thou always gave them an expectation of, and which they justly claim as a Point of Right; not for the Sake of Honour, but for the Suppressing of Vice. . . .[75]

The compiler of these acts adds that it would take too long to enumerate all the details of this quarrel which flared up several times and lasted until Gookin was dismissed in 1617 [1717] and replaced by William Keith. A full account would be tedious for the reader and painful for the writer.

[75] *Votes and Proceedings*, 1:180–81.

We have said enough to show how **Penn** was followed by his flock to Pennsylvania as if he were a kind of patriarch. We described the causes for their complaints against him, and an analysis of the proceedings of the assemblies which fomented the quarrel at various times will be sufficient to justify their conduct.

## Note B (see page 59)

### Declaration of Independence
### 4 July 1776

[Omitted]

## Note C (see page 72)

Reply of the Governor of Virginia [Lord Dunmore] to the Message Sent Him by the Council and House of Representatives in Reply to the Note His Excellency Left When He Withdrew to the Warship *Fowey* [10 June 1775]

Gentlemen of the Council, Mr. Speaker, and Gentlemen of the House of Burgesses.

In answer to your joint Address, presented by your deputies yesterday, I acquaint you, that it appears to me the commotions among the People, and their menaces and threats (an enumeration of which I forbear, out of tenderness) have been of such public notoriety, that you must suppose many of his Majesty's subjects in this Colony, whether they meditated or not, have at least manifested, such an inveteracy as justifies my suspicion that they would not hesitate to commit a Crime, which, horrid and atrocious as it is, I had just ground to apprehend. And when the disposition which the House of Burgesses have shown towards me, the returns they have made to the respect and civility which I have been forward to offer to them, the countenance they have given to the violent and disorderly proceedings of the People, his Majesty's magazine having been forced and rifled in the presence of some of the members of the House of Burgesses, and, by the information of the Committee of the House appointed to inspect the Magazine, no other endeavours have been used than to prevail on the People to return the Arms taken out, but not to commit the Persons in whose possession they were found, in order that they might be brought to the punishment due to so heinous an offence, no less against the peace and good order of the Country than the dignity and authority of the King; when a body of men assembled in the City of Williamsburg, not only to the knowledge, but with the approbation of every body, for the avowed purpose of attacking a party of the King's forces, which, without the least foundation, it was reported were marching to my protection, and which, if true, ought to have been approved and aided, not opposed and insulted, by all good and loyal Subjects; when especially the House of Burgesses, or a committee of the House (which is the same) has ventured upon a step fraught with the most alarming consequences, in ordering and appointing guards, without even consulting me, to mount in the city of Williamsburg, as is pretended, to protect the Magazine, but which may well be doubted, as there then remained nothing therein which required being guarded; but if otherwise, this step nevertheless shews a design to usurp the executive power, which, if it be persisted in, subverts the constitution; I say, when these circumstances are duly considered, I may submit it to your own Judgment whether I could reasonably expect any good effect from communicating the ground of my uneasiness to you.

But as you are pleased, Gentlemen, now to assure me, that you will cheerfully concur in any measure that may be proposed proper for the security of myself and family, I leave to your own consideration whether that can be effected any other wise than by reinstating me in the full powers of my office, as his Majesty's representative, by opening the Courts of Justice, and restoring the energy of the Laws, which is all the security requisite for all parties; by disarming all independent companies, or other bodies of Men raised and acting in defiance of lawful authority, and by obliging those who have taken any of his Majesty's public store of Arms to deliver them up immediately; and, what is not less essential than any thing by your own example, and every means in your power, abolishing that Spirit of persecution, which, to the disgrace of humanity, now reigns, and pursues with menaces and acts of oppression, all persons who differ from the multitude in political opinion, or are attached from principles and duty to the service of their King and government; by which means, the deluded People never hearing but the disfigured side of a Story, their minds are continually kept in that ferment which subjects them forever to be imposed upon, and leads to the commission of any desperate Act, and endangers the general safety. For the more speedy accomplishment of these ends, and the great object and necessary business of the Sessions, I shall have no objection to your adjourning to the Town of York, where I shall meet you, and remain with you till your business be finished.

With respect to your entreaty that I should return to the Palace, as the most likely means of quieting the minds of the People, I must represent to you, that, unless there be among you a sincere and active desire to seize this opportunity, now offered to you by Parliament, of establishing the freedom of your Country upon a fixed and known foundation, and of uniting yourselves with your fellow subjects of Great Britain in one common bond of interest, and mutual assistance, my return to Williamsburg would be as fruitless to the People, as, possibly, it might be dangerous to myself. But if your proceedings manifest that happy disposition, which is to be desired ardently by every good friend to this as well as the Mother Country, I assure you, in the warmth of my heart, that I will return, with the greatest joy, and shall consider it as the most fortunate event of my Life if you give me an opportunity to be an instrument of promoting your happiness, and a mediator between you and the supreme authority, to obtain for you every explanation of your doubts, and the fullest conviction of the sincerity of their desire to confirm to you the undisturbed enjoyment of your rights and liberty; and I shall be well pleased, by bringing my family back again, that you should have such a pledge of my attachment to this Country, and of my wishes to cultivate a close and lasting intimacy with the inhabitants.

Dunmore [76]

### Address of the House of Representatives to John Lord Dunmore

[The House resolved itself into a Committee of the whole House.]

To His Excellency, Lord Dunmore, Governor of the Colony and Commonwealth of Virginia,

*Resolved*, that it is the Opinion of this Committee that an address be presented to his Excellency, the Governor, to inform him that we have taken into our Consideration the joint Address of the two Houses of Parliament, his Majesty's Answer, and the Resolution of the Commons which his Lordship has been pleased to lay before us. That wishing nothing so sincerely as the perpetual continuance of that brotherly love which we bear to our fellow subjects of Great Britain and still continuing to hope and believe that they do not approve the measures which have so long oppressed their brethren in America, we were pleased to receive his Lordship's notification that a benevolent tender had at length been made by the British House of Commons towards bringing to a good end our unhappy disputes with the Mother Country: that next to the possession of liberty, we should consider such Reconciliation the greatest of all human blessings. With these dispositions we entered into consideration of that Resolution; we examined it minutely; we viewed it in every point of light in which we were able to place it and with pain and disappointment we must ultimately declare it only changes the form of oppression, without lightening its

[76] *Journals of the House of Burgesses of Virginia, 1773-76*, ed. John Pendleton Kennedy (Richmond, 1905), pp. 212-14.

burthen. That we cannot close with the terms of that Resolution for these Reasons.

Because the British Parliament has no right to intermeddle with the support of civil government in the Colonies. For us, not for them, has government been instituted here; agreeable to our Ideas provision has been made for such Officers as we think necessary for the administration of public affairs; and we cannot conceive that any other legislature has a right to prescribe either the number or pecuniary appointments of our Offices. As a proof that the Claim of Parliament to interfere in the necessary Provisions for support of civil Government is novel and of a late Date we take leave to refer to an Act of our Assembly passed so long since as the thirty second Year of the Reign of King Charles the second intituled *An Act for raising a public Revenue and for the better support of the Government of this his Majesty's Colony of Virginia.* This Act was brought over by Lord Culpeper then Governor under the great Seal of England and was enacted in the name of the "King's most excellent Majesty by and with the Consent of the General Assembly."

Because to render perpetual our exemption from an unjust taxation, we must saddle ourselves with a perpetual tax adequate to the expectations and subject to the disposal of Parliament alone. Whereas, we have right to give our money, as the Parliament does theirs, without coercion, from time to time, as public exigencies may require, we conceive that we alone are the judges of the condition, circumstances, and situation of our people, as the Parliament are of theirs. It is not merely the mode of raising, but the freedom of granting our Money for which we have contended. Without this we possess no check on the royal prerogative, and what must be much lamented by dutiful and loyal subjects, we should be stript of the only means, as well of recommending this Country to the favour of our most gracious Sovereign as of strengthening those bands of Amity with our fellow subjects which we would wish to remain indissoluble.

Because on our undertaking to grant money as is proposed, the Commons only resolve to forbear levying pecuniary taxes on us; still leaving unrepealed their several Acts passed for the purposes of restraining the trade and altering the form of Government of the Eastern Colonies; extending the boundaries and changing the Government and Religion of Quebec; enlarging the jurisdiction of the Courts of Admiralty, and taking from us the right of trial by jury; and transporting us into other Countries to be tried for Criminal Offences. Standing armies too are still to be kept among us, and the other numerous grievances of which ourselves and sister Colonies separately and by our representatives in General Congress have so often complained, are still to continue without redress.

Because at the very time of requiring from us grants of Money they are making disposition to invade us with large Armaments by Sea and land, which is a stile of asking gifts not reconcileable to our freedom. They are also proceeding to a Repetition of injury by passing acts for restraining the commerce and fisheries of the Provinces of *New England,* and for prohibiting the Trade of the other Colonies with all parts of the world except the islands of Great Britain, Ireland, and the West Indies. This seems to bespeak no intention to discontinue the exercise of this usurped Power over us in future.

Because on our agreeing to contribute our proportion towards the common defence, they do not propose to lay open to us a free trade with all the world: whereas to us it appears just that those who bear equally the burthens of Government, should equally participate of its benefits. Either be content with the monopoly of our trade, which brings greater loss to us and benefit to them than the amount of our proportional contributions to the common defence; or, if the latter be preferred, relinquish the former, and do not propose, by holding both, to exact from us double contributions. Yet we would remind Government that on former emergencies when called upon as a free People, however cramped by this monopoly in our resources of wealth, we have liberally contributed to the common defence. Be assured then that we shall be generous in future as in past times, disdaining the shackles of proportion when called to our free station in the general system of the Empire.

Because the proposition now made to us involves the interest of all the other Colonies, we are now represented in General Congress, by members approved by this House where our former Union it is hoped will be so strongly cemented that no partial Application can produce the slightest departure from the common Cause. We consider ourselves as bound in Honor as well as Interest to share one general Fate with our Sister Colonies, and should hold ourselves base deserters of that Union, to which we have acceded, were we to agree on any Measures distinct and apart from them.

To observe that there was indeed a plan of accomodation offered in Parliament, which tho' not entirely equal to the terms we had a right to ask, yet differed but in few Points from what the General Congress had held out. Had Parliament been disposed sincerely as we are to bring about a reconciliation, reasonable man had hoped that by meeting us on this ground something might have been done. Lord Chatham's bill on the one part and the terms of the Congress on the other would have formed a basis for negotiation which a spirit of accomodation on both sides might perhaps have reconciled. It came recommended too from one whose successful experience in the art of Government should have ensured to it some attention from those to whom it was tendered. He had shown to the world that Great Britain with her Colonies, united firmly under a just and honest government, formed a power which might bid defiance to the most potent enemies. With a change of Ministers however a total change of measure took place; the component parts of the empire have from that moment been falling asunder, and a total annihilation of its weight in the political scale of the World seems justly to be apprehended.

To declare that these are our sentiments on this important subject, which we offer only as an individual part of the whole empire. Final determination we leave to the General Congress now sitting, before whom we shall lay the Papers his Lordship has communicated to us. To their wisdom we commit the improvement of this important advance; if it can be wrought into any good, we are assured they will do it. To them also we refer the discovery of that proper method of representing our well founded grievancies which his Lordship assures us will meet with the attention and regard so justly due to them. For ourselves, we have exhausted every mode of application which our invention could suggest as proper and promising: we have decently remonstrated with Parliament; they have added new injuries to the old; we have wearied our King with supplication; he has not deigned to answer us: We have appealed to the native honour and justice of the British nation; their efforts in our favor [have so far been unavailing]. What then remains to be done? That we commit our injuries to the even-handed justice of that being who doth no wrong, earnestly beseeching him to illuminate the Councils and prosper the endeavors of those to whom America hath confided her hopes; that thro' their wise direction we may again see reunited the blessings of Liberty, Property, and Union with Great Britain.[77]

# Letters from a Citizen of New Heaven[78] to a Citizen of Virginia on the Futility of Dividing the Legislative Power among Several Bodies

[Omitted]

[77] Ibid., p. 241.
[78] Marie Jean Antoine Nicolas de Caritat, marquis de Condorcet, philosopher and politician.

# Observations

# Addressed to the Inhabitants of the United States by the Author of the *Researches*

The legislative power will be approximately the same in all states. You will notice, to some degree at least, the disadvantages I have always observed in Virginia. At the beginning of the sessions the least important matters are discussed; some men do not even bother to come, others are afraid they will arrive before there are enough members to begin, so that a great deal of time is wasted.

When the session becomes interesting, constant attendance is required, and this puts a strain on the health of some members, for discussions often continue into the night. Certain matters have to be examined in committee before they are taken to the floor. This means that committee members have to work late at night, early the following morning and then go to the house without a moment's rest. When these men have put their resolutions in legal form to be discussed by the house, they are so tired they cannot examine the proposed changes carefully. Although these were dictated for the purpose of improving the resolution, they may well change or obscure its meaning. The General Assembly often has to wait for a committee before discussion can start. Sessions frequently last longer than they should, and some men become so exhausted that they make decisions on crucial matters without adequate consideration.

It would be wise to establish a permanent committee of six men whose responsibility would be to prepare the material for the next session of the General Assembly. A large amount of the work could thus be done in advance, laws would be better written, and it is probable that everything would proceed more expeditiously, although the assembly could, of course, change or reject the proposed articles and deliberate on other matters as well. The president of the University of Williamsburg [79] had this idea, which he passed

[79] Bishop James Madison was president of the College of William and Mary from 1777 until 1812.

on to me two years ago. I liked it, but it seemed to me that these six men could perform other functions as well.

In order to maintain a free government, it is very important for its agents to have just the right amount of power. Too much promotes tyranny; too little, anarchy. I believe power should reside in the legislative body and that the committee of six, whom we might call the guardians of liberty, should be highly esteemed.

In order to prevent the house from passing or revoking laws too easily, the six could give their objections to the legislative body in writing, and these objections could be overruled only by a vote of two-thirds or three-quarters. Whenever the legislative body refused to examine laws proposed by the six or rejected by them (which would require a simple plurality), or whenever the requisite plurality of two-thirds or three-quarters proposed or revoked others against their wishes, the committee and the legislative body should inform the people at once so that the voters might reach a decision before the next session.

If there is a difference of opinion between the bodies, I think that the number of votes for and against should be published, together with the name of each representative, so that the people may be informed of the intentions of each voter.

Our constitutions state that the legislative, executive, and judiciary branches should be absolutely independent, but they do not tell how to settle arguments which might arise between them. In such an event, the nation would have to elect a convention and there might be long delays. If the committee of six were established, these differences could be settled by them and by an equal number of members from the neutral department, appointed by their colleagues.

The six could also intervene in civil and criminal private suits, if one of the parties was judge in a supreme court. Partiality can cause criticism of a virtuous judge in whose favor a case has been decided. In such an instance I should like to have each one of the parties demand that the affair be judged by the six and an equal number of judges from the various supreme courts.

The six could also be useful in the executive department, where they could give advice to the chief magistrate of the republic whenever it was requested. I have already explained my reasons for thinking that the chief magistrate should be free to act without his councillors.* Since the six, by reason of their functions, would have

---

* The colleagues of the chief magistrate in the executive department are called councillors.

to reside in the capital, it would be easy to consult them, and the chief magistrate would seldom need to consult his colleagues. This would free them to look after their own business, and instead of a salary, they could be paid for whatever time they devoted to public service.

A revision of the constitution may be necessary for several reasons. It may prove insufficient, and dangerous innovations may be inserted into it. Anyone has the right to inform his fellow citizens of this and to request that a convention be convoked, but it would take a long time before the majority of the counties in a state reached this decision. A man would hesitate to express his views because the people have such confidence in their representatives that they would tend to disregard the opinion of a few individuals.

Pennsylvania wisely thought this should be an obligation, not a right. It therefore decreed that every seven years a council of censors should be elected, whose principal duty would be to see if the constitution needed to be reformed. If they decided in the affirmative, they would order that a convention be convoked. Although this is good theoretically, it is dangerous to set a time for such an operation. Discontent and a desire for change are enhanced by the certainty of revision, and intrigues begin several years in advance. Vigilance should be continuous, not periodical. This task should be entrusted to people like the six, who are always available, and to the three branches of government. Two of the four bodies would have the right to order the chief magistrate to call a convention to examine the constitution. In the legislative body a simple plurality should be adequate for this, while in the others two-thirds would be needed. Every citizen may ask his fellows to call a convention, but the right to convoke it should not be given to too small a group.

The six ought to be elected by the legislative body and none of them discharged without a verdict of the judges of all the supreme courts. As they would devote all their time to serving their country, their salaries should be adequate to ensure a decent living for them and their families. These six posts would be regarded as an honorary retirement for men distinguished by their talents and virtues, and there is every reason to believe that the people's representatives would elect as fathers of the nation citizens they venerated and who would not be apt to arouse jealousy.

The spirit of economy, which governs public expenses in America, need not fear the cost involved in establishing this body, for the savings resulting from a prompt expedition of business in the legislative department would compensate for it.

One of the salutary precautions our ancestors brought from England was the appointment of grand jurors, without whose approbation no one can enter an action which might lead to capital punishment. The little republic of Lucca has a similar requirement for civil cases which I should like to see adopted. Six men distinguished for their character are charged with examining a case before it can be taken to court. Their opinion carries such weight that many cases have been settled out of court by this means.

# PART II

## Reply

## To the *Observations* of Abbé Mably, Together with a Discussion of Some Important Matters Pertaining to the Government of the United States

One of the numerous errors of Abbé Mably in his *Observations on the Government and Laws of the United States of America* is very curious. He claims we have no laws other than those dealing with the constitution, which puts us in a pitiable state of ignorance. On the other hand, he tells us (p. 4): "People are astonished and edified that your thirteen republics have known the dignity of man and have drawn from philosophical sources the human principles by which they wish to govern themselves." Such a contradiction on our part would be monstrous.

In general, his praise, like his blame, is either undeserved or exaggerated. His principles are often obscure, occasionally contradictory. For example, on page 20 he is annoyed because we are too attached to English laws, and on page 22 he fears we have departed too far from them; on page 24 he advises us to avoid aristocracy, and elsewhere he recommends it and predicts it is inevitable. He wants to prevent the wealthy from acquiring an authority which should not belong to them; yet he thinks they should be granted privileges unfair to the poor, etc.

Mably pretends we have no laws to administer justice and subscribes to the common European fallacy that England rightfully had sovereignty over our colonies before the Revolution. He believes the English ministers when they insinuate we wanted the Revolution; he imagines that our division of states into counties or districts, the election of representatives, and the establishment of juries are all modern institutions.

The abbé fears the consequences of equality in the rights of the citizen and expresses concern about the effects of religious liberty.

He frequently harps on the need for establishing an aristocracy, criticizes freedom of the press, and thinks merit should not be preferred to fortune. In short, his maxims are such that any philosophical legislator would reject them with scorn.

The lack of clarity and precision in his book makes it impossible to refute it in an orderly fashion. We have to quote the text to keep from being accused of partiality. This is lengthy, but there is no other way to clear up so much confusion. Before examining his critical observations on our governments we shall glance at his first letter. This serves as an introduction, and in many places he appears to favor us.

# Chapter 1

# General Observations of Abbé Mably

Page 4: "It is fortunate for you that the English kings, when they were guided by ambition and avarice, gave your fathers charters for your colonies. While they were disposing of a throng of citizens who irritated them, they foresaw new provinces which would augment the majesty of the British empire. They also flattered themselves that they were opening a new source of wealth for British commerce and hoped to make you prosper so that they could enjoy, to an even greater extent, the advantages of your prosperity." Such motives were quite normal on the part of those who founded plantations, although the abbé seems to consider the kings unusual in this respect. The truth is, of course, that the colonies were not established by the kings, and in any event, whatever their opinions may have been, Americans never complained about their charters. In some colonies they objected when the charters were abolished or changed or when their terms were not observed.

It is difficult to guess the abbé's meaning when he speaks of the throng of citizens who irritated the English kings. This kingdom has never, at least since the discovery of America, needed to decrease the number of its inhabitants. The proclamation of 30 April 1637 forbidding emigration to America is a good indication that the throng of citizens was not very irritating. It was the emigrants who were irritated, and they determined to leave England to seek the liberty and happiness they despaired of enjoying in their homeland. So we should believe the opposite of what Mably said.

Page 6: "After the last war, which made the French lose all their possessions on your continent, you understood that your masters had grown feeble by their very conquests and you finally felt your strength." The abbé had probably read the report published by the ministerial party in England, and as he did not write his book until long afterward, he praised Americans for a principle far removed from their manner of thinking. As for the expression "your masters," he did not have to consult colonial history to discover that England had no rights over America. The Declaration of Independence, alluding to the approval the king gave Parliament to subdue the colonies, states: "He has combined with others to subject us to a Jurisdiction foreign to our Constitution, and unacknowledged by our Laws; giving his Assent to their Acts of pretended Legislation."

Page 6: "Since England, they said, claimed the right to banish the Stuarts in order to put the House of Hanover on the throne, why would we be forbidden to throw off the yoke of George III, whose ministry, more inflexible and cruel than that of James II, takes cruel advantage of our generosity and zeal?" No one, save the author, appears to have reached this conclusion; Americans justified their conduct by reason, not example.

Page 8: "Fortunately the thirteen states did not confuse their rights, independence, and liberty at the time they established one republic with the same laws and magistrates." If anyone had made such a statement in America, even the most poorly educated individual could have shown it to be absurd. The author spends two pages praising us for not having blundered.

Page 11: "May all the provinces with definite boundaries, like Massachusetts, Connecticut, Rhode Island, New Jersey, Delaware, and Maryland, be afflicted by the only calamity which honors nations; I refer to the large population which, while a tribute to the government, proves a burden at times." It is doubtful whether any country ever had a real need to dispose of inhabitants, and it is certain that many centuries have passed with no symptoms of such a disease; but to tell us about it and how to deal with it—as he does—makes one think he jests. Among the states which already had definite boundaries when he wrote (and in Mably's list Massachusetts should be replaced by Pennsylvania and New Hampshire),* the one with the largest number of inhabitants could easily triple its population without finding it a burden.

The scarcity of inhabitants, which makes labor very expensive, is the only reason why factories are not being established and goods have to be imported from Europe. We agree that the American population has increased considerably, but many years will pass before it becomes dense in any particular region. As long as men can obtain land cheaply, they will do so. The territory of the United States is vast, the cultivated portion very small. As the artisan earns more than his European counterpart, he hastens to

---

* Pennsylvania and New Hampshire have always had definite boundaries, whereas Massachusetts has never recognized that its boundaries were any more fixed than those of New York, Virginia, Georgia, and the two Carolinas.

buy land to be independent; elsewhere a man with a small piece of property sells it to get a larger holding in a more remote area.

Page 11: "Let these states I have just named renew the spectacle of ancient Greece, whose happy colonies created a new homeland everywhere. I hope that Americans will not seek to make conquests but will settle the provinces where farmers are needed." The author's pompous advice is childish and out of place. Men emigrate because they want to acquire as much land as possible, and Americans can easily move from one state to another, since Article 4 of the Articles of Confederation assures them of the rights of citizenship everywhere.

Page 13: "The ancient republics were enclosed within city walls and had a very restricted territory." Unless we assume that the abbé was referring to the boundary limits within which men had to live in order to vote, it remains to be determined whether Rome and Carthage should be put in the same category as modern republics, or whether the empires and kingdoms they were said to possess were poetic fiction.

Page 13: "The American population will be less bold, less imperious, and less fickle because the extent of each republic and the number of its citizens make it impossible for them all to assemble in the same place." Without asking how fickleness can be the result of an imperious, bold spirit, I can state that there are several reasons why all the inhabitants of our republics do not assemble to discuss political matters. Our ancestors brought from England the custom of selecting representatives. Then, our common man is far better educated than his European counterpart, and an illiterate peasant is a phenomenon. Most important, however, is the fact that Americans are accustomed from childhood to deliberate. If they were asked to discuss governmental matters, they would raise several objections, beginning with their own incapacity.

Page 14: "You have adopted the modern method of dividing the country into counties or districts, where citizens discuss their affairs and appoint those they consider best qualified to represent them in the legislative assembly of the Republic." The method of dividing the country to facilitate voting, to settle litigation and other municipal matters, as well as the custom of naming representatives, was copied from English usage and has always been in force. One useful innovation we have made since the Revolution is the annual election; another is the statute which decrees that the representatives of each county or district must be chosen from the inhabitants of the district.* In several states very large counties are divided; other regulations are designed to make the rights of suffrage and representation more uniform. Can we conceive what the author means with his "modern method"? Furthermore, he predicts the beneficial results of regulations we have always enjoyed.

Page 15: "I see with pleasure that in all your constitutions you religiously respect the rights you have recognized in the working class. You even protect the slaves; you have attached them to the fate of the republic by giving them an opportunity to earn money and to get a job which will raise them to the rank of citizens." Here the author is apparently not referring to Negroes, but there are no other slaves in the United States. Since the Revolution their fate has been improved to a certain extent, and it is intended to abolish slavery everywhere as soon as circumstances permit.† They have, however, no legal means of obtaining money so that they can become citizens. I believe Spain is the only country where slaves can become citizens.

The condition of freemen bound to others depends on an agreement between the two parties. Poor Europeans lacking funds to emigrate usually bind themselves out to the captain or to another passenger, with the promise that they will serve him for several years on condition that they are housed, fed, and clothed. The new master sells this paper in America and generally makes a profit. You must keep in mind, however, that he has run the risk of disease and death and that the purchaser is exposed to the same hazard. In my opinion, the poor man is the one who gains the most, since his master is obliged to provide him with everything and to take care of him if he becomes ill. He has an opportunity to make contacts, and when the time of his service has expired, he can better his position. It is true that he has not saved anything, but people who go to America without enough money for their passage probably would have had a harder life in Europe than in the colonies. These

---

* This is extremely important, and I hope it will never be set aside. Representatives who live in their districts are under the immediate inspection of their constituents, and as they are scattered throughout the whole state, it is highly unlikely that they could intrigue with their colleagues.

† The evil is so deep-rooted in the southern states that it will take time to overcome. This would not be the case if the English government, which wished to favor the London African Company, had not constantly refused to sanction laws passed by different colonies to stop its profitable slave trade. While we were subject to these inhuman refusals, the King's Bench decided in 1771 that a slave belonging to Sir Charles Stuart of Maryland became free on setting foot in Great Britain. The contrast is thought provoking.

contracts are individual matters, not regulated by law unless one of the parties takes the other to court. The only legal requirement is that the service cannot extend more than a given time. In Virginia this is five years, and it is the limit prescribed for those who did not sign a contract before leaving Europe. Only minors may be obliged to serve until they are twenty-one. They may be apprenticed by their father or guardian to a master, who is obliged to teach them to read, write, do arithmetic, and ply a trade. At the end of the term of service he must give them, like the servants, a new suit of clothes or money to purchase it. The word *slave* has never been used either in this connection or in speaking of the criminals brought from England before the Revolution, and contracts dealing with servants or apprentices are the same as they have always been.

Page 15: "As a result of these humanitarian principles, you have adopted the best jurisprudence men have devised, that of jurors, which is the wisest practice yet known to promote true equality." Page 16: "You will always remember that England tried to submit you to its tyranny by depriving you of the safety of your jurors." Why praise us for not abolishing an institution we prized? Could we have done anything else in reason, and does he think we were making some great sacrifice when we were acting for our own good? Between these two quotations he lists several advantages of jurisprudence, as if we knew nothing about it. Finally he takes the trouble to put us on guard against several maxims we formally condemned in our constitutions.

Page 18: "You will agree with me that democracy must be handled with the utmost prudence. An ignorant and degraded multitude has neither the time nor the opportunity to adopt the principles of a sound political doctrine." The man on the street does not need to be versed in politics to choose his representatives. He needs only honesty and sound judgment.

The author, with his hazy democracy, has become lost in a labyrinth. On page 19 he says of the common people: "They cannot help envying their superiors." That is impossible in America, where the people, being sovereign, cannot have any superiors. Obedience is due only to the laws, which are the same for everyone. The men who carry out these laws are agents of the people, not their superiors. Those who make the laws are also agents, chosen by the people and dismissed if they are not satisfactory. Assembled, they represent sovereign power; when the session is over, they are ordinary citizens. Subordination among individuals performing some public duty does not prove superiority or inferiority, but it is essential to good order. Soldiers on review * obey their officers, but when the review is over, subordination disappears. Wealthy men may be ordinary soldiers, and their stewards or other employees officers in the same companies.

After discussing the evils which he fears may be rooted in the people's power, the abbé asks, page 23, whether we did not "promise them more than we wished and could give them." As the people in the United States are the nation, it is difficult to see who could have promised or given them power. If any ambitious citizen entertained such an insidious thought, he never dared reveal it.

Page 24: "The American constitutions may well put you in the position of the Romans after they had driven out the Tarquins. The patricians made the populace magnificent promises to interest them in the cause of liberty. They then seized all the public power, while the plebeians flattered themselves they were only obeying the laws. All the dissensions of the marketplace rose from these conflicting interests." This comparison is vicious. The Romans were divided in two distinct classes; we have one. Their patricians had hereditary privileges; all our citizens are born with the same rights. The patricians wielded public power from the time of Romulus. They took advantage of the expulsion of the Tarquins to seize it all, and the populace was degraded. In the United States no citizen has any power unless it has been given to him by his peers. He can enjoy it only for a specified time, and everyone is eligible for every position,† whether salaried or honorary. Finally, an intelligent nation cannot be compared to a multitude shrouded in ignorance and superstition and dominated by oracles.

The abbé has such boundless respect for the Ancients that he magnifies their virtues and is oblivious to their faults. He believes, page 24: "Any nation could console itself for resembling the Romans in their mistakes, provided it could resemble them in their deeds of greatness, wisdom, and magnanimity."

The Romans were ambitious and wanted a universal empire. We want the whole world to be free. The Romans made slaves of their peers and slaughtered some of them for sport. Our slaves have been

---

* Every citizen is obliged to serve from the time he is 18 until he is 50. No one is exempt unless he has an infirmity or holds public office.

† No one should object to the law prevailing in most states that requires a man to have a small capital to vote or to be a representative. Some states demand a larger amount for the latter or for certain other posts. Although I consider this system unfair to those who have nothing, a hardworking man can obtain enough money to enjoy every privilege.

brought from distant lands, and we want to give them their liberty as soon as possible. Although a great many people regard these unfortunates as a very inferior race, we treat them as kindly as we can.

The Romans refused the right of citizenship to men who had helped them conquer a large part of the world; we give it to every inhabitant of the globe. Blinded by ambition, the Romans wanted a single government; we divide our territory into states.

They were motivated by a fanatic enthusiasm; the American compass is reflection. To the Romans the state was a divinity which promised eternal happiness to those who sacrificed their lives for her; Americans are peace loving, but they are patriotic and seek danger when duty requires it.*

We shall now discuss Abbé Mably's remarks about our governments and his claim that we do not have enough laws.

* See Note D, with several deeds evincing intelligent patriotism.

# The Nature of the Governments
# and Characteristics of the Inhabitants
# of the United States

It is evident from what has been said about the state governments that the people have universally abandoned all legislative, executive, and judiciary power, as well as the election of the judiciary. In several states they elect only the legislative body, and the state of Connecticut is the only one where the inhabitants reserved the right of election for two offices among all those which depend on the legislative and executive branches.

This is still not enough to calm the fears of Abbé Mably, who is concerned about "the excess of power in the hands of the people." On page 23 he says: "If it is true that, because of your connections with England, you have a tendency toward aristocracy, would it not be unwise to establish too complete a democracy?" And on page 34 he asks: "Do you believe that the prejudices you developed under the English will make it possible for you to aspire to a pure democracy?"

It is difficult to surmise what he means by a "complete" or "pure" democracy. If a democracy is a constitution in which every citizen who has a right to vote expresses his opinion on specific cases and judges his magistrates, we do not have a democracy; the power reserved by the body of citizens to elect legislators in every state, and certain other officials in some states, is far from constituting a pure democracy. This explains why most Europeans believe our states are aristocratic.

It is a common failing for people to get lost in a dispute over names when they are discussing the nature of our governments. In point of fact they are neither aristocratic nor democratic, but if you do not take the trouble to examine them carefully, you use the term which best fits the characteristics you have noticed. As we have no distinction of rank and no citizen is excluded from any office and as citizens entrust their representatives with almost all the power they exercise personally in democratic governments, neither term is suitable unless we call them limited, or rather rational, democracies.

On page 23 the author says: "It seems to me that instead of arousing the people's hopes, it would have been preferable to free them from the English yoke and have them obey magistrates whose mediocre fortunes would keep them modest and zealous for the public weal."

If the American public had not penetrated the intentions of the English government, there would have been no revolution, or it would have been stillborn. As to his suggestion that the public be placed under the tutelage of magistrates, the inhabitants would be forced to deprive themselves of their power to vote or promise to vote only for men with mediocre fortunes. They would have to order their representatives to do the same as long as it seemed prudent to exclude from the bench those above and below mediocrity. It would also be very difficult to persuade a nation to be satisfied with promises when the people have and wish to preserve the right to elect the candidates they choose.

On page 45 he fears the power of the people, whom he calls "ignorant, imbecile, and inclined to prejudice." It is strange that he speaks of Americans with so much assurance when he has not taken the trouble to become acquainted with them. Any American in Paris could have told him that there are no distinguished civil servants in the United States other than those elected by the people. Many citizens who have served their country for a long time desire to rest and enjoy domestic life, which, for an American, is the greatest bliss. Some are obliged to refuse another post to attend to their own business, and I am sure that the majority of the revolutionary leaders prefer the simple pleasures of home to any kind of position. I know a number in Virginia, including the author of the Declaration of Rights and General Washington. Dr. Franklin resigned his appointment as minister plenipotentiary at the court of France to spend the rest of his days in Pennsylvania. Later, at the age of eighty, he yielded to the demands of his fellow citizens to be chief magistrate of the state.

The author was wrong in comparing our people to the populace of other nations, for Americans differ from all others. It is a moral difference, not a physical one based on soil or climate. There has never been a republic where the whole population exerted so much influence on the government and where everyone could aspire to honors and wealth. Before the Revolution the distinction between classes was much smaller than it has been and still is in other countries. It is therefore not surprising that popular disorders, which occur in other countries, do not break out here. It is also easy to understand why the American public, although hardworking and less wealthy, is fairly well educated. Men wish to learn about public affairs when they realize that it is in their interest to do so, and since the beginning of the Revolution, Americans have made astonishing progress in their ability to discuss these matters.

The useful sciences are encouraged by the lack of vain honors, such as titles, crosses, and ribbons, and by the fact that few men are wealthy. Whenever there is a superior class there must be a large number of unfortunates, and knowledge will be restricted largely to the middle class. The poor cannot acquire it, while the wealthy obtain far more from their titles than by science or virtue. If a great lord has both, he should be admired far more than those who need these qualities to attain distinction.

# Chapter 3

# Admission to Citizenship, Suffrage, etc.

On page 31 Abbé Mably condemns the Pennsylvania constitution because it gives a man the right to be a representative after a residence of two years. "This test is not long enough to gain my confidence, for a man can conceal his true nature without much difficulty for such a short period of time." I know no remedy to the misfortune of being unable to win the author's confidence, but there is otherwise nothing to fear. To begin with, it is difficult to wear a mask for two years. Such a new resident would need outstanding qualifications to be elected in preference to other candidates, and, finally, one or two votes could not endanger public safety when such large numbers are involved.

On the following page he writes: "All the states require their representatives or electors to have a certain sum of money; Pennsylvania alone accepts those who have paid taxes for a year. It seems that the legislator would pay more attention to merit than to money, and at first glance this appears highly estimable, but are there not circumstances where the highest good cannot be attained and where it is wisdom to be satisfied with a less perfect system?"

It is inaccurate to say "for a year" because Pennsylvania requires two, and how could the author fail to know this when he himself quotes the law on the preceding page? Then it is horrible to hear him talk about sacrificing merit to money. He says "at first glance this appears highly estimable." It not only appears more estimable, but it is more estimable. The paths of justice are straight. Let us follow them and learn from experience the best policy. If political expedients can lure us away, any crime can be committed with impunity.

The Pennsylvania constitution, like all the others, has some faults, but the abbé does not refer to them, for he is too busy criticizing its good points. On page 30 he censures balloting: "I think there are men of sufficient importance in their cities and counties to be humored; it would also be difficult to find any electors there who dared express their opinion freely." He then tells us that "the wisest politicians of antiquity condemned balloting." And finally he recalls that "Cicero said the Roman republic was divided by parties which it was dangerous to offend." Although the author contradicts himself at frequent intervals, he never fails to regard the Ancients as infallible, and he is not concerned by any relation of cause and effect.

The use of the ballot, which he seems to have noted only in the Pennsylvania constitution and which he apparently considers an indication of our decadence, was the work of the first immigrants and of William Penn. It exists in nearly every state, and New York, which did not have it, has passed a constitutional law so that it will be tried there.

In Virginia the General Assembly has always used a secret ballot, and the legislators now plan to introduce it for popular elections. The advantage is obvious, for many good people lack the courage to displease a relative or friends. Few men are unmoved when they hear these individuals vote for others, and there are numerous instances where private feelings have conflicted with public duty. It is wise not to put them to a test.

The abbé seems aware of only four human motives: opulence, poverty, thirst for tyranny, and fear. Although our customs are not so corrupt as those in Europe, we do not flatter ourselves that we are perfect—as he thinks the citizens of a free country should be. He apparently has little knowledge of men, for he wants what has never been and never can be. It is true that since the revolutionary period public welfare has often taken precedence over everything else, but we must realize that such self-sacrifice is rare save in critical times. Passions rule the human heart and the strongest always prevails.

Justices of the supreme courts are nominated by the legislative or executive branches, or sometimes by both, and they are among the most virtuous and enlightened of our citizens. If one of them has a personal interest in a case, he must step down from the bench.* A justice renowned for his virtue is often challenged, but no one is perturbed because it is a well-known fact that one can be partial without meaning to be so. Had the author observed this, he would have concluded that our justices are fearfully corrupt, since he regards precautionary measures as an indication of evil.

On page 44 he is raging because the Pennsylvania constitution provides a means of preventing the public from being deprived of legislative power in case certain cities or counties do not elect representatives. He seems extremely surprised at this, although the

---

* The same is true of justices of the peace.

South Carolina constitution contains the same clause. He claims it indicates "a monstrous indifference, which is a forerunner of the dissolution of the republic." This is an example of the abbé's sad prophecies, but there is so little foundation for this one that we need not fear it will materialize.

We have seen that Pennsylvania requires a year's residence to vote and two to be a representative. The author criticizes this stipulation, which, according to him, is extremely dangerous. Page 42: "You are too liberal to grant this privilege to any adventurer who has paid state taxes for a year. A crowd of young men who do not enjoy citizenship anywhere will take refuge in Pennsylvania, where they will sell themselves to different parties, and nothing good will come from these intruders."

In some districts, where voting is public, intruders could get a drink, and in a few they might be able to obtain a meal, but that is all. As no other profit could be made from selling their votes, it is hardly worthwhile. It is curious that Abbé Mably picks a state where there can be no buyers for votes, since the ballot is secret. He chose the very state he had condemned for using a secret ballot.

I omit numerous other points, for the reader, I am sure, has already noted more than one inconsistency.

# Chapter 4

# Constitutional and Common Legislative Power

Two of the reprimands addressed by Abbé Mably to the legislators who wrote the Pennsylvania constitution are especially interesting, both for their ideas and for the astonishing contradiction between them. After observing that one of the fundamental principles of this constitution is that the General Assembly cannot change it, he states, page 40: "That is a strange law. Did this assembly believe itself infallible? What power superior to or even equal to the legislative assembly did the first legislators assume to force the assembly to do what they ordered?" *

Here the author blames the Pennsylvania constitution for a wise precaution taken by other states as well. If ordinary legislative power could abrogate the constitution, the foundations of government might be changed whenever the legislative body met. Citizens are extremely careful about electing representatives to examine or correct the constitution. It is at such times, or when the safety of the republic is endangered, that they seek distinguished men who have retired from public life but who accept new tasks for such an important cause.

Even more surprising is the way the abbé censures the writers of the constitution for restricting legislative power, which, according to him, is unlimited. If this were the case, the founders could have transferred to the legislature more authority than they themselves received from the people. On page 49 he writes: "I should like to ask why the legislators assembled in Philadelphia did not prescribe any rules either for the General Assembly or the executive council. Philosophers show their disciples the road they should follow in quest of truth; should legislators not be equally careful to establish patterns leading to justice and public welfare?"

We do not know on what basis he condemns the writers of the constitution for not prescribing, since the constitution was the only document they had the right or the obligation to prepare. They

* The constitution requires that every seven years two representatives shall be chosen by each city and county to form the Council of Censors. Their chief duty is to examine the constitution and to see that necessary improvements are made. The abbé himself refers to this on p. 79.

fixed the duties of the executive power and the method of electing judges in the various departments. Yet he asks why they failed "to establish patterns leading to justice"!

We do not know whether he believed the General Assembly had to attend to any business other than legislation, whether he attributes the functions of the judiciary power to this assembly or to the executive power, or whether he thought that the first legislators, instead of laying the foundations for government, should have written *in-folio* volumes to deal with the special business of each department. Several of these departments have subordinate officers who are much more competent to handle these details than the greatest philosophers and legislators.

After observing (on the next page) that the council election is triennial, he adds: "But that does not reassure me. The magistrates of a budding republic need a longer term to provide the principles best suited for its happiness." Thus he would like to see these constant principles only in the executive department, and he implies that the foundations of the constitution should be subject to change (page 40), since he does not permit any limitation of the legislative power.

This kind of reasoning does not make him qualified to teach the inhabitants of the thirteen states how to govern themselves, and he treats the wisest citizens like schoolboys. He quotes Cicero (p. 31), Plato, and Aristotle and tells us what books to consult. But, if we failed to remember his observations, we should merely have to talk to our young people in the classroom. The philosophers whom Abbé Mably quotes are as respected in America as elsewhere, but we do not wish to be dazzled by their authority, and they made mistakes too.

We agree that men are always the same, but they act differently at different times. On page 99 he says: "The ancient republics which deserve our admiration were not governed in this way." When the new governments were being established in America, every gazette carried a description of the horrors committed in these old republics. Someone then analyzed them and found that their problems were caused by conditions that have never existed in America. Like Abbé Mably, we have always believed their example is one to be admired, but this does not necessitate following it. If it were true, which it is not, that the ancient legislators did the best they could, they would certainly not have done the same thing for us, since the situation is altogether different.

# Chapter 5

# Liberty of the Press

Abbé Mably threatens us with a multitude of evils in connection with our liberty of the press. On page 100 we read: "Rome considered the verses of the Sibyls as a sacred book, to be consulted in emergencies, but they were entrusted to magistrates and not to the populace, which would have been incapable of understanding them and interpreting them in accordance with the maxims of the republic." These mysteries, so useful to the superstitious Romans, would be considered childish by Americans.

The abbé does not like freedom of the press, which every state has established as a fundamental law. He thinks there should be distinctions, the nature of which can be appreciated by these passages. On page 98: "Grant everything to the savants who are studying the secrets of nature and who seek truth in the ruins of antiquity and the shadows of modern times." On page 100: "If the ancient republics had known the art of printing, it is unlikely that they would have permitted bold writers to publish dangerous paradoxes. These stir up trouble and rouse men incapable of thought against those entrusted with government and public welfare." And on page 102: "I should like to see every writer obliged to sign his work; if he violated the laws or the respect due to magistrates charged with the executive power, he should be subject to their displeasure."

He ought to have told us why he speaks only of the magistrates charged with executive power, as if all individuals were not entitled to respect. Moreover, we could scarcely submit the guilty to these magistrates, since no one can judge his own case.

The abbé considers the works of antiquity so luminous that they cast modern knowledge into the shadow. But when you think of the useful discoveries made by science, you realize we have emerged from the shadows and that the light is brighter every day. The author wants us to admire the great men of antiquity without attempting to equal them. Although we owe much to Euclid, today it is possible to go far beyond his discoveries. Newton would not have done so much had he not been preceded by Galileo. He pushed back boundaries as his followers have moved back and con-

tinue to move back those he established. It is possible that none of
the best clockmakers today could have invented this marvelous
mechanism; yet the most ignorant of them all would be ashamed to
produce one which was not vastly superior to the first clock made.
If we could have an ocular and geometrical demonstration of all
the sciences, no one would blindly venerate the knowledge of
antiquity.

If bold writers published forbidden material, they would be
punished. Abbé Mably did not see the laws governing these crimes
because he was not looking for them. If the author's name does not
appear, the printer is obliged to denounce him or suffer his punishment as well. Although liberty of the press does not permit publication of books capable of fomenting insurrections, it is subject to
certain restraints, like all the best laws, since nothing can be
perfect.

At the beginning of the Revolution it was said that worthless
books could be published without breaking the law. People thought
the author's fear of spoiling his own reputation would prove to be
a powerful brake, but it was finally decided, almost unanimously,
that the production of books of no value was of no significance in
comparison with the loss of some that could be useful.

The author calls himself a zealous partisan of the republican form
of government, but the principles he advocates are diametrically
opposed to it. Nothing is more important for this kind of government than freedom of the press. It is essential to extend useful
knowledge, to correct abuses, to lay bare governmental vices, to
ascertain the wishes of the people, and to prepare them for needed
reforms. In our country the legislative power has no right to attack
this freedom, as we see in the Declaration of Rights, which, up to
the present, seems to have been approved by everyone except the
abbé.

In his fear lest bold writers do harm to "customs, the majesty of
the laws, and the respect due to magistrates charged with executive
power," the abbé recommends a procedure which would discourage sensible writers. Prohibition would not only encourage
temerity but would embolden malice and ignorance. As soon as
anything is forbidden it appears good, and prohibition causes the
worst books to be sought avidly. They are regarded as a triumph
over the shackles with which men had attempted to chain the mind.
However just a criticism may be, it would be scorned if the author
failed to treat the people he was discussing respectfully. But if the
press were not free, the more injurious the criticism, the more it

would be applauded. Crude and absurd books are unusual in the United States, for good sense hastens to reject them. But if our press were not free, good writers would be afraid of being accused of selling their pens to powerful men. When the press is free, the slanderer is banished from good society. If it is fettered, people run after unjust criticisms, even libels. If a writer is punished, compassion replaces justice because of hatred for the law. If his condemnation is arbitrary, he wears a martyr's crown. Certain writers who can win fame no other way aspire to this. Shackling the press corrupts men by making trickery and ruse profitable; it opens the door to a favoritism which administrators can practice without being punished.*

These are some of the evils Abbé Mably did not foresee. A little study would have made him realize the difficulty of finding men capable of resisting the numerous temptations involved. What he fears could be harmful is the only thing that would be useful. With freedom of the press, those who govern are defended against calumny; without it they are exposed to slander.

* When government is in the hands of a single individual, administrators are restrained by a fear that would be impossible in a republic. The prince can punish their lies as he wishes. But in a free state where it is necessary to prove a crime any power that could be so easily undermined would have disastrous consequences.

# Chapter 6

# The Rights of the Citizen in the Republic

On page 37 the author quotes the following passage from the Pennsylvania constitution: "the people have a right to assemble together, to consult for their common good, to instruct their representatives, and to apply to the legislature for redress of grievances by address, petition or remonstrance."[1] The author, who believes that the voice of the people, like the press, should be shackled, adds: "I confess that it is difficult for me to understand this law. It is just and reasonable for the people to consult about their interests and to give instructions to their representatives when they meet to appoint them. But I question the wisdom of letting citizens assemble whenever they wish, without being subject to any law or under the eyes of a magistrate. If that is the meaning of the law, it is anarchical, and I can see that the legislative assembly will be exposed to the whims of a tumultuous assembly carried away by the eloquence of some bungler or malcontent."

This law is expressed in the same terms in the Massachusetts constitution, which, to a considerable extent, was the work of the gentleman to whom the abbé addresses his remarks.[2] The people have this sacred and inalienable right everywhere. If the assembly were tumultuous, the guilty would be punished in accordance with laws existing in every state, although the author imagines there are none. But I hope that America will never produce an individual so opposed to liberty or so ignorant of its basic principles that he believes a man does not have the right to consult his fellow citizens whenever he wishes on any subject he considers useful or harmful to the common weal. The best road to tyranny would be to shackle freedom of the press or freedom of speech, especially when it involves informing the people about the conduct of their representatives in the legislature. On page 40 the abbé says: "It seems to me that it is a universally accepted axiom that legislative power should not be limited in any way, unless you want to destroy it." If that is an axiom, you will never find an absurdity.

[1] *The Constitution of the Commonwealth of Pennsylvania* (Philadelphia, 1776).
[2] John Adams.

Where would liberty be if the legislative body had unlimited power and the people could not assemble without the consent of a magistrate? Could an all-powerful body not inspire the magistrates with fear and prevent them from authorizing assemblies? But he believes the legislative assembly will be exposed to the eloquence "of some bungler or malcontent." On page 139 he asserts: "A skillful orator is all that is needed to pit citizens against one another and to produce anarchy, which leads only too often to despotism."

Let us see what a skillful, sly, and eloquent American Gracchus could do. The people's vote in a state consists of the votes of the plurality of the electors in the plurality of the districts. Let us suppose that a malcontent rouses the inhabitants of his district against the legislative power and makes them write a remonstrance devoid of the respect due an assembly representing the government. The legislature will table the remonstrance, which means there is to be no further discussion, or have it thrown under the table to indicate contempt; or it will put a resolution in the papers saying the district has acted unwisely; if laws have been broken, it will pursue the guilty and force them to explain their behavior.* In the first instance, the matter is settled. In the second and third, it is probable that the wisest and most prudent inhabitants of the district would protest against the remonstrance, if they had not already done so, to uphold the honor of the district. The imprudent would probably see that they were wrong, and our Gracchus would be isolated. In the fourth instance, let us suppose that the men resisted, but what could they do against the militias of all the other districts?

Unless a Gracchus had lost his mind, he would realize that here, where all the inhabitants are interested in maintaining order, where a private insurrection would be quelled before it even got started and a general one would require several months to organize, his enterprise would be so dangerous and difficult that he would have to be eager to seek an ignominious death.

A general uprising would require a Gracchus in each district, or at least in the majority of the districts, and they would have to speak calmly and reasonably or no one would listen. If they succeeded in making most of the citizens believe the legislative power was endangering public safety and passing laws opposed to liberty, no one would take arms. Would it not be ridiculous for the greater part of the citizens in a state to arm against their deputies, that is,

---

* This does not mean that the legislative body has the right to serve as a tribunal. See Note E.

against 150 or 200 men? After counting the votes, to be sure of a plurality, these men would be dismissed from public service and new representatives would be chosen for a convention, at which everything would be set in order. In this instance the public would be grateful to the Gracchi, but if it appeared that the alarm had been sounded needlessly, the troublemakers would lose public favor and the representatives would be regarded even more highly. If we do not make the legislature all powerful, the abbé predicts that we shall suffer from the disorders which plagued the ancient republics; to assure liberty he advises us to relinquish its basic principles.

If the author were better informed about the gentle, calm nature of the American people, he would have urged them to keep an eye on the conduct of their representatives, since overconfidence tends to cool their zeal while vigilance revives it.

The enthusiasm of our author often caused him to fear events which should have reassured him. After telling us that he has a map of our possessions and that he cannot think without fright of the vast extent of Pennsylvania,* he continues, on page 36: "All you need is a bold and enterprising man to stir up a revolution there. But, without speaking of these adventurers, some rich merchant may take advantage of the jealousies and hatreds always present in a democracy to fan the flame of civil discord and establish his tyranny."

Here as in so many other places, the author seems persuaded that any kind of cause can produce any sort of effect. Can this fear, which might be justified in a small state, have any foundation in one so large that he is alarmed by its very size? Democracy, which tends toward equality, becomes, according to the abbé, one of the causes of financial inequality. As to the tyranny of "some rich merchant," whenever the country is large and sovereignty is in the hands of the whole population, you will find few men timid enough to seek protection from a wealthy individual, who would probably not be known by a fortieth of the inhabitants.

The author adds: "People will perhaps tell me that I invent chimeras to have the pleasure of combatting them." He should have omitted the "perhaps." Here is one more proof: "I beg you, sir, to reread the history of Florence, and you will be afraid lest some Medici arise in Pennsylvania, who will go from his bank or counter to the throne." The Florentines, at the time of the repub-

---

* It is 136 miles from south to north (2 degrees 16 minutes in latitude); from east to west it is 5 degrees in longitude.

lic, had the world's most lucrative commerce. Little attention was paid to agriculture because the profits from manufacturing and trade were so immense. Wool was made nowhere else, Florence was the best market for precious stones, and the only bankers in Paris and London were Florentines. It is therefore not astonishing that one family succeeded in accumulating enormous wealth, far more than any other family has ever possessed.

But today commerce is so extensive that it would be foolish to try to acquire even a tenth of the Medici fortune. In this country, moreover, the extent and fertility of the soil turn men against commerce, which is attractive when land is scarce and sterile.

In principle the Florentine government was aristocratic, even after commoners had snatched it from the hands of the nobility. The whole organization seemed designed to produce bickering. A huge bell, far larger than necessary, rang to summon the rulers of the city, who lived within the radius of a mile and could have gathered in a drawing room. The size and government of Pennsylvania are so well known that the reader will see how ill advised is this comparison with the republic of Florence.

# Chapter 7

# The Aristocratic Principles of Abbé Mably

Although it is apparent that the author's principles are aristocratic, hence opposed to the rights of the people, at times he presents a different point of view.

On page 34 he says: "One of the most dangerous stumbling blocks in politics is the attempt to unite establishments which are good in themselves but cannot be associated. Pennsylvania law favors democracy, but this very partiality frightens the rich, who will never consent to have no prerogatives other than those enjoyed by the poor." I leave it to the reader to determine those "establishments which are good in themselves but cannot be associated." It seems to me the abbé is showing a great predilection for the aristocracy when he uses the term "partiality" for what tends toward equality. Later he writes: "I believe America is being driven toward aristocracy by a superior force which will destroy the laws that would like to oppose it." This sort of prophecy has no foundation whatsoever.

On page 48 he thinks representatives should be obliged to select the executive council from their own number. He adds: "The body acting as trustee for the laws would thus be composed of outstanding men, and this would temper, to a certain degree at least, the inconsiderate and intriguing nature of the democracy." We have already noted that he thinks a small number of the elect can absorb the science and virtue of all the inhabitants. It is not surprising that he makes the executive council depository of the laws, since he has so frequently demonstrated he considered it unnecessary to get information before writing his book; but he goes a little too far when he attributes the intriguing nature of the aristocracy to the democracy.

On page 62: "I see with pleasure, sir, that the Massachusetts government keeps at a safe distance those men who have no wealth other than their hands and who would cause dissension in the administration if they had any authority." The same partiality with regard to these "men who have no wealth other than their hands" is only too evident in almost all the other states. It is not surprising that he is pleased, as he likes the rich and has supreme scorn for the poor. No barbarous law keeps them out of office; poverty alone is quite sufficient, unless circumstances are very favorable and they are extremely gifted.

On pages 137 and 138 he declares there will certainly be an aristocracy. "But in the second or at least the third generation how will children born in wealthy homes feel about equality? They will fail to understand these inalienable rights you have given the people."

It is worth noting that the author attributes a right common to all men to the generous imprudence of a small group of individuals. He also derides the most sacred principle of liberty and criticizes us for respecting it. Yet on pages 7 and 15 he applauded us, saying: "I see with pleasure, sir, that all your constitutions respect the people's rights. You have made it a fixed axiom that all political authority is derived from the people. . . . You recognize the dignity of men and have bound all citizens together by a love of country and of liberty. May these ideas influence all your deliberations and daily consolidate the foundation of your federative republic!" The abbé could not state anything more contrary to the principles professed throughout his whole work.

The flattering observations and undeserved praise at the beginning of his book apparently are intended to prepare us to receive good-naturedly what he says later. I beg the reader to compare the passage I have just quoted with his remarks on page 137: "Since wealth has always been the source of nobility, should it not separate American families into different classes? Why should wealth, which marks the greatest difference between men, permit the poor to enjoy the same advantages as the rich? As I can foresee revolutionary clouds gathering, I prefer the legislation in Massachusetts, which sets more definite limits to democracy and prepares the way for the inevitable transformation of the republic into an aristocracy. It does so without exposing the state to the convulsive movements which will probably hurl Pennsylvania under the yoke of an oligarchy or a tyrant."

Without discussing the imaginary sources of all these prophecies, I may say that the Massachusetts constitution does not prepare for an inevitable transition to an aristocracy. We have seen that although every citizen does not possess the right to vote and to be a representative, the path is open, and not a single state has an aristocratic class. In South Carolina there are actually more barriers than in Massachusetts. In Maryland and New Jersey the right to vote is a little more liberal, but it is harder to be a representative. In New York, where the right to vote carries the privilege of being a representative, as in Virginia and several other states, requirements for election to the Senate are more restricted than in Massachusetts. If our governments were so corrupt that a revolution seemed imminent, as the abbé says, it would seem that the reverse of his prediction might occur, in other words that Massachusetts would fall "under the yoke of an oligarchy or a tyrant," and that Pennsylvania would have an aristocratic government. In Massachusetts the constitution puts too much emphasis on the position of governor, and in Pennsylvania the balance of power inclines too far toward legislative power in a single chamber. The intentions of the founders were completely honorable, and whatever faults remain are due to old prejudices, several of which were supported by famous writers.

I have already mentioned the spirit of equality in Massachusetts, and everyone knows that its citizens were zealous for the glorious cause of liberty. While our enemies were in Boston, the Massachusetts deputies stated that if Congress approved, they would burn the city to ashes.

The passages we shall now quote deserve special attention as they contradict the preceding.

Page 23: "People should have blocked the aristocracy and passed laws to prevent the rich from buying an authority which should not belong to them." * "Instead of aspiring to a pure democracy, would it not be better to provide only those laws necessary to prevent the aristocracy from giving vent to its natural ambition?" On page 145 he advises us to "shackle the ambition of the wealthy, who think that everything belongs to them." On page 89: "But when a different order of classes is established, as will happen only too soon . . ."

These last passages, especially the expression "only too soon," seem to indicate that he is not very enthusiastic about the distinction he tells us to establish. Some may say he considered aristocracy an unavoidable evil and that he was trying to tell us how to cope with it. Elsewhere he speaks of an aristocratic government as the best. On page 51 we see: "If you analyze, sir, the histories of Lacedaemon and Rome, you will find that the virtues of these republics, their wisdom, and everything we admire can be traced to the establishment of the self-perpetuating senate which was their soul."

---

*All states have similar laws, but the abbé has the idea that every law is or should be in the state constitutions.

Far from accepting the common maxim that it is better to serve one master than several, he uses the expression "to be hurled under the yoke of a single master" in tracing a parallel between the monarchical and aristocratic forms of government. But even the most favorable interpretation of these contradictions reveals that the abbé is not teaching us anything. Common sense shows that a number of men with some authority can usurp the rest much more easily than if they did not have any. Fortunately my fellow citizens are convinced that the serpent's egg must be destroyed before it is hatched.

# Chapter 8

# Administration and Education

It is claimed that these observations were intended for Europeans, but on page 168 he apologizes: "Excuse me, sir, for spending so much time on this subject, but all Americans do not have your intelligence and I am writing for them." So he is writing for us, that is to give us lessons, and he is kind enough to tell us frequently that we need them. We must not forget what he calls the necessity of increasing the size of the executive department. He declares that the number of advisers fixed by the constitutions is not sufficient to handle all the administrative business, which he doubtless believes he understands better than we do.

The legislative body meets for only a few months during the year, but during this time the representatives are extremely busy. Judges of two of the supreme courts, common law and chancery, have a great deal of work when the courts are closed, and a thousand tasks when the courts are in session. In the executive department work is continuous, but there is so little to be done that the governor could attend to it without devoting more than three or four hours to the task several times a week. He has advisers, so that the authority is divided. In Virginia, the largest and most densely populated of the thirteen states, the governor can do almost nothing without his council, a group of eight men with very little work to perform. Pennsylvania has twelve advisers and the abbé does not consider it enough. On page 48 he writes: "It is very difficult for these twelve to handle all the business of administration." On page 64 he adds: "After what I said about the Pennsylvania council, you will not be surprised, sir, if I take the liberty of condemning the one in Massachusetts, which is even smaller and renewed each year." *

He must attribute functions of which we know nothing to these councillors. According to the figures given to Congress, Pennsylvania had 320,000 inhabitants on 18 April 1783. On this scale the French king would require more than eight hundred advisers to

---

* There are nine councillors in Massachusetts; they are elected for a year but may continue to serve indefinitely.

handle his administrative affairs, for if twelve are not enough for 320,000 Americans, the number would be even less adequate for 320,000 Frenchmen, as they would have to handle the legislative and at times the judiciary branches as well.

On page 52 he notes he "is very pleased that the New York constitution provides for a council of twenty-four members"; this is incorrect, for these twenty-four men are senators, who form one of the branches of the legislative power and are not members of the executive.

As the abbé does not distinguish between the executive and judiciary power and refers to the former as the depository of laws, he may think our councillors are judges—and that is why he considers the number twelve inadequate. We could tell him that this number would be considered too large in any tribunal except the court of appeal. Experience shows us that men become audacious in a large group. Those who are protecting the people's rights should be numerous and armed with courage; administrators of justice should fear public censure.

It is hard to believe the author could flatter himself he knew our business better than we do. It is equally incredible that his zeal led him to treat us so severely and with so much injustice. On page 74 he says: "The three republics which I have the honor to describe (Massachusetts, Georgia, and Pennsylvania) are the only ones which have felt the value of a good education, or at least which mentioned it." This is false, because every state speaks of it. He continues: "The Massachusetts legislators wish not only to enlarge our knowledge; they want to engrave in the hearts of children the principles of 'Humanity and general benevolence, public and private charity, industry and frugality, honesty and punctuality in their dealings, sincerity, good humour and all social affections and generous sentiments.' " [3] He adds: "I shall consider this nothing but a vague assertion unless the republic puts its fine theory into practice by establishing schools in the very near future."

The writers of the constitutions only laid the foundation stones, and they were not supposed to do anything more. Fundamental principles should be clear, definite, and as brief as possible. If the author had examined our codes, he would have realized that the objective of our education is not "vague assertion," and if he had read the constitutions and the Declaration of Rights attentively, he

---

[3] *A Constitution . . . of Massachusetts-Bay . . .* (Boston, 1780), chap. 5, sec. 2.

would have found that every republic had imposed this obligation on the legislative powers.

As I am not very well informed about other states, I shall merely say that Virginia has a college supported by the public and other educational institutions to which the state contributes. At the close of the Revolution we proposed to establish as soon as possible other colleges and public schools located so that everyone could send his children to school daily. The law governing these establishments was prepared by the citizens entrusted with a revision of the code of the General Assembly, and we believe it will soon go into effect.

The preamble of this law reads:

Whereas it appeareth that however certain forms of government are better calculated than others to protect individuals in the free exercise of their natural rights, and are at the same time themselves better guarded against degeneracy, yet experience hath shewn, that even under the best forms, those entrusted with power have, in time, and by slow operations, perverted it into tyranny; and it is believed that the most effectual means of preventing this would be, to illuminate, as far as practicable, the minds of the people at large, and more especially to give them knowledge of those facts, which history exhibiteth, that, possessed thereby of the experience of other ages and countries, they may be enabled to know ambition under all its shapes, and prompt to exert their natural powers to defeat its purposes; and whereas it is generally true that that people will be happiest whose laws are best, and are best administered, and that laws will be wisely formed, and honestly administered, in proportion as those who form and administer them are wise and honest; whence it becomes expedient for promoting the publick happiness that those persons, whom nature hath endowed with genius and virtue, should be rendered by liberal education worthy to receive, and able to guard the sacred deposit of the rights and liberties of their fellow citizens . . . ; but the indigence of the greater number disabling them from so educating, at their own expence, those of their children whom nature hath fitly formed and disposed to become useful instruments for the public, it is better that such should be sought for and educated at the common expence of all, than that the happiness of all should be confided to the weak or wicked.[4]

For the sake of brevity we are omitting the law which traces all the means of reaching this goal.

[4] Jefferson, *Papers of Jefferson*, ed. Boyd, 2:526.

# Chapter 9

# Salaries, Entails, etc.

On page 76 the author complains because the Massachusetts constitution orders that the governor should receive an honorable salary to "maintain the dignity of the commonwealth." He says: "As posts become more important, I should like to see salaries decline; I should even like the incumbents to serve without salary."

In no state are financial rewards large enough to arouse greed. They are sufficient to support men without private fortunes, but the author, who has vowed not to approve any good thing we have done, does not reflect that his method would foster an oligarchy. He claims we have "opened the door to avarice," and concludes on page 77: "Let the Republic of Massachusetts have the courage to destroy the law I am complaining about." This emphatic tone would seem more appropriate if he were dealing with an exorbitant sum rather than the suppression of the salary attached to a position. I hope that my compatriots will not be misled by a false spirit of economy into preventing men of merit but modest means from seeking public office. This would be the end of liberty.

On page 113 Mably asks: "Why do other states not follow Georgia in forbidding entails?" In the Pennsylvania and North Carolina constitutions, which the author tells us he has read, entails are also proscribed. As several states never had entails, it seemed unnecessary to mention them. In Virginia they were forbidden by the General Assembly after the formation of the present government, and I am informed that the same thing occurred in all the other states. Instead of asking an idle question, the abbé could have given us a bit of good advice by suggesting they be proscribed by constitutional law so that the legislative body, which he would like to make all powerful, cannot establish them.

In all states I think there is unjust partiality in favor of the eldest son when parents die intestate. In New England and Pennsylvania, for example, the eldest receives twice as much as any of his brothers; in Virginia and several others he inherits all the real property. The revised code to which we referred establishes equal rights without distinction of primogeniture or of sex. We must hope the General Assembly in Virginia will not hesitate to adopt such a just law * and that a wise philosophy will dissipate the shadows of error in every state.

If the abbé read our constitutions as attentively as he claims, he forgot them when he began to make his analysis. We said, in describing the governments, that the Georgia constitution submits the deliberations of the legislative power for revision by the members of the executive power, but not by the governor. Article 22 says: "The Governor may preside in the Executive Council at all times, except when they are taking into consideration, and perusing the laws and ordinances, offered to them by the House of Assembly." [5] In speaking of the same constitution, the abbé writes on page 70: "The laws passed by the House of Representatives will be submitted to the examination of the governor and his council, who are responsible for the executive power. Their remonstrances will be carried to the legislative body by a committee which will explain the clauses demanded by the governor and the reasons that make them necessary." Yet on page 73 the author declares that the Georgia constitution is one of the three he "studied with particular care."

On page 109, in discussing a paradox he ascribes to a Massachusetts law, he writes: "May I say, sir, that one finds in this American constitution several laws one cannot help but approve and condemn simultaneously." After this precise declaration, he continues: "The Republic of Massachusetts orders that as, 'in time of peace, armies are dangerous to liberty, they ought not to be maintained without the consent of the civil authority.' It adds: 'Military power must always be subordinate to the civil authority.' This law sees the danger but does nothing to prevent it. Why does it refer only to peacetime? Are armies more inclined to submit to civil authority during war? People who know will have trouble accepting this paradox." It will probably be still more difficult to persuade them that the word "always" means only in peacetime. In all the constitutions it is stated that standing armies are not to be kept in peacetime, since they are a menace to liberty, and that the military power should "always" be subordinate to the civil power.

* It seems incredible that this reform encountered any opposition among those appointed by the General Assembly to revise the code. The single dissenter thought the eldest should have at least twice as much as the others, and he regarded this as a natural right. He was told that this distinction would be admissible when nature made the eldest twice as large as the other children, when he ate twice the amount consumed by the others, and when he was so constituted as to double them in all the natural functions.

[5] *The Constitution of the State of Georgia* (Savannah, 1777).

# Chapter 10

# Justices of the Supreme Courts

The writer who condemns us for not having made positions in the executive branch and terms of members of Congress more permanent, and who believes that a "perpetual senate" should be established to preserve "the virtues, politics, constancy and character" of the free states, devotes three pages to a demonstration of how wrong we are to keep justices of the supreme courts in office as long as they behave well. He must be eager to criticize everything, for as their functions do not concern national matters, how can they menace liberty? * It is advisable to read the entire text (p. 105) in order to judge the cogency of his reasoning: "Before concluding this long letter, permit me, sir, to examine several articles in the American constitutions which do not seem to foresee the abuses with which you are threatened. For example, do you approve the law ordering that justices of the supreme court shall retain their offices as long as they behave well? At first glance, this seems like a wise regulation, but I have some scruples."

Before examining the writer's objections, it is pertinent to see why it was decided that no justice of the supreme court of judicature can be dismissed as long as his conduct is exemplary. It is obvious that they must be chosen from among those lawyers outstanding for both knowledge and character. If these men are in business, they must abandon their profession to be justices. A dismissal after several years would require them to rebuild their practice, and no successful man would agree to serve under such conditions.

"I am afraid that men who aspire to these benches will set traps

* In at least three states, Massachusetts, New Hampshire, and Maryland, they can be removed by the governor of the republic on the demand of the two houses which form the legislative body. In Maryland a two-thirds vote is required. It is unlikely that such a removal from office would be demanded without good reasons. The New York constitution forces judges to retire at the age of 60. While it is true that the mind and body usually begin to weaken at this age, I think it unwise to leave the continuance of appointments to the discretion of the legislative power.

for those whose positions they covet and make enemies for them."
The author's zeal is extraordinary. He is concerned not only about
the problems of all the ancient and modern republics but about
those facing absolute monarchies as well. Since the law states that
no judge can lose his post as long as he behaves properly (and this
is what the abbé condemns), he faces dismissal only if he is accused
and convicted of a crime. Everyone knows how cases are tried in
America, and even the abbé praised the Declaration of Rights for
guaranteeing the accused every opportunity to defend himself. I do
not believe the writer realized that a case of this kind would attract
a huge audience and occupy the leaders of the state. Nor do I believe he recalled reading in the constitution that justices of the
supreme courts are elected by the legislative body, by the executive, or by them both. In this case, even if the judge were voted
guilty, it would be the task of those who appointed him to decide
if he should be removed from office. But it seems to me the abbé
could tell us why an intriguer should have a better chance in a case
against a judge than in many others. A judge's salary is not large
enough to tempt a lawyer to intrigue at the risk of losing his reputation.

"If this magistrate under attack relies on his probity and loses, his
successors will soon believe that virtue is powerless, and one intrigue will follow another." But how will the victorious intriguer
get himself elected by men so respectable that the author doubts
their ability to retain their posts for a considerable period or to
have much authority? The writer should have told us.

"People will try by insidious means to obtain friends and powerful protectors; justice will no longer prevail, and there is nothing
worse for public morality than the corruption of magistrates. It
will then be easy to evade laws by pretending to improve them."
The flattery of judges seeking powerful protectors could produce
nothing save sentences unfair to the weak. After he spends so much
time praising our jury system, as if we had invented it, it is strange
to suppose that judges could engage in corrupt practices so easily.
It would be a waste of time to discuss the remarkable conjectures
the author draws from this supposition.

"My fear, or rather my zeal, may exaggerate the dangers. Let us
assume that the spirit of intrigue, so common in Europe, is unknown in America. What will happen? At first the chief justices
will be most attentive to their duties. No one will be dismissed, and
as they hold office for life, people will become accustomed to think

that the position is permanent. The successors of these admirable men will be flattered by this idea, which appeals to their vanity, and will readily accept it."

I have already had the occasion to observe that the abbé always goes to extremes. We do not flatter ourselves that we are, or ever shall be, free from the faults that are too common among men. Our ancestors naturally brought some vices from Europe, and our continuing relationship with Great Britain fostered them. Our only consolation on this point is the quantitative difference. As governments influence education, we may hope that these vices will not attack us so promptly or in such numbers as they have attacked other nations, especially if we continue to improve our governments. At the present time not a single one of them has ministers sufficiently powerful to sacrifice innocence to intrigue.

But the most astonishing thing in the last passage is the supposition that little by little the successors of these admirable men will become accustomed to thinking that their offices are for life, an idea, the author adds, "which appeals to their vanity," although his whole criticism tends to condemn the law which makes lifetime appointments and to predict its dire consequences.

I assume the abbé knew you cannot deprive judges of their posts without a trial during which it is decided they are unworthy to keep them. But if he imagined judges could lose their positions through the caprice of some individual, which would be possible in an absolute monarchy or under a despot, it would be one more proof that the author wrote without knowing the facts and confused the principles essential to liberty with those of despotism.

Mably continues: "Then the evil begins, and these magistrates are less attentive. Slight mistakes will at first be condoned because removal from office would appear too severe a punishment." Justice demands "would be," not "would appear." All men are capable of making mistakes, and they may do so involuntarily. It would be hard to be deprived of one's job for a small error. Moreover, harsh punishments make men worse, and the penalty should be suited to the crime. Although these axioms are incontestable, the author has his own opinion; so he makes several doleful predictions which we shall not bother to repeat.

# Chapter 11

# The Written Law and the Equity Tribunal

After criticizing the justices, without being so kind as to suggest any better system, the abbé threatens us with serious trouble if we let the chancery court, that is, the equity court, continue. He concludes: "It is important to the citizens' safety and tranquillity that no court of justice have jurisprudence which can easily degenerate into tyranny."

This obvious truth, which he could have saved himself the trouble of stating, has nothing to do with the matter. In almost every state, as in England, the legal system is divided into two departments, common law and chancery, or equity. Far from worrying lest the court of equity "degenerate into tyranny," we know by experience that this court prevents tyranny. The court of common law, on the other hand, cannot avoid being tyrannical in certain instances, as it has to follow the literal meaning. The author is mistaken in thinking that this court is not bound by any rule. But, as the subject is interesting, the reader will perhaps not be sorry if we go back to show the distinction between the two courts. This involves a bit of English history.

The tribunal of common law includes all written law, the code dating from the period of the heptarchy as well as parliamentary law, or the statutes. Before the existence of the chancery or equity court, judges in lower courts took the liberty of applying all laws to cases where the principle was understood. That was called the law of equity, but because people had long since begun to revere fixed law, judges were obliged to limit themselves to cases where the intention of the legislators was clear. The intention is expressed in legal terms, and it is only when these terms are ambiguous that you can have recourse to precedents provided by the history of the period when the law was passed and the circumstances responsible for it.

In early days, when contracts and deeds of sale were still unusual, the imperfections of a legal administration obeying the letter of the law were not so apparent; but as commerce developed, the injustices perpetrated or upheld by courts obeying the letter of the law reached a point where something had to be done. Historically it seems that appeals were first taken to the kings, who judged them themselves or, more frequently, turned the adjudications over to the chancellor. This person was almost always a priest, since the little knowledge which enlightened these centuries was in the hands of the clergy.*

As priests always favored Roman jurisprudence, the forms of procedure in the chancery were similar to Roman law. The distinction between the *jus praetorium* and general law is widely known. Among the Romans, and in most modern countries, both were and still are exercised by the same person, but as English chancellors found the lower courts administering general law, they gradually seized the magistrate's law and made the chancery a court of conscience or equity. The story of the arguments between the courts of common law and the chancery court does not belong here. I shall merely say that the chancellor's interventions became more frequent and were tolerated rather than authorized by law. Lord Bacon [6] was the first to introduce regularity into their proceedings, and during the reign of Charles II, Finch (earl of Nottingham) [7] developed this system, which has not changed substantially.

This court has the power to judge in the following instances: (1) where there is no remedy in common law; (2) where the remedy is imperfect; (3) where it would be unjust to take in the literal sense of the law what is contrary to the spirit and intent of the legislator.

The chancery encountered serious obstacles, especially in the national veneration for fixed law, the only one which runs no risk of favoritism. The chancery was forced to erect a barrier against itself, and it cannot cross this without causing the general court of judicature to take note of its transgressions and to nullify its decisions. The general court in England is the House of Lords; in Virginia it is the Court of Appeals.

These limitations are: (1) it must not deal with any case where justice can be obtained by common law; (2) it cannot render justice in any case against the literal sense when the latter is clear or against the intent of the legislator; accordingly, if the legislator passes an unjust law, the chancery has no power to remedy it; (3) it must not hear any case which is not included in some general

* See Note F.
[6] Francis Bacon, English philosopher.
[7] Daniel Finch, second earl of Nottingham.

definition and whose remedy cannot be found by means of some general rule.

This third restriction is to prevent partiality. It was considered a lesser evil to allow a rather extraordinary case to remain without a remedy than to give the court of chancery authority to render biased decisions and to excuse them on the pretext of the unusual circumstances that human subtlety can always invent. Thus all cases within the competence of the chancery are specific, and this tribunal has no opportunity to enact laws according to whim. If a case for which there was no remedy should occur with sufficient frequency so that the court of equity could submit it to a general definition and show the necessity for a regular remedy, a new category is established and it is subject to the chancery court, whose responsibilities follow step by step the progress of commerce and the refinement of morals.

It seems to me that one more operation would enhance the usefulness of this court. When a category has been established, when the frequent decisions of this court have showed it in every combination, and the rules to judge it have been carefully examined, if the legislators reported it in a document which they deposited in the department of common law, then the chancery would be a nursery where new plants could be raised for the common law.

More than once it has been predicted in England that the chancery would swallow up the court of common law, but the latter does not seem to have suffered during the past several centuries; rather it has gained through new laws. Jealousy and fear, carried away by a lack of reason and experience, see certitude where only possibility exists. It is also true that some people consider the court's power more dangerous than useful. I have heard that in one or two states people abolished, or wished to abolish, this tribunal. If this should happen, either the cases now handled by the court of chancery would remain unsettled and cries for justice would force its reestablishment, or the court of common law would be forced to take over the judge's law hitherto exercised by the court of equity. To achieve this end the court of common law would have to adopt all the rules of the court of chancery with the consent of the legislative power. If the legislators refused, it would be obliged to extend the law to equity in many cases. This would be a case of Scylla and Charybdis, for at present about nine-tenths of the cases are referred to the court of common law, and as the judges of this court must follow the literal meaning, most cases rest on a solid basis; but if the judges were required to decide some cases on the

basis of equity, the whole system would become a mass of incerti-
tudes, as it is in every country where the two departments are
combined.

It is probable that the administration of justice in England can be
traced to the separation of these two departments. Unfortunately a
very dangerous change was recently introduced. Lord Mansfield,[8]
chief justice on the King's Bench, a man remarkable for the breadth
of his knowledge and eloquence, comes from a country * where the
two courts are united. He has persuaded his colleagues that they
should interpret common law according to the principles of equity.
This makes the law less definite on the pretext of interpreting it in a
more reasonable way. It is possible that since he has extraordinary
talents, justice has gained more than it lost; but the advantage is
temporary, and permanent harm may be done if the old system is
not restored. His decisions will be valuable in states which do not
have a court of chancery, but all English decisions dating from the
time he assumed office should be proscribed in those where the two
departments are distinct.

Lord Mansfield's plan to render the chancery useless by administering justice by its rules in the courts of common law was upheld
by his famous contemporary and colleague, Dr. Blackstone,[9] who
undertook to prove that the jurisprudence of the chancery was too
chaotic to systematize and that it could not be defined or explained.
If this were true, it would be a monster which should not be tolerated in a free country, where any power is dangerous if it is not
restricted by definite laws. The legislative assembly in Virginia
took all possible precautions by introducing jurors to decide factual
questions without renouncing the advantages inherent in this court.

It would be impossible for me to say anything on the other side,
as I am convinced that the two-department system is preferable.
The abbé merely says: "I like to have judges follow the letter of the
law. If it seems obscure or unjust, let them consult the legislative
power."

The equity court does not prevent anyone from referring to this
body as a means of preventing future problems. But the writer errs

* Scotland

[8] William Murray, first earl of Mansfield.

[9] Sir William Blackstone's *Commentaries on the Laws of England* (1765–69) has
been called "the most ambitious and most successful effort ever made to reduce
the disorderly overgrowth of English law to an intelligible and learnable system"
(David Hawke, *The Colonial Experience* [Indianapolis: Bobbs-Merrill, 1966], pp.
445–46).

in thinking it can be invoked when cases are pending, for friends of liberty and justice will never permit the legislative power to take control of the judiciary.[10]

[10] At Mazzei's request, Jefferson wrote an essay on the origin and object of the American court of chancery. He authorized Mazzei to "extract such of these details as will fulfill your object," and Mazzei incorporated the greater part of the essay in his book. See Jefferson, *Papers of Jefferson*, ed. Boyd, 9:67–72.

# Chapter 12

# Religious Liberty

After predicting all the evils imaginable (and many are so contradictory that they would destroy one another), the abbé consoles us to a certain degree by saying on page 150: "My friends tease me at times by calling me a prophet of misfortune."

But before we rejoice, let us examine what he says several pages earlier about freedom of conscience. The reader must not expect it to have better treatment than civil liberty. On page 82: "Your fathers laid the foundations of your colonies at a time when England, like the rest of Europe, was torn by religious wars. They fled from a country where fanaticism was rife, and they felt that freedom to worship was the greatest happiness one could desire. This became the cardinal principle of their doctrine, which they inculcated in their children. Although it seems from your constitutions that this liberty is still the basis of your republics, circumstances have changed. Since you no longer obey the English, you are obliged to govern yourselves, and it is possible that in granting these same rights to all the different sects, you should have restrained your extreme tolerance to prevent abuses."

Here we should make three observations: (1) the injustice of depriving a number of citizens of the sacred right of freedom of conscience; (2) the monstrous temerity of even considering such an act at the very time when everyone was risking his life and property in the glorious cause of liberty; (3) the falsity of his statement, since freedom of conscience was much more restricted before the Revolution in America than in England. Pennsylvania, New York, and Rhode Island were the only colonies where freedom of worship was permitted. Penn's indulgence was limited to Christians, and no Catholics were tolerated in New York or Rhode Island. About a hundred and fifty French families from Nova Scotia wanted to settle in Virginia, but the religious obstacles they encountered made them decide to go to Pennsylvania instead. The New England colonies were remarkable for their intolerance. Abbé Raynal discusses this at length, while adding some facts that are pure fiction. These ancestors of ours, the very ones whom Mably esteems for their liberty of conscience, may well be reproached for introducing a spirit of vengeance into their new country. This plague was an inheritance from the intolerance that had harassed them in England.

In order to understand the influence of the Revolution on religious and civil liberty in America, we must consider both periods. To explain the situation before 1776 I shall quote what a friend and fellow citizen,* author of the Declaration of Independence and several other important documents, said in a book entitled *Notes on the State of Virginia*. This was printed in 1782 but has not yet been published.

The first settlers in this country were emigrants from England, of the English church, just at a point of time when it was flushed with complete victory over the religious of all other persuasions. Possessed, as they became, of the powers of making, administering, and executing the laws, they shewed equal intolerance in this country with their Presbyterian brethren, who had emigrated to the northern government. The poor Quakers were flying from persecution in England. They cast their eyes on these new countries as asylums of civil and religious freedom; but they found them free only for the reigning sect. Several acts of the Virginia assembly of 1659, 1662, and 1693, had made it penal in parents to refuse to have their children baptized; had prohibited the unlawful assembling of Quakers; had made it penal for any master of a vessel to bring a Quaker into the state; had ordered those already here, and such as should come thereafter, to be imprisoned till they should abjure the country; provided a milder punishment for their first and second return, but death for their third; had inhibited all persons from suffering their meetings in or near their houses, entertaining them individually, or disposing of books which supported their tenets. If no capital execution took place here, as did in New-England, it was not owing to the moderation of the church, or spirit of the legislature, as may be inferred from the law itself; but to historical circumstances which have not been handed down to us. The Anglicans retained full possession of the country about a century. Other opinions began then to creep in, and the great care of the government to support their own church, having begotten an equal degree of indolence in its clergy, two-thirds of the people had become dissenters at the commencement of the present revolution. The laws, indeed, were still oppressive on them, but the spirit of the one party had subsided into moderation, and of the other had risen to a degree of determination which commanded respect.[11]

* Mr. Jefferson, who is now minister plenipotentiary of the United States at the court of France.

[11] *Notes on the State of Virginia*, ed. William Peden (Chapel Hill: University of North Carolina Press for the Institute of Early American History and Culture,

As soon as they had resolved to change their government, the first step was the examination, determination, and declaration of the natural rights of man, rights which imply liberty of worship. Although tolerance is always preferable to persecution, they felt it was out of the question in a free country, since it indicates an arrogant pride. To give any religion the right to tolerate others, you have to prove that it is the only one valid. The most enlightened European nations do not agree on this point, for the same religions are tolerant or tolerated as they go from one country to another. Every man believes his own religion is the best. The word *tolerance* is insulting; so it was by inadvertence that it was used in several constitutions.

After the government was established in Virginia, five citizens were charged with a revision of the code of laws. Although their task was completed in 1779, the General Assembly did not consider the document until 1784. Copies were then printed so that the people could express their opinions before the assembly convened. As I think it will be of interest, I am quoting the article about religion. The law itself is expressed in a few precise words, but the preamble, which justifies it, cannot be so short, and form required that it be contained in a single sentence.*

Well aware that the opinions and belief of men depend not on their own will, but follow involuntarily the evidence proposed to their minds; that Almighty God hath created the mind free, and manifested his supreme will that free it shall remain by making it altogether insusceptible of restraint; that all attempts to influence it by temporal punishments, or burthens, or by civil incapacitations, tend only to beget habits of hypocrisy and meanness, and are a departure from the plan of the holy author of our religion, who being lord both of body and mind, yet chose not to propagate it by coercions on either, as was in his Almighty power to do, but to extend it by its influence on reason alone; that the impious presumption of legislators and rulers, civil as well as ecclesiastical, who, being themselves but fallible and uninspired men, have assumed dominion over the faith of others, setting up their own opinions and modes of thinking as the only true and in-

---

Williamsburg, 1955), pp. 157–58. Jefferson wrote his notes in 1781 and revised them in 1782; on his arrival in Paris he had 200 copies printed for private distribution in 1785, carrying the composition date of 1782 on the title page. A French edition was published in 1786, and the first public English edition was printed in London in 1787.

* This is from the pen of Mr. Jefferson, who offered to write it and several other articles when the five revisers divided up the subjects.

fallible, and as such endeavoring to impose them on others, hath established and maintained false religions over the greatest part of the world and through all time: That to compel a man to furnish contributions of money for the propagation of opinions which he disbelieves and abhors, is sinful and tyrannical; that even the forcing him to support this or that teacher of his own religious persuasion, is depriving him of the comfortable liberty of giving his contributions to the particular pastor whose morals he would make his pattern, and whose powers he feels most persuasive to righteousness; and is withdrawing from the ministry those temporary rewards, which proceeding from an approbation of their personal conduct, are an additional incitement to earnest and unremitting labours for the instruction of mankind; that our civil rights have no dependance on our religious opinions, any more than our opinions in physics or geometry; that therefore the proscribing any citizen as unworthy the public confidence by laying upon him an incapacity of being called to offices of trust and emolument, unless he profess or renounce this or that religious opinion, is depriving him injuriously of those privileges and advantages to which, in common with his fellow citizens, he has a natural right; that it tends also to corrupt the principles of that very religion it is meant to encourage, by bribing, with a monopoly of worldly honours and emoluments, those who will externally profess and conform to it; that though indeed these are criminals who do not withstand such temptation, yet neither are those innocent who lay the bait in their way; that the opinions of men are not the object of civil government, nor under its jurisdiction; that to suffer the civil magistrate to intrude his powers into the field of opinion and to restrain the profession or propagation of principles on supposition of their ill tendency is a dangerous falacy, which at once destroys all religious liberty, because he being of course judge of that tendency will make his opinions the rule of judgment, and approve or condemn the sentiments of others only as they shall square with or differ from his own; that it is time enough for the rightful purposes of civil government for its officers to interfere when principles break out into overt acts against peace and good order; and finally, that truth is great and will prevail if left to herself; that she is the proper and sufficient antagonist to error, and has nothing to fear from the conflict unless by human interposition disarmed of her natural weapons, free argument and debate; errors ceasing to be dangerous when it is permitted freely to contradict them.

We the General Assembly of Virginia do enact that no man shall be compelled to frequent or support any religious worship, place, or ministry whatsoever, nor shall be enforced, restrained, molested, or burthened in his body or goods, nor shall otherwise suffer, on account of his religious opinions or belief; but that all men shall be free to profess, and by argument to maintain, their opinions in matters of religion, and that the same shall in no wise diminish, enlarge, or affect their civil capacities.

And though we well know that this Assembly, elected by the people for the ordinary purposes of legislation only, have no power to restrain the acts of succeeding Assemblies, constituted with powers equal to our own, and that therefore to declare this act irrevocable would be of no effect in law * yet we are free to declare, and do declare, that the rights hereby asserted are of the natural rights of mankind, and that if any act shall be hereafter passed to repeal the present or to narrow its operation, such act will be an infringement of natural right.[12]

Up to the present, several religious laws, diametrically opposed to what is contained in the Declaration of Rights, have not been revoked. They will probably not be changed until the legislative branch reforms the entire code. As they have been out of use for a long time, no one thinks about them, and it would be hard to make anyone in Virginia believe, unless he saw the text, that a father can be deprived of the right to raise his own children because he is a heretic; other regulations deprive a man of his rights as a citizen, and still others could condemn an individual to be burned.† They should be repealed, although we may consider them revoked by disuse, the will of the people, and the maxims in the Declaration of Rights.

The Anglican religion was dominant until the Revolution, and those who did not profess it were forced, like the Anglicans, to contribute to the church. At the first meeting of the assembly, held in October 1776, all parliamentary acts pertaining to religion were revoked, but no one thought of these barbarous regulations which sully the municipal code as well as common law.‡ All religions were placed on the same footing, and salaries, which hitherto had been granted by law to ministers of the Anglican church, were suspended, a suspension declared permanent § by action of the assembly in October 1779. As Anglican ministers were not satisfied with voluntary contributions, although those of other faiths never had any others, they asked the assembly to provide for ministers of the

---

* It is clear that if this were a constitutional law, it could not be revoked by ordinary legislative power, despite Abbé Mably's protests.

† These laws were enacted by our ancestors, who, according to the abbé, established liberty of conscience.

‡ Common law refers here only to the code of English laws preceding the Magna Carta, which, if you except the laws pertaining only to England, was adopted in toto and not in part, like the acts of Parliament.

§ Permanent means it will be in force until revoked by another assembly.

[12] Jefferson, *Papers of Jefferson*, ed. Boyd, 2:545–47.

Gospel and to grant members of the Anglican church the right to form a body and pass laws to govern their sect. The second request was granted in the October 1784 session, but it was made clear that other sects could obtain this privilege if they desired. The first request was copied and distributed to the people, who expressed their feelings at length in the manner characteristic of free citizens.*

As the abbé wished to censure the religious liberty he calls "tolerance," he stated that our fathers, fleeing the religious persecutions which were tearing England apart, established "unlimited liberty of conscience" in America. He wants to prove they were right to permit complete tolerance, since the English provided for their safety, but he says we were wrong to follow their example, because we have to govern ourselves.

On page 81: "You can obtain almost no advantage from religion; yet politicians of every nation have considered it one of the most powerful springs which drive the human heart." We know only too well the power of this spring. The death of Socrates alone would serve as a sad reminder, and the atrocities perpetrated in its name are so numerous and revolting that humanity shudders to think about them. Religious fanaticism can help a villain achieve his ends. No virtuous man will have recourse to it, for virtue seeks calm and reflection. The only use we can make of the author's doctrine is to express the hope that no American government will ever be sufficiently barbarous to use religion for politics.

On page 87 he asks: "Why do I read in the Pennsylvania constitution 'Nor can any man, who acknowledges the being of a God, be justly deprived or abridged of any civil right as a citizen, on account of his religious sentiments or peculiar mode of religious worship: And that no authority can or ought to be vested in, or assumed by, any power whatever, that shall in any case interfere with, or in any manner controul, the right of conscience in the free exercise of religious worship'?" If he seriously condemns such wise institutions, his censure should be taken for praise. He continues: "Is there any reasonable doubt that Christianity does not offer enough sects to satisfy everyone? On the pretext of populating your territory more rapidly, do you want to summon religions from the most remote countries? I dare not express my thoughts about such a project."

This frightening reticence does not impress us because we are not afraid of hobgoblins. On the contrary, we are convinced that

* See Note G.

no religion will be harmful provided the government does not tamper with it. We have also observed that Muhammadans are not inspired to emigrate; the poor Jews have not caused any trouble anywhere, and their sordidness is a result of the persecution and contempt from which they suffer. Finally, experience has taught us that religious novelties are like a torrent whose damage is proportionate to the dikes erected to stop it.

Since the abbé thinks we are motivated by a desire to populate our territory rather than by principles of justice, I shall observe that after the Revolution we abolished land grants and other encouragements formerly given to immigrants. "The greatest legislators," he continues, "have always been less interested in attracting large numbers of men than in forming good citizens and uniting them with the same kind of thinking." After drawing from somewhere the idea that "the character of our confederation is still only sketched, and that a seven-year war has not given our states a national consciousness," he adds: "Under these circumstances it would be a great misfortune if a large number of strangers arrived with their prejudices since they would delay the growth of a public morality which should unite citizens in mutual confidence."

We fail to see why it is necessary to be a great legislator to prefer good citizens to hordes of bad ones, or why the author takes the trouble to tell us things which have no more connection with liberty of conscience than a savage from the Strait of Magellan with the Tatar khan.

On page 85 he asks why we have "stigmatized ministers." "It would be enough to let them vote in your elections and to exclude them from public office, on the pretext of not distracting them from their important functions. Europeans have occasionally used this method to dispose of priests who were too powerful or who were forgetting the saintly character of their ministry." To appreciate the utility of this lesson you should know that ministers enjoy the right of suffrage, like other citizens, and that they were excluded from public office seven years ago for the very reason he suggests. He must have found this in several constitutions, notably that of New York, which states: "And whereas the ministers of the gospel are, by their profession, dedicated to the service of God and the cure of souls, and ought not to be diverted from the great duties of their function; therefore no minister of the gospel, or priest of any denomination whatsoever, shall, at any time hereafter, under any pretence or description whatever, be eligible to, or capable of holding, any civil or military office or place, within this state." [13]

His criticism is now turned (p. 90) against the legislators of South Carolina, who, he says, "have departed even further than all the others from the principles permitted by a healthy political structure forced to tolerate several religions." He quotes the law stating that "whenever fifteen or more male persons, not under twenty-one years of age, professing the Christian Religion and agreeing to unite themselves in a society for the purposes of religious worship, they shall (on complying with the terms herein after mentioned) be, and be constituted a Church." [14]

This law really does not deserve any praise, since it requires the consent of fifteen persons for something any individual should be able to do if he wishes to construct a church and has the means to do so. It also favors the Protestant church, but the author, instead of censuring the law for intolerance, goes in the other direction. On the following page he says: "Any scatterbrained young man of twenty-one, by using his imagination and the ignorance of fourteen other people as scatterbrained as he, can aspire to the honor of being leader of a sect." South Carolina seems more reprehensible to him for this assumed liberality than the other states in which a single scatterbrained individual, whether Protestant, Catholic, Muhammadan, Jew, pagan, or nothing at all can do what in South Carolina is only permitted to fifteen scatterbrained Protestants of the same sect.

The author considers intolerance in religious matters essential to the existence of free governments. He thinks it is a mistake to tolerate various religions and gives us a very curious recipe for stopping this evil (page 92): "I believe the ministers of these religions should have liberty to teach their doctrine. But I should like to see each church compelled to preserve the dogmas and discipline set forth in its catechism without making any changes on the pretext that it is explaining its truths more clearly." This is another lesson we could never put in practice because the American people, not believing itself infallible, would never consent to an irrevocable decision about religion or any other matter.

The writer would also like each government to have its political and moral catechism, and he adds: "It would be a task worthy of the Continental Congress"; but, lest the wisdom of the Continental

---

[13] *Constitution of New York* (Fishkill, 1777), Art. 39.

[14] South Carolina, General Assembly, *A Bill for Establishing the Constitution of the State of South Carolina* (Charleston, 1777).

Congress be inadequate for such an important document, he devotes a page and a half to it. He begins majestically: "This respectable body of magistrates which is responsible for the prosperity of the thirteen United States of America would declare that 'The Holy Scriptures, etc.'" and "'It is just and pious that all the American religions, while adoring the wisdom of God's judgments, etc.'"

It seems unnecessary to quote his remarks about deism, the apple of discord which, according to him, will come from the new religions, etc. The principles in the preamble to the proposed law about religion or in the Declaration of Rights could serve as a reply to all the abbé's arguments. I hope, however, that I may be excused for inserting at this point some pertinent reflections by the author of the *Notes on the State of Virginia.*

The rights of conscience we never submitted, we could not submit. We are answerable for them to our God. The legitimate powers of government extend to such acts only as are injurious to others. But it does me no injury for my neighbour to say there are twenty gods, or no god. It neither picks my pocket nor breaks my leg. If it be said, his testimony in a court of justice cannot be relied on, reject it then, and be the stigma on him. Constraint may make him worse by making him a hypocrite, but it will never make him a truer man, It may fix him obstinately in his errors, but will not cure them. Reason and free enquiry are the only effectual agents against error. Give a loose to them, they will support the true religion, by bringing every false one to their tribunal, to the test of their investigation. They are the natural enemies of error, and of error only. . . . Was the government to prescribe to us our medicine and diet, our bodies would be in such keeping as our souls are now. Thus in France the emetic was once forbidden as a medicine, and the potatoe as an article of food. Government is just as infallible too when it fixes systems in physics. Galileo was sent to the inquisition for affirming that the earth was a sphere: the government had declared it to be as flat as a trencher, and Galileo was obliged to abjure his error. This error however at length prevailed, the earth became a globe, and Descartes declared it was whirled round its axis by a vortex. The government in which he lived was wise enough to see that this was no question of civil jurisdiction, or we should all have been involved by authority in vortices. In fact, the vortices have been exploded, and the Newtonian principle of gravitation is now more firmly established, on the basis of reason, than it would be were the government to step in, and to make it an article of necessary faith. Reason and experiment have been indulged, and error has fled before them. It is error alone which needs the support of government. Truth can stand by itself. Subject opinion to coercion: whom will you make your inquisitors? Fallible men; men governed by bad passions, by private as well as public reasons. And why subject it to coercion? To produce uniformity. But is uniformity of opinion desireable? No more than of face and stature. Introduce the bed of Procrustes then, and as there is danger that the large men may beat the small, make us all of a size, by lopping the former and stretching the latter. Difference of opinion is advantageous in religion. The several sects perform the office of a censor morum over such other. Is uniformity attainable? Millions of innocent men, women, and children, since the introduction of Christianity, have been burnt, tortured, fined, imprisoned; yet we have not advanced one inch towards uniformity. What has been the effect of coercion? To make one half the world fools, and the other half hypocrites. To support roguery and error all over the earth. Let us reflect that it is inhabited by a thousand millions of people, that these profess probably a thousand different systems of religion. That ours is but one of that thousand. That if there be but one right, and ours that one, we should wish to see the 999 wandering sects gathered into the fold of truth. But against such a majority we cannot effect this by force. Reason and persuasion are the only practicable instruments. To make way for these, free inquiry must be indulged; and how can we wish others to indulge it while we refuse it ourselves. But every state, says an inquisitor, has established some religion. No two, say I, have established the same. Is this a proof of the infallibility of establishments?

Our sister states of Pennsylvania and New York, however, have long subsisted without any establishment at all. The experiment was new and doubtful when they made it; it has answered beyond conception.* They flourish infinitely. Religion is well supported; of various kinds, indeed, but all good enough; all sufficient to preserve peace and order: or if a sect arises, whose tenets would subvert morals, good sense has fair play, and reasons and laughs it out of doors, without suffering the state to be troubled with it.[15]

Although this truth has been demonstrated in all the states since the Revolution, it is surprising that it was not more generally foreseen. If everyone can obtain satisfaction for his wrongs, public tranquillity will be assured; when free discussion is permitted, reason dominates. But if certain individuals have civil rights that are denied to others, the latter will be opposed to the system, which will then be on the defensive. The same situation prevails when

---

* Although liberty of conscience was greater in these two colonies and Rhode Island than elsewhere before the Revolution, it was not comparable to what is found today in any state. These good results came from the perfect agreement and equality of all religions.

[15] *Notes*, ed. Peden, pp. 159–61.

there are religious distinctions; if the government recognizes only one sect, the others are jealous.

Although religious liberty is on a better footing everywhere than in Europe, each state could improve it. Freedom of worship exists; no state has a dominant church, and in no state are there distinctions about the form, size, and location of the buildings. But in Massachusetts, New Hampshire, and South Carolina, Protestantism is favored. In Massachusetts non-Christians cannot be representatives, and they are excluded from other posts in Maryland and Delaware. Catholics cannot fill some positions in New Hampshire, New Jersey, North Carolina, and Georgia. The Pennsylvania constitution excludes non-Christians, although the second [third] article of its Declaration of Rights states that "all men have a natural and indefeasible right to worship Almighty God according to the dictates of their own consciences." This proves that although reason triumphed theoretically, it was often forced to yield to prejudice.

We cannot deny the injustice of depriving a citizen of his natural rights on account of his way of thinking. And it is a serious mistake to attempt to cover this injustice with a veil of political precaution. If non-Christians are few in number, it is unlikely they would be preferred unless they have extraordinary ability; and in this case it would be idiotic not to take advantage of it. If they are numerous, their displeasure can produce trouble, and if they are numerically superior to the Christians, they will do justice to themselves unless they are kept in a state of ignorance, which might dishonor the state.

# Chapter 13

# The Revolutionary Period

The American Revolution came at a most opportune time. Had it been earlier, we should probably have lacked the strength necessary to win; had it been later, the British government might have introduced family distinctions and division among us. Even the abbé appears to agree (p. 12): "I note with pleasure that you are in a more fortunate situation than the old republics whose wisdom we admire; you will be able to give your institutions a character of stability which makes the laws more revered." It is true that he also says (p. 116): "We must admit, sir, that Americans established their independence under unfortunate circumstances."

This contradiction is not nearly so astonishing as his explanation of this assumed misfortune. "The time has vanished when strong and courageous souls were capable of both violent injustice and exemplary virtue." So the author mourns the age of ignorance, superstition, and enthusiasm because violence and injustice, by inflaming human passions, produced heroic traits. He considers it a misfortune to live in the century of philosophy, when good sense, moderation, and enlightened reason perform frequent acts of humanity and virtue.

Anyone imbued with such ideas about happiness and unhappiness should not write legislative treatises. It is cruel to write glowingly about ancient civilizations, since it makes us envy periods far less fortunate than ours. A real friend of mankind would exhort his fellow citizens to think about the advantages we enjoy today. Men forget past troubles, and their imagination enhances pleasant memories as they become more remote in time and space. The exaggerated virtues of the Ancients and the happiness they seem to have enjoyed provide misanthropes with an opportunity to rail at the present century. No one can deny that philosophy has made considerable progress and that the inhabitants of the polite world are far happier than ever before, although we are still a long way from the degree of science and contentment to which we can aspire.

My subject does not permit a full comparison of the benefits and evils of antiquity and modern times. But I should have the courage to contend against anyone who wishes to prove by force of reason that there has ever been any century as happy as our own.

# Chapter 14

# The Confederation

The abbé advises us to give Congress, or our "amphictyonic council"[16] as he calls it, command of our troops. This is what we have always done. He thinks, however, that the power of this body should be unlimited,* and that is contrary to our conception of liberty. Finally on page 169 he tells us (to prove we are mistaken in changing our delegates so frequently): "You only need a skillful, obstinate, and eloquent man to upset everything." This would be an excellent reason to deprive him of his power.

The abbé's method of expressing himself is inexcusable. All the republics had the wisdom to reserve the privilege of recalling their delegates from Congress at any time. On page 161 he writes: "What does this law mean? Your enemies, sir, will say that the states arbitrarily reserved the right to recall their ministers because they were ambitious. If these deputies are not sufficiently sly and opinionated to get their own way, they can be replaced by men capable of playing power politics in an association which can be useful only if there is equality. Such a false and shameful political system implies that Americans suffer from the same ambition which caused the downfall of the Amphictyonic Council."

On page 169 he is under the impression that we change representatives annually: "The term of these new magistrates will expire before they have time to become acquainted. If you are afraid to have fixed administrative principles, you cannot establish a better rule."

Mr. Hayley†[17] calls the abbé a "dogmatic and insolent author" who has treated the most distinguished English historians, especially his friend, Mr. Gibbon,[18] indecently. I shall let the reader

* On p. 167: "You cannot give too much authority to your amphictyonic council, since it cannot abuse it."

† See Note H.

[16] The Amphictyonic Council was the council of deputies in a league of Greek tribes. It protected and maintained worship in the temple of a deity.

[17] William Hayley, poet, dramatist, and critic.

[18] Edward Gibbon, *The History of the Decline and Fall of the Roman Empire* (London, 1776–88).

decide for himself, but I may surely be excused for not always remaining as calm as I had promised to be.

It is inaccurate to say that members of Congress are replaced every year. They are elected for a year but can be returned for three consecutive years, after which they are ineligible for the same space of time. Pennsylvania differs slightly on this point, for its constitution decrees they cannot serve more than two years, after which they are ineligible for three, as in most states. They usually serve the maximum term permitted, unless they ask to be excused, which frequently happens. Three years is a long time for a man to be absent from his wife and children. Few individuals can afford to neglect their business for that period, and members of Congress work such long hours that many of them have been unable to stand the physical strain involved.

As for the right to recall delegates from Congress, the author does not admit the possibility that a group of men could make a poor choice or that a man could become mentally or physically ill. In short, he does not recognize any of the common, natural vicissitudes; yet he thinks we should fear the dire result of evils which may not have existed even as figments of his imagination.

The wise precautions taken to ensure that the same delegates cannot be elected for more than three years out of six and that they can be recalled at any time appear in Article 8 [5] of the Confederation and were adopted by Congress. The men who wrote it were thinking about their descendants, not about the prestige of the body they constituted.

The Confederation provides that any quarrel which might arise between two or more states shall be judged by Congress in accordance with certain rules.* This law is necessary to preserve the union. The author would also like Congress to know about certain private matters, but as he does not divulge their nature, we cannot profit by his advice. After predicting that we should encounter the same troubles they had in Geneva (and he fails to take into consideration the prodigious difference between the two), he says (on p. 166): "I see, sir, only one recourse for the Americans, and that is to make Congress the supreme judge over all differences of opinion which might arise between different social classes." He then explains the reasons why the governments should agree to this proposal and adds: "If the wealthy objected, it would be an indication that they were already formulating ambitious projects."

* See Note I.

If, as he believes, this is really our "only recourse," we are lost. No state would permit Congress to adjudicate personal matters, and Congress would refuse to do so. However, one hope remains, that we shall never have any of these disorders between social classes, since we have only one class. So the law proposed by the author is subject to two little difficulties: the first is that neither party would agree to it, and the second is that it would be useless.

On page 159 he proposes another after discussing Congress: "This august assembly has been the chain linking the thirteen states and binding them together. We may be sure that if each republic had acted individually, there would have been no unity and you would have succumbed." No one will argue this point, but he might have saved himself the trouble of mentioning it, since no American would have been foolish enough to believe he could resist England without a perfect union.

The law proposed by the abbé is as follows: "I should like each republic to limit membership in the Continental Congress to those citizens who have distinguished themselves in the executive branch. I should like public opinion to foster the idea that the greatest honor to which a citizen can aspire is to be a delegate to the council of your amphictyons." A little reflection will make it apparent that it would be almost impossible to have enough amphictyons. Furthermore, it would be unjust to exclude worthy citizens from representing their state because they have not served in the executive branch. As for the honor, we believe that a citizen is honored by any post his country confers upon him, and the magnitude of the honor depends upon the way he fulfills his responsibilities.

The author wishes to give Congress too much power. On page 121 he writes: "It seems to me that none of your republics has anything to fear from what I propose. Is it conceivable that the Continental Congress should take advantage of its power?" And on the next page: "If they were foolish enough to form a conspiracy, their fortresses, castles, and garrisons could do little against the militia of the thirteen republics."

According to the abbé, therefore, an almost limitless power, granted by the unanimous consent of the states, would be useless against troops of the thirteen republics, troops which he calls up easily, although they are scattered over a territory with a circumference of about 42,500 miles. On the other hand, he believes a state would be powerless against the eloquence of his Gracchus, who could be easily curbed by a justice of the peace. This is remarkable logic.

It is impossible to recall everything the author tells us about his amphictyonic council. If the reader wishes to read it all, he should consult pages 156–74 of the abbé's book and several other places. On page 165 he has qualms about the appointment of magistrates: "I am afraid your tribunes might resemble the seditious individuals who, in the last days of Rome, sacrificed the republic to their own interests." For this reason he recommends a powerful Congress to protect the people against the people.

The attentive reader may find the author's ideas generally obscure, but he cannot deny that some of them are very clear. He states that a single member of Congress can "upset the entire body"; yet he admits this is impossible unless they all agree. Again, on page 160, he seems to approve the annual election of the amphictyons, although elsewhere he regards this as a source of fearful disasters. It would be impossible to record all the author's contradictions, but I shall close with one of the strangest. After showing three of our republics how they should act to serve as a model for the others, he remarks on page 74: "However, if any more troubles arose, the others would offer to mediate, and little by little peace would reign throughout the whole confederation." On page 156: "Someone may tell me that if one of your provinces is torn by dissension, neighboring states will mediate to restore peace and harmony. This is a vain hope!" And on page 176: "Do not flatter yourself that any neighboring state would intervene to settle differences." According to the first statement, they will make peace; according to the second, they could not make peace if they tried; and according to the third, they would not even try.

An inattentive reader would not suspect so much negligence on the part of a writer who admits on page 111: "It is useless for me to study the legislation of your republic; I do not find the harmony which keeps all the parts of the state in balance and gives them the same character." We cannot say that the dire predictions of the abbé are founded on feeble bases, since they have none. His prophecies about dissensions between city and country inhabitants prove only too clearly that they rest on fantastic suppositions.

# Chapter 15

# The Dire Prognostications of Abbé Mably

After noting on page 42 that sons of property owners in Pennsylvania can vote although they have not paid taxes, he says on the next page: "I see the formation of a hereditary nobility forbidden by American laws." If his prophecy comes true, the noble class will include about half the inhabitants (when the country is well populated). It would number approximately seven-eighths of the present population.

But on page 138 he writes: "At the moment I believe farmers are so busy clearing land and harvesting that they are quite satisfied. Provided they get a good price for their crops, they will give little thought to what is happening in the cities. But when these men can take pride in their leisure, their numbers, and their wealth, will they not begin to think of liberty? Will they be indifferent to the pretensions of city dwellers? They were not thinking about freedom when they relied on the equality established by law. But if they have reason to fear that the city dwellers want to seize public power, will they patiently consent to become subjects of an aristocracy?"

So the author now finds that an aristocracy is about to be established in the cities, while farmers are not even thinking about their freedom. This is a bit difficult in view of the fact that representatives have to be elected each year, and since those chosen in country districts have a role in public affairs, just as city representatives do, how could such a change be wrought in the constitution without their knowing it? This would be impossible without their consent, and it is unlikely they would approve anything harmful to their constituents or to themselves. Even if they consented, the legislative power cannot change the constitution.

To make sense out of this passage we must assume he used the word *aristocracy* in the sense of "administration." Farmers do not seek posts because they are devoting all their time to their business. Later, when they "can take pride in their leisure, their numbers, and their wealth," they want to have a part in the government. What harm is there in this, and who can prevent them? His expression "begin to think of liberty" must refer to administration or it has no meaning. And when he says that "they were not thinking of freedom," I see no connection with what follows unless he meant that they did not fear to lose their liberty because they relied on the equality established by law.

On page 147 he continues his observations on city inhabitants: "As soon as your city dwellers have been corrupted by wealth, will they not regard country dwellers and artisans with scorn, and will legal equality not be useless? These favorites of fortune will aspire to form dynasties." After all the writer has said about equality, it is apparent that he confuses equal rights with equal wealth. Equal rights are just and easy to maintain when they have been well established; equal wealth is neither practical nor desirable. The abbé often tells us that wealth is incompatible with liberty; yet he advises us with equal frequency to grant special privileges to the rich. Again he speaks of wealth as if it were pernicious on account of the sums involved rather than their unequal distribution. He seemingly has not realized that if only one million dollars were in circulation, a penny would have the same value as a dollar if there were a hundred million.

Let us return to the difference between the city and country inhabitants. On page 148: "We may be sure that the [country] inhabitants will not consent to be treated as subjects; indignation will give them courage, and they will demand their inalienable rights. Then, in their anger, they will treat the magistrates as insolent and unfaithful servants. If democracy triumphs, anarchy will result; but if aristocracy rises on the ruins of liberty, it will abuse its authority. Perhaps it will degenerate into an oligarchy, and the triumvirs will dispute the honor of conquering on the pretext of avenging the people."

In addition to the quarrels scheduled to take place between two nonexistent classes, the author, with his customary clarity, lets us guess what is meant by these magistrates against whom the country inhabitants will rise in their indignation. Either the magistrates and the wealthy are one and the same, or they are in cahoots. In either case it is hard to see how there could be so many of them in the cities or how they could mistreat any citizens when the magistrate's power is restricted to executing the orders of the legislative branch. The following observations would have dissipated his fears.

The government in Great Britain is a little better than that of the old republics because the people exercise their rights through representatives. Whatever national liberty exists is in the House of

Commons, for the two hereditary branches of the legislative power contribute nothing to liberty. One third of this is vested in a single individual and another third in some two hundred others. It is obvious that the basis for liberty becomes increasingly solid as the right to elect representatives and to be elected is equalized. Although this right is not so equal in any state as it could and should be, even before the Revolution the situation was much better than in England, and since then it has greatly improved. The United States has taken the good points of the English constitution and avoided its worst faults.

The facts that we recognize no hereditary privileges, that we have greatly extended the right to vote and to be a representative, and that each representative is required to live in the district he represents are enough to preserve us from the misfortunes which the abbé says are inevitable. While he threatens us with all the evils of the other republics, he seems persuaded we are quite incapable of enjoying any of their advantages.

This prophet of doom claims we are in the same situation as the Romans were after the expulsion of the Tarquins. According to him, only the Ancients could aspire to have a free government. In a word, he condemns everything which does not conform to the principles of the old republics, especially Sparta; yet predicts we shall suffer from all the ills to which they were exposed.

When the old republics were established, most nations were divided into different classes which were constantly bickering. Equal rights did not exist, and revolutions served to favor the ambition of an individual or a small group; they never represented the wishes of the whole population.

Before the American Revolution a truly rational republic never existed. The principles of such a government were developed in England under James I and Charles I and matured in America. The ambition of Cromwell prevented the establishment of true republican principles and roused the desire to reestablish the heredity rights of the monarchy. The English who emigrated to America were imbued with republican ideas which were not affected by the glamor of the throne and the aristocracy. The loss of hereditary rights inspired the citizens with the idea of correcting the faults of the constitution when an opportunity rose. The greatest obstacle was their fondness for the country of their ancestors, but English ministers destroyed this.

The inhabitants of the thirteen colonies were free, without a government, interested in public welfare, and, on the whole, well informed about the rights of man and the principles of a free government. The Revolution was not produced by domestic factions but by the necessity to cast off a foreign yoke. There was no need to overthrow a system of government or to change principles, for experience had taught that it is impossible to govern without representation. With all these advantages we should have attained a point closer to perfection, but we are not so far from it that we need fear the dire prophecies of Abbé Mably. Our governments may be changed but not overthrown. If the voters wish to change them, they can do so legally, as stated in the Declaration of Rights.

Someone may say that the representatives might make bad use of the power entrusted to them; if this could be done, which is highly doubtful, the trouble would be short-lived because at the end of the year the people would elect representatives whose views would be more in line with those of the majority.

During the war the gazetteers, who repeated whatever the English government wanted to circularize in Europe, said that nine-tenths of the inhabitants were in favor of the former government. If there had been a majority of even one member in most of the districts, why did England have to send armies to subdue them? English ministers persuaded the journalists to write falsehoods. It is surprising that they have found some credence, but it is even more amazing that men writing about our governments assume they could be overturned by a few citizens. The people do not need to resort to violence in order to change the government; if any other power wished to attempt it, force would be needed, and the larger number would win. Here force and the law would be on the same side. Although it is difficult to conceive a revolution, it is not impossible; furthermore, human prudence cannot imagine a law which would destroy the possibility of one.

The author's interest in our prosperity makes him believe that one day we shall see events inevitable in any human society. On page 163 he warns: "As the inhabitants of America have professions, rights, customs, and different ways of envisaging their interests, the various passions will excite murmurs and complaints." Earlier he had told us we were threatened with "troubles, divisions, and domestic disorders," and finally he repeats in a threatening fashion: "What outlets have you prepared to prevent these seeds from fermenting and doing serious damage to the social structure? If citizens who think they have just cause for complaint are not provided with legal means to be heard, they will go to extremes."

In a word, he has the kindness to inform us that we have not passed a law to repair social disorders, and he seems to insinuate, although in a circuitous fashion, that the difficulties which have arisen elsewhere because of the diversity of social classes will be created in America by our equality.

The evils he declares inevitable are so numerous they would frighten a superficial reader; this same terror will, however, reassure anyone who reads carefully. Not content with predicting that we shall suffer the fate of Florence, Geneva, and all the ancient republics (which we should imitate, however), he threatens us with the problems encountered by monarchies. He even takes us to Sweden (p. 160) to show us the decline of his dear aristocracy, which we regard as a blessing for the kingdom.

Finally, on page 125, he tells us: "Plato would doubtless think your republics could not remain prosperous for long even if they immediately corrected all the negligences which escaped their legislators and which I have taken the liberty of calling to your attention in my previous letters."

If our country must remain in a desperate plight despite the remedies, what is the use of all the wise counsel he has taken the trouble to give us?

# Conclusion

Before taking leave of Abbé Mably, I have several more observations to make.

Although it is true that the political errors so frequent throughout his book do not affect the good moral philosophy he warmly recommends, any intelligent man knows it is salutary to have laws designed to discourage vice and favor virtue, and it seems scarcely necessary to write a book on the subject. We should have been grateful for a demonstration about how to practice these worthy principles, but he keeps stony silence on this point, although convinced that we have failed to accomplish anything. On several occasions he states that his book is intended for our instruction, but he teaches us nothing unless we can regard as lessons his censure for what we have done well or his advice to do worse when we have committed an error.

The abbé advises us to proscribe commerce and the arts, to defend wealth, to shackle the press; religious liberty should be banned and tolerance not extended too far; citizens should not be permitted to assemble without permission from a magistrate; and, finally, censors should again have the power to regulate the conduct of citizens. If we wanted to convert the republics into religious communities, his lessons might provide some useful ideas.

It is possible that his intentions were good, but it is not in our province to scrutinize intentions. Our duty is to judge facts. Those who know the author may be persuaded that his errors spring from excessive zeal, but these men constitute a small group in comparison to those who can only judge by what he has written. What will the latter think of the way he treats us on page 161, where he begins: "Your enemies, sir, will say"? This singular approach reveals his design of veiling his own feelings to soften the bitterness. Readers will think he was well informed and will imagine he soft-pedaled our faults instead of exaggerating them.

And who will not believe we are as grossly ignorant as he pretends, since the gazettes report that we requested his advice? At the beginning of his book he says to Mr. Adams, one of our ministers plenipotentiary in Europe: "Since you request it, I shall have the honor of addressing my remarks to you." So the book is dedicated to him.

His fatherly solicitude extends to such minutiae that it would offend schoolboys. On page 172, for example, he invites us to celebrate every ten or twelve years "the day when we declared we were free from the English yoke"; this day, which we call Independence Day for the sake of brevity, is celebrated every year. He spends a page and a half telling us how to thank God for this event, how to plan the celebration, and he holds our hand until nothing remains save to blow out the candles. He closes saying: "We have senses and we must stimulate them in order to have a deeper reverence for the truths we need and which the multitude does not understand."

The people, whom the writer did not take the trouble to know, has, among its senses, one called common sense. It would be stimulated in a very disagreeable fashion if the men to whom the direction of the most important national matters is entrusted celebrated with solemn pomp these childish events he considers so important that he thinks every state ought to send ambassadors to the ceremony.

I shall close by quoting what Mably says (p. 126) about the savages, whom he introduces in a rather singular way: "Plato might have had the audacity to tell you that the savages who wander along your frontiers are closer to the principles of a good civilization than men who engage in commerce and cherish wealth. Savages do not reason about the rights of man, but all the principles are engraved in their souls and they will not fear any virtue whose usefulness has been made clear to them." It is good to note that his conception of the savages, like ours, is diametrically opposed to what has been said and written in Europe. But since the abbé honors us with his approval and supposes that Plato himself would have agreed with us, it is difficult to understand why he seems so dissatisfied.

After picturing us as prey to the most horrible anarchy, he continues on page 179: "No one, sir, is more interested than I in your liberty, and in the glory of your legislators. There will be no reason to reproach them if it is evident that they have recognized all the reefs on which a republic can run aground." This is a modest way of saying that all will be well if the lessons in his letters are heeded. We have every reason to hope that "the negligences" which he states (p. 125) "have escaped our legislators" will also escape our descendants. May they never believe that to preserve liberty, you must proscribe everything which makes men more civilized.

Some men believe the last works of Abbé Mably reflect the decadence of age. I have no concern with his other productions, as my sole object has been to warn the public about his observations on the governments and laws of the United States. I undertook this because I love truth and I am an American citizen; furthermore, I should like to observe that when a writer is well known, it is all the more necessary to refute his errors.

# Notes D-I

## Relative to the Reply to
## the *Observations* of Abbé Mably

### Note D (see page 123)

In Europe it is said that soldiers want war; in America they wanted peace. Men had no desire to risk their lives, but they never ran away from danger. When the enemy invaded, the inhabitants deplored the evils of war. At the same time they armed before being called for duty, and those not yet summoned often followed their comrades as volunteers.

There was a time when the enemy tried to frighten us by broadcasting the idea of their strength and our weakness. What happened? So many volunteers hastened to camp from all sides that in the early days of 1777 the state governments sent out word that General Washington did not want any more volunteers. The enemy then circulated exaggerated reports of our strength, and Americans refused to enlist on the grounds that it was wrong to neglect their business and increase public expenses when the commander had more men than he needed. Some distinguished citizens had to go with the officers to military reviews and other assemblies to explain that more recruits were required.

When the last English governor of Virginia seized the gunpowder in a public storehouse and put it on board a warship, several companies of volunteers requested an explanation. I saw a number of old men accompanying their sons for miles on this expedition to praise and bless them. One was William Wood of Albemarle County.[19] In 1777, when Admiral Howe and General Howe[20] went to Head-of-Elk [Elkton] near Chesapeake Bay to invade Virginia, this good old man took his rifle, left the Blue Ridge Mountains with his three sons, and walked two hundred miles to the sea. All were married and had left their wives to care for the children, the house, cattle, and crops. It was a broiling summer, almost unendurable for mountaineers. After a compaign of

[19] This may have been the William Woods who emigrated to America when he was 17, settled in Pennsylvania, and then moved to Virginia (Neander M. Woods, *Woods-McAfee Memorial* [Louisville, Ky., 1905], p. 56).

[20] Admiral Richard Howe, first Earl Howe, and his brother, Sir William Howe, fifth Viscount Howe.

five months William, in his eighty-first year, left for home suffering from smallpox. He died on his arrival.

On 19 April 1775, when the English began hostilities without provocation, the last royal governor of Massachusetts, General [Thomas] Gage, sent a detachment of nearly a thousand men from Boston to Concord with orders to destroy a supply of cannon and ammunition the Americans had assembled. As they passed through Lexington, they fired on a company of militia who were drilling and killed seven or eight men. The news spread like wildfire, inhabitants hurried to the spot from all directions, and the Redcoats lost more than two hundred men before Lord Percy [21] arrived to facilitate their retreat to Boston. On this occasion the Americans did their duty as citizens, and their actions show they had no other motive. When Mr. Hasket Darby of Salem [22] was warned by signals, he went home and looked sadly at his children, the eldest of whom was just thirteen. His wife came downstairs, took his musket from the wall, handed it to her husband with his cartridge pouch, and he left. This silent drama lasted not more than twenty or thirty seconds.

On 12 October 1776 the British army, under command of General Howe, landed at Frogs Point [Throgs Neck], a peninsula near Westchester, New York. Mr. John Smith [23] fled to New Rochelle with his seventy-year-old mother-in-law, his wife, and ten children, the eldest of whom was not yet twenty-one. As there was no time to take any of their possessions, they passed overnight from a position of wealth to one of adject poverty. But this was not all. Within a few days the rapid progress of the enemy forced this unhappy family to separate. The eldest son, William S. Smith, who was in the care of a surgeon because he had been wounded 16 September in the battle of Harlem Heights, succeeded in making his escape with his father and two of his brothers, but the rest of the family was captured by the enemy. They were taken to New York, where for a week they had no food save potatoes. After the loss of Fort Washington and most of the American forces, young Smith, now cured of his wound, appeared at the enemy advance post with letters to General Howe from Generals

[21] Hugh Percy, son of the earl of Northumberland.

[22] Elias Hasket Derby married Elizabeth Crowninshield 23 April 1761 (*Vital Records of Salem, Massachusetts* [Salem, 1924], 3:292).

[23] John Smith was a prosperous New York merchant. His eldest son, William S. Smith, married Abigail Adams (*New York Genealogical and Biographical Record* 25 [Oct. 1894] 153–54).

[Charles] Lee and [John] Sullivan demanding the release of the Smith family. It was a bold gesture in view of the situation. Family friends urged the ladies to remain in New York, where they felt safe. Mrs. Smith was the daughter of an English officer, but she was determined to do her duty, and she resolved to leave if permission could be obtained. She went to see General Howe, who received her graciously, told her that he had taken up quarters in her home, and knew that her oldest son was a major in the provincial army. He said the boy, if he wished, might be an officer in His Majesty's service, and he gave her his word "as a gentleman and a soldier" that if she returned with her whole family, all their possessions would be restored. Mrs. Smith thanked him but replied she would have to act in accordance with the wishes of her family.

Meanwhile young Smith was awaiting the answer at Kingsbridge, where a brave young Scotsman, Colonel [Colin] Campbell, was in command. A fellow student, who had become an officer in the British army, got Smith alone and attempted to win him over. Smith replied: "I do not recall ever doing anything that would make you think me capable of abandoning a cause because the wheel of fortune was turning against it. You may leave." Two days later the British commander's reply was brought to him about midnight, and at the same time several acquaintances sent word that they would come for lunch with his mother the next day. Smith was afraid the family misfortunes had been too much for his mother; so he asked for guides and left at midnight. His mother and the other children crossed to the American side and joined his father in Connecticut. She begged him to accept General Howe's offers, but he refused to express an opinion until he had heard his oldest son. That evening, when they were all assembled, the mother described in frightening colors the strength of the British army, repeated the advice of her old friends, and closed by saying, "You see, my son, everything depends on you; your reply will determine whether we return to a life of prosperity or remain in poverty." The father walked back and forth, his head down, in utter silence. The unhappy son said: "Tomorrow I shall ride to General Washington, who will, I am sure, grant me a flag of truce with permission to conduct you and the other members of the family to the enemy camp. Then I shall say good-bye for ever." The father embraced his son with pride and gave him his blessing. This same William S. Smith is now secretary of the legation in

London, where he has just married the daughter of Mr. Adams, minister plenipotentiary of the United States at this court.

Everyone knows about the retreat of General Washington across New Jersey in December 1776. Volunteers appeared at the camp from all sides as soon as it was known he had been obliged to cross the Delaware with only 2,500 men. The night of the 26th–27th [24] was bitter cold; snow was falling, but the general again crossed the river to surprise the enemy at Trenton. He sent General Sullivan along the river with some troops, while he took the longer route with General [Nathanael] Greene's forces. General Sullivan stopped two or three miles from Trenton to give General Greene time to catch up. While waiting, he checked the guns and found the humidity had put four out of five muskets out of order. He sent his aide-de-camp, Major Smith (of whom we were just speaking), to the commander with this report. General Washington said firmly: "Tell your general that if the muskets do not fire, they will have to use bayonets. The city must be taken." When the soldiers, who had walked almost all night on snow and ice, heard this, they stuck their bayonets on the end of their rifles, and General Sullivan jumped on his horse. They entered Trenton at one end of the main street, General Greene at the other, and they forced the British to surrender.

At the beginning of the winter of 1778, Colonel—now General —[George Rogers] Clark of Virginia, who had conquered Illinois and set up a small fort there, undertook an important expedition on the Mississippi because he thought this area would be inaccessible to the enemy. Upon his return he found that [Henry] Hamilton, governor of Detroit, had crossed this vast expanse of territory despite the ice and snow and taken refuge in Fort Vincennes with 120 trained soldiers. He had also brought along 300 Indians, whom he dispatched to make forays in the district.

Clark with 150 men armed only with rifles did not try to hide the fact that it would be extremely dangerous to attack the fort without artillery, especially as one could not approach it without getting into water up to the neck. He told his men that all would be lost if they left the fort in the hands of the enemy, and the soldiers assured him they would sell their lives dearly. It was almost a year since the government had received any news of this

[24] George Bancroft corrected Mazzei's date to the night of the 25th–26th in his copy of the *Researches* now in the Rare Book Division, New York Public Library.

area; so, before the attack, Clark sent a dispatch rider to Williamsburg, telling of their decision and asking the government to pardon him if he deprived the country of so many citizens. He captured Hamilton, whom he sent nine hundred miles to the capital in the spring of 1779.

About the first of March in that same year General [Charles] Scott obtained permission to go to his home in Powhatan County, Virginia. When an old neighbor heard of his arrival, he went to ask for news of his two sons, who had been serving for some time in General Washington's army. General Scott, sensitive as he was brave, replied gently that both had died. "My dear general," said the old man, "they lost their lives in a good cause. I have another boy who wants to join his brothers; if you would like to take him when you leave, I shall give him to you."

The following anecdote is an illustration of character which I consider fully as estimable and more unusual than courage in facing death.

Before General Scott returned to camp in the spring of 1779, the enemy made a sudden invasion of Virginia with some 2,500 men, protected by a warship, several frigates, and a number of smaller vessels. As the Americans had no disciplined troops, Mr. Thomas Nelson was put in command. A general of the militia and a member of one of the most distinguished families in the state, he was universally beloved, had represented his state in Congress with distinction, was a member of the General Assembly, and was friendly with the English governors, but when citizens were called to defend their country, his courage and zeal were exemplary.

The General Assembly, in session at the time, decided, however, that in view of General Scott's experience in camp, he should lead the militia. This caused criticism, since General Scott was a much younger man and had never held office. As soon as General Nelson heard that people were blaming the General Assembly, he hastened to say that he would be honored to serve under General Scott, and as long as the invasion lasted, he went to get his orders every morning with that serenity which bespeaks a truly great man.

In the spring of 1781 General Nelson was elected governor of Virginia, and he continued to serve under the marquis de Lafayette as general of militia until the capture of Yorktown. As the enemy had taken up quarters in his home, one of the most beautiful in the country, he offered ten guineas to the first French bombardier who would hit it,* while their officers were saying to one another that the building should not be harmed.

On the fourth day of the invasion, when there were less than eight hundred militiamen at general headquarters in Williamsburg, the government received an urgent appeal for help from the deputy governor of South Carolina. Some four hundred recruits were destined to be sent to this state. At the council meeting the first suggestion was to keep the men in Virginia until after the invasion, but one man said: "If the state militia are not capable of defending the country against a handful of enemy troops, we are not worthy to have it."

A mother's firmness reveals a courage far superior to the often barbaric bravery of the Ancients. While she and one of her daughters were busy mending headgear and other equipment for her two elder sons, neither of whom was twenty, she said: "It is hard to have to spend your time on such things, but it is a consolation for a mother to see that her children do not lack courage to fight for their country." She regretted the fact that the third, who was about thirteen, was not old enough to go. This lady is Anne Randolph of Curles,[25] sister of Colonels Richard and Everard Meade. Their mother, two of whose three children were in the army, was happy and proud to see her grandsons arm and ride off to battle. "Go, my brave children," she said, "chase the incendiaries from our shores." Mrs. Meade was born in England, and I believe her father had been governor of North Carolina. Richard and Everard Meade were captains in the same regiment.[26] At the beginning of the war the General Assembly named Richard a lieutenant colonel, but he lacked the necessary confidence to command a regiment. The members then thought of appointing Everard, but he declined on the grounds that he did not want to

---

* Toward the close of 1784, when he was entertaining a large group in a smaller establishment, he said gaily to the marquis de Lafayette and [Victor Maurice Riquet,] the chevalier de Caraman that if they were cramped, they should blame the marksmanship of the French bombardier. During that same dinner he made several other remarks about how he had always followed the orders of "his brave young commander" with pleasure.

[25] Anne Meade married Richard Randolph, Jr., of Curles (P. Hamilton Baskervill, *Andrew Meade of Ireland and Virginia, His Ancestors and Descendants* [Richmond: Old Dominion Press, 1921], p. 5).

[26] Colonel Richard K. Meade was a captain in 1775, then aide-de-camp to General Washington from 1777 to the end of the war; Major Everard Meade served from 1776 until the end of the war.

have to give orders to his older brother. The assembly was forced to choose someone else, and Richard left to be General Washington's aide-de-camp.

Before the battle of Monmouth on 28 June 1778, two advance batteries engaged in very active gunfire. As it was dreadfully hot, the wife of one of the cannoneers ran back and forth to fetch water from a spring. As she was approaching her husband, she saw him fall, hastened to help, but realized nothing could be done. She heard the officer give orders to remove the cannon, as he had no one to replace the valiant fellow who had just been killed. "No," cried the intrepid Molly. "The cannon shall not be taken away because there is no one to fire it. Since my brave husband is no longer alive, I shall do what I can to avenge him." Her courage attracted the attention of all the witnesses, and finally of General Washington, who gave her the rank of lieutenant captain at half-salary as long as she lived. She wore an epaulette, and everyone called her Captain Molly.[27]

In March 1783 the American frigate *Alliance* fought a battle with an English frigate on its way from Havana to Boston. A young American, not more than seventeen, was wounded by a ball which broke one of the bones in his leg. He refused to be carried to the infirmary and continued to service the battery until a second bullet broke the other leg. They then carried him to the surgeon. After cutting one leg, the surgeon said he should have removed it closer to the knee. "Cut it again," said the young man. Four days later the other leg was removed, and the boy died shortly after the frigate landed in Rhode Island.

Long before the tragic death of Major [John] André, Captain Nathan Hale of Connecticut, a handsome young man with a lovable character, was taken on Long Island in disguise and sentenced as a spy on the same grounds which later caused the condemnation of the unfortunate André. But André could at least be grateful for the sympathy of the American army and the tact displayed by his severe but fair judges. The young American was insulted until the last moment. "This is a fine death for a soldier," said an English officer derisively. "Sir," replied Captain Hale with astonishing calm, "I only regret that I have but one life to lose for my country." Those were his last words. A generous enemy, Mr.

---

[27] Margaret Corbin's husband was killed during the battle of Fort Washington 16 Nov. 1776. She took his place and fired a small cannon until she was severely wounded. After the war Congress voted her invalid pay, a complete suit of clothes yearly, and the ration of tobacco that the soldiers received.

Taylor, lieutenant in the Regiment of the Guards, was present at this scene and reported the details with feeling to our Colonel Blackdon.[28]

Colonel David Humphreys, who was recently in France as secretary of the legation charged with making treaties with the European powers, was a fellow student of the unfortunate Captain Hale. He told me he had never known a more intelligent and courageous young man or one so universally beloved. When Hale undertook to spy on the enemy, General Washington had no information about their army, though they knew all about ours. Hale inspected everything and was at the last enemy outpost when he was recognized by a first cousin, who had been reared with him by his own father and had joined the enemy just the day before.

Captain Hale was killed without observance of the necessary formalities. Major André had a legal trial with eight officers, including General Greene, the marquis de Lafayette, and Baron [Friedrich Wilhelm von] Steuben. Some of the troops attended the execution under arms, and every one of these brave men was moved with sympathy. The difference in behavior between the two groups is all the more remarkable when you recall that the André trial was subsequent to the Hale catastrophe.

After the defeat of the Indians at Newton on the Susquehanna 29 August 1779, General Sullivan had rations for only twenty-two days. When the guides told him it would take fully this long to reach the farthest post on his expedition to the Genesee country, he summoned his officers and told them he could not execute his orders from Congress unless the army would march on half rations for forty-four days. This meant half a pound of flour, an equal amount of beef, and nothing to drink save water. Each colonel explained the situation and told his regiment that those who wanted to go should cry "Hurrah!" three times. There was a great chorus, but the leaders wanted to be sure. The colonels then said the wounded were to be sent to general headquarters, under the escort of men who did not want to march. The latter were requested to step out of line, but not one of the three thousand men moved, so they had to draw lots.

After the capture of Charleston in 1780 (the English report that 6,000 men did not surrender to 12,000 was inaccurate; a garrison of 1,700 held out for a long time against General [Henry]

[28] Samuel Blackdon, possibly Blagden, major, aide-de-camp to General Wooster 1775, lieutenant colonel 1777.

Clinton's army of 14,000), the enemy kept a considerable force there until the end of hostilities. Some citizens went to prison, and others saw their property destroyed because they refused to be subjects of the English king. The ladies' behavior was even more remarkable. They never received British officers socially, scorned their parties, and journeyed to the neck of land to which the French and Americans had been relegated to share frugal repasts with them. When a French or American officer appeared in the streets of Charleston, they vied with each other in entertaining him, and this annoyed the British no end. Our soldiers were finally forced to join the British army and were shipped off to the islands. The same treatment was accorded the British after Yorktown.

Toward the close of 1780, about two thousand unpaid Pennsylvania soldiers, some of whom had served overtime, left the army and marched in the direction of Philadelphia. As the group did not include a single officer, a council of sergeants was elected and granted full authority. When General Clinton heard about this, he sent emissaries to bribe the men to desert the American cause. They offered money, clothing, and exemption from military service. Sentinels led the emissaries as spies to the sergeants, who cried: "Does Clinton think we are traitors?" They then declared, "We have reason to complain about Congress, but if the English troops leave New York, we shall fight them and then return to settle our differences. We shall make Clinton see that America has produced only one Arnold."

The Pennsylvania officers, including General [Anthony] Wayne, had also left camp and kept within sight of the troops. The council of sergeants finally decided to send Clinton's emissaries to the officers to be judged, and the men were hanged.

The president of Pennsylvania went to see the troops, who received him with full military honors. They wanted to deal directly with Congress, but with the help of General Wayne and several other officers, the president persuaded them to state their case to the representative of the executive branch of their state. The matter was finally settled, and the soldiers no longer insisted on impossible demands.

A short time after Arnold's desertion Baron von Steuben was reviewing the Connecticut troops. He asked a handsome young soldier his name, and when the boy replied "Arnold," the baron said: "It is too bad that a man like you has such an infamous name." The soldier replied modestly that he was sorry it was the only one he had. The baron told him he could use the Steuben name if he wished. The boy got leave, went home, changed his name legally, and returned to the army. The baron became fond of him and gave him a new uniform every year as long as the war lasted.

You can scarcely believe how people hated the name Arnold. In a letter to the marquis de Lafayette, General Washington praised his friend for "refusing to correspond with the traitor Arnold." At the death of General [William] Phillips, Arnold assumed command of the British army in Virginia, a post he kept until the arrival of Cornwallis. When an officer of the militia sent a sergeant to discuss peace terms, Arnold asked what would happen if he fell into the hands of the American army. The sergeant replied: "The leg which was wounded in the battle for liberty would be buried with honor; the rest of your body would be hanged."

At the end of February 1781 the Americans and French proceeded against Portsmouth, Virginia. The French left Rhode Island with a squadron and detachment of land troops, and the marquis de Lafayette marched with twelve hundred light infantrymen from West Point to Elkton, where he embarked for Annapolis. Everyone knows about the naval battle in which M. Destouches[29] distinguished himself against superior forces. But when the English squadron entered Chesapeake Bay, the French returned to Newport, the militia was dismissed, and Lafayette's detachment was blockaded at Annapolis by small frigates. For several hours the marquis drove them off by firing several pieces of heavy artillery placed on flatboats, and he then took advantage of a favorable wind to return to Elkton. The enterprise required secrecy; so his troops left camp without supplies, as they expected to be away three or four days at the most. When they returned after an absence of six weeks, the marquis received orders from General Washington to go back to Virginia and defend it with whatever troops he could assemble. Washington had learned the British were planning to strike Virginia, but he had to keep an eye on the New York army with his troops and those of the comte de Rochambeau[30] while General Greene was in South Carolina, some four hundred miles from the threatened area. Lafayette had no food, no money, and no clothing for his troops. In the nearest city, Baltimore, merchants gave him £50,000 to buy material for

[29] Charles-René-Dominique Sochet, chevalier Destouches, as rear admiral commanded the French fleet 1780–81.

[30] Jean Baptiste Donatien de Vimeur, comte de Rochambeau, led the French troops at Yorktown.

shirts. On the evening of his arrival the marquis attended a ball and explained his predicament, whereupon the ladies at once promised to make the shirts and supply bandages for the hospital.

The marquis was chiefly concerned about desertion. During the three previous nights the soldiers, seeing the army move south at the approach of summer, had departed in large numbers. Even the death penalty had not stopped them. The marquis, who understood his men, sent out word that he "was marching against a powerful enemy; he hoped he would not be abandoned during a long, arduous campaign, and he would discharge any soldier who had committed a serious offense." He thereupon dismissed one soldier, who had been condemned to death. Lafayette now undertook a forced march of nearly two hundred miles. He reached the capital, Richmond, a few hours before General Phillips, saved the city, and kept public stores and government papers from falling into enemy hands. The campaign lasted seven months, and although the soldiers had no pay, were barefoot, and left a trail from their bleeding feet, not a single man deserted.

The English had sent their elite troops with their favorite general, Lord Cornwallis,[31] to conquer Virginia. Success seemed so assured that on 9 June Governor Clinton wrote Lord Germain[32] that Lafayette could not escape. On the basis of this message the minister assumed that Virginia was conquered, our forces in Carolina were destroyed, and the victorious army had advanced into Maryland and Pennsylvania. Governor Clinton's hopes were not unfounded, since at the beginning of the campaign we had only three thousand men, two-thirds of whom were militia, and the number never rose above six thousand. With this little army the marquis reconquered almost the entire province before he was reinforced by three thousand French soldiers the marquis de Saint-Simon[33] brought from the islands. Lafayette then camped at Williamsburg, assembled some more detachments of militia, and blockaded Cornwallis on land, while the French fleet blockaded him by sea at Yorktown. There the English general was captured with more than seven thousand troops and nearly a thousand sailors.

---

[31] Charles Cornwallis, later first Marquess Cornwallis, attacked Charleston, fought in the battle of Brandywine, captured Fort Lee, and commanded troops in the south; he capitulated after the battle of Yorktown.

[32] George Sackville Germain, first Viscount Sackville, secretary of state for the colonies 1775–82.

[33] Claude-Henri de Rouvroy, comte de Saint-Simon.

Before the arrival of the French fleet, it was vital for the marquis de Lafayette to give the enemy false information. Morgan, a soldier in the light infantry, agreed to go on condition that if he were caught, the marquis would have the *New Jersey Gazette* publish a statement saying he had deserted for his country. Morgan went over to the enemy camp, gave a false report, joined Colonel [John Graves] Simcoe's legion, and made the observations he had been ordered to make. When the French fleet arrived, Morgan returned with six Englishmen whom he had persuaded to desert and a German he had taken prisoner. The marquis tried to give him a reward or make him a sergeant, but he declined, saying he could serve his country better as a soldier.

The state of affairs in Virginia was such that the commander of the army had to have unusual power. The General Assembly gave the marquis authority to cope with any situation, and his place in the hearts of Americans shows how well he used it. Although not yet twenty-four years old, he was prudent throughout the long, difficult enterprise.

This work does not include a history of his activities, and I should not even attempt to chronicle them. Here I am merely describing American patriotism. The esteem, affection, and veneration of an entire nation can only be won by a man of most unusual attributes. The marquis's prudence, a virtue which made him the object of admiration throughout America, was well known before this time. There was no military enterprise which General Washington would not have entrusted to him, nor any political decision which Congress and the legislative power of each state would not have turned over to him without hesitation. The legislative body of Massachusetts had given striking proof of its opinion of the young warrior a year before he undertook the Virginia campaign. On his return from a trip to Europe, which he had undertaken to get money, men, and ships to help the Americans, he informed General Washington that the chevalier de Ternay's [34] squadron, with troops under command of the comte de Rochambeau, would leave France shortly. General Washington then sent him to Congress, which recommended to the legislatures of the respective states that they do everything they could to prepare for the next campaign. As one article recommended by Congress was encountering some stiff opposition in the Massachusetts assembly, Mr. Samuel Adams got up and read part of a letter he had received

[34] Charles Louis d'Arsac, chevalier de Ternay.

from the marquis advocating the same action. The proposal was immediately adopted by a large majority.

When Lafayette left Philadelphia to undertake the Virginia command, he received permission to open any letters addressed to Congress, and the delegates of the southern states told him he might read dispatches from their respective states. Because personal letters might contain useful information, these delegates, like the representatives of the other states who were then in Philadelphia, also authorized him to open their letters. The first use to which the marquis put the power which had just been granted him by the General Assembly was to take horses and carriages wherever he could find them. He began with the home of General Washington and the homes of the other wealthiest citizens. He often granted an audience to farmers who came to complain because their carriages and horses had been kept much longer than the time stipulated. Several men told him that the horses they had lent for a few weeks had not been returned in a year or two and that their crops were suffering. The marquis assured them their complaints were just. He then told them he would be in a sorry plight if the equipment were taken away, but he ended by offering to return it. Each man went home happily leaving behind what he had come to claim.

Doctor Ramsay, in his excellent history of the war in Carolina, speaks briefly of what occurred in Virginia in 1781.[35] He notes that the marquis, who had been obliged to wait for the Pennsylvania troops on the Rapidan, a branch of the Rappahannock River, made up the lost time by a forced march. The enemy was waiting for him at an important post, but he stole a march on them by this unexpected maneuver and camped on Mechunk Creek between the enemy and the large warehouse for all the southern states, where he had ordered a corps of riflemen to rendezvous. These worthy mountaineers left their harvests to join the army, and for at least six consecutive weeks the detachment of militia took part in the campaign despite the fact that they were far from their families, they were abandoning their crops, and it was difficult to get food. At this point, Colonel Richard Meade, of whom I have already spoken, arrived in the uniform of a militiaman. He had been aide-de-camp to General Washington for several years, and he did not leave the army as long as conditions were critical.

---

[35] David Ramsay, *The History of the Revolution of South Carolina, from a British Province to an Independent State*, 2 vols. (Trenton, 1785).

One detachment of militiamen had been kept long overtime because new soldiers failed to arrive. They complained more bitterly every day, and the marquis admitted that their grievance was just. He told them he realized they were being subjected to serious inconvenience, especially by this protracted delay which they had been unable to anticipate before leaving home, and which he was unable to explain. He apologized for asking them to stay overtime, said that he could not ask them to remain any longer, and gave them all permission to leave. He added that he could not abandon his post; so he would remain with the small number of regular troops under his command. The marquis understood these men as if he had been born and reared among them. After this talk he would have had trouble making a single man leave without a written order. They said to each other, "What wretch could even think of abandoning the marquis?"

M. de Sacy (12:366), after telling about the capture of Cornwallis, adds: "This was the end of that memorable campaign which decided the fate of North America, upset the plans and hopes of the British government, covered with glory all the generals who took part in the enterprise, especially the man who planned it. His slow, arduous operations, weariness, triumphs, and wise planning were not appreciated by the populace." [36]

M. de Sacy is correct in everything except the last point. His error, a common one, is due to the fact that he judges Americans without knowing them. If he went to the United States, he would hear the least educated citizens pay tribute to the extreme bravery of our young commander and to his extraordinary prudence, which is rarely found in more experienced men.*

No one speaks of patriotism in America; the memory of some acts is already erased by the death of those who witnessed them,

---

* The following resolution was adopted by Congress 9 September 1778: "Resolved: The president is charged with writing to the Marquis de Lafayette; that congress conceives that the sacrifice he made of his personal feelings, when, for the interest of the United States, he repaired to Boston, at the moment when the opportunity of acquiring glory on the field of battle could present itself; his military zeal in returning to Rhode Island, when the greatest part of the army had quitted it, and his measures to secure a retreat, have a right to this present expression of the approbation of congress" [Marie Joseph Paul Yves Roch Gilbert du Motier, marquis de Lafayette, *Memoirs, Correspondence, and Manuscripts*, 2 vols. (Brussels, 1837–39), 1:220].

[36] Claude-Louis Michel de Sacy, *L'Honneur français, ou Histoire des vertus et des exploits de notre nation depuis l'establissement de la monarchie jusqu'à nos jours*, 12 vols. (Paris, 1779–84).

and others are forgotten. My fellow citizens should record these glorious deeds for our revolutionary historians. I may be criticized for not giving more spectacular examples, but I have told only what I saw or learned from trustworthy sources. Furthermore, I have not been able to do any research in America since I began my book.

I shall close with one more story to illustrate what example can do, even at a very tender age. When General Washington was quartered in Philadelphia during the winter of 1782, a fine-looking seven-year-old wearing the South Carolina uniform appeared early one morning and asked the sentries if he might speak to the general. He was sent to the aides-de-camp, who inquired who he was and what he wanted. "My name is Ezechiel . . . ," he replied (Colonel Humphreys has forgotten the surname). "My father was a gunner in Colonel Robert's regiment; [37] he died during the attack on Stono; my mother worked in the hospital, and she died at Gasden's Wharf. I want General Washington to supply me with rations until I am big enough to fight the English and avenge my father." At that moment the officers were summoned to lunch. They presented the boy to General and Mrs. Washington, who had him lunch with them. After caressing the lad, they gave him some money. He looked at it with indifference, then stuck it in his pocket, saying: "I shall give it to the head of the hospital, who is now my mother, for my rations." The general checked Ezechiel's story, found it completely accurate, and instructed the secretary of state in charge of the War Department to provide for the child and educate him.

Some time after finishing these anecdotes, I received the following from Brittany, written by the chevalier de Mauduit Duplessis.[38] As I felt that I ought not to make any changes whatsoever, I should inform the reader that he might have said a great deal more about Captain [Oliver] Clark's part in the Red Bank action. He probably did not do this to avoid praising himself. Count von Donop,[39] who

[37] 182. Owen Roberts of South Carolina was made colonel of the Fourth Regiment of Artillery in 1775; he was killed at Stono Ferry.

[38] General Washington recommended to Congress 19 Jan. 1778 that Thomas-Antoine, chevalier de Mauduit Duplessis, be promoted to lieutenant colonel because of his gallantry at Red Bank (Francis B. Heitman, *Historical Register of Officers of the Continental Army during the War of the Revolution* [Washington, D.C., 1903], p. 444).

[39] Colonel Carl Emil Curt von Donop was a Hessian mercenary who led his troops against the Americans in the battle at Red Bank.

lived three days after this battle, told him he had led 1,200 grenadiers and 1,260 light troops, all elite soldiers. The Americans numbered 352, twelve of whom were incapable of fighting, and 90 matrosses.

(Now the chevalier de Mauduit Duplessis is speaking.)

During the battle of Monmouth many men died from excessive heat, especially among the enemy. I crossed a little creek and found myself on their left flank with eight pieces of cannon. Several of my soldiers fell during this forced march. Someone shouted to a young gunner who was putting his shoulder to the wheel: "Your brother fell, your brother is dying, your brother is dead." The man replied, "I shall spend the rest of my life mourning my brother, but I cannot go to him now; we are attacking." A few minutes later we caught up with the enemy. The young man performed incredible feats during the whole battle, but when it was ended, he became strangely still, and four days later he died.

During the battle at Red Bank a Rhode Island captain was stationed with his company at the most dangerous point. This man was a god, inspiring his men. Suddenly a bullet struck his throat. I ran to him and said in English: "Dear Captain Clark, give me your hand. I am going to get help." He replied: "Good François, I am beyond help, but get ammunition for my poor children, ammunition for them, ammunition . . . ," and he died, repeating "ammunition" for the fourth or fifth time. I looked at the pouches of his soldiers, found that they had only one or two bullets, and had some distributed at once. We may well owe our safety to the heroism of this brave man.

During the retreat at Brandywine an American soldier was struck by a bullet. I went to him, and the man said: "Leave me sir, I am only a plain soldier, but save our general, our leaders, our cannon." The enemy was gaining on us so rapidly I was forced to abandon him.

I was going to visit a battery I had set up above Billingsport across from the enemy. To my astonishment, I found a dozen gunners repairing a breastwork under heavy fire. I ordered them to come down, but at that very minute a chain shot hit one, blowing off both of his hips. This unfortunate fellow fell, almost lifeless, on the platform. A young man rushed up in sorrow, despair, and anger, crying: "My father died to save me! Oh mother, what will become of you?" The father regained consciousness, clasped his son's hand, and said: "My son, I have done my duty, now you do yours. I ordered you to let me take your place because your career is beginning; mine is coming to an end. Take my place, my son, beside your mother and my other children, but, above all, defend your country's liberty."

## Note E (see page 136)

The reader will recall that the Declaration of Rights states that the three powers, legislative, executive, and judicial, must be separate and distinct.

During the spring of 1784, while the General Assembly of Virginia was in session, an impudent man spoke in a very insulting way about the House of Delegates. The house then assumed a power it did not have (like the House of Commons in England); it sent an officer to arrest the man and ordered him to post bail. The behavior of this man, an English lawyer, had angered every good citizen, but now even those who disliked him most took up his defense, and everyone criticized the unwarranted action of the house. The members finally admitted they had made a mistake, and the order was rescinded.

During these debates resentment against the lawyer was forgotten, but as soon as he was set free, people treated him with even more contempt than before. He was, for example, forced to leave a dinner because one lady declared she would not dine with such a man. If governments knew how to make use of public opinion, which is always more powerful than laws, men would risk fewer injustices and criminals would never go unpunished.

## Note F (see page 152)

Originally the law was held, that no man should be admitted to the privilege of clergy, but such as had the *habitum et tonsuram clericalem.* But in process of time a much wider and more comprehensive criterion was established: everyone that could read (a mark of great learning in those days of ignorance and her sister superstition) being accounted a clerk or *clericus,* and allowed the benefit of clerkship, though neither initiated in holy orders, nor trimmed with the clerical tonsure. But when learning, by means of the invention of printing, and other concurrent causes, began to be more generally disseminated than formerly; and reading was no longer a competent proof of clerkship, or being in holy orders; it was found that as many laymen as divines were admitted to the *privilegium clericale:* And, therefore, by statute 4 Hen. VII. c. 13, a distinction was once more drawn between mere lay scholars, and clerks that were really in orders. And, though it was thought reasonable still to mitigate the severity of the law with regard to the former, yet they were not put upon the same footing with actual clergy; being subjected to a slight degree of punishment, and not allowed to claim the clerical privilege more than once. Accordingly the statute directs, that no person, once admitted to the benefit of clergy, shall be admitted thereto a second time, unless he produces his orders: And, in order to distinguish their persons, all laymen who are allowed this privilege shall be burnt with a hot iron in the brawn of the left thumb. This distinction between learned laymen, and real clerks in orders, was abolished for a time by the statutes 28 Hen. VIII. c. 1, and 32 Hen. VIII. c. 3. but is held to have been virtually restored by statute 1 Edw. VI. c. 12 which statute also enacts that lords of parliament and peers of the realm, having place and voice in parliament, may have the benefit of their peerage, equivalent to that of clergy, for the first offence, (although they cannot read, and without being burnt in the hand) for all offences then clergyable to commoners, and also for the crimes of housebreaking, highway robbery, horsestealing and robbing of churches.

In the twenty-first year of James I's reign women began to share the privilege, but not to the same extent as men who could read. In the fourth year of William and Mary's reign they were given equal rights, and in 1707, the fifth year of Queen Anne's reign, the same privilege was extended to men who were illiterate. It was finally recognized that ignorance should explain and excuse crime rather than aggravate it.

In general, the clergy of the dominant religion continue to enjoy this privilege to the fullest extent; next come the peers of the kingdom, and all others, men and women alike, enjoy it equally.[40]

## Note G (see page 161)

### To the General Assembly of the Republic of Virginia
### A Memorial and Remonstrance

We the subscribers, citizens of the said Commonwealth, having taken into serious consideration, a bill printed by order of the last session of the General Assembly, entitled, "A Bill establishing a Provision for Teachers of the Christian Religion," and conceiving that the same, if finally armed with the sanctions of a law, will be a dangerous abuse of power, are bound as faithful members of a free state, to remonstrate against it, and to declare the reasons by which we are determined. We remonstrate against the said bill,

BECAUSE, We hold it for a fundamental and undeniable truth, "That religion, or the duty which we owe to our Creator, and the manner of discharging it, can be directed only by reason and conviction, not by

[40] Blackstone, *Commentaries* 4 (Worcester, Mass., 1790): 366.

force or violence." * The religion then of every man must be left to the conviction and conscience of every man; and it is the right of every man to exercise it as these may dictate. This right is in its nature an unalienable right. It is unalienable; because the opinions of men, depending only on the evidence contemplated by their own minds, cannot follow the dictates of other men: It is unalienable also; because what is here a right towards men, is a duty towards the Creator. It is the duty of every man to render to the Creator such homage, and such only, as he believes to be acceptable to him; this duty is precedent, both in order of time, and in degree of obligation, to the claims of civil society. Before any man can be considered as a member of civil society, he must be considered as a subject of the Governour of the Universe: And if a member of civil society, who enters into any subordinate association, must always do it with a reservation of his duty to the general authority, much more must every man who becomes a member of any particular civil society, do it with a saving of his allegiance to the Universal Sovereign. We maintain, therefore, that in matters of religion, no man's right is abridged by the institution of civil society; and that religion is wholly exempt from its cognizance. True it is, that no other rule exists, by which any question which may divide a society, can be ultimately determined, but the will of the majority; but it is also true, that the majority may trespass on the rights of the minority.

Because, If religion be exempt from the authority of the society at large, still less can it be subject to that of the legislative body. The latter are but the creatures and vicegerents of the former. Their jurisdiction is both derivative and limited. It is limited with regard to the co-ordinate departments; more necessarily is it limited with regard to the constituents. The preservation of a free government requires, not merely that the metes and bounds which separate each department of power be invariably maintained, but more especially, that neither of them be suffered to overleap the great barrier which defends the rights of the people. The rulers who are guilty of such an encroachment, exceed the commission from which they derive their authority, and are tyrants. The people who submit to it are governed by laws made neither by themselves, nor by an authority derived from them, and are slaves.

Because, It is proper to take alarm at the first experiment on our liberties. We hold this prudent jealously to be the first duty of citizens, and one of the noblest characteristicks of the late revolution. The freemen of America did not wait until usurped power had strengthened itself by exercise, and entangled the question in precedents. They saw all the consequences in the principle, and they avoided the consequences by denying the principle. We revere this lesson too much soon to

* Declaration of Rights, Article XVI.

forget it. Who does not see that the same authority which can establish Christianity, in exclusion of all other religions, may establish, with the same ease, any particular sect of Christians, in exclusion of all other sects? That the same authority which can force a citizen to contribute three-pence only of his property for the support of any one establishment, may force him to conform to any other establishment, in all cases whatsoever.

Because, The bill violates that equality which ought to be the basis of every law; and which is more indispensible, in proportion as the validity or expendience of any law is more liable to be impeached. If "all men are by nature equally free and independent," * all men are to be considered as entering into society on equal conditions, as relinquishing no more, and therefore retaining no less, one than another, of their rights. Above all are they to be considered as retaining an "*equal* title to the free exercise of religion, according to the dictates of conscience." † Whilst we assert for ourselves a freedom to embrace, to profess, and to observe the religion which we believe to be of divine origin, we cannot deny an equal freedom to those whose minds have not yet yielded to the evidence which has convinced us. If this freedom be abused, it is an offence against God, not against man: To God therefore, not to men, must an account of it be rendered. As the bill violates equality by subjecting some to peculiar burdens, so it violates the same principle, by granting to others peculiar exemptions. Are the Quakers and Menonists the only sects who think a compulsive support of their religions unnecessary and unwarrantable? Can their piety alone be intrusted with the care of publick worship? Ought their religions to be endowed, above all others, with extraordinary privileges, by which proselytes may be enticed from all others? We think too favourably of the justice and good sense of these denominations, to believe, that they either covet pre-eminences over their fellow-citizens, or that they will be seduced by them, from the common opposition to the measure.

Because, The bill implies, either that the civil magistrate is a competent judge of religious truth; or that he may employ religion as an engine of civil policy. The first is an arrogant pretension, falsified by the contradictory opinion of rulers in all ages, and throughout the world: The second an unhallowed perversion of the means of salvation.

Because, The establishment proposed by the bill is not requisite for the support of the Christian religion. To say that it is, is a contradiction to the Christian religion itself; for every page of it disavows a dependence on the powers of this world: It is a contradiction to fact; for it is known that this religion both existed and flourished, not only without the support of human laws, but in spite of every opposition from them; and not only during the period of miraculous aid, but long

* Declaration of Rights, Article I.
† Article XVI.

after it had been left to its own evidence, and the ordinary care of Providence: Nay, it is a contradiction in terms; for a religion not invented by human policy must have pre-existed and been supported, before it was established by human policy. It is moreover to weaken in those who profess this religion, a pious confidence in its innate excellence, and the patronage of its author; and to foster in those who still reject it, a suspicion, that its friends are too conscious of its fallacies, to trust it to its own merits.

Because, Experience witnesseth, that ecclesiastical establishments, instead of maintaining the purity and efficacy of religion, have had a contrary operation. During almost fifteen centuries, has the legal establishment of Christianity been on trial. What have been its faults? More or less in all places, pride and indolence in the clergy; ignorance and servility in the laity; in both, superstition, bigotry, and persecution. Inquire of the teachers of Christianity for the ages in which it appeared in its greatest lustre; those of every sect point to the ages prior to its incorporation with civil policy. Propose a restoration of this primitive state, in which its teachers depended on the voluntary rewards of their flocks; many of them predict its downfall. On which side ought their testimony to have greatest weight, when for, or when against their interest?

Because, The establishment in question is not necessary for the support of civil government. If it be urged as necessary for the support of civil government, only as it is a means of supporting religion; and it be not necessary for the latter purpose, it cannot be necessary for the former. If religion be not within the cognizance of civil government, how can its legal establishment be said to be necessary to civil government? What influence, in fact have ecclesiastical establishments had on civil society? In some instances they have been seen to erect a spiritual tyranny on the ruins of the civil authority; in many instances they have been seen upholding the thrones of political tyranny; in no instance have they been seen the guardians of the liberties of the people. Rulers who wished to subvert the publick liberty, may have found an established clergy, convenient auxiliaries. A just government, instituted to secure and perpetuate it, needs them not. Such a government will be best supported by protecting every citizen in the enjoyment of his religion, with the same equal hand, which protects his person, and his property; by neither invading the equal rights of any sect; nor suffering any sect to invade those of another.

Because, The proposed establishment is a departure from that generous policy; which, offering an asylum to the persecuted and oppressed of every nation and religion, promised a lustre to our country, and an accession to the number of its citizens. What a melancholy mark is the Bill of sudden degeneracy. Instead of holding forth an asylum to the persecuted, it is itself, a signal of persecution. It degrades from the equal rank of citizens all those whose opinions in religion do not bend to those of the Legislative Authority. Distant as it may be, in its present form, from the Inquisition, it differs from it only in degree. The one is the first step, the other the last, in the career of intolerance. The magnanimous sufferer under this cruel scourge in foreign regions, must view the Bill as a beacon on our coast, warning him to seek some other haven, where liberty and philanthrophy, in their due extent, may offer a more certain repose from his troubles.

Because, It will have a like tendency to banish our citizens. The allurements presented by other situations are every day thinning their number. To superadd a fresh motive to emigration, by revoking the liberty which they now enjoy, would be the same species of folly, which has dishonoured and depopulated flourishing kingdoms.

Because, It will destroy that moderation and harmony which the forbearance of our laws to intermeddle with religion, has produced among its several sects. Torrents of blood have been spilt in the old world, by vain attempts of the secular arm to extinguish religious discord, by proscribing all differences in religious opinion. Time has at length revealed the true remedy. Every relaxation of narrow and rigorous policy, wherever it has been tried, has been found to assuage the disease. The American theatre has exhibited proofs, that equal and complete liberty, if it does not wholly eradicate it, sufficiently destroys its malignant influence on the health and prosperity of the State. If, with the salutary effects of this system under our own eyes, we begin to contract the bounds of religious freedom, we know no name that will too severely reproach our folly. At least let warning be taken at the first fruits of the threatened innovation. The very appearance of the Bill has transformed "that Christian forbearance, love and charity," which of late mutually prevailed, into animosities and jealousies, which may not soon be appealed. What mischiefs may not be dreaded, should this enemy to the publick quiet, be armed with the force of law?

Because, The policy of the Bill is adverse to the diffusion of the light of Christianity. The first wish of those who enjoy this precious gift, ought to be that it may be imparted to the whole race of mankind. Compare the number of those who have as yet received it, with the number still remaining under the dominion of false religions; and how small is the former? Does the policy of the Bill tend to lessen the disproportion? No: It at once discourages those, who are strangers to the light of revelation from coming into the region of it; and countenances, by example, the nations who continue in darkness, in shutting out those who might convey it to them. Instead of levelling as far as possible, every obstacle to the victorious progress of truth, the Bill, with an ignoble and unchristian timidity, would circumscribe it, with a wall of defence, against the encroachments of errour.

Because, Attempts to enforce by legal sanctions, acts obnoxious to so great a proportion of citizens, tend to enervate the laws in general, and to slacken the bands of society. If it be difficult to execute any law which is not generally deemed necessary or salutary, what must be the case, where it is deemed invalid and dangerous? And what may be the effect of so striking an example of impotency in the government, on its general authority?

Because, A measure of such singular magnitude and delicacy ought not to be imposed, without the clearest evidence that it is called for by a majority of citizens: And no satisfactory method is yet proposed, by which the voice of the majority in this case may be determined, or its influence secured, "The people of the respective counties are indeed requested to signify their opinion respecting the adoption of the Bill to the next session of Assembly." But the representation must be made equal, before the voice either of the Representatives, or of the counties, will be that of the people. Our hope is that neither of the former will, after due consideration, espouse the dangerous principle of the Bill. Should the event disappoint us, it will still leave us in full confidence that a fair appeal to the latter will reverse the sentence against our liberties.

Because, Finally, "The equal right of every citizen to the free exercise of his religion according to the dictates of conscience," is held by the same tenure with all our other rights. If we recur to its origin, it is equally the gift of nature; if we weigh its importance, it cannot be less dear to us; if we consult the "declaration of those rights which pertain to the good people of Virginia, as the basis and foundation of government," * it is enumerated with equal solemnity, or rather studied emphasis. Either then we must say, that the will of the Legislature is the only measure of their authority, and that in the plenitude of this authority, they may sweep away all our fundamental rights; or that they are bound to leave this particular right untouched and sacred: Either we must say, that they may controul the freedom of the press, may abolish the trial by jury, may swallow up the Executive and Judiciary Powers of the State; nay, that they may despoil us of our very right of suffrage, and erect themselves into an independent and hereditary Assembly; or we must say, that they have no authority to enact into law the Bill under consideration. We the Subscribers say, that the General Assembly of this Commonwealth have no such authority: And that no effort may be omitted on our part against so dangerous an usurpation, we oppose to it this remonstrance; earnestly praying, as we are in duty bound, that the Supreme Lawgiver of the Universe, by illuminating those to whom it is addressed, may on the one hand, turn their councils from every act which would affront his holy prerogative, or violate the trust committed to them: And on the other, guide them into every measure which may be worthy of his blessing, may redound to their own praise, and may establish more

* Preamble to the Declaration of Rights.

firmly the liberties, the prosperity and the happiness of the Common-wealth.[41]

## Note H (see page 168)

William Hayley, Esquire, author of poems and comedies printed in six volumes at T. [Thomas] Cadell's on the Strand in 1785, re-proaches the abbé for having called Mr. Gibbon a "pedantic writer" when he has read none of his works save one extract in translation. Can we be surprised when the abbé himself confesses he has not read Robertson's history of America,[42] which he criti-cizes?

Without posing as a judge of Mr. Gibbon's books, which are fairly well known, I shall merely say that if the abbé had taken the trouble to read the first book Mr. Gibbon wrote in French as a youth, he would have realized this author could never be pedantic in his own language. The blind respect the abbé has for the An-cients seems to have made him dislike the moderns.

## Note I (see page 169)

The united states in congress assembled shall also be the last resort on appeal in all disputes and differences now subsisting or that hereafter may arise between two or more states concerning boundary, juris-diction, or any other cause whatever; which authority shall always be exercised in the manner following. Whenever the legislative or ex-ecutive authority or lawful agent of any state in controversy with another, shall present a petition to congress, stating the matter in question and praying for a hearing, notice thereof shall be given by order of congress to the legislative or executive authority of the other state in controversy, and a day assigned for the appearance of the parties by their lawful agents, who shall then be directed to appoint by joint consent, commissioners or judges to constitute a court for hearing and determining the matter in question; but if they cannot agree, congress shall name three persons out of each of the united states, and from the list of such persons each party shall alternately strike out one, the petitioners beginning, until the number shall be reduced to thirteen; and from that number not less than seven, nor more than nine names as

---

[41] *Memorial and Remonstrance Presented to the General Assembly of the State of Virginia at Their Session in 1785* (rept., Worcester, Mass., 1786).

[42] William Robertson, *History of America* (Dublin, 1777).

congress shall direct, shall in the presence of congress be drawn out by lot; and the persons whose names shall be so drawn, or any five of them, shall be commissioners or judges, to hear and finally determine the controversy, so always as a major part of the judges, who shall hear the cause, shall agree in the determination: and if either party shall neglect to attend at the day appointed, without shewing reasons which congress shall judge sufficient, or being present shall refuse to strike, the congress shall proceed to nominate three persons out of each state, and the secretary of congress shall strike in behalf of such party absent or refusing; and the judgment and sentence of the court to be appointed, in the manner before prescribed, shall be final and conclusive; and if any of the parties shall refuse to submit to the authority of such court, or to appear or defend their claim or cause, the court shall nevertheless proceed to pronounce sentence, or judgment, which shall in like manner be final and decisive, the judgment or sentence and other proceedings being in either case transmitted to congress, and lodged among the acts of congress, for the security of the parties concerned; provided, that every commissioner, before he sits in judgment, shall take an oath, to be administered by one of the judges of the supreme or superior court of the state, where the cause shall be tried, "well and truly to hear and determine the matter in question, according to the best of his judgment, without favour, affection, or hope of reward:" provided also, that no state shall be deprived of territory, for the benefit of the united states.

All controversies concerning the private right of soil claimed under different grants of two or more states, whose jurisdictions as they may respect such lands, and the states which passed such grants are adjusted, the said grants or either of them being at the same time claimed to have originated antecedent to such settlement of jurisdiction, shall on the petition of either party to the congress of the united states, be finally determined, as near as may be, in the same manner as is before prescribed for deciding disputes respecting territorial jurisdiction between different states.[43]

[43] Articles of Confederation and Perpetual Union, between the States of New-Hampshire, Massachusetts-Bay, Rhode-Island and Providence Plantations, Connecticut, New-York, New-Jersey, Pennsylvania, Delaware, Maryland, Virginia, North-Carolina, South-Carolina and Georgia, in the *Constitutions of the Several Independent States of America* (Philadelphia, 1781), pp. 191–99.

# PART III

## Observations on
## the *Philosophical History of the Two Indies*
## Relative to United States of America

The title *History* proclaims a work consecrated to truth. The title *Philosophical History* implies that the author has added cause to remember what he owes to truth. If this writer makes mistakes, they will be all the more dangerous, since he is thought incapable of making any. But if he turns these mistakes into axioms and blinds his readers with his magic style, then you must tear the veil away to show them how far they have strayed from the facts.

These are the reasons which have led me to publish some observations on Abbé Raynal's account of the United States of America.[1] I have selected what seem to be the outstanding details and have organized the material as clearly as possible without restricting myself to places, persons, or things.

[1] See Part I, note 4.

# Chapter 1

# Founding Period of the First Colonies

Abbé Raynal's description of the first settlements in North America cannot give an exact picture because he confuses matters to such an extent that he implies Sir Walter Raleigh's plantations were established at the same time as the New England settlements.* Then, instead of following a chronological order, he begins with the New England colonies and discusses them from north to south.

In describing these colonies he writes (8:445): "Discovered at the beginning of the past century and named North Virginia, they did not receive any Europeans until 1608." Yet speaking of Virginia (9:63), he says: "The English landed on this wild beach in 1606, and their first settlement was at Jamestown."

His discussion of North Carolina omits the Roanoke settlements, and after listing the causes which prevented the Spaniards and French from settling in the Carolinas (9:85), he adds: "Some Englishmen replaced them toward the close of the sixteenth century, as an inexplicable whim made them abandon the young plantation for a less fertile soil in a colder climate." He continues: "Not a single European was in Carolina when Lords Berkeley, Clarendon, Albemarle, Craven, and Ashley and Messrs. Carteret, Berkeley, and Colleton obtained this fine country from Charles II in 1663."

To be convinced that it took "an inexplicable whim" to make them abandon this settlement, it is good to see what the author says of the region (p. 94): "The soil is generally flatter, more sandy, and with more salt marsh than in South Carolina. These sad plains are covered with pines or cedars, indicating an infertile soil; at intervals they are dotted with a few oaks too oily for shipbuilding. The coasts, which are usually obstructed by a sandbank that repels navigators, are no more inviting than the interior. Finally, the area is more exposed than adjoining regions to hurricanes from the southeast." The necessity of leaving such an area seems scarcely an inexplicable whim, especially when he adds: "These characteristics doubtless drove the English from North Carolina, although it was the first beach they glimpsed in the New World."

* In Part I of this book the reader saw the difference between these dates.

The abbé provides no information about the first colonies or about the dates when they were established. Any suppositions based on his remarks would be completely erroneous.

It is difficult to believe he supposed there could be such variation in climate and soil between North Carolina and Virginia, since they border one another. Between Roanoke Island, in Carolina, where Raleigh's men landed, and Jamestown, Virginia, which was settled by the London Company, there is a difference of only one degree eight minutes of latitude, less than a hundred miles. We also saw that all the immigrants left on Roanoke Island perished, except those whom Sir Francis Drake took back to England, while those who landed at Jamestown stayed there. Hence we do not know what Englishmen left Carolina or where they went.

# Chapter 2

# New England

Abbé Raynal writes (8:445): "The English Presbyterians, who had fled persecution in Holland, decided to found a church in another hemisphere. In 1621 they purchased the rights of the English company in North Virginia, as they were not poor enough to await prosperity as a reward for their patience and virtue."

Robinson's companions, who sailed from Holland to Southampton and from Southampton to America, were Independents, not Presbyterians. Hence the Independents have always claimed the honor of being the first to bring the Gospel to this part of the world. The Independents were schismatic Brownists, as Brownists were schismatic Puritans. It has already been noted that these brave adventurers revived the hope of establishing a colony in these northern regions, but it seems unlikely that they were capable of purchasing the company's rights. Neal (1:85) says they spent about £700 sterling in Southampton for food and other necessities and about £1,700 for merchandise.[2] Their greatest asset appears to have been their firm resolution to withstand any kind of hardship.

We have seen that the first Plymouth Company gradually dwindled away and that the charter for the second was dated 3 November 1620. By this time the settlers were already on the American coast, for they landed at Cape Cod on the eleventh of that month. We also saw it was the London Company, not the Plymouth, which granted them a tract of land, and that they knew before sailing that the territory described in the act of donation was not under the jurisdiction of this company. It is useless to repeat all the details; the important thing is that the company's charter was brought to America by the men who founded the colony of Massachusetts nine years later.

Abbé Raynal continues ([8:]448): "The inhabitants of New England lived peacefully for a short time without bothering to choose a form of government, although this was duly authorized in their charter, and London was not sufficiently interested to urge

[2] Daniel Neal, *The History of New-England*, 2 vols. (London, 1747).

them to assure their tranquillity. Not until 1630 did they feel the necessity of adopting a form of government for the colony."

This passage cannot refer either to the people who really had the charter or to the little colony at Plymouth. The founders of this colony, who came from Holland, never received a charter for the territory they occupied. One can scarcely accuse them of not bothering about their form of government, since they prepared an act on shipboard and ratified it before landing.

The majority of the colonists who brought the charter to America with the privilege of establishing a government (which they obtained from the Plymouth Council in 1629) did not arrive before 1630. So it is not astonishing that the settlers did not think of making use of their prerogative until that time.

On the previous page the abbé states that at the beginning of 1629 "there were only three hundred settlers." A few lines later we read: "The only immigrants to America were a few clergymen, who had been deprived of their living for their opinions, and some humble sectarians attracted by the new dogmas." If the immigrants prior to 1629 had been limited to these two groups (which they were not), could one blame them for not thinking of establishing a government? Moreover, how can the abbé reconcile this statement with what he says two pages earlier: "In 1621 they purchased the rights of the English company in North Virginia, as they were not poor enough to await prosperity as a reward for their patience and virtue"? We could also ask him why he says that the capital was "not sufficiently interested to urge them to assure their tranquillity." He had read their charter, for he speaks of it several times; was it possible he did not know that England had no right to intervene?

The following statement does not show any more scrupulous attention to exactitude. "The following year (1630) so many immigrants arrived that it was found necessary to make them disperse." Does this sound like men who leave the amenities of civilization and endure countless privations to enjoy liberty?

After blaming the inhabitants of New England for waiting until 1630 to establish a government, and saying (p. 449) that they had agreed "to have a yearly meeting of deputies appointed by the people," * the author tells us that "two remarkable laws were passed at the same time. The first set the price of wheat, and the

---

* No form of government was established until 1634 because the immigrants were not sufficiently numerous at first and had to get settled.

second decreed that the savages were to be deprived of whatever land they did not cultivate." If such laws had been enacted, which they were not, they would be remarkable only for their absurdity.

The second law, moreover, would have been the signal for a declaration of war that would have destroyed all the Indians. They do not want to be farmers; their land is fallow, and they would rather die than leave the forests. As they live chiefly by hunting, they need a very large territory, and a nation consisting of a thousand families may occupy more space than the largest province in France. To the Indian, farming is a shameful occupation. The women sow very small quantities of Indian corn, beans, pumpkins, winter squash, and long potatoes,[3] all of which are native plants; if a young man wants to help his sweetheart or his wife, he is treated with scorn by the men and the women laugh at him.

All well-known writers say the colonial governments tried to maintain a peaceful relationship with the natives. Furthermore, it would have been impossible for a handful of men to deprive so many nations of their immense territory, and several million laborers would have been needed to farm it. Hutchinson, who examined the archives and read as many manuscripts of this period as he could obtain, shows clearly that there is no shadow of truth in this strange law. After exposing the European system of seizing lands, he adds (2:266): "The first settlers of the Massachusetts and Plimouth were not content with this, but made conscience of paying the natives to their satisfaction for all parts of the territory which were not depopulated or deserted and left without a claimer."

I refuted Abbé Mably's statement that our ancestors were extremely tolerant, but Abbé Raynal goes too far in the other direction. He exaggerates the laws about religion and customs in New England and describes some that never existed, as when ([8:]461) he writes about the immolation of ten-year-old children. Superstition brought men to erect scaffolds, where innocent citizens were tortured for pretended witchcraft. This is sad enough, but the author of the *Philosophical History* implies that no part of the world ever witnessed worse atrocities.

Although Hutchinson was partial * to England, he says (2:15 [–16]): "The great noise which the New England witchcraft made throughout the English dominions proceeded more from the gen-

* He was governor of Massachusetts at the beginning of the Revolution and died in London in 1780 [1786].
[3] Long potatoes: a form of radish.

eral panick with which all sorts of persons were seized, and an expectation that the contagion would spread to all parts of the country, than from the number of persons who were executed, more having been put to death in a single county in England, in a short space of time, than have suffered in all New England from the first settlement until the present time." He continues (p. 23): "From 1694 to 1701, there were eleven persons tried for witches before Lord Chief Justice Holt, all of whom were acquitted. In Scotland seven were executed for witches in 1697, upon the testimony of one girl about eleven years old."

On page 457 Abbé Raynal is apparently trying to paint the inhabitants of Massachusetts as villains. "The Quakers were imprisoned, whipped, and banished (for having behaved in an edifying manner). The proud simplicity of these new enthusiasts, who blessed heaven and mankind in the midst of their torment, inspired veneration and multiplied the number of their converts. This success angered their persecutors and inspired them to wreak bloody deeds of vengeance."

Douglass (1:447) states that in 1656, 1657, and 1659 the Quakers committed such excesses in the Massachusetts colony that laws were passed against them. Although Abbé Raynal describes their conduct as gentle and peaceable, Douglass says they shrieked like madmen during the assemblies, insulted judges on the bench, interrupted church services, and sneered at the ministers. They seemed to have inherited a good part of the fury of the Anabaptists from whom their sect sprang. The magistrates ordered them to leave and told them not to return under pain of death. They came back, nevertheless, and behaved even worse than before. Several went so far as to run nude into churches to threaten the congregations with hellfire.

Several Quakers were hanged and the law is to blame, for they should have been put in an insane asylum and restored to sanity by bloodletting and a rigorous diet. But Abbé Raynal is equally at fault for giving us such false information about both the Quakers and the New England colonial governments. He not only ignores the contraventions of the Quakers; he says of the magistrates: "They had five of these unfortunates hanged when they slipped back furtively from exile." Does this not imply that they were arrested in some quiet spot where they were hiding? Especially as he adds (9:13): "They were devout men whose crime and madness consisted in excessive reason and virtue."

We should also observe that they were not persecuted everywhere in New England. Hutchinson quotes (1:526) a letter written 13 October 1657 by the Rhode Island colonial government to the Massachusetts General Court. It censures the conduct of the Quakers but states that it does not want to exile them. The letter concludes by saying the matter will be submitted to the General Assembly in March. Quakers were never persecuted in Rhode Island. They went to Massachusetts to get converts, for had they wanted peace, they would have remained in Rhode Island.

Abbé Raynal implies ([8:]450) that witchcraft, blasphemy, adultery, and false witness were all capital crimes, punishable by death. False witness was a capital crime if it led to the conviction of an innocent person; similarly, adultery, witchcraft, and blasphemy were capital crimes in certain cases. "Children," he continues, "perverted to the extent of striking or cursing their parents, received the same punishment." No crime was judged capital unless the children were over sixteen, they had not been provoked, and their education had not been neglected.

It is undeniable that laws were more severe than they should have been, although, on the whole, they were less stringent than in England, but Abbé Raynal never gives any precise information and what he says is always grossly exaggerated.

Instead of speaking scornfully about the law dealing with false witness, the abbé might well have praised the men who enacted it. As legislators in England did not foresee all the consequences, false witness was never considered a capital crime. Less than thirty years ago five miscreants were convicted of causing the death of some innocent people because they had borne false witness, but they could not be condemned to death. The citizens of London took the matter in their own hands, and during the two days when the men were in the pillory, they threw such a prodigious quantity of filth at them that one man died each day.* This led to the enactment of a law during the next session of Parliament which makes false witness a capital crime whenever it leads to the death of an innocent person. Abbé Raynal should have been grateful to the New England legislators for foreseeing more than a century before the British the dire consequences of bearing false witness.

He calls (pp. 465–66) our predecessors "monsters" because the colonial governments offered a reward to anyone who killed an Indian; he adds that in 1724 this sum was raised to £2,250 per

* They were to be attached to the pillory five times, but after the second day, the government changed the sentence because it did not want to accustom the people to meting out justice. The other three were given life imprisonment.

scalp. One several occasions some of our frontier ancestors, who had become as savage as the Indians, behaved so badly that wars resulted. In general the governments treated the Indians with justice and consideration. If they could have punished the guilty, who had escaped into the wilderness, many skirmishes would have been avoided.* The French, who lived to the north of our colonies, tried to attract as many Indians as they could; our ancestors did the same, and this was another source of trouble.

When an Indian faces his enemy he is astonishingly brave, but he believes trickery to be a warrior's chief asset. If the abbé had studied the history of this period, he would have seen that governments offered rewards only to avoid even more serious difficulties. The abbé speaks of these rewards as if they were commonplace, which was not the case. Furthermore, he has not taken into consideration that a reward of £2,250 for each Indian scalp would soon have exhausted a treasury far larger than that of our ancestors.

Had he not known about fluctuations in value of paper money, we might assume he was taking these pounds for pounds sterling. But it is evident that he understood their value, for he says (9:211) that by using cash Massachusetts "got a sum twelve times the amount in paper."

In accordance with the initial agreements, he claims ([8:]476 [-79]), New England was to restrict its commercial dealings to the mother country, serious crimes were to be judged there, and the colonies submitted only to the extent of recognizing the English king as their sovereign. All of this is false, but he is correct in stating that the Massachusetts charter granted the colony more privileges than the others and that it was annulled for this reason. Charles II undertook this act of despotism in 1684 and it was completed by James II two years later.

Before saying (quite wrongly) that the colonists were subject to English courts for serious crimes and deprived of freedom of commerce, the abbé had remarked that "they were almost independent."

He pretends (pp. 474 ff.) there is a dearth of building materials for shipping in New England, that the soil is poor and the fishing fabulous. He mentions a prodigious amount of sturgeon, which no one recalls ever finding north of New Jersey, although it is abundant in Delaware and Virginia rivers.

I shall close with an account of the Polly Baker story, which the

---

* In 1636 three Englishmen were hanged in New Plymouth for killing an Indian near Providence.

abbé (p. 466) claims to be true. "Laws are still too severe in these areas. Their rigor can be gauged from the speech a girl made recently to the magistrates when she was convicted for bearing her fifth illegitimate child." Polly Baker's speech produced, he said, "an astonishing revolution in New England. The court did not punish her, she was not even fined, and as a final triumph, she married one of her judges."

One day at the close of 1777 or early in 1778 the abbé called on Dr. Franklin and found Mr. Deane [4] with him. "We were speaking of your book," said Mr. Deane, "and saying you were poorly informed about America, especially about New England." As the abbé wished to argue the point, Mr. Deane quoted several passages in which there was not a word of truth. They then discussed the Polly Baker anecdote and here the debate grew more serious, because the abbé insisted he had found the story in an authentic report. After some time Dr. Franklin spoke: "Sir, I am going to give you the facts. When I was young at times I lacked material to fill the pages of my gazette, so I amused myself by writing stories and the yarn about Polly Baker is one of them." "Well," replied the abbé, "I prefer to have your stories in my book than truth from many other people."

I shall let the reader decide to what extent a historian should copy gazettes. This yarn should have been deleted in the last edition, or the author might have inserted a note explaining that it was an ingenious satire composed by Dr. Franklin, who was trying to be useful and to amuse his compatriots. As the abbé is forever telling us that he worships truth, and that nothing can prevent him from telling it, he could have informed his readers that the rigors which existed at the time of the first edition of his book had finally been forced by the Revolution to give way to a sensible indulgence.

[4] Silas Deane was sent to Paris by the Continental Congress in 1776.

# Chapter 3

# New Jersey

The six pages devoted to New Jersey show that the author knows nothing about it.

"Fields ([8:]508) are covered with flocks and planted with grain. Hemp thrives better than in any adjoining region. A mine of excellent copper has been opened. The coasts are accessible, and the capital, Perth Amboy, has a fairly good harbor. New Jersey lacks nothing to make it prosperous; yet the colony has always been very obscure. The name was almost unknown in the Old World and is scarcely more familiar in the New. However, I do not consider this a cause for unhappiness."

The facts are quite different: Navigators avoid the New Jersey coast because it is dangerous. There is not a single port capable of receiving a medium-sized vessel, and the general feeling is that human industry will never be able to construct one. Egg Harbor, the only port on the long coast, is suitable only for very small craft, but access is dangerous and difficult even for them. The Perth Amboy harbor, on the Raritan River, the best one in the state, has no more than eight or nine feet of water at high tide. Hemp grows in New Jersey but not so well as in Pennsylvania, Maryland, and Virginia. There is plenty of grain and you see herds of cattle, but neighboring states have them too. Copper mines are not unusual in this part of America; those in New York are much larger, but the abbé fails to mention them.

After expressing his opinion about the brilliance and obscurity of various peoples, he makes an unexpected transition: "Whatever may be the causes of the obscurity of New Jersey, we owe it our advice both on its present and its future state." You can see (p. 511) how he pays this unnecessary debt. The abbé could scarcely have found a worse style, for dogmatism among either philosophers or historians is not fashionable in America. True philosophers are modest and afraid of making mistakes. Anyone who pontificates is regarded as a complete ignoramus.

As for the author's proposition that direct commerce is more profitable than indirect, probably every workman in the state is aware of this, and if he needed advice, he would consult well-informed men in his hometown or professors at Princeton rather than a writer who lives more than twenty-five hundred miles away and obviously does not know what he is talking about.

# Chapter 4

# Pennsylvania

"Pennsylvania," says Abbé Raynal (9:21), "is bordered on the east by the ocean, on the north by New York and New Jersey, on the south by Virginia and Maryland, and on the west by lands occupied by Indians. On all sides it is surrounded by friends, and within its borders it is protected by its virtuous inhabitants. The coasts, which are very narrow, broaden gradually to a width of 120 miles." Between the Atlantic Ocean and Pennsylvania you find most of New Jersey and the tip of one of the angles of New York. New Jersey borders almost the whole eastern side of Pennsylvania, a little of the south, but none of the north. At its closest point, Pennsylvania is nearly a hundred miles from the sea. It is impossible to guess what the author had in mind by "narrow coasts which broaden gradually" unless we assume he was thinking of the banks of the Delaware River and the Bay, which occupy most of the area between Pennsylvania and the ocean. But one of these banks belongs to the state of Delaware and the other to New Jersey.

Mr. Paine, author of the pamphlet *Common Sense*, makes the following observation in his letter to Abbé Raynal, written in Philadelphia in 1782. Paine wrote: "In the geographical account which the abbé gives of the thirteen states, he is so exceedingly erroneous, that to attempt a particular refutation, would exceed the limits I have prescribed to myself." [5]

The abbé (8:504) tells us that "the merchandise exported from New York in 1769 amounted to 4,352,446l.t. 17s. 9d., while (p. 511) "the exports from New Jersey were worth only 56,965l.t. 19s. 9d.," and (9:81) "Virginia and Maryland together sold 16,195,-577l.t. 4s. 7d. worth of merchandise." He lists (p. 123) the exports from Georgia as amounting to 1,625,418l.t. 9s. 5d. and, finally, declares (p. 137) that Florida "exported only 673,209l.t. 18s. 9d. worth of goods." The author's scrupulous exactitude for figures is no less astonishing than his negligence in geographical matters. It

[5] Thomas Paine, "Letter to the Abbé Raynal, on the Affairs of North America: in Which the Mistakes in the Abbé's account of the Revolution of America Are Corrected and Cleared Up," *The Complete Writings of Thomas Paine*, ed. Philip S. Foner (New York: Citadel Press, 1945), p. 250.

would have been quite as easy to have located places accurately as it must have been difficult to make these calculations in French currency.

We find (p. 379): "The population of the thirteen provinces rose to 2,981,678 people, including 400,000 Negroes." [6] In view of the fact that most of the colonies have not as yet started taking a census, this exactitude appears even more remarkable than his financial calculations.

The abbé took the trouble to describe the climate of each colony as if he were distinguishing Russia from Spain. There is a great difference between America and Europe in winter, for rivers in America frequently freeze at lat. 37°, but the difference from one colony to the next is slight.

The abbé says (p. 22) that in Pennsylvania "the seasons contribute considerable variety to the year. Winter, which begins on the first of January, lasts until the end of March." Actually the Pennsylvania winter starts earlier than in Maryland and Virginia, and in Virginia there are few years when you do not feel the cold in early November.

It is possible the abbé was too ready to accept the tales of ignorant travelers, or he may have had a penchant for the odd. He reports (p. 29) that "women bear children earlier and for a longer time than in Europe." If he had said earlier than in Norway and later than in Sicily, he would have been correct; but then the reader would have traced the cause to climatic differences, and the marvelous element would have vanished.

The abbé describes the "Dumplers" [Dunkers] in detail to arouse the curiosity, or rather the admiration, of the reader. Most of his statements are exaggerated, and some completely untrue. The Dunkers are a strange people whose life is a web of sadness and melancholy. They are neither harmful nor useful to society, and they could exist only in a land where they are protected.

On page 39 we read that every house in Philadelphia "has its own garden and orchard." Few have an orchard, let alone a garden, for land is too costly, especially in the center of town and near the river, which is the commercial area. He assures us (p. 40) that the City Hall is magnificent and calls the public buildings of Williamsburg, Virginia, the finest on the northern continent (p. 83). Lest the reader assume we have produced some noteworthy

[6] Evarts B. Greene and Virginia D. Harrington, *American Population before the Federal Census of 1790* (rept. Gloucester, Mass.: Peter Smith, 1966), p. 6, lists a total of 2,312,000 people for 1770, including 1,850,000 whites and 462,000 blacks.

edifices, I should warn him that, architecturally, we have scarcely reached mediocrity.

After reporting that Dr. Franklin was born in Philadelphia (p. 42), the abbé discusses religious freedom and declares that Pennsylvania is "the only country in the world where people will not fight over words." Dr. Franklin, who was born in Boston of an old Bostonian family, was over twenty when he settled in Philadelphia. When the last edition of the *Philosophical History* was published, Virginia had been ahead of Pennsylvania in the matter of religious liberty for five years. As a historian the abbé should have known this.

"Philadelphia," we read (p. 44), "like other cities in Pennsylvania, is entirely open. The whole region is unprotected." The author often refers to things common to all the states as if they were limited to one of them. Here he continues: "This is a necessary corollary of Quaker principles." As a historian, should he not know that no American city was ever walled and that the other twelve states are quite as lacking in fortifications as Pennsylvania?

A complete refutation of the *Philosophical and Political History* would require an analysis of the entire book. I shall take pages 30, 31, and part of page 32 as a sample.

"The economy of the Pennsylvanians does not prevent both sexes from being well dressed." It is evident from his previous statements, as well as from what follows, that the author is referring to a praiseworthy economy. How could it prevent citizens from being well dressed? The author has already discussed six states without making any reference to clothing. Does he find anything remarkable about the dress of the Pennsylvanians? It is decent, but so is the attire in the other states.

"Food is superior to dress." We may say, in praise of Pennsylvania, that there are fewer luxurious tables here than elsewhere. "The poorest families have bread, meat, cider, beer, brandy with sugar." This is noteworthy exaggeration. The "poorest families" in Pennsylvania, as elsewhere, have bread as the staple of their diet. Rum ("brandy with sugar") is uncommon, and it would be even rarer if it were made of sugar, since that would raise the cost. Rum is made from the dregs of sugar and the canes.

"A large number of inhabitants habitually use French and Spanish wines, punch, and more expensive liqueurs. They are less apt to drink to excess than residents of other areas." Before the Revolution, French wines were very costly because they had to go to America by way of England and were excluded from the drawback.* Madeira, which the author does not mention, has always been the favorite for several reasons. It is the only wine which does not require a good cellar, which improves in a broached cask, and before the Revolution, it was the only one which Great Britain permitted Americans to import directly. It is still preferred, although a taste for French wines is growing daily.

"The delicious spectacle of this abundance is never saddened by beggary. Pennsylvania does not have a single pauper, and those whom birth or ill fortune left without resources are cared for by the public treasury." Every state has the same method of caring for the poor, and it is a much more sensible one than drawing on the public treasury.

"Pennsylvanians extend the most cordial hospitality. A traveler can stop anywhere without fear of occasioning any sorrow other than the regret caused by his departure." This is not strictly true. It is possible that the first immigrants settled so close together that they had few opportunities to be hospitable, or the great diversity of national customs may have made entertaining difficult; in any case, inhabitants of other states have always complained that they find less hospitality in Pennsylvania than elsewhere. The abbé probably relied on some European traveler who had not visited any other area.

"The tyranny of taxes does not poison the colony's felicity. In 1766 they did not exceed £280,140, and the majority, destined to heal the scars of war, were supposed to cease in 1772. If there was no relief at this time, it was due to the extraordinary expenses occasioned by Indian wars." The reader will recall (p. 20) a sentence beginning "this republic without war." On p. 45 he will find the contradiction, couched in a much more pompous style. "Go warlike peoples, slaves and tyrants, go to Pennsylvania; you will find all the doors open and everything at your disposition; there are no soldiers, and there are numerous merchants or laborers. But if you torment them or irritate them or vex them, they will flee, leaving their fields fallow, their factories in ruins, and their shops empty. They will go to cultivate a new land; they will travel around the world and die on the way before they will cut your throat or obey you."

"The inhabitants would be consoled for having to pay taxes if, as justice required and they demanded, they could have forced

* The term *drawback* refers to the restitution of fees paid by foreign merchandise on entering the country. It was designed to encourage export of these products.

Penn's family to contribute to public expenses in proportion to the revenue it derived from the province." In describing the settlement of Pennsylvania I have already said that Penn's family inherited this unjust privilege from the founder, whom the Abbé Raynal describes as the soul of generosity and a model of moral perfection.

"The Pennsylvanians, tranquil possessors of a land which always rewards their labors, are not afraid to bear children. There is scarcely a bachelor in the province." Lest the reader, on the strength of this "always," think it is a promised land, I should warn him that Pennsylvania, like other states, is as subject as Europe to bad weather and poor crops. For obvious reasons bachelors are less numerous than in Europe, but Philadelphia has more than any other American city. In other parts of Pennsylvania they are in the same proportion as elsewhere.

"Marriage is more sacred. Its liberty, like its sanctity, depends on the contractants, who take the judge or priest as witness of their engagement. If two lovers encounter opposition, they elope, the boy riding behind his sweetheart. When the girl tells the magistrate she has kidnapped her lover to marry him, no one can refuse her request or trouble her afterwards." A statute of the third year of Henry VII's reign states that if anyone kidnaps a girl, widow, or woman possessed of moveable or immovable goods, or likely to inherit some, and if this elopement is "against her will," and afterwards she is married to this miscreant, or by his consent to another, and if she is dishonored, this man and all his accomplices will be judged guilty of a capital crime. By a statute dating from the third year of Elizabeth's reign, all the guilty are deprived of benefit of clergy, except for accomplices after the crime.

It is evident that this English law, promulgated two centuries before the settlement of Pennsylvania, was designed to protect women who had, or anticipated having, some money, since the action is criminal only when it is "against the wishes" of the woman. Whenever a minor is unable to obtain the consent of her parents or guardian, she declares she has kidnapped the man to prove she has not been raped. This is doubtless what led to the passage of the *Philosophical History* I have just quoted, and the reader can take it for what it is worth.* It is not necessary for

* About twenty years ago there was a proposal in England to add a supplement to this law, since several daughters of noblemen had married far below their social rank. The duke of Bedford replied to this in the House of Lords, and his words do honor to his memory: "It is of no significance when a duke's daughter marries a lackey or a butcher; the important thing is to have a large number of marriages."

the couple to elope with the boy riding behind his sweetheart; the lovers can escape in any way they please.

"If the head of a family is in financial straits, he has the right to bind his children over to his creditors. This punishment should make a loving father careful with his money. A man receives £112 10s. per year of service; a child under twelve is obliged to serve until he is twenty-one for the same sum. It is like patriarchal customs in the Orient." These statements are completely inaccurate. The writer gives us an exact account of the right which belongs to the father, a right he calls punishment as if the father might be forced to exercise it. A yearly salary of £112 10s. would be extremely unfair in a country where men are scarce and labor is expensive. The truth is that all contracts are free, but the author attributes absurd laws to Penn in his effort to paint him as a sublime legislator. It is said that apprentices can be bound to their masters until they are twenty-one. In England the master usually receives a specified sum, the amount varying according to the profession or trade he is going to teach the apprentice and the service he hopes to get from him; board and room are also included. In America young people are placed without payment, and the master often pays to have them. But the father has no right to bind his son unless the boy is to be taught a profession or trade.

These details suffice to show the accuracy of the abbé's assertions; they also prove that it would be a herculean task to refute the entire book.

## Chapter 5

# William Penn

The ninth volume of the *Philosophical History* begins with a description of two imaginary governments, one of which was to be the worst possible and the other the best. After observing that some nations have resembled the former, others the latter, the author states (p. 4): "Among the latter is Pennsylvania."

William Penn, founder of this colony, is praised for having been the first to buy land from the Indians. "His arrival in the New World was marked by an act of justice which made everyone love him and admire his principles. As he was not satisfied with his claim to the land ceded by the British ministry, he resolved to purchase from the natives the enormous territory he proposed to settle. We do not know what price was asked by the savages; but although they are accused of stupidity for selling what they should never have transferred,* Penn had the glory of giving America an example of justice and moderation which Europeans had never even imagined" (p. 15).

In our account of the first colonial settlements we saw that the immigrants purchased land from the savages not only before Penn came to America but long before he was born. This was the policy of the founders of the Plymouth Colony, which dates from the beginning of 1621, as well as of Wheelwright and Company, whose much larger purchases were made in 1629. Some merited particular attention, such as the purchase of Sheepscot, or Nagwasac, from Robinhood in 1639, Naumkeag [Salem] in 1649 [1626], the island of Cononicut in 1657, the land acquired from the Sachem of Narragansett by John Parker the same year, the even larger Pettaquamscutt bought by another company, the land north of Pettaquamscutt bought by Athernon and Company in 1659, Misquamicut in 1669, etc.

In short, if we wish to list all the sales made by the Indians to our predecessors before Penn's arrival, even the most patient reader would be bored because the state archives are full of them. One

---

* We do not know who can accuse the Indians of stupidity for selling land they could not defend.

of the leading jurists of Massachusetts told me that there are few territorial suits in New England which do not go back to contracts with Indians. The author of *Notes on the State of Virginia*, who, as governor, examined the public records, wrote of the Indians: "That the lands of this country were taken from them by conquest, is not so general a truth as is supposed. I find in our historians and records, repeated proofs of purchase, which cover a considerable part of the lower country; and many more would doubtless be found on further search. The upper country, we know, has been acquired altogether by purchases made in the most unexceptionable form." [7]

The southern part of the country was owned entirely by the colonists before Penn came to America.

The abbé talks about the charters with so much assurance one wonders how he failed to see that the territory given by Charles II to the Rhode Island colony in 1662 had been purchased from the Indians. Hutchinson (1:249) says the king's commissioners met in 1665 in Providence and Warwick to examine the titles. On page 251 of the same volume he quotes a letter by Josiah Winslow, governor of Plymouth, written 1 May 1676: "I think I can truly say that before these present troubles the English did not possess one foot of land in this colony but what was fairly obtained by honest purchase of the Indian proprietors."

What follows will give an even more precise idea of the colonists' wish to buy land and not hurt the Indians. While New Jersey was under Dutch control, Augustin Herman, a Hollander, purchased from the Indians a vast area containing over four hundred thousand acres of excellent soil. When the country yielded to the English, Herman abandoned this territory; it was claimed the land belonged to the crown and that the Indians no longer had any right to it. Nevertheless, John Bailey, Daniel Denton, and Luke Watson of Long Island, together with several of their associates, asked Governor [Richard] Nicolls for permission to repurchase the tract from the natives. This was granted 30 September 1664; the sale took place on 28 October; and Douglass tells us (2:277) that the price, which consisted of blankets, clothing, axes, guns, gunpowder, lead, etc. (of which he gives the amount), was paid in two installments, as agreed.

"Penn's humanity," continues the abbé ([9:]16), "was not limited to the savages but extended to all those who came to inhabit

[7] Jefferson, *Notes*, ed. Peden, p. 96.

his empire. As man's happiness would depend on legislation, he based his on property and liberty, which determine the splendor of the states and the felicity of their citizens." The abbé borrows the language of fables to describe this era, which he calls fabulous; he believes that, thanks to Penn, the reign of innocence and peace will be reborn; the writer and his reader will be recompensed for the horror and sadness inspired by modern history, especially by the European settlement of the New World. Up to the present, barbarians have depopulated before possessing, ravaged before cultivating. It is time to see the seeds of reason, happiness, and humanity sown in the ruin and devastation of a hemisphere still reeking with the blood of its native peoples.

"The virtuous legislator established tolerance as the keystone of society. He wanted every man who recognized a god to have the rights of a citizen * and every Christian to share authority." "Penn wanted the ownership of the establishment he had created to remain forever in the hands of his family, but no decision could be made without the help of delegates elected by the people." "This true philosopher ceded for £450 a thousand acres of land to those who could pay the price. Any man who did not have this sum obtained for his wife, every child over sixteen, and each servant † fifty acres at a perpetual rent of 1s. 10½d. per acre.‡ Fifty acres were also guaranteed to those who, on becoming of age, would agree to an annual tax of £2 5s."

When you invent facts it is easy to manufacture the marvelous. In praising Penn's legislation, the writer should have specified the period he was describing. As this famous promoter succeeded, by trickery, in changing the charter several times, it would have been beneficial if the *Philosophical History* had stated whether the writer was referring to the first charter, written in London; to the second, composed upon Penn's arrival in America; to the third, dating from 1683; or to the final one of 1701.

The reader will recall that the laws which Abbé Raynal attributes to the wisdom, goodness, virtue, and generosity of William Penn were, for the most part, contained in the royal charter or the one which the first immigrants forced him to sign before they embarked. Tolerance, without which the Quakers would never have

---

* He should have said "the right to vote."

† It is difficult to believe that men unable to purchase land at this figure had servants.

‡ This does not speak highly for the generosity of the legislator-proprietor, as it was a very high rent for land and was intended for the poor.

come to America, had been granted in London, but Penn's role was to diminish it by the charter of 1701.* As to the innocence and peace which the abbé claims prevailed in the colony, there were constant quarrels between Penn and the colonists; these lasted from 1682, when he founded the colony, until his death in 1718.†

Penn's generosity in ceding land consisted of selling it at a much higher rate than prevailed in other colonies. Some of them gave a tract of fifty acres to every immigrant, without regard for age or sex. Article 6 of the capitulation between the inhabitants of Virginia and Cromwell affirms that "the privelege of having fifty acres of land for every person transported in that colonie shall continue as formerly agreed."

Other colonial governments forbade individuals to purchase land from the Indians without permission in order to avoid legal disputes; Penn forbade it so he could have a monopoly. If land was sold at a higher rate in Pennsylvania than elsewhere, we may attribute it to the favorable circumstances surrounding the settlement of the colony, circumstances which also proved profitable for Penn's heirs. They are not to blame, but it is wrong to paint as a model of generosity a man who was crazy for money and always in need of it.

Penn cannot be excused for leaving large blocks of land unsold for his own use. The assembly reproached him for this in the remonstrances of 1704 and 1707. Aside from the fact that it is always inconvenient to be too far from neighbors, it was dangerous, since men could not unite to defend themselves against Indian attacks. The immigrants knew that lands are more valuable when adjoining properties are inhabited. When they went to see Penn, he promised to sell all the lands save the tenth he had the privilege of reserving for himself. But he paid no attention to these agreements and left large tracts empty.

As for the assertion that "Penn wanted the ownership of the establishment he had created to remain forever in the hands of his family," only an attack of apoplexy prevented him from signing the deed of sale he had arranged to transfer the colony to George I.

The abbé (p. 19) insinuates that Penn rendered justice in a manner worthy "of a true philosopher," "forbidding those who were to judge cases from demanding or even accepting any salary" and decreeing that "every district should name three arbiters or peace-

* See Note A.
† See Part I, pp. 37–43.

makers who were to try to reconcile differences in a friendly fashion before they were taken to court."

A more precise picture emerges from the remonstrance of 1704,* in which the people's representatives address Penn as follows: "Therefore we propose that a man learned in the laws of England may be commissioned by the Queen to determine all matters, wherein thy tenants have just cause to complain against thee, thy deputies or commissioners; or else restore the people to the privilege of electing judges, justices and other officers, according to the direction of the first Charter, and intent of the first adventurers, and as the people of New England have by King William's Charter."

So justice was administered less fairly in Pennsylvania than in Massachusetts, even after the granting of King William's charter, which, as I have said, was not so liberal as the one arbitrarily annulled by Charles and James. To see how little the Pennsylvania system deserved the abbé's praise, you have only to look at Dr. Franklin's report of the committee to the assembly in 1757 and their unanimous request to George II that the government be administered by the crown.

The abbé attributes to Penn several laws in which he had no part. Page 20: "It was decreed that every child over twelve, rich or poor, should be obliged to have a profession." Although the author draws excellent conclusions from this, Penn was quite incapable of adopting any requirement so contrary to his interests. A regulation of this kind would have driven all friends of liberty from Pennsylvania.

On the same page the abbé writes: "Perhaps virtue had never inspired legislation more conducive to happiness." And he adds, as proof, that there were no wars in Pennsylvania. Actually there were quite as many as in other colonies, but Europeans were quick to believe that perpetual peace reigned between the Pennsylvanians and the Indians because Quakers are forbidden to fight.

People thought the Quakers made up more than half the population, although it was really only a fourth. This error may be traced to the fact that about three-quarters of the members of the assembly have always belonged to this sect. Douglass (2:346) says the Quakers owed this preponderance to their politics. They intimated to the numerous Germans and Dutch that if other religions had a majority in the assembly, they would establish a compulsory

* See Note A.

militia, which they described as the worst thing they had had to suffer in Europe. But the principal cause was the method of selecting representatives. The territory around Philadelphia, inhabited to a large degree by Quakers, was divided into smaller counties than the others. Furthermore, these counties had the right to elect a larger number of representatives; some appointed six, others eight, while more distant ones could name only two, without regard for their population.

When Pennsylvania was at war, the assembly devised an expedient to allay the religious scruples of the Quakers. The money which they had to raise was ostensibly designated for the king, but the governor used it for war. William Penn, who has been called both a Jesuit and a Quaker, realized that war was inevitable; so he got himself endowed in the royal charter with all the power of a commanding general. Article 16 entitles him to "levy, muster and train all sorts of men, of what condition soever, or wheresoever born, in the said Province of Pennsylvania for the time being and to make war, and to pursue the enemies . . . as well by sea as by land even without the limits of the said province, and by God's assistance to vainquish and take them etc."

We see that wars soon broke out with the Indians, for in the remonstrance of 1704, the assembly refers to the vast sums it had supplied Penn for "the administration and defence of this government since the year 1682, though we know thy stay here at first coming was not above two years." *

This is enough to point out the inaccuracies in the information which has been circulated and to show how writers are at fault when they state facts without taking the trouble to examine them.

* See Note A.

## Chapter 6

# The Quakers

The abbé's description of Quaker character at the beginning of volume 9 is no less exaggerated than his portrait of the Dunkers. An excessive zeal, enthusiasm, and fanaticism usually accompany every young sect, but violence cannot endure. Religious fanaticism feeds on persecution; if you leave it alone, it soon loses force.

Page 11: "If you slapped a Quaker, he turned the other cheek; if you asked him for his coat, he offered his vest as well." If this were true of Quakers, those in London could not go out in winter without running the risk of freezing to death, for at every step they would encounter "friends" who would ask for all their clothes. And I do not advise anyone to slap a Quaker either in England or America. There are stories about people who paid dearly for taking too many liberties with them.

Before the Revolution an English sailor, who may have imagined that American Quakers were more patient than those in England, decided to put the matter to a test. When he found a Quaker sitting beside the fire in an inn with a group of people, he gave the man a fairly hard blow on his shoulder and observed that this would give him an opportunity to practice the tenets prescribed by his faith. The Quaker was one of those tremendously strong men who consider themselves natural prodigies. He rose, opened the first two fingers of both hands, picked the sailor up by his waist, lifted him, carried him over to the wall, and squeezed him until the poor man prayed for help. As the suppliant reminded the Quaker of his religion, he replied: "It is true that my religion prevents me from beating you, but it does not prevent me from squeezing you." After squeezing the man so that he would never forget the lesson, the Quaker set him down and returned to the fire.

We fail to see why the author writes (p. 12): "Temples were in their eyes quackery-shops." Like other sects, they have their own meetinghouses everywhere.

His statement on the following page is no more accurate: "While all the other new sects were encouraged, these people were tormented." At the time when Quakers were persecuted in New

England, all those who did not observe the dogmas of strict Congregationalists were subjected to similar treatment. The author
himself says (8:450): "It is a fact that Puritans were forbidden,
under pain of death, to worship images." The law decreed capital
punishment for all dissidents, and any men suspected of tolerance
were exposed to such cruel annoyances that they were forced to
flee from their new asylum.

The books of the Muggletonians[8] were burned by the execu-
tioner in the Boston public market in 1654, the year when the first
Quakers appeared in New England. As Congregationalists became
more tolerant, Quakers received better treatment.

For no reason whatsoever the abbé claims the Quakers are disin-
terested. Like other sects, they have peculiarities, but their chief
assets are their economy and industry. No one would deny their
superior talents in the marketplace, where they excel at driving
hard bargains. They are about average in hospitality and generosity; a few scrupulously honest men scorn hypocrisy, but they are
rare. Their manners resemble so closely those of the Jesuits that
they are often called Protestant Jesuits.

Some of their men are very distinguished. One, whom I know
well, said to me: "My friend, believe me, our apparent simplicity
and our scorn for display only enhance our pride. Passions are
often cloaked with different colors." Quakers do not take their hats
off to anyone and always use thee and thou. However, if any non-
Quaker addresses them in this manner, they are annoyed. They say
that as members of other sects are not obliged to depart from common usage, they should not treat the Quakers in a different way
from everyone else. While granting them this point, we must comment that it gives no indication of the resignation and humility for
which they are noted.

In speaking of slavery (9:185) the writer again alludes to the
Quakers: "Some Christians who sought virtues rather than dogmas
in the Gospels have often wished to set their slaves free but were
restrained by a law which ordered that freedmen should receive an
income adequate for their subsistence." If the author had examined
the law more attentively, he would have seen that it is inspired by
justice and humanity. This law, which still exists, does not order
the owners to provide an income for former slaves, but it requires
them to support those who, because of illness or old age, are incapable of earning their living. This is to prevent men from putting

[8] This sect was named for Ludowick Muggleton about 1651.

on the shoulders of the community a burden which they themselves should bear.

One of the good qualities of the Quakers, which the abbé fails to mention, is that they never say anything without proof. I should be sorry if anyone thought me incapable of recognizing their virtues. If it were possible to compare them with other sects, I am sure the Quakers would appear no better and no worse than the rest, but their character has been poorly represented.

Quakers cannot justify the role they played during the Revolution, when they denied their own principles and used their religion to mask insidious politics. A declaration they addressed to the American people with the title *The Ancient Testimony and Principles of the People Called Quakers Renewed* was one of the principal motives which led Mr. Paine, author of the pamphlet called *Common Sense*, to write them a letter containing the following passages:

This epistle is not so properly addressed to you as a religious, but as a political body, dabbling in matters, which the professed Quietude of your Principles instructs you not to meddle with. But be ye sure that ye mistake not the cause, and ground of your Testimony. Call not coldness of soul, religion; nor put the Bigot in the place of the Christian.

O ye partial ministers of your own acknowledged principles. If the bearing arms be sinful, the first going to war must be more so, by all the difference between wilful attack and unavoidable defence. Wherefore, if ye really preach from conscience, and mean not to make a political hobby-horse of your religion, convince the world thereof, by proclaiming your doctrine to our enemies, for they likewise bear arms. Give us proof of your sincerity by publishing it at St. James's, to the commanders in chief at Boston, to the admirals and captains who are piratically ravaging our coasts, and to all the murdering miscreants who are acting in authority under whom ye profess to serve. Had ye the honest soul of Barclay * ye would preach repentance to your king; Ye would tell him his sins and warn him of eternal ruin. Ye would not spend your partial invectives against the injured, and the insulted only, but, like faithful ministers, would cry aloud and spare none. Say not that ye are persecuted, neither endeavor to make us the authors of that reproach, which ye are bringing upon yourselves; for we testify unto all men, that we do not complain against you because ye are Quakers, but because ye pretend to be and are NOT quakers.

If these are really your principles why do ye not abide by them?

* Mr. Paine alludes to the noble words addressed to Charles II by a Quaker named Barclay.

Why do ye not leave that, which ye call God's Work, to be managed by himself? These very principles instruct you to wait with patience and humility, for the event of all public measures and to receive that event as the divine will towards you. Wherefore, what occasion is there for your political testimony if you fully believe what it contains? And the very publishing it proves, that either, ye do not believe what ye profess, or have not virtue enough to practice what ye believe.

How can ye on the ground of your principles, justify the exciting and stirring up the people "firmly to unite in the abhorrence of all such writings, and measures, as evidence a desire and design to break off the happy connexion we have hitherto enjoyed, with the kingdom of Great Britain, and our just and necessary subordination to the king, and those who are lawfully placed in authority under him." What a slap of the face is here! the men, who in the very paragraph before, have quietly and passively resigned up the ordering, altering, and disposal of kings and governments, into the hands of God, are now, recalling their principles, and putting in for a share of the business. Is it possible, that the conclusion, which is here justly quoted, can any ways follow from the doctrine laid down? The inconsistency is too glaring not to be seen; the absurdity too great not to be laughed at; and such as could only have been made by those, whose understandings were darkened by the narrow, and crabbed spirit of a despairing political party.[9]

Mr. Paine was correct in speaking of a political party, for not all the Quakers behaved in the same fashion. Some deserved the gratitude of their country. Quakers, like Jesuits, can be divided into three classes. The Jesuits included: politicians who governed, philosophers who were interested only in learning, and men of good faith who were passive. The Quaker classes are the politicians, the patriots, and the religious. During the Revolution the patriots took arms to defend their country; the religious prayed and did charitable work, without becoming involved in either war or politics; and the politicians, who formed a much larger class than the others combined, ran business affairs and did everything they could to harm the American cause. Under any other government such conduct would have been severely punished.

In general, writers have paid tribute to Penn and the Quakers together. The custom has become so deep-rooted that it is unusual to hear one praised without the other. If a blind veneration for errors that have become axioms does not permit anyone to say that Penn's character has been falsely interpreted and that of the Quakers

[9] Paine, "Epistle to Quakers," *Complete Writings*, pp. 56–59.

greatly exaggerated, it must be granted that the remonstrances of 1704 and 1707 were either just or unjust. In the first instance Penn was quite unlike the opinion commonly held of him; in the second, the representatives, who were almost all Quakers, were impostors and slanderers, since not one of them opposed the remonstrances.

# Chapter 7

# Maryland, Virginia, etc.

According to the abbé ([9:]52): "Many inhabitants of Maryland are Catholic and many more German. Their customs are characterized by gentleness rather than energy, but this may be due to the fact that women are not excluded from society, as in most parts of the continent."

I leave it to the reader to decide whether the contrast between Catholic and German is natural, as if Catholic could be a national title or German could designate some religious characteristic. Germans are actually much less numerous than Catholics. As the adjoining states have many more than Maryland, we fail to see why the abbé makes special reference to this group.

The degree of gentleness or energy among Americans could not be calculated according to the abbé's yardstick, since there is no area in the United States where women are excluded from society. If men linger at table, women usually leave because they do not like to drink heavily and because they are busy. Our women run the household, usually with great care. They have all the keys, look after everything, and it would be a very good thing if Southerners paid as much attention to their business and were as economical as their wives.

Page 63: "Two centuries ago England proposed to occupy no part of North America save Virginia. Today this designates only the area between Maryland and Carolina." It would be difficult to guess what the writer means by "no part of North America except Virginia." The reader would have been spared these ambiguities had he been told that the territory claimed by Raleigh, and which he named, now designates the area bounded by Maryland, Carolina, the sea, and the Mississippi, for kings granted the remainder of the country under different charters. We do not know where the author learned what England proposed to do. Judging from history, she had no plans. Raleigh obtained from Queen Elizabeth a charter for the whole country he would control and appropriated the area from lat. 25° to the Gulf of St. Lawrence.

Page 65: "The company etc. was dissolved when Charles I ascended the throne." The charter was annulled by his father. "Then

Virginia got an English government." It had been established four years before, and the company had the privilege of approving or rejecting laws it submitted to the king. "The crown only charged 2s. 5d. for each hundred acres under cultivation." This tax, called a quitrent, was not regulated by the number of acres a man cultivated but by what he owned; the number of cultivated acres was very small in comparison to what had been appropriated, but quitrents were charged indiscriminately for everything.

"Until this time colonists had no real property. Everyone wandered around or settled wherever he liked without title to the land." The company had been selling and granting property in fief for years; it has been said that men holding property in fief paid for the first settlements in 1617.

Page 66: "But some inhabitants, who saw the Protector's (that is, Cromwell's) forces supported by a powerful fleet, delivered the colony to him." This implies the surrender of an important fortress by men who had been seduced by the enemy, but the country was unable to protect itself. The only opposition was a refusal by the inhabitants to accept harsh conditions; yet they consented when it was necessary.

On page 71 the author is discussing tobacco: "It was thought that nothing would help the foundering business more than to ship to Europe what Maryland and Carolina sent to Virginia." The abbé should have told us where he found this law. The inhabitants of North Carolina, which borders Virginia, have always taken and continue to take their tobacco there since they have no harbors. Residents of Maryland would be foolish to imitate them, since ships pass easily through Chesapeake Bay and along the Potomac River.

The writer speaks (p. 74) of the right of appeal to the General Assembly. The General Assembly has never been a legal tribunal.

Page 77: "As there were no women in the province, they paid £2,250 for every young woman the company brought from Europe with a certificate of good character. This custom did not last long." It would have been better to say it never began. At the beginning the company sent only its own employees, and as soon as the system changed, whole families began to emigrate. In the opening pages of this book, there is a reference to 1,216 men, women, and children who sailed in 1619 in eleven vessels.

It would be exceedingly difficult to note all the abbé's mistakes about Virginia. I shall close with a passage so different from the rest that friends of truth will wish he had drawn all his information from this source.

Page 83: "Men who prefer the tranquillity of country life to the hubbub of cities should be economical and industrious, but such was never the case in Virginia. Its inhabitants have always spent a great deal of thought on furnishing their houses. They have always loved to entertain their neighbors frequently and lavishly and to bedazzle visiting English navigators with their luxury. They were always lazy, a characteristic of regions where there is slavery; so the province owed large sums of money. At the beginning of the troubles these debts were estimated at £25 million.* This prodigious amount was owed to British merchants for slaves or other items. The confidence of these bold lenders was based on an unjust law which guaranteed they would be paid before any other debts were settled."

Negligence, indolence, and luxury have been the curse of this country. The chief causes are, as the abbé says, slavery and the English government's concern lest the inhabitants become involved in public affairs. Today young men are spurred to take an interest by openings in all departments of the government and by the zeal of their fellow citizens. The fertility of the soil makes life easy and contributes to heedlessness. Since one of the women's major responsibilities is to receive strangers hospitably, they are only too ready to go along with their husbands in setting a table covered with so much food there is no room for the plates. As men are obliged to have overseers for their property, they gradually turn responsibilities over to them and little by little adopt such slothful ways that it takes a shock to stir them into any kind of activity.

When the abbé discusses the eight proprietors of Carolina, he states (p. 90): "The first act of these sovereigns was to create three orders of nobility. They called barons those who received twelve thousand acres; caciques got twenty-four thousand; and the two landgraves received eighty thousand acres each." We do not know why the author mentions only two landgraves. Is he speaking of the whole country or of each county? In the first case, it is too few; in the second too many. As he states (p. 85) that the legislative system of the new state was developed by the famous Locke, he might have taken the trouble to read it. He would then have seen that there was to be one landgrave per county; that each one

* They were very much larger, unfortunately.

was to have forty-eight thousand acres, not eighty; that the proprietors could sell or give their lands to the nobles; that there were to be two orders of nobility, not three; and finally, that barons are not even mentioned.

Page 92: "In 1728 Parliament finally decided to restore this beautiful domain to the nation and to grant its first masters £540,000 in damages." George I took over the government in 1722 at the request of the inhabitants; the nation had no right to it, and Parliament had nothing to do with it.

Page 93: "The two areas together stretch more than four hundred miles along the coast and about two hundred miles into the interior." They extend about six hundred miles to the west, or inland. On the coast they used to stretch five hundred miles, but that has been cut in half since the formation of the state of Georgia.

Page 94: "North Carolina is one of the largest provinces on the continent." This would not be true if the western portion did not extend to the Mississippi but only two hundred miles inland, as the abbé states on the preceding page, since North Carolina is less than a hundred miles in width.

Page 95: "Much later a few vagabonds settled there." The first colonists were honest, industrious men from the Palatinate, 130 of whom are said to have been massacred by the Indians in a single night. "But in time land became scarce in the other colonies." Nearly a century has passed, and there is still no shortage of territory.

On page 106 the writer discusses funerals in an altogether different way than on pages 33 and 34, where he is describing those in Pennsylvania. His imagination produces some dreadful scenes, which the Carolinians fortunately have never witnessed.

On page 131 the abbé begins to write about the two Floridas which belonged to England. At that time it was difficult to foresee they would be ceded to Spain, although hostilities had already begun between the two countries. He regarded the Floridas as a kind of promised land, although he admits the soil in the western part is "much too sandy." He believes "that the Floridas have a great advantage over the rest of the continent and that it is likely grapes, olives, cotton, and other delicate plants will thrive there better than in the adjoining provinces." What he says about cotton is true. Experience proves that it requires heat, like sugar and coffee. But grapes become too sweet in Florida, and the olives have a strong, disagreeable flavor.

The fact that a few Tories sought refuge in Saint Augustine

doubtless led the abbé to mention some Americans who decided to retire there, but his description makes one fear an emigration to this terrestrial paradise that would be detrimental to the United States. After reporting that Dr. Turnbull brought a number of Greeks, he asks: "Why should Athens and Sparta not be reborn in North America?" [10]

He makes some really curious observations in connection with these immigrants. "Women who seldom gave birth are now very fertile thanks to the change in climate, and it is assumed that the children will be taller." It would have been a good idea to explain this theory of sterility, assuming it was true, and the notion about the children's height. Finally he says that the little group "received from its founder institutions they approved; it is like a family in which the spirit of peace will endure." At the very time when the abbé was writing, there were troubles, and the little group dispersed. Dr. Turnbull left Florida before the end of the war and for several years has been renowned as a physician in Charleston. The author of this book knew him in Smyrna long before he went to Florida.

[10] Dr. Andrew Turnbull was a Scottish physician who married a Greek.

# Chapter 8

# Climate, Soil, etc. of the United States

The simplest way to show the author's inaccuracies in his descriptions of climate, soil, etc. is to give the facts.

Anyone who has traveled in Europe and Asia and observed the causes of tertian fever and other diseases will readily imagine that the same situation prevails at a similar degree of latitude in America. Great lakes never infect the air, but stagnant water does. In any area where there is more land than can be cultivated, there are bound to be pockets in which rainwater collects, since it is impossible to level the soil or provide good drainage. In Virginia there is probably not a single field without such pockets except in naturally sloping areas, which constitute the major portion of the terrain. In woods where the soil preserves its natural state, stagnant pools are even more numerous, and we have already noted that the amount of fallow land is far larger than the cultivated areas. A similar source of trouble is water from mills, which often floods thirty or forty acres. Very few millers channel it into canals because so much land is available and also because they are afraid of a shortage during periods of drought. Not everyone has learned that evaporation over such a large surface constitutes a greater loss than would occur in canals.

Although many people complain about sudden changes in climate, I have heard similar stories in both Europe and Asia. Furthermore, in the United States, Asia Minor, Italy, and southern France the temperature never shifts from hot to cold and from cold to hot three or four times in the same day as it does everywhere in Europe from lat. 47° to lat. 55°. The same winds do not always have the same effects. The one blowing from the pole may not be the coldest, nor the one from the equator the warmest.

Cold in the United States is occasionally much more intense than at the same latitude in Europe. This is caused by the northwest wind traversing an immense, uncultivated continent. This wind destroys fruit in the central states, for it often brings a spring freeze. Spring comes later to the northern states, so that fruit is not exposed, and the sun counteracts the wind's force in the southern region.

At the beginning of May 1774 this wind blew for thirty-six hours, and on the morning of the fifth some parts of Virginia were covered with a layer of ice over two inches thick. The oldest inhabitants had never seen anything like it.[11] New leaves dried up on old trees in the forests and saplings two or three years old withered. Wheat was generally ruined; in places it was given to cattle, and what was left in the fields produced a very poor crop. Some farmers plowed the fields and sowed Indian corn. Nearly all the fruit was destroyed.

Every year the vegetation contradicts Abbé Raynal, who claims it is slow to appear in this climate. At the time of the freeze bunches of grapes were already very long, but all the new shoots dried up, and some vines even lost the adjacent portion of old wood. Both domestic and wild vines recovered to produce their usual crop at the normal time.

Here I should warn the reader that the virtues attributed by the abbé to Indian corn should be added to his list of imaginary curiosities. After carefully describing this plant ([9:]157), as if it were unknown in Europe, and telling us how to cultivate it, he concludes: "It may be frozen two or three times in the spring without affecting the crop." When a freeze occurs, the farmers plow and sow again, because frozen seed produces a very poor harvest.

Excessive cold does not last long. The northwest wind rarely blows more than three days in succession, but it often returns before the thaw. Thawing takes time unless southern winds bring rain. If the cold persists without long intervals of mild weather, spring is late and fruit does not suffer.

The first stories sent back to Europe by colonists were similar to those told by Abbé Raynal. Men who landed on fertile ground talked as if they had found the Promised Land, while others thought it was like the Arabian Desert. Toward the close of the last century, Hubbard and several others gave more accurate accounts, and contemporary travelers do not encounter any of the amazing phenomena spawned by ignorance, a taste for the miraculous, or a desire to boast.

There are all kinds of land, from the best to the most impoverished. The upper stratum of soil is transported by rains from mountains and hills to adjacent plains, valleys, and riverbeds. New land

---

[11] *Journals of the House of Burgesses of Virginia, 1773–76*, pp. 110–11, May 19, 1774: "The late frost hath destroyed all the grapes in the public vineyard which was in a very flourishing state before."

is fertile the first year if it is well cultivated, but this seldom happens because labor is expensive while land is cheap. In consequence, new land usually has a better yield the second year, and occasionally the third is better than the second. When soil becomes impoverished it is fertilized or left fallow.

According to Abbé Raynal, New England produces no grain save a very small amount of Indian corn. He claims the population would starve to death were it not for fishing. The major drawback in the soil of three New England states is the abundance of stones. Otherwise, soil is generally fertile and crops are normal for various local conditions at this latitude.

Kentucky, a district in western Virginia which may become a separate state, has the finest soil found in the United States to date. I say "to date" because the country has not yet been thoroughly examined. Specialists divide Kentucky soil into six categories, the poorest of which is above average for other parts of the United States. In order to reach this excellent and very large region, you have to cross more than a hundred miles of such poor soil to the east that it is believed the area will never be inhabited. These extremes seem to indicate that nature, on the whole, tried to be impartial.

Animals degenerated in places where they were neglected but thrived if given proper care. Rhode Island is outstanding for the size of its horned cattle and Virginia for its beautiful horses. In Rhode Island the climate, soil, and other local conditions may contribute to the unusual size of the cattle. I believe the superiority of Virginia horses is due to the care devoted to breeding and improving the stock.

Pigs are easier to breed here than in Europe because we have so many forests. Sheep thrive everywhere, especially if they are frequently moved. They degenerate if kept too long in the same spot.

The subject is a big one, and much could be said about it. However, as Mr. Jefferson discusses the matter much better than I could, I refer the reader to his *Notes*. They contain the best description of Americans and American animals; the latter are compared with European species, and he points out mistakes made by various writers, including M. de Buffon himself. Mr. Jefferson pays this celebrated naturalist a well-deserved tribute, however, when he says: "The wonder is not that there is yet something in this great work to correct, but that there is so little." [12]

[12] Jefferson, *Notes*, ed. Peden, p. 55.

I wish I could make the same observation about Abbé Raynal, but my respect for truth forces me to say just the contrary. Mr. de Pauw is the only writer surpassing Abbé Raynal in the number of his errors about America.[13] Convinced that the New World is inferior in every way to the Old, Mr. de Pauw hunted for details to support his theory. He produced three volumes in which you have to read a number of statements in order to find a single one that is true, although practically all of them rely on some authority. The author evidently worked very hard on this book, but most of his sources were gazetteers or ignorant travelers. I have heard that Mr. de Pauw has finally realized his own errors, and we may hope he will share this discovery with the public.

The abbé's statement about the degeneration of seeds and plants is no less fantastic than many of his other assertions. There are few plants used for food in the most favorable European climates that I have not tried in America. Some improved, others remained the same; not one degenerated. This does not prove any superiority of soil or climate, since the same thing occurred when I shipped several from America to Europe. It has now been established that moving is usually beneficial to species of both the animal and vegetable kingdoms. This would suggest that peasants should exchange seeds from their harvests for others grown at some distance.

It may be said that on several occasions the experiment failed when goods were shipped from Europe to America, or vice versa, or when they came to us from Asia or Africa. But how were these experiments conducted? If a plant requiring a cold climate is sent from England to Georgia, if rice and indigo are transported from Georgia to England, or if laziness and ignorance replace intelligence and skill, the plant will certainly degenerate.

A considerable number of layers of Tuscan grapes shipped in late 1774 did not arrive in Virginia until the latter part of June 1775. Even if they had been in good condition, it would have seemed futile to plant them at this season. However, an attempt was made, and about fifteen hundred of those not totally dried up were planted in various places. More than half took root, and the layers the second year were so long and thick that Italian peasants said the story would not be believed in Tuscany. They produced grapes with more flavor and substance than those grown in Italy, possibly because they were about five and a half degrees closer to

[13] Cornelius de Pauw, *Les Recherches philosophiques sur les Américains* (Berlin, 1770).

the equator. In Tuscany these vines usually produce a smaller yield the third year than the second; in Virginia, it was larger. The fourth year brought an enormous harvest, but the growers were absorbed by political events, and the vines were finally destroyed.

Before this occurred, a number of layers were transported to a better location on Mr. Jefferson's land. After the harvest in 1783, some vines grew up again and by the middle of October the grapes were two-thirds normal size, but as Mr. Jefferson went to the meeting of Congress and then to Europe, he did not ascertain whether they matured fully.

Lemon and orange seedlings of various sizes from the vicinity of Genoa were shipped before the grapes. About 120 were planted, nearly all took root, more than half of them blossomed, and about 20 bore fruit. Toward the end of October, these oranges and lemons were two inches in circumference, but during the winter almost all the seedlings died back. They were moved to what seemed a better location, carefully protected from the cold, but within a few years they all withered. Olive trees met the same fate. In the spring they put out new shoots, even sturdier than they would have been in Italy, but they perished during the fourth year. Fig trees do fairly well in lowlands but die if planted on hillsides, even though the elevation is lower than it would be in Italy and they are six degrees closer to the equator.

We are not sufficiently acquainted with the character of the soil to select the best locations. I think it is only a matter of time before we know where to plant fruit to make it ripen several weeks earlier or how to protect it from the cold. But I question whether any spot is sufficiently protected from northwest winds to grow oranges and lemons if it is north of lat. 36° and east of the Alleghenies.* These mountains, although some of the highest yet known in North America, are not to be compared with the Apennines. It is true that Pisa, a Tuscan city, lat. 43°20', which grows oranges, lemons, and other delicate plants, is protected from north winds by a mountain not nearly so high as the Apennines. But we must recall that the atmosphere is never so cold as it is in America and that the cold never arrives so suddenly as when it is brought by our northwest wind.

It is said that two or three hundred miles west of the Alleghenies and south of the Ohio River this wind does not prevail and the seasons are much more temperate, particularly in Kentucky; in time,

---

* The Allegheny Mountains are called the Appalachians in France.

perhaps, an area will be found here where these plants could grow outdoors. However, since in warmer climates than on the Gulf of Genoa, in Tuscany or Naples, lemons have a thicker peel and less delicate flavor, I believe Europe will continue to outdo America in this, just as Italy will always surpass other parts of Europe. The situation may be different with regard to oranges, for those from Malta are slightly better than the ones grown in Pisa. The latter are the finest on the European continent and only slightly inferior to those of Tripoli.

It is still too soon to determine the natural resources of this country, especially of southern areas, which so far have been cultivated by men from such different climates. English and Scottish gardeners had not been able to grow edible chicory in Virginia; when it was cultivated by Italian peasants, it was as good as any you would find in Europe. Some people claimed the seeds came from Italy, but they were brought from Williamsburg by a Scottish gardener of Lord Dunmore's because the Italian seeds spoiled during the voyage. The famous Dr. Fothergill [14] told me one day that a Scottish acquaintance of his, who had settled in South Carolina, planted an almond tree against a wall with a southern exposure, where it was soon burned by the hot sun. People err in following the customs of their mother country, in not learning from experience, and in not seeking better plants. Virginia vineyards have no grapes other than English varieties; fig trees thrive there as well as in Provence, Italy, and Asia Minor, but there are only two or three species and none of the best. In the vicinity of Richmond, they are not even trained to grow as trees.

In most parts of the United States, but especially in Virginia, nature seems to favor vineyards. I have never seen such perfect, varied, and abundant wild grapes. In 1775 and 1776 I selected some of the best and made about three hundred bottles of wine, which was far better than ordinary Italian wine or what is produced near Paris. As these vines are cultivated, the new shoots are stronger every year and the grapes larger and better, but I believe it will take several generations of plants to perfect them, because the first layers are very thin. Despite their natural advantages, I do not expect grapes to be grown in quantity as long as land is cheap. Since labor is proportionately dear, farmers will not wish to expend it on a plant which requires rather exacting care and does not begin to bear for four or five years.

[14] Dr. John Fothergill, an English scientist.

These details may appear trivial to some of my readers, but I have not hesitated to give them, for they are useful. I am writing for the small group who desire to learn. That is my one purpose, and I am not interested in applause or in the criticism of those who want people to tell them only what they want to hear—not how things really are.

It is time now to examine the philosophical and political principles of Abbé Raynal during the American Revolution.

# Chapter 9

# The Behavior of France

The author begins by declaring (9:342) that it is his earnest desire to be impartial: "Here our task becomes increasingly difficult. Since our sole object is to be truthful, we scorn any party spirit which blinds and degrades leaders and those who aspire to learn. We love our country and pay homage to justice."

The author's intentions could not be better; we can only find fault with their execution. It is possible that the abbé was afraid of being partial because of his patriotic zeal, and it may be that his very delicacy made him go to the opposite extreme. Praiseworthy actions, of both France and its allies, are described coldly or falsely interpreted. The behavior of the French government appears quite different from what it actually was, for in his pages its moderation becomes fear, its generosity imprudence, its courage and frankness temerity and insolence.

He makes Americans on the field of battle resemble Arabs or a herd of cattle, while General Washington plays the role of a militia sergeant. Since he also complains about not being able to find adequate terms to extol certain actions of the English ministers that would seem insignificant to anyone else, we must assume that the same principle was involved.

This reasoning must also explain why he was so ready to believe British statements, even if there was no basis for them. After saying that "the delirium which caused the British ministry to attack its colonies forced it to declare war on France" (because France and Spain were, in his opinion, in a deplorable state); after saying that "it was important for England to deprive its rebellious subjects of the only support promised them and this would have lessened indignation roused by the violation of solemn treaties"; he concludes (p. 340): "George III saw nothing of that. The secret assistance granted by the Court of Versailles to the provinces armed to defend their rights * did not open his eyes."

If this secret assistance had been really sent, we should have wel-

---

* As the author admits we were defending our rights, he might have omitted the word "rebellious"; it is difficult to reconcile the two.

comed it gladly. The abbé was assured of the contrary by well-informed persons, but he repeats his statement several times, and on page 357 makes it even more authoritative: "We know today that this crown, which had rendered clandestine help to the Americans from the beginning of hostilities, etc."

At the beginning of 1756 the British ministers continued to flatter the French ambassador with peaceful overtures even after their warships had already seized some twenty-two thousand French sailors. On that basis this secret assistance would not have been so out of place, but the fact is that the Court of Versailles did not want war, and it therefore treated the English ambassador with more consideration than was pleasing to French pride.

Circumstances made this absolutely necessary, since Louis XIV had frightened Europe. The terror spread by his schemes still prevailed, and enemies of France took advantage of it. Suspicion, which gave credence to stories and exaggerated reports, encouraged impostors to spread tales about the excessive ambition, subterfuges, and intrigues of the French government. But France, which was convinced that true greatness must be based on national esteem, felt it had to give proof of its new policy to destroy the widespread prejudice. The results of this wisdom were beneficial, although the abbé did not approve of them.

We cannot help admiring the blindness he attributes to George III, who saw, or thought he saw, that France was giving us secret assistance, if we can judge by all the remonstrances of his ambassador at Versailles.

As long as General Paoli [15] was in Corsica, he received help from England. We must not conclude this was sent by the court, for the money and arms came from individuals as gifts, whereas we purchased the weapons and other merchandise we received. The English court did not oppose shipments; the court of France shackled them.

It was claimed the French court had authorized shipments to America. If we admit that the government did not use every precaution to prevent them, we are not implying that they were approved and certainly not that the crown gave secret assistance to the Americans. Furthermore, it is doubtful whether this assistance could have been prevented, since everyone favored it, and universal approbation is a powerful passport.

Dr. Franklin had been in France for a year, but no one listened

---

[15] Pasquali Paoli, a Corsican patriot.

to him until the government learned the English court had resolved to reunite with the colonies and wage war on France. So it was likely that if France continued to reject the American offers, they would accept those from England. This would have brought to an end the internal schism between Britain and its colonies and united all its forces against the House of Bourbon.

What would the world have said had France failed to help separate two countries that would be formidable if united, and if it had neglected the opportunity to avenge the affronts it had received? War was inevitable. The alternative was whether to join America against England or to fight England and America together.*

At this time Abbé Raynal was in Paris. Despite his efforts to ascertain what was happening, he seems to have known nothing of the complaints of the British ambassador, although they were very frequent. One of the singular demands of this gentleman was that Mr. Deane should be turned over to England as a rebel or banished from France.

The abbé (p. 341) says: "To rouse Saint James's from its lethargy, Louis XVI had to announce on 14 March [1778] that he had recognized the independence of the United States." England assumed this was a declaration of war. The author then continues: "It was impossible for a nation, more accustomed to sin than to be sinned against, to permit its subjects to be freed from their vow of allegiance and raised to the rank of a sovereign power."

These expressions "subjects to be freed" and "raised" are noteworthy, since it was almost two years since the Americans had freed and raised themselves, and the abbé has already indicated he was quite aware of the fact. He adds (p. 342): "It was not known that a fleet from Toulon was ordered to fight the English in North America or that London had issued orders to drive the French from the East Indies. Without being initiated into these perfidious mysteries, which politicians have termed great achievements, enlightened men viewed hostilities as inevitable."

The author is correct. Enlightened men do not need to be initiated into perfidious mysteries, but they must pay some attention to chronology. The departure of the fleet from Toulon did not take place until after England had termed the French declaration a declaration of war. The orders to drive the French from the East In-

---

* See Note K, "Reflections on the Way France and Spain Should Regard the Consequences of the Quarrel between Great Britain and Its colonies." The author, M. Turgot, did not share the opinion of those politicians who thought France could choose between war and peace.

dies were issued before Saint James's was roused from its lethargy. The abbé seems to assume the English court was asleep when it ordered the arming of warships.

In the same volume he says (pp. 352 [–53]): "France has become embroiled in a disastrous war, whereas it should bend every effort to heal the wounds of a reign, the latter half of which was vile and weak. The nation reproaches the ministers for using a timidly audacious language in their dealings with England, a language which seems to deny the projects that have been formed, the feelings we cherish; this language can only debase the speaker without deceiving the hearer, and it casts dishonor that is useful neither to the minister nor to the state."

The moderate but certainly not timid replies of Louis XVI to the Court of Saint James's said in substance that he did not want to close his ports to Americans or forbid his subjects to have commercial dealings with them; that he had given orders to prevent smuggling, insofar as possible; that France had observed the Treaty of Utrecht and would continue to observe it.

These replies prove that Abbé Raynal was mistaken both with regard to the Court of Versailles and the lethargy of Saint James's.* As French conduct has won universal approbation, it would not have been wise to change everything to please the author of the *Philosophical History of the Two Indies.*

As for the reproaches he claims were addressed to the government, he should tell us what war ever pleased a nation. It is natural that commercial transactions should play a part, both with individuals and the government, because the latter has no right to involve the nation in a war which will not benefit the public.† It is praiseworthy to reconcile this public advantage with humanitarian sentiments and prudent generosity. That France did this for us is evident in the treaty of alliance and commerce based on equalitarian principles and drawn up at a time when we desperately needed help and when it alone had acknowledged our independence.

The abbé complains that France fettered itself to Congress, which it could have controlled by adequate and regular subsidies. I shall not even attempt to guess what he means by fettering France to Congress.

As my reflections on this passage are similar to those of Mr.

* See Note L.

† In Part IV we shall comment on the causes hindering commercial transactions between France and America.

Paine, I shall quote his words. "When an author undertakes to treat of public happiness he ought to be certain that he does not mistake passion for right, nor imagination for principle. Principle, like truth, needs no contrivance. It will ever tell its own tale, and tell it the same way. But where this is not the case, every page must be watched, recollected, and compared like an invented story. I am surprised at this passage of the Abbé's. It means nothing or it means ill; and in any case it shows the great difference between speculative and practical knowledge." [16]

If France had followed the philosophical lessons of the abbé and tried to keep the Americans in a dependent state, it would have transgressed the laws of good politics. Alliances are not enduring unless they are established on a basis of reciprocal convenience, and a people that risks everything for liberty is entitled to gratitude, not submission.

"Finally," continues the abbé [p. 356], "as the principal object of philosophy is to see that all governments are just and all peoples happy, it seeks the motive of this alliance between a monarchy and a people defending its liberty. Human happiness cannot be involved because if the Court of Versailles had been motivated by love of justice, it would have decreed in the first article of its treaty with the United States that all oppressed peoples had the right to rebel."

This is not necessarily the case. The Americans were careful not to add any superfluous articles, especially one which would have provoked long and thorny discussions. The difficulty is not so much in the principle as in the right to make decisions. For example, who will decide in a monarchy whether the people are oppressed? To find out, you would have to change governments, including that of Great Britain, where, according to James Burgh,* the population numbers about six million, but less than six thousand voters elect half of the representatives.

Since France did not insert in the first article of its treaty with the Americans a maxim which might have displeased all the European powers, the abbé concludes that the happiness of humanity was not involved. The reader will wonder how this same happiness

---

* This celebrated writer says that "254 members [of the House of Commons] are actually elected by 5,723 votes . . . and the greatest part of these illustrious 5,723, who have the power of constituting lawgivers over the property of the nation, are themselves persons of no property" [*Political Disquisitions* (Philadelphia, 1775), pp. 45–46].

[16] Paine, "Letter to the Abbé Raynal," *Complete Writings*, p. 245.

would have been involved if France had kept the United States in a state of subordination.

As for the motive sought by the philosophical author, one might believe the lethargy he attributes to the Court of Saint James's had taken possession of his philosophy, since anyone who was awake could easily perceive the wise and just motives on which the alliance was based. Not the least of these was to attract a nation which would otherwise have joined forces with the enemy. All Europe knows that Louis XVI found the French navy in a very bad state. During the first years of his reign mariners rose from a state of degradation to one of glory. Had the abbé been less scrupulous, he might have made several observations to honor his prince, but he was afraid of being considered a Francophile.

He writes (p. 340): "all the French were concerned about the navy" (in 1775), and four pages later, "France began the war with tremendous advantages" (in 1778). He might have used the interval between these passages to inform the reader what produced such a transformation in three years. Instead he criticizes public administrators. He says he speaks to the nations and to posterity,* that the just and magnanimous are his fellow citizens, that he honors virtue, and that he will be just to the living as he has been to the dead.

After these observations, which might have been omitted without harm to either philosophical history or modesty, the abbé undertakes to persuade his readers that France had decided to fight England at the beginning of the Revolution. "The place, the time, the circumstances, it had chosen everything. It was only after making its leisurely preparations and building its forces to the requisite size that it appeared on the battlefield." The truth is that it had no desire to wage war.

A writer less fearful of being accused of partiality would have said that France had not forgotten the fatal blow it suffered in the loss of about twenty-two thousand sailors while its ambassador in London was assuring the Court of Versailles of the peaceful intentions of the British government. This contributed heavily to the disasters which followed and to the shameful treaty of 1763. It would have been easy to take vengeance, especially on the American coasts and in the islands, but France refused to do so.

Abbé Raynal may be correct in saying the royal vessels did not

---

* On p. 376 and in a number of other places the author declares he is writing for posterity, but a love of truth and distaste for bombast are growing daily.

afford sufficient protection to merchant shipping. I shall not claim
the discipline was perfect, but remind you that several years earlier
it did not even exist. It is possible the conduct of the ministers was
not always exemplary; but where will you find a minister, an admiral, or a general who does not make mistakes? A sidelight on the
way our enemy did business is revealed in the American remark
that their forces should erect statues to Lord North, Lord Sandwich, Lord Stormont, and Lord Germain.[17]

The abbé's anger and credulity are boundless. When he criticizes the navy (p. 347), he reveals that he was gullible or that enthusiasm had confused his ideas. "Until that time the ministry had
directed naval operations in accordance with its political objective.
This authority now passed, almost imperceptibly, to those who
were to execute the operations." The government has always directed plans, and commanders have carried them out as circumstances permitted. If he intended to say the commanders acted as
if they had full authority, he relied on false information. If he
condemns their flexibility, his judgment is at fault. It is most imprudent to direct operations from a distant office, and governments
which have attempted it have suffered the consequences. England
has always granted its commanders freedom to act and has never
regretted it.

The author was also misinformed about the conduct of the
French toward the Spanish court (p. 358). "The Court of Versailles did not inform Madrid it was notifying Saint James's that it
had recognized the independence of the colonies." The Spanish
king was always informed about everything. Again the abbé was
incorrect in his discussion of the suggestions made by the Spanish
king to England. "This monarch realized the arrangement gave
Great Britain an opportunity to become reconciled with its colonies. He was aware that he was wounding the dignity of his royal
nephew—but he wanted to be just." [18] According to the treaty of
alliance between France and the United States, neither party could
make peace or agree to a truce without the consent of the other.
Louis XVI freed the United States from this obligation by au-

[17] Frederick Lord North was British prime minister from 1770 until he resigned
in 1782 after the surrender of Cornwallis. John Montague, fourth earl of Sandwich,
was first lord of the admiralty during the American Revolution. David Murray,
seventh Viscount Stormont and second earl of Mansfield, was British ambassador
in Vienna and at Versailles. For Germain, see p. 190 and note above.

[18] Philip V, duke of Anjou and later king of Spain, was a grandson of Louis
XIV and uncle of Louis XVI.

thorizing the Spanish ruler to propose that the king of England should have the authority to deal directly with the Americans.

The English ministers acknowledged this in a derisive memoir asserting that the French king was pretending to do the king of England a favor by granting him "permission to deal with his rebellious subjects." If the abbé had taken the trouble to read this memoir, instead of committing the error for which he is being reproached, he might have been able, without running the risk of being accused of Gallomania, to point out the absurdity of sneering at a proposal which so honors its author. He could have proved that the absurdity consisted rather in applying the term *subjects* to the inhabitants of the United States at this time.

The British navy was at the peak of its power when Louis XVI assumed command of the piteous French fleet, although the number of vessels it contained was not so small as had been believed. If we compare the lack of experience of the French to the recognized skill of British admirals and captains, the French would have covered themselves with glory had they merely defended themselves. They would, however, have had an unbroken string of victories were it not for one serious error, attributed to the misplaced courage of a commander.

It has been claimed that the English had to fight four enemies, and this four-to-one ratio is likely to impress the superficial observer. But because the Americans had no vessels other than several small frigates, they could not reinforce the French navy. The Dutch did not bother the English nearly as much as their French allies, since the latter had to defend their possessions in America and the East Indies. English ships occasionally lost fighting time in provisioning Gibraltar and reinforcing their garrison there, but the French lost considerably more in carrying out the wishes of the Spanish court.

An impartial examination of the belligerents reveals that England was fighting only one enemy on the high seas. The Americans fought on land, but they would not have scored their victory so quickly without assistance from the French navy. We should also note that because the Americans were fighting a purely defensive war, the aggressor had the advantage of being able to select the time and place to attack.

After saying that "the Spanish court espoused the Versailles quarrel, and consequently the American cause," Abbé Raynal quotes historic events to prove that a lone power which plans and executes projects independently has numerous advantages over allied forces, whose operations are subject to all the annoyances caused by a conflict of interests. Yet the same writer, in discussing the British ruler's rejection of the proposals of mediation offered by the Spanish monarch, could say (p. 360): "When pride vanquishes terror, the greatness of a nation is revealed. If anyone were to ask me how the present English firmness will be regarded in a few years, I should answer that I do not know. But I am sure the world's annals rarely afford the august and majestic spectacle of a nation which sacrifices its life to its glory."

Even Lord North must have laughed at this. Mr. Paine at the beginning of his letter wrote: "The abbé in the course of his work, has, in some instances, extolled without a reason, and wounded without a cause. He has given fame where it was not deserved and withheld it where it was justly due." [19] He has gone further, for the praiseworthy has often been the object of his censure.

If the author had not said "we love our country and pay homage to justice," we could almost suspect him of being an Anglophile. Certainly no English minister dreamed that his country was in danger of perishing from the earth. England did not doubt its superiority over the combined forces of France and Spain. "Peace with America and war with the House of Bourbon" was the slogan of the famous earl of Chatham, who was carried to Parliament to advise the nation a few days before his death.[20]

Since the prime minister, Lord North, and the first lord of the admiralty, Lord Sandwich, had not hesitated to assure Parliament that England's naval strength surpassed that of France and Spain, they could scarcely have believed they were risking the very existence of their country by declining the offers of the Spanish ruler. This threat to England appears all the more extraordinary since the author seems to think the union of the allied powers will be of short duration (p. 364); elsewhere (p. 368) he considers it unlikely the other powers will permit the House of Bourbon to become more powerful than England, and he had already stated that Europe must decide whether, in helping America, France did not increase English strength.

The English were convinced that war with Spain would be beneficial, since piracy in wartime is protected by law. Ever since 1745, when Admiral Anson [21] got so much loot, war with Spain had

[19] Paine, "Letter to the Abbé Raynal," *Complete Writings*, p. 215.
[20] William Pitt.
[21] George Anson, Baron Anson, British admiral known as the Father of the Navy.

been considered an easy method of reaping an abundant harvest, and the capture of the *Endymion* in 1762 confirmed this.*

If further proof is needed that England did not share the abbé's views, you will find it in its decision to attack Holland, for it preferred a state of war to neutrality. As good politicians had predicted, England had little to fear from this adversary.

I trust the reader will not be sorry to see some of Mr. Paine's reflections on the astonishing passage I have just quoted.

In this paragraph the conception is lofty and the expression elegant, but the coloring is too high for the original, and the likeness fails through an excess of graces. To fit the powers of thinking and the turn of language to the subject, so as to bring out a clear conclusion that shall hit the point in question and nothing else, is the true criterion of writing. But the greater part of the abbé's writings (if he will pardon me the remark) appears to be uncentral and burdened with variety. They present a beautiful wilderness without paths; in which the eye is diverted by everything without being particularly directed to anything; and in which it is agreeable to be lost, and difficult to find the way out. . . . [England had high expectations of subjugating America and had no other naval force against it than that of France; neither was England certain that rejecting the mediation of Spain would combine that power with France. It felt superior to both and had no idea of renouncing its own existence.]

But if the Abbé is delighted with high and striking singularities of character, he might in America have found ample field for encomium. Here was a people who could not know what part the world would take for, or against them; and who were venturing on an untried scheme, in opposition to a power against which more formidable nations had failed. They had everything to learn but the principles which supported them, and everything to procure that was necessary for their defense. They have at times seen themselves as low as distress could make them, without showing the least decrease of fortitude; and been raised again by the most unexpected events, without discovering an unmanly discomposure of joy. To hesitate or to despair are conditions equally unknown in America. Her mind was prepared for everything; because her original and final resolution of succeeding or perishing included all possible circumstances.

The rejection of the British proposition in the year 1778, circumstanced as America was at that time, is a far greater instance of un-

---

* The treasure from this galley, estimated at £700,000, was borne to the Bank of England with solemn pomp to the accompaniment of cannonades, martial music, and the pealing of bells.

shaken fortitude than the refusal of the Spanish mediation by the Court of London.[22]

The parallel drawn by the abbé (p. 366) between the national characters of the French and the English is no less astonishing than the so-called act of moral greatness we have just discussed. "If we consider the mentality of the French in contrast to that of the English, we shall see that the Frenchman is quick to be enthusiastic and to lose interest; he expects miracles at the beginning but loses heart when he encounters an obstacle; he needs to be successful if he is to continue. The Englishman, on the other hand, is less presumptuous at the beginning, but he can struggle courageously and rise to the occasion in a time of danger and disgrace. He resembles the robust oak to which Horace compared the Romans, which grew beneath blows of the axe and gained new vigor from its wounds."

Without examining how far national character exerts an influence on court behavior, I shall merely comment that the writer confuses the qualities of the body with those of the mind, and that his comparison to Horace's oak tree is out of place.

I agree that Frenchmen show more ardor than other soldiers at the beginning of a battle. I must therefore admit that the enemy's resistance tires them more rapidly. The second concession is a necessary result of the first. But this does not prove they have lost courage; quite the contrary. After the disastrous battle of Minden in 1760, the decision to send the royal guard into the army restored national valor. I crossed France in September of that year and observed a universal confidence mixed with joy.

The English, with more prudence and less ardor, can resist for a longer period but are cast down for a longer time by the memory of their defeats. At the beginning of the war of 1756 the failure of the expedition against Cherbourg and the loss of Port Mahon upset the English to such an extent that you could not take a step in London without seeing it on all faces. The consternation occasioned by the progress of the Pretender in 1745 ended by giving George II power equal to that of a dictator.

If the author was anxious to put Horace's oak on the stage, he could very well have placed it on the other side. His ideas are so confused that neither his criticism nor his praise is appropriate.

[22] Paine, "Letter to the Abbé Raynal," *Complete Writings*, pp. 246–48.

Chapter 10

# American Behavior

Americans, according to the abbé, should be regarded with contempt because they tried to maintain their independence. "Budding authority had to deal with cowardice, not audacity" (p. [9:]330). This language seems to be that of misinformed or very prejudiced individuals. He describes (p. 311) General Howe's landing on Long Island in these terms: "On 28 August he landed without opposition on Long Island under the protection of a fleet commanded by his brother, the admiral. The Americans did not show much more vigor inland than on the coast. After a mediocre resistance with fairly heavy losses, they took refuge inland with an ease which a conqueror would not have permitted if he could have followed up his advantage."

"The new Republicans abandoned the city of New York even more readily than they had evacuated Long Island." A well-informed officer gave me the following statement: "It would have been more just to pay homage to General Washington for the Long Island retreat, which was dangerous and so well planned it was a tribute to his courage, prudence, and talents. As to the English landing, it would not be surprising if Abbé Raynal knew nothing of the terrain or even the point where the Howe brothers landed their troops. This information was important to the Americans in deciding what they should do."

In this area the Long Island terrain is such that troops protected by a fleet can land without opposition. Masters of the sea, the English could select the site for the attack, land in several places simultaneously, or keep their forces together. General Howe landed thirty-two thousand men on Long Island, where the Americans never had over ten thousand. They were under command of General [Israel] Putnam, while General Washington's army was on the mainland. An account of this engagement appears in the *Annual Register* for 1777.* I shall merely give an extract.

* The *Annual Register* is an anthology published annually in London [by Edmund Burke from 1759 to 1788] with an account of the most remarkable events which occurred during the previous year. It is believed the history of the war was written by Mr. Edmund Burke, which indicates that it is well written. The only

According to the English historian, the officers sent by Putnam to seize passes were not very clever. General Howe sent Lord Cornwallis with the reserve corps and some other troops to a place called Flatbush, where, as the Americans occupied the pass, he waited as ordered. When the whole army had landed, General [Leopold Philip von] Heister went to Flatbush with the German troops and General [James] Grant with a detachment of English troops. Grant commanded the left wing, which extended to the coast.

The next morning the attack began, and for several hours the artillery and musketry of both sides fought valiantly. Suddenly, from behind the Americans appeared General Clinton, Lord Cornwallis, and Lord Percy with the main portion of the English army, which had come around to the right during the night without our knowing it. The warships attacked as soon as it was light, and one battery was located above Red Hook to distract the soldiers fighting General Grant and to keep the others from seeing the troops approaching behind them. The following paragraphs I quote from the English historian are quite different from the description written by Abbé Raynal three years later:

> Those who opposed the Hessians in the left and center were the first apprized of the march of the British army and of their own danger. They accordingly retreated in large bodies, and in tolerable order, with their artillery, in order to recover their camp, but soon found themselves intercepted by the King's troops, who furiously attacked and drove them back into the woods. In these desperate circumstances some of their regiments, overpowered and outnumbered as they were, forced their way to the lines through all the difficulties and dangers that opposed and surrounded them. Others, perhaps not less brave, perished in the attempt.
>
> General Washington passed over from New York during the engagement and is said to have burst into a poignant exclamation of grief when he beheld the inextricable destruction in which some of his best troops were involved. Nothing was now left but to preserve the remainder of the army on Long Island. He knew the superior power of the royal artillery.[23]

After painting the critical situation of General Washington, which was aggravated by the threat that with a favorable wind the English vessels might cut off all communication, the same historian

---

fault one could find is that the historian could not avoid partiality, but he was writing at a time when it was very difficult to get reports from both sides.

[23] *Annual Register for the Year 1776* (London, 1777), pp. 170–72.

relates how he got out of this dilemma. He concludes: "It must be acknowledged that in the course of this campaign, and more particularly in this part of it, he fully performed the part of no mean commander." [24]

As to the evacuation of New York, a subject which the abbé seems to have enjoyed because it gave him an opportunity to speak scornfully of the "new Republicans," a little knowledge of topography reveals that the city could be burned in less than half an hour by anyone controlling the heights of Long Island. It is not true, however, that New York was abandoned as precipitously as the writer would like us to believe, because General Washington withdrew the last pickets on 15 September, or fifteen days after the retreat. During the interval he kept the army in a safe place about two miles away. Moreover, the English commander, who was certain the American general would soon have to abandon the city, was anxious to preserve property which would be useful.

Not content with misleading his readers from the landing of the English troops on Long Island to the evacuation of New York, the abbé continues in the same inaccurate vein: "The Americans withdrew to Kingsbridge, where everything seemed ready for a stubborn resistance. If the British had followed up their initial successes with the energy demanded by the circumstances, the new recruits opposing them would inevitably have dispersed or been forced to lay down their arms. They were given six weeks to consolidate, and they did not abandon their entrenchments until the night of the first to the second of November, when military movements convinced them that their camp was finally going to be attacked."

The author, who does not spare us his reflections but is less generous with facts, suppresses them altogether here. The inaction, which seems to displease him, was quite imaginary. The English took possession of the city of New York the day it was evacuated; the following morning (16 September) they set out to attack, but the Americans pushed them back two miles with heavy losses. The battle of Harlem Heights, which the abbé considers of no significance, drew the attention of the British historian, who was not convinced the British would inevitably have forced the new recruits to lay down their arms.

On 12 October the English embarked on the river and arrived at Throgs Neck, ten miles behind our camp, where they were

[24] Ibid, pp. 178–79.

stopped by Washington's forces. On the eighteenth they set out again and went to Pelham; no sooner had they landed than they were attacked by troops under Colonels [John] Glover and [William] Shepard. This attack forced the light infantry of the enemy to draw back to the right, and General Howe took up his position between Pelham and New Rochelle instead of moving inland as he had apparently intended.

The enemy's new location made General Washington decide to retreat twelve or fifteen miles. On the twentieth and twenty-first of the month he set up camp at White Plains, at a spot almost parallel to the English camp. The next day (the twenty-second) General Howe attacked him with twenty-two thousand élite troops. The action began three miles outside the lines, between the English infantry and the American militia, which could not bear the brunt of the attack. However, because the infantry was exhausted by so much marching, it was relieved by German troops. General [Alexander] Macdougall withstood their attack and finally repulsed it. Then General Howe, who had opened a path between them, advanced at the head of the English grenadiers and forced General Macdougall, who resisted, to withdraw inside the lines. The rest of that day was marked only by sporadic artillery fire, and during the next four days the two armies remained facing each other. Since General Washington had changed his position slightly to put his magazines in a safer location, General Howe was unable to drive him out. This is enough to prove that Abbé Raynal was incorrect in blaming the English general for six weeks of inactivity.

The English army then moved toward New York in search of winter quarters, but the unexpected seizure of Fort Washington and its consequences made General Howe decide to go in the direction of Philadelphia instead. Everyone knows General Washington was obliged to retreat across the Jerseys, because he had only twenty-five hundred men, with whom, Abbé Raynal says (p. 312), "he was only too happy to be able to escape across the Delaware."

After reproaching the English commander for not taking advantage of the opportunity to "stifle the new republic," a task which apparently did not seem so easy to General Howe, who was on the spot, as to the author in his study, the abbé concludes by saying that General Howe settled negligently into winter quarters (p. 313). "This gave heart to the militias of Pennsylvania, Maryland, and Virginia, which had united for their common safety. On

25 December they crossed the Delaware and attacked Trenton, which was occupied by fifteen hundred of the twelve thousand Hessians who had been sold to Great Britain by their greedy master. These troops were massacred, captured, or dispersed. A week later three English regiments were also driven from Princeton, although they put up a better fight than their foreign mercenaries."

The officer whom I have already quoted comments:

The Trenton affair is poorly explained and the battle of Princeton not explained at all. A week after the battle at Trenton, General Washington returned to the Jerseys and took up quarters in this same city. At nightfall twelve thousand English arrived to attack him. The American general, who was greatly outnumbered, outwitted the enemy by lighting fires whose smoke covered his retreat; he made a diagonal march of about eighteen miles and reached Princeton, twelve miles behind the enemy, at dawn. Here he captured a regiment which had been left as liaison. These men did not put up a fight, and the commander, instead of withdrawing into the college courtyard, went out into the main street, where he could offer no resistance. General Washington's maneuver does him great honor among military men. As this forced the English to withdraw, he ended by recovering the Jerseys and establishing winter quarters.

Although the Germans posted at Trenton were surprised, they fought and did not surrender until their commander, Colonel [Johann] Rall, had been gravely wounded by three bullets. I got this detail from several people who were present, among them Colonel Smith,[25] who took care of him.

The account which follows (p. 315) is no more accurate: "The 1777 campaign began very late. The English army, despairing of finding a route through Jersey to Pennsylvania, finally embarked 23 July and sailed through Chesapeake Bay to a region which their generals should have invaded the previous year. Their progress was not interrupted until they reached Brandywine. There they beat the Americans on 11 September and arrived in Philadelphia on the thirtieth."

The author's style is truly curious. I recall Mr. Paine's remark: "He hastens through his narrations as if he was glad to get from them, that he may enter the more copious field of eloquence and imagination."[26]

[25] Probably William S. Smith, who later became Washington's aide-de-camp. See pp. 181–83 above.
[26] Paine, "Letter to the Abbé Raynal," *Complete Writings*, p. 222.

The same officer, who saw bloodshed several times before the English army reached Philadelphia and who was wounded himself, gave me the following report, which, once again, does not agree with that of the abbé.

The British advance was stopped at Christina Creek, where our light troops engaged their vanguard in a skirmish. The Brandywine cannonade began at nine o'clock in the morning at Chadds Ford, though the light troops had started firing at daybreak. The affair at the right at the Wilmington church began at four o'clock with musketry and grapeshot cannon. As new lines formed behind those which were repulsed, the combat lasted until dark. We were beaten; we lost some men; but our enemies lost more because we killed a number during the attack and our retreat was protected. This is the information we got from our surgeons, who were summoned by General Howe because his doctors were too busy taking care of their own wounded.

The enemy must have found this affair much more tiring than Abbé Raynal because they did not proceed to Darby the next day. That would have been highly embarrassing for us. It is about two days' march from Brandywine to Philadelphia; so there must have been some other activity between the eleventh and the thirtieth. Some very interesting things happened, and if our numbers had not been inferior, Howe would never have crossed the Schuylkill.

On the same page the abbé tells us his "victor" left Philadelphia because he was bored. "Bored by a nine-months' confinement, he decided to return to New York by way of Jersey, and under the command of Clinton, Howe's successor, he carried out this long and dangerous retreat with fewer losses than would have been incurred had he been fighting a more experienced enemy."

The one man we could criticize for not taking more advantage of this retreat (which from our point of view was not so admirable) was our only experienced general, General Lee. If Washington's orders had been obeyed, Clinton would have been in a tight fix, although this seems inexcusable for a "victor" seeking relief from boredom.* The truth is that the English were having a good time in Philadelphia, and it was the French fleet, under command of the comte d'Estaing,[27] not boredom, which made the English decide to take the wise precaution of crossing the Jerseys.

When the enemy had evacuated Philadelphia, General Washing-

---

* From time to time the reader can make reflections which apparently do not occur to the abbé; they would do little honor to the men he wants to praise.

[27] Charles Hector Théodat, comte d'Estaing, arrived off New York harbor on 11 July 1778 with a fleet of 17 French ships.

ton left the Valley Forge camp and crossed the Delaware twenty miles above the city. Although his army destroyed roads in the Jerseys, it did not stop the advance of Generals Clinton and [Wilhelm von] Knyphausen, who had sent their sick and some of their equipment by sea. Some time later General Clinton moved toward Freehold, where it was difficult to attack him. The two armies were about the same size, with approximately fourteen thousand men. We had fifteen hundred to two thousand militiamen, who tried to harass the enemy, but our advance was delayed by inadequate provisions and, to an even greater extent, by the uncertainties of a council of war. General Lee had persuaded the majority of the officers that they should go directly to White Plains without risking a battle. General Washington, however, decided to give the marquis de Lafayette some four thousand men to pursue the enemy. General Lee now demanded the detachment he had previously commanded; he left with a thousand men, joined the marquis, who was under his orders, and detached the militia, which was supposed to attack from the front while he attacked the rear guard. On the morning of 28 June he was within range of the enemy, which had united in a single column, while their rear guard was cut off. Instead of taking advantage of this, General Lee moved back until he was attacked by the entire army. He was retreating in confusion when General Washington arrived at a gallop, sent him to the rear, and organized the vanguard troops under Generals Lafayette, [Henry] Knox, and Wayne. Washington then returned to his army and ordered the vanguard to retreat. They had barely time to do so. The two armies, separated by a small valley, cannonaded each other for a long time with great success. The enemy was hit in the flank by a battery of General Greene's right wing under command of Lieutenant Colonel Mauduit Duplessis. They attempted to go around our left, but the general sent the marquis de Lafayette there at a right angle to them with the second line. Lord Stirling [28] took up two positions at the back of the battlefield, and then the American army advanced. When night fell, General Clinton withdrew to the Minisink Hills, leaving the wounded behind.*

On the next page the author tells about General [John] Bur-

---

* General Clinton wrote the court he had taken advantage of the moonlight, but it was a new moon and below the horizon. It is inconceivable that he could have been bedazzled to this extent.

[28] William Alexander, known as Lord Stirling, commanded the First New Jersey Line.

goyne's expedition and describes his arrival at Ticonderoga in a way that discredits General [Arthur] St. Clair, in command of the fort. "As he approached, a garrison of four thousand men abandoned their important post, losing their artillery, ammunition, and rear guard." If an English general had seen that Ticonderoga could not be defended against an army from Canada in control of Lake Champlain, and if this general had sacrificed his reputation in order to save two or three thousand men, who later formed the kernel of the troops which captured Burgoyne at Saratoga, the abbé, who is always ready to commend enemy maneuvers, would have praised him to the skies; this is what General St. Clair did.

The writer then describes General Burgoyne's maneuvers and concludes: "Gathering their courage, Americans surrounded him on 13 October at Saratoga, and people learned with astonishment that six thousand of the best soldiers of the Old World had laid down their arms before the farmers of the New under the lucky [General Horatio] Gates. Those who recalled that the hitherto invincible Swedes of Charles XII capitulated before the barbaric Russians did not blame the English troops but the poor judgment of their general." *

The poor Americans, whether soldiers or commanders, have never been able to arouse the author's eloquence. He scarcely mentions the capture of Burgoyne, and the strategy of those who captured him is not worthy of his attention.

Abbé Raynal is singularly inclined to believe we received secret assistance, but I can assure him that unfortunately for us, the aid from the English party of the opposition, which he suspected, was no less imaginary than that of the French government which he was sure about.

According to his views, it was also a taste for luxury that prevented the English from defeating the colonies. "On leaving the coasts they would have been forced to abandon their pleasures; so they had no inclination to pursue an enemy which was always ready to bury itself inland." The word "bury" conveys the impression that Americans resembled a flock of sheep which sought shelter the instant a wolf appeared. I should like the reader to recall, however, that it was indispensable for the patriots to draw the enemy into the interior, because they could never hope to win on the coasts.

When Milord Cornwallis was in Yorktown, he could have

---

* The author seems unaware that half of the captured troops were German.

thumbed his nose at a hundred thousand picked soldiers if the French fleet had not been present. As soon as the situation became dangerous he would have embarked on the York River and within a few hours reached another spot he could pillage for several weeks without interruption. The English could never remain for any length of time in the interior; they laid it waste with their forays but weakened themselves. Their great asset was their ships, and they lost this advantage as soon as they left the coasts and navigable rivers.

Americans were guided less by enthusiasm than by an intelligent patriotism. From this point of view they might have merited the abbé's praise if a scrupulous delicacy had not led him to fear being accused of partiality. To avoid any doubt on this score, he first accuses us gratuitously of "cowardice" and then continues (p. 330) with his picture of the "birth of authority." "The new government prescribed the death penalty for desertion and soiled the standard of liberty by assassinations." Some writers think a revolution is like a riot and that an army resembles a small clique. All nations need tribunals for a period of ten years, and there are miscreants in every army. When foreigners, or occasionally Americans, deserted, they were punished; that is what the abbé politely terms an "assassination."

English prisoners were exchanged for Americans; the English wanted to give us a number of men they had deposited dead or dying on shore, some of whom perished during the crossing from New York to New Jersey. General Washington could not accept them. The English also offered to exchange private citizens for English soldiers, and they refused to exchange General Lee until 1778.

All navies and many armies conduct an investigation when a ship or post is lost. It is less a method of punishment than a justification, and the more men prize public opinion, the more they request this type of inquiry.

Raynal claims the government refused to permit an exchange of prisoners lest the troops develop a "tendency to surrender instantly." Such a tendency never existed, and the enemy never dared boast of such a thing. The facts are quite different. From the beginning of the war until August 1779, American prisoners were treated in a barbarous fashion, but officials could never bring themselves to take reprisal on the innocent. When I was a prisoner in New York, during the summer of 1779, I walked one day with

Mr. Cammel, a captain of infantry in the English army,[29] toward the Hudson through the section of the city which had been burned. He told me sadly that we were passing over the graves of about four thousand Frenchmen and Americans who had died because they were imprisoned in churches throughout the summer heat. They were packed together so closely they were suffocating from lack of space and air. Furthermore, because their sole nourishment consisted of a small quantity of spoiled food and a minute amount of brackish water, they suffered horribly from thirst.*

The British held their prisoners in two converted warships. On the third day they developed a pestilential fever, which brought delirium and death to the majority, while the survivors had little hope of recovering. One day when I was on board the commodore's vessel, I saw the bridge of a small craft covered with men who had just been taken from the prison ships. "There are about 150 exchanged prisoners," a marine lieutenant told me, "but a scant 20 will live to see Boston." "Why?" I asked. "Because they have death in their blood." I surmised from his manner that he was sad, and I was not mistaken. His compassion contrasted with the air of satisfaction I had seen half an hour before on shore. One Scot, looking at the ships through his binoculars, said gaily to another, "We got men and we are giving cadavers in exchange."

From the outbreak of the war we heard reports about the inhumane treatment to which our prisoners were subjected. Several times I heard brave men protest they would not enlist unless it was agreed that no one would give or receive any quarter. "It is the only way," they said, "because we cannot bring ourselves to do what they do. What is the use of living if you have to suffer to such a point that you want to die?" Such convictions are quite different from the "tendency to surrender instantly."

This barbarous treatment was brought almost to a halt in August

---

* Mr. Cammel belonged to a Scottish family which had settled in North Carolina several years before the Revolution. When the war broke out, he joined the English, leaving his father, mother, brothers, sisters, and all his possessions in Carolina. He told me several times that his conscience made him march under the royal flags, although he often disapproved of the behavior of the king's ministers and officers. He believed the English would win, and he flattered himself he would be useful to his family, who did not share his political views.

[29] Mr. Cammel may have been Captain Colin Campbell of the Eighty-fourth Regiment under command of Sir Henry Clinton (Worthington C. Ford, comp. *British Officers Serving in the American Revolution, 1774–1782* [Brooklyn, 1897], pp. 40–41). See also p. 182 above.

1779, thanks to M. [Conrad-Alexandre] Gérard, minister plenipotentiary of the king of France in the United States. He sent a
messenger from Philadelphia to Staten Island for a two-day conference with the English commissioner. It is thought that one important factor contributing to this change was the news that the
comte d'Estaing had just fought Admirals [John] Byron and
[Samuel] Barrington and had captured Saint Vincent and Grenada.
A defeat usually inspires moderation in the English, as victory inspires humanity and generosity among the French.

There are, of course, always exceptions, and I know our enemies
performed more praiseworthy acts than the blameworthy ones of
our allies. Some Englishmen in New York were diametrically opposed to the spirit prevailing at the Court of Saint James's. But I
shall tell just one story to illustrate the greatness of soul of a simple
sailor.

Toward the close of 1777, a French captain was sentenced to
death by a British court-martial in New York because he had continued to fight and had killed a man after his vessel had been
boarded. The fact is that the flag was still flying. He was to be
executed the following day, but during the night an English sailor
managed to help him escape. The two arrived safely in Williamsburg, where the captain had French friends. They made the sailor
several generous offers, but he declined them, saying to the captain: "You are brave and I thought your sentence unjust. I risked
my life to save you and I should do it again because I could not
bear to see a brave man perish miserably. I was already unhappy
about what my compatriots in New York were doing and wanted
to leave. Now all I ask is the means to return to England so that
no one can think me disloyal to my country." His wish was
granted.

I return to my author. After taxing us with "cowardice" and
saying (p. 331) that few Americans were capable of heroic feelings,* he continues: "The intoxication was never widespread, and
it could be only short lived, for not a single motive for revolution
existed in North America. Religion and the legal system were upheld. No citizens had perished on the scaffold. No cherished
customs had been desecrated. Not a single inhabitant had been
taken from his home and thrown into prison. The principles of

---

* Elsewhere he wrote (p. 269), however: "It was said Americans were only a
flock of cowards who would yield to any threat; but you encounter worthy men,
real Englishmen."

administration and government had not changed. It all came down to the question whether England had the right to put a small tax, directly or indirectly, on the colonies, and this question, almost metaphysical in nature, was not one to rouse a multitude."

When the writer published his historical reflections, the "intoxication," to use his expression, had lasted for six years and was still almost universal. It is true that up to that time, no inhabitant had been imprisoned, but an order of Parliament had sanctioned this procedure, and the author would have paid more just homage to the impartiality he prizes if, instead of denying the existence of any cause for revolution, he had commended the Americans for not awaiting the consequences of this act. He speaks of the Declaration of Independence as if it were a naïve manifesto, since the complaints it lists were, according to him, all based on the question, "almost metaphysical in nature," whether England had the right to put a small tax on the colonies. The discussion of the true cause of the Revolution reveals that the question was by no means a metaphysical one, and the complaints listed in the Declaration of Independence all referred to incontrovertible facts. The abbé now addresses himself to the English (p. 259) and discusses their attitude toward Americans: "When did they refuse you until you held a bayonet against their chests and threatened, 'Your wealth or your lives; die or be my slaves'?" In view of this admission, it is difficult to see how "not a single motive for revolution existed in North America."

As this matter is discussed in Mr. Paine's letter, I shall quote several passages pertaining to this dearth of motives.

In speaking of the Stamp Act, which was passed in 1764, he styles it "an *usurpation* of the Americans' *most precious and sacred rights.*" Consequently he here admits the most energetic of all causes, that is, *an usurpation of their most precious and sacred rights,* to have existed in America twelve years before the Declaration of Independence, and ten years before the breaking out of hostilities. . . .

The Stamp Act, it is true, was repealed in two years after it was passed, but it was immediately followed by one of infinitely more mischievous magnitude; I mean the Declaratory Act, which asserted the right, as it was styled, of the British Parliament, "*to bind America in all cases whatsoever.*"

If then the Stamp Act was an usurpation of the Americans' most precious and sacred rights, the Declaratory Act left them no rights at all; and contained the full grown seeds of the most despotic government ever exercised in the world. It placed America not only in the lowest, but in the basest state of vassalage; because it demanded an unconditional submission in everything, or as the act expressed it, *in all cases whatsoever:* and what renders this act the more offensive, is, that it appears to have been passed as an act of mercy; truly then may it be said, that *the tender mercies of the wicked are cruel.*

All the original charters from the Crown of England, under the faith of which the adventurers from the Old World settled in the New, were by this act displaced from their foundations; because, contrary to the nature of them, which was that of a compact, they were now made subject to repeal or alteration at the mere will of one party only. The whole condition of America was thus put into the hands of the Parliament or Ministry, without leaving to her the least right in any case whatsoever.*

There is no despotism to which this iniquitous law did not extend; and though it might have been convenient in the execution of it, to have consulted manners and habits, the principle of the act made all tyranny legal. It stopped nowhere. It went to everything. It took in with it the whole life of a man, or if I may so express it, an eternity of circumstances. It is the nature of law to require obedience, but this demanded servitude; and the condition of an American, under the operation of it, was not that of a subject, but a vassal. Tyranny has often been established *without* law and sometimes *against* it, but the history of mankind does not produce another instance, in which it has been established *by* law. It is an audacious outrage upon civil government, and cannot be too much exposed, in order to be sufficiently detested.[30]

Abbé Raynal is incorrect when he declares (p. 333) that the English and the colonists resolved to use the savages "for their mutual destruction." On the following page, after stating that the Indians rejected General [Guy] Carleton's proposal, he gives what he says was the Oneida reply to the American deputies. He is mistaken, for the Oneidas sent a protest, not a reply.

Discourse of the Chiefs and Warriors of the Indian Tribe of Oneidas to the Four Provinces of New England; This Was Addressed to Governor Trumbull,† Who Was Charged to Forward It to Them

As . . . younger brothers of the New England Indians, who have settled in our vicinity, are now going down to visit their friends, and

---

* Mr. Paine evidently thought it unnecessary to observe that it is far worse for a nation to be under the yoke of a foreign country than of a foreign despot.
† Trumbull was governor of Connecticut.
[30] Paine, "Letter to the Abbé Raynal," *Complete Writings,* pp. 216–17.

to move up parts of their families that were left behind . . . with this belt by them,* I open the door wide, clearing it of all obstacles, that they may visit their friends and return to their settlements here in peace.

We Oneidas are induced to this measure on account of the disagreeable situation of affairs that way; and we hope, by the help of God, they may return in peace. We earnestly recommend them to your charity through their long journey.

Now we more immediately address you, our brother, the Governor, and the chiefs of New England.

*Brothers:* We have heard of the unhappy differences and great contention between you and Old England. We wonder greatly, and are troubled in our minds.

*Brothers:* Possess your minds in peace, respecting us Indians. We cannot intermeddle in this dispute between Two brothers. The quarrel seems to be unnatural. You are *two brothers of one blood.* We are unwilling to join on either side in such a contest, for we bear an equal affection to both you Old and New England. Should the great king of England apply to us for aid, we shall deny him; if the Colonies apply, we shall refuse. The present situation of you two brothers is new and strange to us. We Indians cannot find, nor recollect in the traditions of our ancestors, the like case, or a similar instance.

*Brothers:* For these reasons possess your minds in peace, and take no umbrage that we Indians refuse joining in the contest. We are for peace.

*Brothers:* Was it an alien, a foreign nation, who had struck you, we should look into the matter. We hope, through the wise government and good pleasure of God, your distresses may be soon removed and the dark clouds be dispersed.

*Brothers:* As we have declared for peace, we desire you will not apply to our Indian brethren in New England for their assistance. Let us Indians be all of one mind, and live with one another; and you white people † settle your own disputes between yourselves.

*Brothers:* We have now declared our minds; please to write to us, that we may know yours. We, the sachems and warriors, and female governesses ‡ of *Oneida*, send our love to you, brother governor, and all the other chiefs in New England.

* The wampum belt was a gift of friendship designed to help open the road, etc. The Indians use a number of metaphors and often repeat, probably because of the inadequacy of their language.

† As they are much darker than we, they call Europeans "white men" and Americans are "men who came from Europe."

‡ The word *rulers* is incorrect, for no one commands among the Indians, and every question is settled by majority vote. The word *sachem* is applied to their chiefs, whose power is determined by their reputation in the nation or tribe.

Kananoorohara [Oneida], June 19, 1775

Signed by $\begin{cases} \text{Thomas Yoghtanawa} \\ \text{Adam Ohonooraro} \end{cases}$

and ten other chiefs and warriors of the Oneida tribe.
Translated into English by the missionary Samuel Kirkland.[31]

Until this time neither the English nor the Americans had requested aid from the Oneidas. The chief of the Shawnee tribe told the deputies from Virginia he could not guarantee the behavior of his young braves, and he begged them to take three or four hundred into the American army to prevent them from joining the English. The deputies refused to do this and urged the Indians to remain neutral.

It is probable that General Carleton also recommended neutrality, but other English officers used every device to stir up the Indians against us and succeeded only too well. Actually the Indians were of little assistance, for we could use them only against English soldiers, while our homes, our wives, and our children were exposed to their raids. Eventually we took a few into the army to serve as guides on the long marches we had to make against the enemy on our frontiers, but it is probable that less than six Englishmen were killed by our Indians during the entire war.

The abbé next discusses our poverty with the contempt of a Croesus: "Paper replaced silver. To bestow some dignity on this new currency, it was surrounded by emblems intended to remind people of the value of liberty and the necessity of persevering. This trick was not successful, and the new currency depreciated. Congress, indignant, thereupon declared that anyone who refused to take it at face value was a traitor." The history of paper money at the end of my book proves that this ideal wealth was not scorned. Furthermore, Congress never made the declaration to which the abbé refers because no legislative body had the power to do so.

After stating (p. 337) that "Great Britain had intercepted American navigation with Europe, the West Indies, etc.," he adds: "The Americans then said, 'We solemnly abjure the English name, which has made us odious. We are friends of all nations, and all flags can visit our ports.' But people did not accept the invitation." This is ridiculous. Americans simply took advantage of the liberty they had acquired through their Declaration of Independence.

---

[31] William L. Stone, *Life of Thomas Brant—Thayendanegea,* 2 vols. (New York, 1838), 1:62–63.

According to the abbé (p. 339), Congress had the courage to refuse the English offers because of the treaty with France, but that Congress knew nothing about this at the time is evident from Mr. Paine's letter. The English historian we mentioned also thought Congress knew about this treaty, but he was also aware that Americans had little confidence in the sincerity of the English offers and were resolved never to abandon liberty. Abbé Raynal, who should have realized the treaty had nothing to do with the American refusal, assures us it was the sole cause: "Congress, the generals, troops, the adroit or bold men who had seized authority in every colony had all recovered their courage thanks to a treaty of friendship and commerce between the United States and the Court at Versailles which was signed 6 February 1778." English ministers kept reiterating that "adroit men had seized authority in every colony." It was to their interest to say so, but the astonishing thing is that Abbé Raynal believed it. Dr. Franklin, Mr. Adams, or any other well-informed American could have told him that the best way to ruin a reputation in the United States is to intrigue for public office.

Now let us examine the reasons why the abbé thought the allies could not remain united. "Is it possible," he writes (p. 364), "that a close union can last between confederates as different as the excitable and scornful French, the slow, haughty, jealous and cold Spaniards, and the Americans, who keep secretly turning toward their mother country and who would rejoice over any disasters to their allies that did not affect their own independence?"

This is an altogether gratuitous assumption of American perfidy, while his criticism of the national character of our allies is quite uncalled for. I shall not discuss national characteristics, nor shall I ask why he calls the Spaniard jealous or cold. I shall merely observe that he accuses us—quite unjustly—of being completely ungrateful.

Even if we were capable of such treachery, we should have lost our minds had we rejoiced over any disaster that struck our allies. It is important for us to keep in touch with France, the only power which could help in case Great Britain attempted to reconquer America, and it will be at least a generation before that idea is abandoned. We must be extremely economical if we are to prosper. It would be hard to resist the temptation to order the English luxuries with which we are familiar, but it will be easy to get along without French ones we scarcely know.

The disharmony which the abbé predicts between the allied

nations is the fruit of his imagination. The Spaniards and the French have been most friendly, as have the Americans and the Spaniards. French and Americans have always showed high regard for one another and proof of a real affection.* Two facts attest to this national esteem. The French were dismayed by the capture of Charleston, while the unfortunate affair of 12 April[32] spread consternation in America. I could discuss this passage at great length, but the reader will surely be more interested in Mr. Paine's observations.

To draw foolish portraits of each other, is a mode of attack and reprisal, which the greater part of mankind are fond of indulging. The serious philosopher should be above it, more especially in cases from which no good can arise, and mischief may, and where no received provocation can palliate the offense. The Abbé might have invented a difference of character for every country in the world, and they in return might find others for him, till in the war of wit all real character is lost. The pleasantry of one nation or the gravity of another may, by a little pencilling, be distorted into whimsical features, and the painter becomes so much laughed at as the painting.

But why did not the Abbé look a little deeper, and bring forth the excellencies of the several parties? Why did he not dwell with pleasure on that greatness of character, that superiority of heart, which has marked the conduct of France in her conquests, and which has forced an acknowledgment even from Britain?

There is one line, at least (and many others might be discovered), in which the confederates unite; which is, that of a rival eminence in their treatment of their enemies. Spain, in her conquest of Minorca and the Bahama Islands, confirms this remark. America has been invariable in her lenity from the beginning of the war, notwithstanding the high provocations she has experienced. It is England only who has been insolent and cruel.

But why must America be charged with a crime undeserved by her conduct, more so by her principles, and which, if a fact, would be fatal to her honor? I mean the want of attachment to her allies, or rejoicing in their disasters. She, it is true, has been assiduous in showing to the world that she was not the aggressor toward England, and that the quarrel was not of her seeking, or, at that time, even of her wishing. But to draw inferences from her candor, and even from her justification, to stab her character by (and I see nothing else from which they can be supposed to be drawn), is unkind and unjust.

* See Note M.

[32] On 12 April 1782 the French fleet under command of Admiral François Joseph Paul de Grasse was defeated by the British under Vice Admiral George Rodney in the West Indies.

Does her rejection of the British propositions in 1778, before she knew of any alliance with France, correspond with the Abbé's description of her mind? Does a single instance of her conduct since that time justify it? But there is a still better evidence to apply to, which is, that of all the mails which, at different times, have been waylaid on the road, in divers parts of America, and taken and carried into New York,* and from which the most secret and confidential private letters, as well as those from authority, have been published, not one of them, I repeat it, not a single one of them, gave countenance to such a charge.

This is not a country where men are under government restraint in speaking; and if there is any kind of restraint, it arises from a fear of popular resentment. Now if nothing in her private or public correspondence favors such a suggestion, and if the general disposition of the country is such as to make it unsafe for a man who show an appearance of joy at any disaster to her ally, on what grounds, I ask, can the accusation stand? What company the Abbé may have kept in France, we cannot know; but this we know, that the account he gives does not apply to America.[33]

* Yorktown was then in British hands and was occupied by Cornwallis's army. [Paine says New York, not Yorktown.]

[33] Paine, "Letter to the Abbé Raynal," *Complete Writings*, pp. 249–50.

# Chapter 11

# Abbé Raynal's Counsel to France, Spain, and the United States

The abbé's zeal for the prosperity of his country is extended to Spain, and he puts both powers on guard lest their relations with the new republics be prejudicial to their best interests. The abbé's reflections are full of contradictions, as the passage on page 369 of volume 9 shows. He says that the United States intends to attract all of North America into its confederation and has already invited Canadians to rebel. Eventually the New World must be separated from the Old, but can Spain and France encourage this separation? America would then become an asylum for seditious European politicians who would turn their attention to conquest. The courts at Madrid and Versailles should endeavor to maintain two powers as a counterbalance in North America, and then their colonial possessions would be at peace.

If the abbé has no trouble stating our intentions as if they were facts, we can risk surmising his without being indiscreet. Mr. Paine observes: "But notwithstanding the Abbé's high profession in favor of liberty, he appears sometimes to forget himself, or that his theory is rather the child of his fancy than of his judgment." [34]

It is difficult to become accustomed to this emigration of seditious, dishonored, or ruined politicians and to the chain of events which follow one another so rapidly. Is it philosophy, politics, or both which caused him to advise France and Spain to postpone the great separation of the New World from the Old, even though he states it is being prepared by the progress of evil in the Old and good in the New?

He does not want the entire North American continent to be free, and advises keeping two powers there "to counterbalance one another," etc. The New World is painted as an asylum for the unfortunate (p. 379): "Oppression and intolerance drove new settlers there daily. The war stopped this emigration, but peace will open the door again, and people will flock there in greater numbers than ever." If the abbé was not mistaken when he wrote: "As soon as the liberty of this vast continent is assured it will become an asy-

[34] Ibid., p. 245.

lum for European politicians," we are forced to believe that the unfortunate will flock to America as long as only part of the continent is free, but that when the entire country has won its liberty, it will be an asylum for scoundrels. If that is not his meaning, his words do not make sense. If that is his theory, he should have indicated what peculiar circumstances attract them.

To frighten Spain and, to a lesser degree, France, the writer gathers all the politicians he can find on the American continent, and this happens so quickly that they have conquered South America before any word of their plans reaches Europe. The abbé was doubtless thinking about the Huns, and he forgot the little bridgeless lake separating the two continents. We have to admire his imagination and how he must have worked to fashion these immense labyrinths in which rumors about these enterprises became lost. These were essential to give the new nation time to build a fleet, attack defenseless seas, land its armies in surprise attacks, and conquer South America before Europe knew anything about it.

After giving advice to France and Spain, the abbé turns a kindly eye on the United States (p. 373): "If the real friends of the Americans consider the matter, they will see that the only way to prevent quarrels among these states is to have a powerful rival on their frontiers, one who will always be ready to take advantage of their dissensions." He continues in a fatherly way: "There is great jealousy between the northern and southern states. Political concepts vary from one river to the next. Citizens of a town, even members of a family, quarrel with one another." The truth is just the opposite.

The constitutions of the thirteen states reveal that political principles are the same everywhere. The jealousy between the colonies that England had fomented vanished several years before the Revolution, so that the Union was founded not only on sound politics but on a fraternal affection of the citizens of each state for those of the others. This is stronger than politics, while family unity is such that Europeans are constantly admiring it.

After saying that Europeans were aroused in favor of the American cause, the abbé concludes his reflections on the United States by showing how easy it is to be misled by illusions. The "courage of philosophy," he declares, is necessary to combat them.

The abbé next measures the area occupied by the thirteen republics; these figures, however, are not rigorously exact because he obviously did not waste any time looking at maps. He also gives a detailed description of the soil, which, were it accurate, would make Americans move to another country. "If ten million people can ever make a living in these provinces, it will be a large number. The country should, however, be able to provide for most of its needs if the inhabitants are economical and content with a mediocre standard of living."

Finally he warns us to fear an abundance of gold, "which brings corruption and scorn for the law." If we accept his description of the country, it seems unlikely that our descendants will ever have to worry about this. Fortunately for us, the author is quite as wrong on this point as on many others. The reader has seen this in chapter 8, where there is a rather detailed description of the soil. As to population, the state of Georgia alone, by virtue of the territory it obtained in the charter of 1732, could support the ten million who the abbé believes might barely eke out a living in the entire country.

# Chapter 12

# Abbé Raynal's Contradictions

We have seen how the author rejoices that America offers an asylum to the unfortunate; yet elsewhere he speaks of poor Europeans who sign up for several years' service as if they were going to a servitude worse than that in Siberian deserts. He is especially sorry for some Germans who were lured by flattering promises, taken to Amsterdam and Rotterdam, and then put on shipboard. "America," he says ([9]:179), "gets recruits for farming as princes raise armies for war. The same tricks are used, but the purpose is less honest and perhaps even more cruel, as no one lists those who die and those who survive their shattered hopes. The illusion persists in Europe because care is taken to destroy any letters which could reveal the iniquity."

America does no recruiting in Europe, has never done any, and has always welcomed poor Europeans with the utmost kindness. It would be difficult to find masters who have not taken pains to see that the letters written by their servants reached relatives or friends. In this instance self-interest may play a part because German servants do their duty while patiently awaiting the day when they will be landowners themselves. They are totally unlike those immigrants who expect to pass suddenly from poverty to wealth simply because they are honoring the New World with their presence. It is natural, therefore, that the colonists should like these servants and want more of them. If the abbé visited the parts of America inhabited chiefly by Germans, he would learn that letters written by these servants do more to encourage immigration than any tricks of imaginary recruiters.

When General Burgoyne's army was imprisoned in Virginia, we placed the German officers in two counties where some inhabitants had come from Germany. The soldiers who had an opportunity to chat with their former compatriots decided to make every effort to stay in America and inspired their fellows to do the same. The officers can say how many deserted, despite all the precautions taken to prevent it. The comte de Deux-Ponts[35] visited several

[35] Christian de Forbach, marquis des Deux Ponts, was colonel-proprietor of the Deux-Ponts Regiment.

Pennsylvania counties where the inhabitants have all the necessities as well as some luxuries. They have preserved their customs to such an extent that a newly arrived German is scarcely aware he has left Europe.

The author's style in this passage reveals that, once again, he does not want to displease those who prefer bombastic eloquence to simple logic. The contradictions I have noted are such that we cannot consider them intentional unless we assume the author was attempting to please everyone. The following passages, which *all* deal with the same subject, illustrate this point:

The author calls (p. 189) English legislation "the best which has ever existed."

Page 266, in addressing the English at the beginning of the Revolution: "The king of England has the negative power. No law can be passed without his consent. Why should Americans grant him this privilege which you regard as a daily nuisance?" * The abbé then continues: "Someday, if your government is improved, you too will deprive him of this privilege. In the meantime, what would be gained if Americans were subjected to a defective constitution?"

Aside from the fact that it is impossible to reconcile the idea of a "defective constitution" with "the best legislation that has ever existed," these questions prove the author believed the colonial constitutions were free from the vices of the English one. Let us see how this agrees with what follows.

After discussing the faults of English laws, he says (p. 209): "Because they were dependent and ignorant, the colonies blindly adopted this unformed and poorly digested mass which oppressed their former country." Elsewhere he refers to English laws as models of legislation. After explaining how good governments are formed, he concludes (p. 199): "From them are derived all the governments which free and thoughtful Englishmen established in North America." But three pages later he contradicts himself again: "This governmental diversity was not the work of the mother country. It does not bear the mark of a reasonable, uniform, and regular legislation. This bizarre collection of constitutions was produced by chance, by climate, by the prejudices of the times and the founders. Men shipwrecked on deserted beaches are not equipped to devise legislation."

---

* It is surprising that a "daily nuisance" should be a feature of "the best legislation which has ever existed."

We saw (p. 266) that the author is convinced that American constitutions did not recognize the negative power of the English king; yet he observes (p. 201) that the Connecticut and Rhode Island colonies could "pass all the laws they deem suitable without the monarch's approval; he had no authority over them." This implies that the other eleven were subject to the royal veto.

Does such exactitude authorize a writer to instruct princes and nations and to censure the behavior of governments severely and dogmatically? The abbé frequently states that he intends to instruct not only his contemporaries but posterity so that future generations may be on their guard. He asks (p. 180): "Should we reveal the snares which may be laid to deprive nations of their liberty?" He is going to raise an altar to truth, as if she were his goddess and the one who guided his fulminating pen. "Our duty," he says (p. 375), "is to combat any kind of prejudice, even one that satisfies our heart's desire. Above all we must be true and not betray the pure and upright conscience dictating all our judgments. It is possible that we shall not be believed today, but a bold prophecy fulfilled several centuries later does more honor to a historian than a long series of proven facts; I am writing not only for my contemporaries, who will survive me for only a few years; I am entrusting my ideas to posterity and to time, for it will be their task to judge me."

It scarcely seems necessary to let centuries elapse before evaluating the *Philosophical History*. Even a cursory examination of the way in which the author deals with the past and present casts doubt on his competence as a prophet. His language impresses superficial readers, but real philosophers express themselves without ostentation.

I shall not comment on the great variety of contrasting styles in the *Philosophical History*. No microscope is needed to distinguish the colors, but it would be impossible to catch all the contradictions without rewriting the entire volume. If anyone has the patience to plough through it, he will be convinced the best remedy would be to change the title.

# Conclusion

In the letter we have quoted several times Mr. Paine takes leave of the abbé in these terms: "Though I have already extended this letter beyond what I first proposed, I am, nevertheless, obliged to omit many observations I originally designed to have made. I wish there had been no occasion for making any. But the wrong ideas which the abbé's work had a tendency to excite, and the prejudicial impressions they might make, must be an apology for my remarks and the freedom with which they are made."[36]

When a celebrated writer makes mistakes, he is imitated. The anonymous author of the *Impartial History* owes some errors to Abbé Raynal, for he merely copied the latter's book. In speaking of New England (8:474) the abbé says: "This colony extends at least 300 miles along the seashore and more than 50 miles inland." "New England," writes the author of the *Impartial History* (p. 59) "is fully 300 miles in length along the seashore and stretches over 50 miles inland." New England, which contains four states, New Hampshire, Massachusetts, Rhode Island, and Connecticut, has a shoreline extending from the frontiers of New York State to the mouth of the Saint Croix River, or 560 miles. The Mississippi River was named as its western boundary by the Treaty of Paris. Since the state of Massachusetts ceded some territory to Congress on 19 April 1783, the western limits have been greatly reduced, but the distance is never less than 120 miles.

On page 488 Abbé Raynal states, "The colony of New York occupies a narrow strip 20 miles in length along the shore." His echo writes (p. 67), "New York has only 20 miles of shoreline." Long Island, which is part of New York State, as it has always been, extends over 100 miles along the Atlantic. The coasts bordering the continent of this state stretch for about 50 miles along the ocean, which, thanks to Long Island, forms an enormous harbor communicating with the Atlantic at both ends of the island.

The author of the *Philosophical History* declares (9:21) that "the western frontier of Pennsylvania is determined only by its

---

[36] Paine, "Letter to the Abbé Raynal," *Complete Writings*, pp. 250–51.

population and its farms." The author of the *Impartial History* repeats this verbatim (p. 77). The western frontier of Pennsylvania has always been at long. 5°. Could this boundary be more exact?

Abbé Raynal writes (p. 28), "At the beginning of 1774 this colony had 350,000 inhabitants, according to the congressional census." "According to the congressional census," repeats the anonymous author (p. 76), "its population numbered 350,000." In the first approximate census made by Congress, which was 22 June 1775, and not at the beginning of 1774, the population of Pennsylvania was estimated at 300,000; the second, 18 April 1783, lists it as 320,000.

The *Philosophical History* (p. 38) states: "Philadelphia is located at the junction of the Delaware and the Schuylkill." The *Impartial History* (p. 78) copies this exactly. The writer of these observations was in Philadelphia last year, at which time the city was seven miles above this point. Abbé Raynal says of this same city (p. 43): "It seems certain that in 1776 it had 20,000 inhabitants." The other repeats: "Philadelphia numbered 20,000 inhabitants." Either these historians are mistaken or the Americans are, for the latter thought the population was no less than 50,000.

The author of the *Philosophical History* said of Maryland (p. 52): "According to the congressional census, the population numbered 320,000." The author of the *Impartial History* (p. 80) quotes the same figure. In 1775 the estimated population was 250,000, and in 1783 it had declined to 220,700.

"Chesapeake Bay," writes Abbé Raynal (p. 60), "extends inland 250 miles." The anonymous writer repeats this (p. 50[80]). This bay extends only 190 miles northward along a line almost parallel to the sea. This forms a very long tongue of land called the Eastern Shore.

Abbé Raynal writes of Maryland products as follows (p. 62): "Mr. Stirenwith finally decided to manufacture stockings, silk and woolen fabrics, cotton goods, every form of kitchen utensil, and even firearms. These products, which are now being produced in a single workshop, will spread throughout the province and, after passing the Potomac, will also be used in Virginia." Here the author of the *Impartial History* was not content to copy. In order to produce a more interesting picture, he thought it necessary to describe how the imaginary products would be used (p. 81): "For Barbados rum and Madeira the inhabitants of Maryland exchange silk and wool fabrics, cotton goods, firearms, and all the kitchen utensils they can manufacture."

We have already listed the reasons why factories have not been built and why they will not be constructed for a long time, at least in areas where commerce with Europe is practical. The only articles produced in America, especially in the interior, are crude items which cannot stand the increased prices required for transportation. There have always been people who made lovely things either for themselves or for gifts. A lady on the James River made several yards of silk ribbon, but I do not know, and no one with whom I have talked knows, anyone who has produced even half a yard of silk anywhere in the United States.

As for Mr. Stirenwith, I have never heard of his products either in Maryland or elsewhere. It is possible he manufactured a few pairs of stockings or several pieces of cloth, but that is not what the writer of the *Philosophical History* says. He might be excused for making such a mistake in the first edition of his book, but not in the second. Everyone in Europe knew that the most severe blow we suffered during the war with England was from the scarcity of manufactured products. Forced by necessity, we tried to make a little of everything, but it was very expensive, and not a single item could be produced in sufficient quantity to fill the need. As soon as the war was over, these factories went out of business.

In discussing the population of Virginia, the abbé says (p. 79): "There are 650,000 if the congressional census is exact. This figure includes the slaves, who are said to number 150,000." The echo repeats these figures (p. 82). There is certainly some exaggeration, but not in the two congressional censuses, both of which list the population as 400,000. Recently a census was taken in Virginia with all possible exactitude. It was found that there were 567,614 inhabitants, 270,762 of whom, I am sorry to say, were slaves.

To satisfy the reader's curiosity, particularly with regard to the discrepancy between this census and the conjectural estimates made by Congress, I shall tell what led to the latter. On 22 June 1775 the representatives of the states had to furnish an approximate idea of their various populations, since Congress was going to distribute $2 million in paper money and it had been decided to do this on the basis of the number of inhabitants.

The approximate figures are as follows:

*Inhabitants*

| | |
|---|---|
| New Hampshire | 100,000 |
| Massachusetts | 350,000 |
| Rhode Island | 58,000 |

| | |
|---|---:|
| Connecticut | 200,000 |
| New York | 200,000 |
| New Jersey | 130,000 |
| Pennsylvania | 300,000 |
| Delaware | 30,000 |
| Maryland | 250,000 |
| Virginia | 400,000 |
| North Carolina | 200,000 |
| South Carolina | 200,000 |
| | 2,418,000 |

Later the deputies of New Hampshire declared that their population was somewhat smaller than they had assumed, but as no census had been taken by the other states, the first figure was retained throughout the war. Georgia was added when it joined the Confederation 5 September 1775.

On 18 April 1783 some changes were made, but again it was necessary to rely almost entirely on estimates. The new figures were:

*Inhabitants*

| | |
|---|---:|
| New Hampshire | 82,000 |
| Massachusetts | 350,000 |
| Rhode Island | 50,400 |
| Connecticut | 206,000 |
| New York | 200,000 |
| New Jersey | 130,000 |
| Pennsylvania | 320,000 |
| Delaware | 35,000 |
| Maryland | 220,700 |
| Virginia | 400,000 |
| North Carolina | 170,000 |
| South Carolina | 150,000 |
| Georgia | 25,000 |
| | 2,339,300 |

Everyone knew the population in the five southern states was really larger than this. However, since the only purpose of the estimate was to apportion the expenses of the Confederation among the colonies, and because slave labor was considered less useful by two-fifths than that of free men, the number of inhabitants was reduced proportionately. These five states have at least 650,000 slaves, whereas there are 50,000 at most in the other eight.

The population of South Carolina was first listed as 170,000, but the deputies begged Congress to decrease the figure still further on account of the damage they had suffered; so it was set at 150,000. In order to determine the total estimated population in April 1783, you must add to the 2,339,300 two-fifths of the slaves, or 280,000 and the 20,000 cut from South Carolina. This brings us to 2,639,-300, or 221,300 more than in June 1775. The general opinion is that the thirteen states have at least 3,000,000, but this cannot be checked until all the states have taken a census.

It is thought that the total population doubles every twenty-five years in peacetime. During the eight years of the war it did not increase so rapidly, but the growth was healthy, despite reports of English gazetteers that it had declined tremendously. There are definite proofs of this. In August 1778 I was in Fairfax County, Virginia, at the home of Mr. George Mason. One day he told me that in this little county there were more than 690 soldiers in the militia; in 1775 there had been 612 or 614, and in the meantime, about 300 men had left to join General Washington's army.* On 3 June 1781 Mr. Mason wrote in a letter to his elder son, who had been forced by ill health to leave the army and go to France: "Your Brother William writes you by this Opportunity. He returned some time ago, from South Carolina, where he commanded a Company of Volunteers (75 fine young fellows from this Country)."[37] If 70 young men could leave their families to help their allies five hundred miles away, we must conclude that the population had continued to grow, for this figure is in addition to the number supplied by the county to the army and the militia.

English gazetteers have taken pains to inform Europe that, "according to congressional estimates," the population of the United States declined by 798,509 inhabitants between 1775 and 1783. To get this figure they increased the 1775 estimate to 3,137,809 and left the 1783 one as it was, after deducting two-fifths for the slaves and 20,000 inhabitants from South Carolina.

As for the congressional authority which these gazetteers mention so freely, the estimates were so uncertain that Congress refused to let them appear in its publications. The secretary made an abstract on a loose sheet of paper in order that the charges could be divided among the states, and that is all the official records contain. So where did Abbé Raynal get this information which he, like the gazetteers, attributes to Congress?

---

* General Washington comes from this county.
[37] Mason, *The Papers of George Mason, 1725–1792*, ed. Robert A. Rutland, 4 vols. (Chapel Hill, University of North Carolina Press, 1970), 2:692–93.

I shall close my list of errors drawn from the *Philosophical History* by the following statement about the southern border of Georgia. "This state," says Abbé Raynal (p. 110), "is bounded to the north by the Savannah River and to the south by the Altamaha River." "Georgia," repeats the anonymous writer (p. 90), "has the Savannah River as its northern boundary and the Altamaha on the south." The Altamaha River is approximately in the center of the state.

I should bore the reader if I reported all the mistakes the anonymous author copied from the abbé's book, but they are few in number in comparison to the rest. You can imagine how he discusses political and military matters.*

I have said enough to show the serious consequences that result when famous writers make mistakes. The majority of their colleagues, whether by blind confidence or negligence, are content to draw material from these sources. Thus the error is widely accepted, and many readers, who find it easier to believe a story than to check its validity, repeat these fables with as much assurance as if they were axioms.

* The chevalier de Caluélan wrote the following witty and pungent letter to the Paris newspaper.

"I beg you, Gentlemen, to present my humble reproaches to the anonymous author of the *Impartial History*. He is a wild man who killed me on the *Triton*, where I engaged in a perfectly peaceful campaign. It is true that he made me deliver such an eloquent speech that I hesitated whether I should claim my life at the cost of such a fine demise. But, as I do not like undeserved glory, I shall ask you to publish my letter.

(Signed) the chevalier de Caluélan, former ship captain."

[Longchamps, in his *Impartial History*, 2:6, recounted the following story. Captain de Caluélan had died following a battle with an English vessel near St. Dominica. Although seriously wounded, he had himself carried on deck, where he spoke to the sailors. "My children . . . I have only a few hours to live, but you have only one blow to strike. . . ." The English vessel lowered her flag, and the master of the *Triton* died the following day.]

# Notes K-M

## Note K (page 249)

### Reflections on a Memorandum concerning the Way France and Spain Should Regard the Consequences of the Quarrel between Great Britain and Its Colonies

[Turgot's [38] lengthy paper of 6 April 1776 is omitted, for Mazzei included a brief summary of its essential points.]

### Résumé

#### I

When the comte de Vergennes [39] and I [Turgot] examined the various ways in which we may suppose the quarrel between England and its colonies might end, it seemed to me that in the interest of the two crowns [France and Spain], the best solution would be for England to overcome the resistance of its colonies. If they were brought to their knees by a lack of resources, England would lose the commercial gain it drew from them in peacetime and the use of their forces in war. But if the conquered colonies retained their wealth and population, they would still yearn for independence, and they would force England to use some of its strength to prevent another uprising.

It seems highly probable there will be a total separation between the colonies and the mother country. When the English themselves recognize the independence of the colonies, political and commercial relations between Europe and America will undergo a complete change. It is my belief that all countries will be obliged to give their colonies freedom to buy and sell and will have no bonds with them other than a friendly relationship. If this is an evil, I see no way of preventing it, but there is consolation in the fact that colonies are an advantage.

I have also observed that powers which resist the course of events run a great danger. After ruining themselves, they would lose their colonies anyway and see them as foes rather than allies. It is important for Spain to reflect on the possibility of such an event, and to consider the idea of changing its system of administering commerce and its relations with its colonies.

[38] Anne Robert Turgot, baron de l'Aulne, was a French economist who undertook liberal reforms.

[39] Charles Gravier, comte de Vergennes, was minister of foreign affairs under Louis XVI.

A prompt reconciliation between England and America seems to offer the only imminent danger to France and Spain.

## II

In examining this danger, I noted it could come from either England or Spain. The comte de Vergennes seems convinced the present English government is not hostile, and I agree with him. I think a new ministry would not declare war until England and America were at peace; so I may conclude we have no reason to worry until next year.

I mentioned the seasons during which French and English sailors are alternately exposed to attack by the rival power. This annual procedure determines the dates England chooses to open hostilities, and these precautions make it possible to envisage its projects.

From Spain we can fear overconfidence in its strength, a dislike of the English, a just resentment on the part of the Catholic king against certain acts of the British government, and the obstacles this would create if a dispute arose between Spanish and English commanders.

Finally, I said it is equally important not to be surprised by England or incited by Spain, and I insisted on the necessity of complete confidence between our two courts.

## III

With regard to protective measures, I agree completely with the comte de Vergennes that we should resist any plan of aggression.

1. For moral reasons, which are in accordance with the attitude of both monarchs.

2. Because of the condition in which the king found his finances, the army, and the navy. Time is needed to increase our strength, and we should risk prolonging our weakness if we made premature use of the forces at our command.

3. For the excellent reason that an offensive war on our part would reconcile England and its colonies. It would give the prime minister a pretext for yielding and the colonists an excuse for listening to his proposals while they were consolidating and increasing their strength.

I next discussed the suggestion that we send land troops and squadrons to our colonies to protect them from invasion and took pains to prove that this project was ruinous, inadequate, and dangerous.

It would be ruinous because the expense incurred would last as long as our anxiety; if we added this sum to our current deficit, we should be unable to balance the budget and that might be more embarrassing than war. During a war extraordinary measures are possible, but in peacetime they would completely destroy public confidence.

It would be inadequate because England would not undertake to attack the two crowns [France and Spain] in America without sending squadrons larger than ours. As it has at least thirty thousand men in America, we may assume they could attack any point they chose. It would be impossible for forces even much larger than those we could muster to resist an army of that size.

It would be dangerous because it would force the British government to prepare for a global conflict. This would have the same effect as war itself; it would produce a reconciliation with the colonies and provoke the danger we wish to avoid. Finally, this plan would increase Spanish confidence and lead us inevitably into war.

I concluded that we should restrict ourselves to less expensive precautions which would avoid the appearance of hostility.

1. We should pay attention to any sign of danger. This means watching landfalls near our islands and the entrances to the Gulf of Mexico. This is the purpose of the cruising fleets mentioned in the marquis de Grimaldi's [40] letter and the orders which will go out to our vessels in these waters. We should have frequent reports about what is happening on the Newfoundland Banks. We should keep close watch on troops in England, their armament, public credit, and the ministry. We should also try to ascertain what is happening in the English colonies, but without letting anyone think we are keeping an agent there.

2. Through commercial channels we should help the colonists obtain the munitions and even the money they need but retain our neutral position and not make them outright grants.

3. We should quietly build up our maritime forces, fill our stores, repair our vessels, and make preparations so that we could arm quickly, if necessary, one squadron at Toulon and later another at Brest, while Spain equipped one at El Ferrol.

4. If we had reason to fear anything more serious, we should arm our squadrons but keep them in port.

5. If all signs pointed to imminent war, we should gather a large army on the coast and prepare for an expedition to England. This would force the English to assemble their forces, and we could then seize the opportunity to send troops and vessels to our colonies, if it seemed necessary, or to India. There we should have paved the way by making contact with the natives and reinforcing Mauritius and Réunion Island.

As even a fraction of these precautionary measures would entail considerable expense, I think it vital to do nothing rash, especially with regard to suggestions 4 and 5, unless we had reason to believe that England was planning to attack us.

I cannot close this memorandum without making an observation I consider of the highest importance. Because our interests are the same

---

[40] Don Geronimo, marquis de Grimaldi, was Spanish ambassador to Paris and later minister of foreign affairs in Madrid.

as those of the Spanish court, we should have complete confidence in one another and act jointly. We have, however, good reason to believe that England has spies who obtain many important secrets from the Spanish ministry. There is no harm in sending a communication expressing the resolution of the two monarchs to keep peace or dealing with methods of threatening England. But any item pertaining to Minorca or Gibraltar, or dealing with plans for shipping French and Spanish forces to India, should be entrusted only to the king of Spain and M. de Grimaldi.

6 April 1776

## Note L (see page 250)

The comte de Vergennes, minister of foreign affairs, replied for the king to Viscount Stormont, the English ambassador, 8 July 1777 as follows.

His Majesty will not permit anything which might abrogate the treaties. He is aware of complaints pertaining to the irregular conduct of the three American privateers, the *Reprisal*, the *Lexington*, and the *Dolphin*, and will issue orders that they be sequestered and detained in any French ports they have entered until sufficient security can be obtained that they will return directly to American waters and remain there. These orders are repeated to prevent the sale of prizes these same privateers or others might bring to our ports. They are to leave as soon as the winds and other conditions permit, and the same order extends to any capture whatsoever. The officers have been commanded to deal with them severely under penalty of being held personally accountable, and they are also ordered to see to it that commercial facilities extended to Americans do not exceed what is permitted. If any British subject wishes to bring action against one of the aforementioned privateers, he is at liberty to do so; law, rather than authority, decides matters of contention in France as in England.

This reply was accompanied by several remarks about the numerous complaints which had been referred to the English court. While the king was eager to see that British subjects were treated justly, he hoped the English monarch would "give orders to put a stop to the vexations to which French commerce was frequently exposed. The king does not intend to encourage or protect any traffic prohibited by law," but he could not tolerate "the seizure and confiscation of vessels and cargoes and the harsh treatment and imprisonment of their crews on the pretext that these vessels contain merchandise from North America; such legislation is not in keeping with justice or with the friendly assurances of the London court."

The same message was communicated to the British government by the French ambassador, the marquis de Noailles,[41] and, as the king of England claimed he had forbidden his subjects to export arms and had punished those who gave false designations, the marquis was ordered to reply that "munitions are contraband only to belligerents. Export of firearms has always been permitted to our colonies, to Africa, or wherever they are sold; without this freedom our firearms manufacturers would soon be out of business. It is impossible, moreover, to prevent false designations. English smugglers who ply along the Spanish coasts of America never tell where their cargoes are really going, but not a single one has ever been punished by the English Admiralty for a false declaration. It is patently unfair to complain to us about a practice that is tolerated and even encouraged in England."

When Viscount Stormont claimed on 3 November 1777 that the French king had "seized all the captured vessels the Americans sailed into his ports," Louis XVI replied:

France has such an extensive coastline that some cases of disobedience to orders are unavoidable. The English ambassador is cognizant of the instructions given by His Majesty to ensure that American corsairs do not find refuge in French ports beyond what is required by treaties and humanity, to prevent fraud, and to prevent the sale of captured vessels. Although the king faithfully observes his treaties with England, he cannot neglect the interests of his subjects and the safety of their commerce. If the Americans considered France an enemy, they would prey on French shipping as they do on that of Britain. The king believes he is doing everything for England that justice and friendship permit, and he hopes that, in return, the king of England will give orders to deal with the various complaints, some of which were made a long time ago, and will put an end to the criminal acts which are too frequently perpetrated by British naval officers.

## Note M (see page 274)

When the French landed in Rhode Island, General Clinton decided to attack them. The New England militia was summoned to join the French troops, and a detachment arrived on Conanicut Island

[41] Emmanuel-Marie-Louis, marquis de Noailles, in 1776 was ambassador in London, where he notified the king of the French alliance with the United States.

without provisions or tents. The soldiers, under command of the vicomte de Noailles,[42] saw the situation, took the men into their tents, and every soldier divided his ration with an American.

When the troops of the marquis de Saint-Simon joined the Americans in Williamsburg, the latter lent their horses to the French officers. They refused to have any of their tents brought until all the French tents had been transported, and as provisions were still scarce, the American soldiers asked that the French troops be given wheat flour and a full ration. They took a smaller amount of cornmeal.

Since the marquis de Saint-Simon knew that the morale of his troops was excellent, he kept the two camps as one. Officers and soldiers were always together; there was no bickering, and each side had nothing but praise for the other.

[42] Louis-Marie-Antoine, vicomte de Noailles, first cousin of the marquis de Noailles, accompanied his brother-in-law Lafayette to America.

# PART IV

Continuation of the Political Researches

# Chapter 1

# The So-Called Anarchy in the United States

In no country where men administrate for the purpose of preserving liberty is more public tranquillity enjoyed than on our continent.

European gazetteers claim we are in a state of anarchy and confusion. A few men, jealous, resentful, and impudent, have used these terms to describe a difference of opinion, and others, for lack of sufficient information, have copied them. If you think of the stormy period when our governments were established and realize how the founders of our country were prejudiced from childhood and that we have scarcely had time to attend to our own business since peace was restored, you will conclude that it would be astonishing if no reforms were necessary. Any decision requires the consent of the majority. Although the people entrust this privilege to their representatives, in certain cases you cannot get a majority of the representatives without long discussion; in others it would be unwise to deliberate before every citizen had expressed his opinion. This requires time. Although delays are harmful, they cannot be avoided without risking something infinitely worse. Should one grant unlimited power for a limited term to a small group? History warns this is dangerous. It is better to choose the lesser of the two evils, and in the meantime, we have no cause to fear the outcome.

When all men have the same natural rights, or when there is not enough inequality to disturb the general harmony (as in America today), if a useful law is not passed, it is a sign that the law is unknown to the majority. Political truths are not like geometrical axioms; some are not deemed useful until people have suffered for lack of them. Speeches and articles are often necessary for this purpose. A zealous man tells his compatriots all the dire things that will happen if they do not do what he wants. He includes those evils which are unlikely and even some that are impossible. The author of the *Notes on the State of Virginia* has great hopes for the prosperity of America, especially because of our youth, but in several places he tries to arouse the fear of his fellow citizens because he wants them to turn their attention to what he thinks is best for the country. The duty of the orator is very different from that of the historian, and they should not be confused. If we listen to a preacher, we might conclude this is the worst of all centuries; yet we know this is not true. If England were not better known than America in Europe, parliamentary discussions about the Revolution would have spread the belief that its doom was sealed if it lost the colonies. Both parties agreed on this point for a time, but they were divided about how to keep the colonies and, having lost them, whether they should use force or persuasion to get them back.

No sensible man would ever imagine that America was a burden to England; yet this has been claimed since the peace. It is true, however, that Great Britain can be quite happy if it does not own an inch of land outside its island. Those who sought to shield their country by exaggerating the evils threatening it deserve praise, but the means currently used to console England for its loss do not merit the same indulgence. Writers pretend Great Britain is better off without its colonies, that we already regret our emancipation, and that we shall soon be reduced to a point where we shall beg in vain to be taken back under what they call its "protection." Surely these writers could make better use of their pens, for were they correct, the nation spent more than a £100 million and sacrificed many lives to preserve something not only useless but harmful. It is astonishing how quickly one acknowledges past wrongs to gain credence in present circumstances.

To give substance to the reports now being circulated to discredit the United States, someone conceived the idea of quoting passages from American gazettes which coincided with his particular views. In the best society and among the most virtuous men, few points on which everyone agrees will be found. This is almost inevitable unless the subject is geometry. In a fairly large legislative assembly, where highly abstract matters are discussed, it would be miraculous if all members agreed. Differences in approach lead to arguments, and the opposing parties are often excited in proportion to their zeal for public welfare. The purer their intentions, the more they try to arouse fear so that right will prevail. Every citizen is involved in the discussion because he has the right to express an opinion orally and in writing. These debates instruct the inhabitants, teach them to reason, and put them on guard against anyone who might try to upset public tranquillity in order to satisfy personal ambition.

As differences of opinion are inevitable and freedom of discussion is complete, two men could paint totally divergent pictures by quoting true statements. Although this causes unfortunate delays, no one thinking of the future is worried, because the longer the discussion, the better understood are the facts, and the more solidly they are established. Men are more willing to accept inconveniences if they recognize their necessity; thus, if you weigh the advantages and disadvantages of temporizing, you may find that in a free country it is sometimes better to wait until men ask for remedies than to provide them with antidotes.

As for the anarchy and confusion said to prevail in the United States, I can state that up to the present no citizen of any state has been molested either in his person or his property. Not a house has been burned nor a window smashed since the enemy ceased his devastations. A difference of opinion does not lead to quarrels; it does not even affect friendships. British gazetteers are writing in a country where one can scarcely take a step without being robbed, where the best of all possible governments cannot prevent violence, insults, and all the disorders which follow a parliamentary election, where the populace delights in breaking windowpanes, setting fire to the capital, menacing the men chosen to represent the nation, and seizing foodstuffs in country houses. These "zealous and truthful" gazetteers could not discover a single one of these disorders caused in America by the so-called anarchy. If, in spite of that, we are living in anarchy, let us pray God to preserve it and deliver us forever from the best of all possible governments.

Our confederation and governments need to be strengthened. The power of Congress is too restricted in some matters; in others it requires clarification. Until 1785 the number of men who feared congressional power constituted a majority. Although I held a different opinion from the beginning, I always have respected the reasoning which led to the opposite point of view. These men believed too much power in the hands of Congress might lead to a situation for which no cure could be found. Too little power, on the other hand, could be easily rectified. The need to increase congressional authority is recognized, but there is as yet no agreement about how it should be done. The longer the delay, the more difficult the problem will probably be. This will, however, hasten the remedy; so little harm will have been done.

# Chapter 2

# The So-Called Disagreement about the Division of the States

It would be simply amazing if a good picture of the current situation in America could be obtained from the gazettes, for news is fabricated in a country where there are numerous reasons for disguising the truth.

In discussing the first colonial settlements, I said that when the duke of York became proprietor of New Belgium, he tried to enlarge it as much as he could. At this time Vermont was included in New York. Until the Revolution, English monarchs continued to give patents for lands that did not belong to anyone. Some residents of New York City and others in royal favor obtained vast tracts in Vermont, where a number of families had been living for some time. When the bearers of patents arrived, the occupants found themselves faced with the unhappy alternative of moving away or purchasing land whose value had been greatly increased by their own toil. Opposition was so strong that the patent holders and their agents were forced to leave. The angry Vermonters then held a meeting at which they resolved they would no longer be subject to the government of New York.

During the Revolution, Vermont soldiers fought valiantly for liberty; afterward they appealed to Congress to be received into the Confederation as an independent state, but Congress had no right to interfere in such an affair, and up to the present the New York assembly has refused to recognize the independence of Vermont. The number of favorable votes is growing, however; so we believe the matter will soon be settled to everyone's satisfaction.

It is a general principle that states should not be too large. Virginia ceded a considerable portion of its territory to the Confederation on condition that it be divided in such a way that none of the new states should extend more than two hundred miles in any direction. The old charters give Massachusetts and New Hampshire some rights to the territory of Vermont. That might be an additional factor in bringing New York to recognize its independence, if the assembly is not influenced by more laudable motives. This dispute between the states does not prevent the inhabitants from seeing each other, doing business, and being even more intimate than they were before the Revolution.

Let us now compare the facts with stories that have been circulated. The worst yarn held that Vermont's claim was an effect of the Revolution. It was invented to make people think we could not remain united. Before the Revolution the English governor of New York proposed to wage war on the inhabitants of Vermont. The latter declared they would defend themselves; therefore the only result of the change in government has been to spare blood the English governor was quite willing to shed.

The gazetteers transformed the time, nature, and results of the Vermont dispute, but the Kentucky quarrel was made up out of whole cloth. This area, which now has about thirty thousand inhabitants, did not have a single family in 1774. Its rapid growth is due to an extremely fertile soil. As the territory of Kentucky is in the state of Virginia, the inhabitants belonged to one or several frontier counties, depending on latitude; longitudinally, these counties extended west to the Mississippi, so that when their inhabitants were summoned to the county tribunal, they were forced to travel over four hundred miles.

As soon as they thought their population large enough, they elected two men to the General Assembly and asked them to request that Kentucky become a new county. The request was so just it encountered no opposition. As the number of inhabitants increased, new counties were formed until there were five, whose ten representatives had to travel nearly twelve hundred miles back and forth, largely through wilderness, every time they attended a General Assembly session. Everyone thought Kentucky should become independent as soon as the inhabitants could support a government. When Virginia ceded an immense territory to the Confederation, its injunction confirmed the general feeling about very large states, and in 1776, when it was decided to move the seat of government from Williamsburg to a more central and convenient location, no thought was given to counties so remote it seemed as if nature had not intended them to be part of the state.

In the constitution of North Carolina, dated 18 December 1776, Article 25 of the Declaration of Rights determines the boundaries and states that the present declaration "shall not be construed so as to prevent the establishment of one or more governments westward of this State, by consent of the legislature." [1] It would be

[1] The Constitution of North Carolina in *The Constitutions of the Several Independent States of America* (London, 1783), p. 297.

difficult to find much opposition to this principle in any state.

Before leaving Virginia last year I often saw representatives from the district of Kentucky, and we spoke of their future emancipation as of something generally accepted. I was therefore greatly surprised, on my arrival in Europe, to find the gazettes carrying stories about the so-called Kentucky disputes. As this territory was recently emancipated, I can quote the act. Like a wise father, the Virginia General Assembly follows the child step by step and does not give him complete control until he can walk alone.

### An Act concerning the Erection of the District of Kentucky into an Independent State

WHEREAS it is represented to be the desire of the good people inhabiting the district known by the name of the Kentucky District, that the same should be separated from this Commonwealth whereof it is a part, and be formed into an independent member of the American confed[e]racy, and it is judged by the General Assembly that such a partition of the Commonwealth is rendered expedient by the remoteness of the more fertile, which must be the more populous part of the said District, and by the interjacent natural impediments to a convenient and regular communication therewith;

BE it *enacted by the General Assembly,* That . . . [five] Representatives . . . to compose a Convention . . . shall be elected by [each of the nine counties]. . . . The said Convention shall . . . be [held in] Danville, on the fourth Monday of September [Hening: 20 July next] . . . , to consider, and by a majority of voices, to determine, whether it be expedient for, and be the will of the good people of the said District, that the same be erected into an independent State, on the terms and conditions following:

*First.* That the boundary between the proposed State and Virginia, shall remain the same as at present separates the District from the residue of the Commonwealth.

*Second.* That the proposed State shall take upon itself a just proportion of the public [Hening: and domestic] debt of this Commonwealth.

*Third.* That all private rights and interests in lands within the said District, derived from the laws of Virginia, prior to such separation, shall remain valid, and secure under the laws of the proposed State, and shall be determined by the laws now existing in this State.

*Fourth.* That the lands within the proposed State of non-resident proprietors, shall not in any case be taxed higher than the lands of residents at any time prior to the admission of the proposed State to a vote by its Delegates in Congress, where such non-residents reside out of the United States; nor at any time either before or after such admission, where such non-residents reside within this Commonwealth, within which this stipulation shall be reciprocal; or where such non-residents reside within any other of the United States, which shall declare the same to be reciprocal within its limits. . . .

*Fifth.* That no grant land, nor land warrant to be issued by the proposed State, shall interfere with any warrant heretofore issued from the Land-Office of Virginia . . . on or before the first day of September, one thousand seven hundred and eighty-eight [Hening: 1790].

*Sixth.* [Omitted; an elaboration of the preceding article.]

*Seventh.* That the use and navigation of the River Ohio, so far as the territory of the proposed State, or the territory which shall remain within the limits of this Commonwealth lies thereon, shall be free and common to citizens of the United States, and the respective jurisdictions of this Commonwealth, and of the proposed State, on the River aforesaid, shall be concurrent only with the States which may possess the opposite shores of the said River.

*Eighth.* That in case any complaint or dispute shall at any time arise between the Commonwealth of Virginia and the said District, after it shall be an independent State, concerning the meaning or execution of the foregoing articles, the same shall be determined by six Commissioners, of whom two shall be chosen by each of the parties, and the remainder by the Commissioners so first appointed. [This article is omitted from Hening.]

*And be it further enacted,* That if the said Convention shall approve of an erection of the said district into an independent State, on the foregoing terms and conditions, they shall . . . fix a day posterior to the first day of September, one thousand seven hundred and eighty-seven [Hening: 1 November 1790], on which the authority of this Commonwealth . . . shall cease . . . over the proposed State, and said articles become a solemn compact mutually binding on the parties, and unalterable by either without the consent of the other. *Provided however,* that prior to the first day of June, one thousand seven hundred and eighty seven [Hening: 1 September 1790], the United States in Congress shall assent to the erection of the said district into an independent State, shall release this Commonwealth from all its federal obligations arising from the said district, as being part thereof, and shall agree that the proposed State shall immediately after the day fixed to be as aforesaid, posterior to . . . [Hening: 1 September 1790], or at some convenient time future thereto, be admitted into the Fœderal Union. And to the end that no period of anarchy may happen to the good people of the proposed State, it is to be understood that the said Convention shall have authority to take the necessary provisional measures for the election and meeting of a Convention at some time prior to the day fixed for the determination of the authority of this Commonwealth, and of its laws over the said district, and posterior to . . . [Hening: 1 September 1790], aforesaid, with full power and authority to frame and establish a fundamental constitution of government for the proposed State, and to declare what laws shall be in force therein, until the same shall be abrogated or altered by the legislative authority, acting under the constitution, so to be framed and established.

This Act shall be transmitted by the Executive, to the Delegates representing this Commonwealth in Congress, who are hereby instructed to use their endeavors to obtain from Congress a speedy Act, to the effect above specified.

> *Jan. 6, 1786. Passed the House of Delegates.*
> *Jan. 10, 1786. Passed the Senate.*
> [Hening: Passed the 29th December 1788.] [2]

The only dispute, if it can be called that, about the division of the states since the Revolution is the Franklin affair.[3] North Carolina ceded to the Union the territory west of the Allegheny Mountains. The next assembly thought it perfectly legal to revoke the act, since Congress had not accepted the land. The eastern portion of this territory is fairly well settled; the inhabitants have declared themselves independent of the Carolina government and have called this district the state of Franklin. Their claim that the cession is valid is perfectly reasonable, and it is believed that the Carolina assembly will soon grant it; then Virginia will provide the new state with another remote tract like Kentucky.

Massachusetts is, as we know, divided in two parts by New Hampshire. The northern portion, called Maine, has few inhabitants, is about five times the size of the other, and is superior in every way. As soon as it has enough settlers, it will be a separate state. Although seven-eights of the inhabitants are in the smaller or southern part, Maine will soon have a larger population. If the two continued to form a single state, which is unlikely, the inhabitants of the southern part would often be forced to cross New Hampshire, as the seat of government would be transferred from Boston to a city in Maine.

For a country whose fundamental principle is the equality of natural rights, the vast extent of Massachusetts serves no purpose other than the satisfaction of idle vanity. It is detrimental to those who live far from the seat of government and also poor politics,

[2] Broadside, Rare Book Division, New York Public Library; see also Hening, 12:788–91.

[3] The Watauga region south of Kentucky was absorbed into North Carolina in 1776 and remained part of that state until it was ceded to Congress in 1784. While Congress procrastinated about accepting the gift, the Watauga settlers created the independent state of Franklin.

since these citizens could gradually become indifferent to the administration of public affairs.

These truths are fairly well known in America, where freedom of discussion will make them triumph if there is time for reflection. But men err if they act too hastily. It follows that we should continue our present system, let the gazetteers accuse our governments of weakness, term our diverse opinions "anarchy" and "confusion," and glory in any agitation caused by inadequate information or the dissatisfaction of a few people who always calm down without creating serious disorder.

# Chapter 3

# Paper Money

Before a discussion of paper money, which we were forced to adopt at the beginning of the Revolution to make up for the shortage of coined silver, the reader will doubtless want to hear about our first experiment with this type of currency.

In 1690 the New England and New York colonies undertook an unsuccessful expedition against Canada. When the troops returned unexpectedly to Boston, they had to be paid, and the public treasury was empty. New taxes were levied, but the impatient soldiers threatened to mutiny; so the Massachusetts Bay Colony resorted to paper money. The new law ordered the treasurer to accept it in payment of taxes and to grant the owner 5 percent interest. This, however, did not prevent the currency from immediately losing one-third of its face value.

The leather money James II had put in circulation in Ireland a short time before, which had depreciated even more, made people afraid, and it is believed that this factor contributed to discredit paper money in Massachusetts.

When tax time came, the new money had an advantage because of the 5 percent interest; so it rose to something above its original value. This encouraged the government to print more, and it was often a convenience rather than a necessity. Other colonies used the same expedient at different periods. For a time the paper was regarded as real money, but corrupt practices produce their effects sooner or later and leave a legacy of ills. It would be tedious to chronicle the increased use of paper money and its pernicious effects. Like those that spring from privileges, prerogatives, and other vicious institutions (which are often based on ignorance), these evils overwhelmed the majority of the inhabitants, and only clever people and scoundrels succeeded in making a profit.

According to the archives, the Massachusetts Bay Colony suffered more than any other from paper money and finally abolished it in 1749. At this time the government received a large sum in silver from the British Parliament in payment for the attack on Cape Breton Island;[4] so the colony recalled its paper money at the current rate, or about one-eleventh of its original value.

[4] Cape Breton Island had been one of the targets of the 1690 expedition.

This was not, however, so unjust as it seems. Let us assume that the British government could and wanted to redeem the debt on which it pays 3 percent interest. For each £100 it received, it would pay only £69, the current rate. It would be unfair to pay 100 percent because the paper has passed through a number of hands, and the government could never reimburse all the creditors who had lost 31 percent. Why reward the current owners rather than the nation, which includes those who suffered the loss?

You may say that the government could pay the current price, like an individual, without obliging its creditors to sell at a fixed sum. But then only the needy would sell, and the wealthy would finally get 100 percent. And as there would not be enough money to redeem all the paper at this figure, more taxes would be levied, and those who were forced to sell at 69 would also have to pay their share.

If England were able to redeem its total debt, which amounts to at least £240 million, by purchasing certificates at various prices that would increase in value as the debt diminished, the tax burden would be unbearable to all but the rich. The reader may decide if equity is not preferable in such a case.

The expedient adopted by the Massachusetts Bay Colony in 1749 was essential to preserve the government and maintain order. The matter was discussed at length in the legislative assembly of the colony as well as by the king's council. The other colonies got rid of their paper money at different times and by various means.

The £10 million debt contracted to help England in the war of 1756 again forced the colonies to have recourse to paper money, but better management and new resources enabled them to withdraw it at the beginning of the Revolution. The principal cause of the scarcity of money in the thirteen colonies was the commercial monopoly exercised by Great Britain. An unfavorable balance forced merchants to send to England not only the small amount of English money brought over by visitors but a large part of the Spanish money that came from commerce with the islands. At the beginning of the Revolution the colonists had to fight without money, without guns, without munitions, without clothing, without manufactured goods; because they had to have currency of some sort, paper money was the only solution.

Paper money's credit depends on the assurance it will be redeemed, but we could not levy taxes, for there was no money to pay them. Fishing was impossible, farming disrupted, the value of our products almost destroyed because of the difficulty and risks of navigation, and everything we had to purchase was exorbitantly priced. Credit for paper money was based, therefore, on our intention to redeem it when circumstances permitted. Every state made paper money for its own needs, and Congress printed a certain amount for the Union.

Congressional bills also circulated in all the states, each state responsible for its share and guaranteeing the whole amount. State bills were intended only for their own territory; their circulation elsewhere depended on commerce and the distance between the state that owned them and the state where they would be used.

At the beginning of the Revolution it was necessary to purchase a great many things, including ammunition, with hard cash in the neighboring islands, but as money grew scarce its price rose in accordance with the law of supply and demand. Patriotism prevented it from rising in proportion to the people's need, for at the end of eighteen months one could get six silver dollars for seven and a half paper ones. Public credit often drops much more rapidly among nations equipped with many advantages we lacked completely, and luxuries may jump 50 to 60 percent in a single day if there is a rumor of impending scarcity.

Some citizens paid in silver at par value for the paper they received. But as this practice was not universal, it could not produce the desired effect. Eventually it would have proved disastrous, for good citizens would have been ruined, and all the money would have fallen into the hands of the fearful, the dissatisfied, and enemies of public welfare. Everyone had to unite to increase the price of merchandise as the price of silver rose, and this caused a drop in the value of paper money. The tricks used to discredit this currency were legion. English merchants had much to do with this, and the Scottish were even worse. The Pennsylvania Quakers, most of whom were wealthy merchants, were the first to demand three or four times more in paper than in silver. Moreover, they bought silver as a commodity, for which they paid in paper currency at this rate.

The common people who found themselves forced to pay such high prices for necessities began to raise the price of foodstuffs and labor. As Congress and the state governments had to buy various items in quantity to supply the armies, a prodigious amount of paper money was required to purchase for three or four dollars an article that had formerly cost one. Soon quantity exceeded the need, and oversupply was one cause for a decline in value, although numerous others were maliciously devised both at home and abroad.

Counterfeiting did a great deal of harm. In several parts of the United States, men had outside sources from which they received equipment. During 1778 an American corsair captured a vessel en route from Scotland to New York with several million counterfeit dollars and the materials necessary to counterfeit paper money as it was printed.

Every expedient that prudence could conceive was tried to remedy this situation. The amount of paper money in circulation was three or four times greater than the sum needed for internal commerce, and fear of counterfeiting made people nervous. Furthermore, it was predicted that future emissions would soon make the paper of no value.

Some men had already begun to demand that taxes be levied, so that the quantity could be reduced to a reasonable amount that would be fully credited. It was impossible either to reduce the amount or to prevent an increase. Taxes, a burden for many, were insufficient because of unequal distribution of money, skillful manipulation on the part of a few individuals, excessive good faith of others, and normal vicissitudes of commerce. Nevertheless, everyone agreed to higher taxes, but the evil continued with ever-increasing counterfeiting. An item that normally cost one silver dollar was six or seven in paper money at the beginning of 1779; in May of that year it had risen to ten or twelve, and by the beginning of 1780 it was thirty or forty. Changes were so rapid and uneven that the price often jumped a third, sometimes a half, and occasionally doubled. Although the large number of prisoners of war brought silver money into the United States, men who owned paper bills fought for the silver, depressing the paper currency still more.

At the beginning of 1780 Congress addressed a recommendation to all the states, urging them to redeem their paper money in a year's time at forty for one, which was considered average in view of the inequality prevailing in various parts of the country. It was hoped that hard cash, which was increasing daily, would supply the needs and that new paper, not to exceed $5 million, could be put into circulation at 5 percent interest. It was a good attempt, but the debt was too large to be redeemed in a single year and the interval between the abolition of the old system and the establishment of the new one was very difficult. Payments were due monthly, and some states were unable to continue after the third. This system would have ruined all but the wealthy because money was so unevenly distributed.

The simple, fair solution was for each man to renounce his claim without checking to see if this cession was larger than the taxes he would have paid to redeem his paper money. This is just what happened. The decline of our paper money was sudden and unexpected, for after dropping to a thousand or two thousand for one, it lost all value and never recovered. The reaction was one of universal satisfaction.

This sacrifice was a tax each man had paid from the beginning, as paper declined in value. It was proportionate to the amount of money which passed through his hands, and this was determined by the size of his business. Those unable to sell their produce had less paper; so they lost less. It would have been difficult to imagine such a fair method as this, which was due to chance and also saved the expense of collecting taxes.

Europeans are attempting to wreak a childish vengeance by making false statements about paper money in the United States. The goal of British politicians is to inculcate the belief that this country was completely happy under its former rulers; so they are exaggerating current problems and attributing them to the Revolution. But let us finish our discussion of paper money.

The general public cooperated in every possible way. Although it is true that the most patriotic citizens are those who suffered, this is true of all revolutions, and these good people are happy about what was accomplished for public welfare. Foreigners who lost because of the paper money had usually made bad investments. The first to take risks were the poor; they made large profits, and several became wealthy. Capitalists were less bold; some lost on account of the paper money, and others through poor judgment. Many men whose business was already in a critical state when they began to speculate took advantage of the paper money to claim large losses.* Those who kept their paper in the hope of converting it into silver at the nominal value were bedazzled by something which would have been completely unjust if it could have been done. Who could agree to a tax that would redeem paper for an equal amount in silver, when a pair of shoes cost two thousand paper dollars, a hat four thousand, etc.? Some will claim they got their paper at a time when it was worth almost as much as silver.

---

* A number bought large amounts of paper for very small sums in silver.

If they can furnish proof of this, they will obtain justice according to the law passed by Congress on 3 June 1784. This states that paper is to be priced at the current value, with an additional 6 percent for interest. But all these demands must be substantiated, or there would be endless cases of fraud.

# Chapter 4

# The National Debt before and after the Revolution

The colonies contracted a debt of nearly £10 million by their efforts to aid Great Britain during the war of 1756. Little more than a decade elapsed between the peace of 1763 and the beginning of the Revolution. Despite annoying commercial restrictions the debt was almost wiped out during this short period. This shows that the current obligations of the United States are small in comparison to its resources, because they amount to less than $11 million abroad and $34 million at home. Furthermore, the territories which some states, notably Virginia, have ceded to the Union will probably be sold and the proceeds applied toward liquidation of this debt. Taxes are small, yet more than sufficient to pay interest and reduce the principal, because both population and the value of real estate are increasing daily. Ordinary expenses of the various governments are trivial and those of the Confederation less than £28,000 annually. It is not fair to judge the future by our accomplishments since peace was declared, for the havoc of war was much greater than is generally realized. In Virginia alone the most conservative figure estimates the damage at more than £3 million. Time is needed to restore things to their former state, especially as there was so much destruction of cattle.

As our war for liberation did not last nearly as long as the one in the Low Countries, it was generally believed we suffered proportionately less. Everyone knows the Dutch enjoyed a flourishing commerce and other advantages during their revolution, while our situation was completely different. As we were plain farmers (with the exception of a few fishermen who were forced to abandon their occupation), we had no means of sending to market the produce we were able to raise. Accustomed to importing all our manufactured goods from England, Scotland, and Ireland, and never having imagined that we should have to wage war against Great Britain, we were without guns, powder, money, or clothing. The state of Virginia could barely scrape together £4,000 to get gunpowder from the nearby islands. Individuals had contracted immense debts to British merchants and manufacturers. Although we had agreed to prohibit importing British goods, we permitted free exports to England for almost a year, so that the debtors would have an opportunity to pay most of their bills. During this period we shipped all the money we could collect to our creditors, together with merchandise. We thus sacrificed every political consideration to our good faith, and British merchants have acknowledged this. The astonishing change in the attitude toward us in Great Britain has given rise to the supposition that the Revolution changed us. That is true, but in the opposite sense from the way the English mean it, for our young people express even more generous ideas than their elders. Others say we have been corrupted by the large number of Europeans in our country. The majority of those who remained in America were German soldiers, nearly three hundred in four counties of Virginia alone, and everyone considers them fine men. The troops of our allies were usually very well behaved, and some of the officers noble as well as highly intelligent. But even if the opposite were true and if we had received the dregs of humanity from various parts of Europe, it is unlikely that these dregs could have acted as swiftly as the plague.

I shall not go into detail about French officers, for it would mean praising too many men, but I cannot refrain from telling one story about the comte de Rochambeau. On his return from the capture of Yorktown he was arrested in New Jersey, where his soldiers had done some damage in a field belonging to a Tory. The law is the same for all; so the police officer had to explain the matter. The comte asked quietly what should be done, and the man replied: "My duty is to take you to prison unless two men guarantee that you will appear at the next session of the court or send someone to reply to the demands of the man who claims to be your creditor and that you will accept the judge's decision." The comte de Rochambeau had no difficulty getting bondsmen, for everyone in the vicinity offered to serve in that capacity. His respect for the law on this occasion won him the heart of more Americans than the great service he rendered during all the time he remained in the United States.

If you think about the enormous taxes the English have been paying for a long time and the repeated demands we made before the Revolution to be on the same footing with them, it will be evident that our present taxes are almost nothing in comparison to the indirect ones we had to pay on commerce. It is true that in some places we have not been able to collect the taxes levied, but that is because a large number of our citizens simply cannot afford to pay them.

Inequality exists not only between the states but between districts in a state and between the inhabitants of a district. During the war, Massachusetts and Pennsylvania contributed the most, and one state that could not pay its share was subsidized by the feeble resources of the Union. Since peace was restored, Virginia and South Carolina have made the largest contributions, for circumstances have favored them as Massachusetts and Pennsylvania were favored during the Revolution.

The causes of our financial troubles are so complicated that I should try the patience of my readers if I catalogued them. Imagine thirteen states that have just shaken off the yoke of tyranny. In the midst of the universal uproar they seize the helm of the ship of state and find themselves forced to steer through a number of shoals they had never before encountered. Contributions of all kinds for the troops necessitated opening accounts between individuals and the public and between the various states and the Union. In several states it was claimed these advances had more than equaled their quota. This allegation, which could only be verified by a general liquidation of accounts, made it impossible to require payment of taxes. Congress was forced to send a body of commissioners to the respective states to settle their bills. Auditing the accounts between the government and the citizens of each state was also a difficult and time-consuming matter.

Although the current situation leaves much to be desired, everyone is zealous about working for the best interests of the country, and delay is occasioned only by a difference of opinion as to the means. We are only beginning to emerge from chaos, and no state has developed a good financial system; yet the taxes collected last year in Virginia were sufficient to pay the ordinary expenses of running the government and interest on the state debt. We also sent a considerable amount to Congress and used the balance to reimburse some of our foreign creditors.

If you wish to understand the inhabitants of a country, you should study their behavior without relying on the complaints of the dissatisfied or the falsehoods of gazetteers. An examination of our governments reveals they cannot endure if the great majority of our citizens are dissatisfied. Furthermore, the wisest laws cannot please everyone, and we are all more impatient at the evils that affect ourselves than at those which strike others. Finally, every corner of the earth resounds with the cries of a few complaining individuals, whereas general satisfaction is quiet and does not attract attention.

# Chapter 5

# Private Debts and Commercial Credit

American indifference to the lies told about the United States in Europe is less reprehensible than one might think. What good would it do to protest? Our adversaries have established their system; their intention is to discredit this country at any price, and if one lie is disproved, they tell a hundred others. They say this harms credit, which is important for commerce. We should be glad if this were true, since the credit we enjoy in Europe is harmful to our economy. When you can buy merchandise on credit, it is only too easy to do so. English gazetteers are trying to deprive us of this privilege, while merchants and manufacturers invite us to take advantage of it. The larger our debt, the more we feel the evil effects of this exchange, which augments the price of what we buy, lowers the value of our merchandise, and, even worse, puts us in a position where we do not dare leave our creditor to make purchases from another source.

To reduce the problems arising from easy credit, the Virginia General Assembly passed a law giving a debtor six months to pay his bill. But this failed to produce the desired effect because merchants who have settled in America know whom to trust; they have learned that the code of honor is more important than law, and in two years or more only one person has taken advantage of this regulation.

Although American citizens paid a large share of their private debts to British subjects at the beginning of the Revolution, it is estimated they still owe at least £5 million. To pay this and to wipe out the national debt contracted in Europe, we must export much more merchandise than we import. Commercial credit has the opposite effect, as it deprives the country of hard cash needed for circulation.

If Congress passes sound legislation, American resources can solve this problem in a short period of time, but the states cannot handle it individually. To strengthen the Union several states have appointed representatives to meet at a designated place and have requested the others to do the same. Permit me to say that all these things take time. We are constantly making improvements, but Europe will not be informed about them until the gazetteers take the trouble to acquire correct information and devote as much energy to telling the truth as they now spend fabricating falsehoods.

Some zealous but misinformed friends of humanity fear certain nightmares that are doubtless very remote, and these are encouraged by the inventions of pedants. Meditating on the disasters of vanished nations, they do not hesitate to predict what will happen to us someday. If they examined the facts, they might be useful, but what is the sense of predicting troubles if they do not provide a remedy? "Things will not always be the same," they cry; "Americans are human like everyone else." We agree completely. No one claims perfection or imagines human institutions, even the wisest, can be eternal. Because it is nonetheless true that the better the foundation, the longer the building will last, barring unforeseen accidents, one just has to do his best and not worry.

It is claimed that the return to peace cooled the enthusiasm necessary to put our new edifice on a solid base. Calm is as essential to complete our task as ardor and courage were necessary to begin it. The diversity of interests which some pretend will cause us trouble need not be feared in our governments, where the titles of doctor, lawyer, merchant, or laborer do not proclaim any class difference. Birth conveys neither nobility nor dishonor. The distinction still accorded in some states to landowners is not one to make us fear the establishment of an aristocracy, especially as principles of equality are stronger every day.

The dissatisfaction of the inhabitants of New England is not an indication of disharmony but the result of our destructive war. Although the balance of the private foreign debt at the beginning of the Revolution was smaller in the four New England states than in Virginia, its effects are more noticeable. African pirates are doing a great deal of harm to New England fishermen, whereas products of the Southern states find a market.

The General Assembly in Virginia decided that debts contracted before the Revolution should be paid in seven years in equal installments and that interest could be extended for that length of time. But in New England, debtors may be forced to pay everything at once. Men who have to sell a piece of property cannot get a fair price for it. Taxes, though modest, are a burden to a man who is in debt, cannot run his business, and finds himself reduced to selling his possessions at a loss. It is hard to be patient about these evils, especially when the money is going to citizens of a country which, by an unjust war, made it impossible for men to pay their bills and which is now stirring up both the Indians and the Barbary pirates against us.

Interruption of employment for more than nine years, destruction of houses, cattle, and agricultural equipment, without counting pillage and other losses, are enough to impoverish any country, especially one already weakened by trying to pay off old debts. But as soon as Congress has the necessary power, and that should be very soon, we shall see that the resources of this country are astonishing. We shall then be able to deal with this deceptive credit and other evils, but this is not the time to discuss that matter.

# Chapter 6

# Reasons for the Slow Development
## of Commerce between
## France and the United States

Europeans claim Americans like the English and do not care for
the French, and that this is why it is difficult to establish a flourishing commerce between France and the new republics.

English gazetteers have constantly dwelt on this theme. Although their statements are too prejudiced to carry much weight,
Abbé Raynal has given credence to the deception. "The American
keeps his eyes secretly turned toward his mother country, and he
would rejoice over any disasters that struck his allies so long as
they did not affect his independence."

There was a time when it was a crime to contradict any statement in the *Philosophical History of the Two Indies*. The abbé's
tone wove a spell of enchantment over the minds of his readers,
but let us examine the statement on page 343 of volume 9: "We
are speaking to nations and to posterity. It is our duty to transmit
faithfully whatever can influence public happiness. We must tell
what has caused mistakes so that men will learn to avoid them. If
we betrayed this noble trust, justice and truth, which are eternal,
would denounce us, and future generations would mention our
name with scorn."

Did anyone ever promise more emphatically to tell the truth?
Mr. Paine was justified in writing Abbé Raynal from Philadelphia
that his mistakes were dangerous. I saw an example of this in 1783,
when I returned to America on the *Comte d'Estaing*, which belonged to M. de Beaumarchais. This vessel was inside the Virginia
capes about the middle of November; although the captain had a
favorable wind, he was obliged to anchor because he lacked a
pilot to take him to Baltimore.*

Several ship's officers who had read the *Philosophical History*
claimed that Americans were pro-English and anti-French. They
quoted the abbé as an indisputable authority and concluded that
the local residents did not provide a pilot because they would
have been happy to see the vessel founder. They wanted to fire

* As this vessel weighed almost 900 tons, it drew a great deal of water. The
captain's decision was not only prudent but in accordance with the law.

on a small boat that was going about its business because, in accordance with their maritime code, any craft was obliged to come alongside at the first shot. The captain did not permit this but, to keep peace, sent his launch to Hampton, some distance away, for a pilot. He finally got two—the launch returned with a somewhat disgruntled individual and the other arrived on a fishing boat.

The war was responsible for the fact there were no pilots outside the capes. In many areas the English had burned or wrecked their houses and taken or destroyed their boats. Some pilots had died and others settled inland. One of the latter heard the cannon and came as soon as possible. The arrival of the disgruntled pilot should have carried some weight, but nothing could change the impression left by Abbé Raynal's book.

If you are prejudiced before you land in a country, you see everything in a false light, and a few ignoramuses can do a great deal of harm. A large number of Frenchmen who have been in America are well informed, but they do not like to talk about themselves.*

In April 1785 I was in York County, Virginia. The entire population was up in arms against an English captain who, on the twelfth, had celebrated with cannonades and flag-flying the anniversary of the Rodney victory.[5] This individual could not be found on a day when court was in session and everyone with business to transact appears. He stayed on board his vessel twelve miles above the city, and it was believed he had to sail without a cargo. He had broken no laws but feared public resentment.

You may say that the example of York County, where Cornwallis's army surrendered—thanks to the help of the French fleet—is not characteristic of American feeling toward the French. I shall give just one illustration to prove it is universal. Americans have always followed the English practice of drinking a toast to the sovereign after dinner. Before the Revolution the first toast was to George III. This was replaced by a toast to the United States and a second to Louis XVI. I had the curiosity to ask inhabitants of various states whether, after peace was restored, anyone drank a toast to the English monarch. They all told me they had never heard one, either in public or in a private home, but that every-

---

* It is worthy of note that the French officers who served in the American army, and whom we have been unable to reward for all their services, are particularly outraged about the lies that are being circulated about us.

[5] Admiral Rodney's victory over the French fleet in the Caribbean took place 12 April 1782.

one drank to Louis XVI. Although this may be regarded as insignificant, it is more indicative of national inclination and dislike than all the information one could cull from acts of Congress or any other legislative body. Public acts may be suggested by politics, but genuine affection appears in private conversation, especially at table.

France is loved in America, and England is not. But we must not confuse the country with its citizens, for Americans respect an Englishman or a Frenchman as an individual. The prevailing affection for France, which is something altogether different, is founded on a just, powerful, and honorable base. If American commerce were regulated by sympathy, it would be with France.

The causes hindering commercial relations between the two countries are very numerous but may be divided into categories as follows:

1. The monopoly of the Farmers General on various commodities, including tobacco, which is the chief American export.
2. The maze of extremely irritating customs restrictions.
3. The difference between commercial regulations.

The following may be regarded as secondary causes; if a remedy were found for the first three, several of these would disappear and the others would be trifling.

1. French factories do not operate according to the American system.
2. Buyers are discouraged because there is no fixed price for merchandise.
3. The language barrier.
4. The difference in currency, weights, and measurements.
5. The American debt to English merchants and manufacturers.
6. The insidious credit which the English continue to extend to Americans.

Several other causes cannot be exactly defined, as they result from temporary conditions. During the stormy times most French merchants who did business with America were desperate men who had nothing to lose. The first to come from the islands brought merchandise that had been given to them on credit because it could not be sold. Even barbers and busboys from Santo Domingo cafés came with their gimcracks, and neither they nor their wares made a favorable impression.

Several times I have made it a point to say to my compatriots that you cannot judge the French by a few individuals scattered around the globe. The opposite is true in England, where the dregs of the country remain at home, while Englishmen who travel for business or pleasure are usually outstanding.*

As long as the war lasted, business remained about the same because of the dangers to which commerce was exposed. There was little risk and the likelihood of an excellent profit, but good merchants were hesitant about becoming involved in these ventures. For the same reason, no leading American merchants came to France. Some men were honest, but the majority got into speculations they could not handle. The despotic monopoly of the Farmers General, the obstacles impeding Franco-American commerce, and troubles resulting from paper money also caused a number to go bankrupt.

As soon as the peace treaty was signed, the English flooded American ports, and even cities in the interior, with merchandise. They encouraged the inhabitants, who needed everything, to take stuff on credit, and adventurers with no hope of obtaining credit received whole cargoes of goods. One young man who saw the names of five commercial firms listed in English gazettes wrote them all to see if one would give him credit; to his surprise, he received five shipments. This extension of credit produced a large number of bankruptcies, but whereas in England only a few suffered, in America the practice helped to keep commerce in its former dependence and stripped the country of its money.

English merchants use every possible device to sell their products and discredit French goods. One of their most successful tricks is to sell all the best items as English, even if they were manufactured in other countries, and to label as French the shoddiest, even if they were made in England. I was shocked by this in America, but then, to my surprise, I discovered the same custom exists in France. A wise Frenchman remarked: "The English are much more exact about their shipments than we are. They know the art of disguising products of other countries under English names, and they apply to commerce the coquetry the French display in society."

The dearth of products suitable for the American market is

---

* In 1777 I met in Williamsburg a Mr. G— from Amiens who had been a dragoon and was now operating a café in Santo Domingo. He was scrupulously honest and so unassuming that I introduced him in the best houses in town to counteract the disagreeable impression which had been made by several other men.

another secondary cause. Anything was satisfactory during war-time, but the war did not last long enough to break habits. After peace was restored, several Frenchmen who had settled in America took samples to France but could not make the manufacturers change their routine. This is not surprising, for reforms, like beginnings, are difficult and expensive; so new enterprises need to envisage a ready and permanent market. If mercantile relations between France and America can be put on a more solid basis, the difference in currencies and in weights and measures will be a small obstacle. The same is true of the language barrier. To learn the language, especially commercial terms, fathers in the two countries should exchange their children. But as long as the big obstacles exist, the little ones will exert a powerful influence.

Knowledge of commercial terms is indispensable. Americans have often complained because they did not receive what they ordered, and correspondence is essential to establish a stable business with a fair profit. The greed of men who wish to make a quick killing has caused Americans to protest about variations in price. If a buyer gives an order in England, he does not have to settle the cost in advance. In France, on the other hand, he will find a difference of 30 to 40 percent between merchants. Although this is one of the most important secondary causes impeding the development of commercial relations between the two countries, it would vanish as soon as the first causes were removed, because the number of men involved would ensure healthy competition.

The old debts to English merchants and manufacturers and the credit the latter continue to extend to Americans are the other secondary causes. New commercial markets must be found, and this matter should be considered by the governments of the United States and those countries with which commerce can be established. But I shall not discuss this subject, since I am merely indicating the problems impeding commerce between France and the United States.

The difference in commercial regulations is one of the three fundamental obstacles I listed. For example, a verbal agreement is valid in America, but in France everything must be in writing if the sum exceeds £100.

Customs regulations are an even greater obstacle than legal differences, and an infinite amount of time is wasted on petty privileges. These are frequently disregarded, fines are imposed, and there are so many quarrels that many Frenchmen want to get out of this business as quickly as possible.* Expenses resulting from these regulations, small as they are, become significant on account of their number. The profit to the crown is so tiny it seems likely some of these abuses were established through ignorance a long time ago, while others were gradually introduced for personal gain. Internal customs are the most dangerous. The arrogance of employees in a position of authority is shocking. When they discover that they have not recognized the rank of the person with whom they are dealing, they drop their insolent pose and cower abjectly. If these vexations are maddening to the French, you can imagine the effect they produce on foreigners who did not know they existed.

Books are an important item in American commerce, but because printing is very expensive, booksellers and authors find it profitable to have their works published in England. Recently someone had the idea that this privilege could be obtained for France, and several distinguished men took the trouble to show what it would mean if this obstacle could be overcome. They wanted to begin with a book that seemed well suited to the United States, and the edition was intended to give Americans a knowledge of French presses. The volume, however, had to be submitted to a censor, who raised difficulties about two expressions. After long delays, permission to publish was finally obtained on condition that every copy should be exported.

If submitting to this condition had paved the way for future operations, all would have been well. But when it was discovered that these same disagreeable rituals would have to be repeated for every single book, the project was abandoned. Even though printing is much less costly in France than elsewhere, no American would want to let his manuscript pass through so many hands, to run the risk of its being lost, and to burden his friends. If laws create obstacles to commerce, we cannot blame our allies for turning elsewhere.†

The Frenchman is witty and industrious. The unfortunate revocation of the Edict of Nantes, which forced so many skilled Huguenots to seek exile in other countries, particularly England, was a serious loss. Labor and raw materials are cheaper in France than in England; yet certain products are more expensive. This

---

* See Note N for some other motives which may make the French want to get out of business.

† See chapter 5 of Part II, which discusses freedom of the press.

makes one question the system, and we may hope it will be revised as soon as circumstances permit.

The worst obstacle is the monopoly, caused by the Farmers General. France loses a tremendous amount on account of their tobacco monopoly. At the beginning of 1785 they made an agreement to purchase twenty thousand casks annually at £36 a hundred from Mr. Robert Morris of Philadelphia; on an average, casks weigh about a thousand pounds.

It would seem at first glance that this should have established commercial relations between the two countries, but it had the opposite effect. If the tobacco were imported by French merchants, or shipped by Americans for their account, it would be paid for in merchandise, and both sides would profit. But the Farmers General pay cash and do not ship a single French article in exchange. This money then goes to Great Britain in bills of exchange or cash to pay for British merchandise sent to America. Thus France loses an opportunity to sell its products; its money goes to England, and America misses a means of strengthening mercantile ties with France. Some men assume the credit of a product is enhanced when one person purchases a vast amount, but the contrary is true. A powerful purchaser who pays cash is courted by salesmen; so he takes advantage of them and keeps the product from reaching a fair price.

The French government has now ordered the Farmers General to purchase fifteen thousand casks a year in France at the price set with Mr. Morris for the remaining two years of their contract. It was thought these would make up the quantity which, by the terms of the agreement between the Farmers General and the government, must remain in the warehouses, and the government gave orders that these casks must be brought from America on French or American vessels.

It was anticipated that the merchants would be exposed to all kinds of annoyances, and this has proved only too true, for commerce cannot flourish unless it is free. Optimists flatter themselves that our troubles will be over when the contract with Mr. Morris expires and the Farmers General have to purchase all their tobacco in France. They are mistaken; the problem will merely be reduced.*

* See Note O for reflections proving that these obstacles will persist until commerce is free.

# Chapter 7

# Immigration

The growth in population caused by an increased birthrate is such that immigration is not an important factor. The reader can see what the author of the *Notes on the State of Virginia* has to say on this subject. The wisest men advise Americans to welcome immigrants, on the principle that everyone has the right to choose his own country, but they say Europeans should not be urged to come. Several years ago Dr. Franklin, who saw that the prevailing ideas in Europe were far from accurate, composed this notice for those who had asked him to help them become American citizens.

### Information to Those Who Would Remove to America

Many persons in Europe having directly or by letters, expressed to the Writer of this, who is well acquainted with North America, their desire of transporting and establishing themselves in that Country; but who appear to him to have formed through ignorance, mistaken ideas and expectations of what is to be obtained there; he thinks it may be useful, and prevent inconvenient, expensive and fruitless removals and voyages of improper persons, if he gives some clearer and truer notions of that part of the world than appear to have hitherto prevailed.

He finds it is imagined by numbers, that the Inhabitants of North America are rich, capable of rewarding, and disposed to reward all sorts of ingenuity; [6] that they are at the same time ignorant of all the Sciences; and consequently that strangers possessing talents in the belles-letters, fine arts, etc. must be highly esteemed, and so well paid as to become easily rich themselves; that there are also abundance of profitable Offices to be disposed of, which the natives are not qualified to fill; and that having few persons of family among them, strangers of birth must be greatly respected, and of course easily obtain the best of those Offices, which will make all their fortunes: That the Governments too, to encourage emigrations from Europe, not only pay the expence of personal transportation, but give lands gratis to strangers, with negroes to work for them, utensils of husbandry, and stocks of cattle. These are all wild imaginations; and those who go to America with expectations founded upon them, will surely find themselves disappointed.

The truth is, that though there are in that country few people so

[6] Mazzei has "industry."

miserable as the poor of Europe, there are also very few that in Europe would be called rich: It is rather a general happy mediocrity that prevails. There are few great Proprietors of the soil, and few Tenants; most people cultivate their own lands, or follow some handicraft or merchandise; very few rich enough to live idly upon their rents or incomes; or to pay the high prices given in Europe, for Painting, Statues, Architecture, and the other works of Art that are more curious than useful. Hence the natural geniuses that have arisen in America, with such talents, have uniformly quitted that Country for Europe, where they can be more suitably rewarded. It is true that letters and mathematical knowledge are in esteem there, but they are at the same time more common than is apprehended; there being already existing nine Colleges, or Universities, viz. four in New-England, and one in each of the Provinces of New-York, New-Jersey, Pennsilvania, Maryland, and Virginia, all furnished with learned Professors; besides a number of smaller Academies. These educate many of their youth in the languages, and those sciences that qualify men for the professions of Divinity, Law, or Physic. Strangers indeed are by no means excluded from exercising those professions; and the quick increase of inhabitants every where gives them a chance of employ, which they have in common with the Natives. Of Civil offices or employments, there are few; no superfluous ones as in Europe; and it is a rule established in some of the States, that no Office should be so profitable as to make it desirable. The 36th Article of the Constitution of Pennsilvania, runs expressly in these words: "As every Freeman, to preserve his Independence, (if he has not a sufficient estate) ought to have some profession, calling, trade, or farm, whereby he may honestly subsist, there can be no necessity for, nor use in, establishing offices of profit; the usual effects of which are dependance and servility, unbecoming Freemen, in the possessors and expectants; faction, contention, corruption, and disorder among the people. Wherefore, whenever an office, through increase of fees or otherwise, becomes so profitable as to occasion many to apply for it, the profits ought to be lessened by the Legislature."

These ideas prevailing more or less in all the United States, it cannot be worth any man's while, who has a means of living at home, to expatriate himself in hopes of obtaining a profitable civil office in America; and as to military offices, they are at an end with the war, the armies being disbanded. Much less is it advisable for a person to go thither who has no other quality to recommend him but his birth. In Europe it has indeed its value; but it is a commodity that cannot be carried to a worse market than to that of America, where people do not enquire concerning a stranger, *What is he?* [7] but *What can he do?* If he has any useful art, he is welcome; and if he exercises it, and be-

---

[7] Mazzei has "Who is he?"

haves well, he will be respected by all that know him; but a mere man of quality, who on that account wants to live upon the public, by some office or salary, will be despised and disregarded. The Husband-man is in honor there, and even the Mechanic, because their employ-ments are useful. The people have a saying, that God Almighty is himself a Mechanic, the greatest in the Universe. . . .

They are pleased with the observation of a Negro, and frequently mention it, that Boccarorra (meaning the white man) make de black man workee, make de horse workee, make de ox workee, make ebery ting workee; only de hog. He de hog, no workee; he eat, he drink, he walk about, he go to sleep when he please, he libb like a Gentleman. According to these opinions of the Americans, one of them would think himself more obliged to a genealogist, who could prove for him that his ancestors and relations for ten generations had been Plough-men, Smiths, Carpenters, Turners, Weavers, Tanners, or even Shoe-makers, and consequently that they were useful members of society; than if he could only prove that they were Gentlemen, doing nothing of value, but living idly on the labour of others, mere *fruges consumere nati,** and otherwise *good* for *nothing*, till by their death, their estates, like the carcase of the Negro's gentleman-hog come to be *cut up*.

With regard to encouragements for strangers from Government, they are really only what are derived from good laws and liberty. Strangers are welcome because there is room enough for them all, and therefore the old inhabitants are not jealous of them; the laws protect them sufficiently, so that they have no need of the patronage of great men; and every one will enjoy securely the profits of his industry. But if he does not bring a fortune with him, he must work and be indus-trious to live. One or two years residence give him all the rights of a Citizen; but the Government does not at present, whatever it may have done in former times, hire people to become settlers, by paying their passages, giving land, negroes, utensils, stock; or any other kind of emolument whatsoever. In short, America is the land of labour, and by no means what the English call *Lubberland*, and the French *Pays de Cocagne*, where the streets are said to be paved with half-peck loaves, the houses tiled with pancakes, and where the fowls fly about ready roasted, crying, *Come eat me!*

Who then are the kind of persons to whom an emigration to Amer-ica may be advantageous? And what are the advantages they may reasonably expect?

Land being cheap in that country, from the vast forests still void of inhabitants, and not likely to be occupied in an age to come, insomuch

---

* There are a number of us born
  Merely to eat up the corn.
                    Watts.

that the propriety of an hundred acres of fertile soil full of wood may be obtained near the frontiers in many places, for eight or ten guineas, hearty young labouring men, who understand the husbandry of corn and cattle, which is nearly the same in that country as in Europe, may easily establish themselves there. A little money saved of the good wages they receive there while they work for others, enables them to buy the land and begin their plantation, in which they are assisted by the good will of their neighbours, and some credit. Multitudes of poor people from England, Ireland, Scotland, and Germany, have by this means in a few years become wealthy farmers, who in their own countries, where all the lands are fully occupied, and the wages of labour low, could never have emerged from the mean condition wherein they were born.

From the salubrity of the air, the healthiness of the climate, the plenty of good provisions, and the encouragement to early marriages, by the certainty of subsistance in cultivating the earth, the increase of inhabitants by natural generation is very rapid in America, and becomes still more so by the accession of strangers; hence there is a continual demand for more artisans of all the necessary and useful kinds, to supply those cultivators of the earth with houses, and with furniture and utensils of the grosser sorts, which cannot so well be brought from Europe. Tolerably good work-men in any of those mechanic arts, are sure to find employ, and to be well paid for their work, there being no restraints preventing strangers from exercising any art they understand, nor any permission necessary. If they are poor, they begin first as servants or journeymen; and if they are sober, industrious, and frugal, they soon become masters, establish themselves in business, marry, raise families, and become respectable Citizens.

Also, persons of moderate fortunes and capitals, who having a number of children to provide for, are desirous of bringing them up to industry, and to secure estates for their posterity, have opportunities of doing it in America, which Europe does not afford. There they may be taught and practice profitable mechanic arts, without incurring disgrace on that account; but on the contrary acquiring respect by such abilities. There small capitals laid out in lands, which daily become more valuable by the increase of people, afford a solid prospect of ample fortunes thereafter for those children. The Writer of this has known several instances of large tracts of land, bought on what was then the frontier of Pennsilvania, for ten pounds per hundred acres, which, after twenty years, when the settlements had been extended far beyond them, sold readily, without any improvement made upon them, for three pounds per acre.[8] The acre in America is the same with the English acre, or the acre of Normandy.

---

[8] Mazzei says that the tracts were bought for £140 per hundred acres and that they sold at £40 per acre.

Those who desire to understand the state of Government in America, would do well to read the Constitutions of the several States, and the Articles of Confederation that bind the whole together for general purposes, under the direction of one assembly called the Congress. These Constitutions have been printed by order of Congress, in America; two Editions of them have also been printed in London; and a good translation of them into French, has lately been published at Paris.

Several of the Princes of Europe having of late, from an opinion of advantage to arise by producing all commodities and manufactures within their own dominions, so as to diminish or render useless their importations, have endeavoured to entice workmen from other countries, by high salaries, privileges, etc. Many persons pretending to be skilled in various great manufactures, imagining that America must be in want of them, and that the Congress would probably be disposed to imitate the Princes above-mentioned, have proposed to go over, on condition of having their passages paid, lands given, salaries appointed, exclusive privileges for terms of years, etc. Such persons, on reading the Articles of Confederation, will find that the Congress have no power committed to them, or money put into their hands, for such purposes; and that if any such encouragement is given, it must be by the Government of some separate State. This, however, has rarely been done in America; and when it has been done, it has rarely succeeded, so as to establish a manufacture, which the country was not yet so ripe for as to encourage private persons to set it up; labour being generally too dear there, and hands difficult to be kept together, every one desiring to be a master, and the cheapness of land inclining many to leave trades for agriculture. Some indeed have met with success, and are carried on to advantage; but they are generally such as require only a few hands, or wherein great part of the work is performed by machines. Goods that are bulky, and of so small value as not well to bear the expence of freight, may often be made cheaper in the country than they can be imported; and the manufacture of such goods will be profitable wherever there is a sufficient demand. The farmers in America produce indeed a good deal of wool and flax; and none is exported, it is all worked up; but it is in the way of domestic manufacture for the use of the family. The buying up quantities of wool and flax with the design to employ spinners, weavers, etc. and form great establishments, producing quantities of linen and woollen goods for sale, has been several times attempted in different Provinces; but those projects have generally failed, goods of equal value being imported cheaper. And when the Governments have been solicited to support such schemes by encouragements, in money, or by imposing duties on importation of such goods, it has been generally refused, on this principle, that if the country is ripe for the manufacture, it may be carried on by private persons to advantage; and if not, it is a folly to think of forcing nature. Great establishments of manufacture, require great numbers of poor to do the work for small wages; these poor are to be found in Europe, but will not be found in America, till the lands are all taken up and cultivated, and the excess of people who cannot get land, want employment. The manufacture of silk, they say, is natural in France, as that of cloth in England, because each country produces in plenty the first material. But if England will have a manufacture of silk as well as that of cloth, and France one of cloth as well as that of silk, these unnatural operations * must be supported by mutual prohibitions, or high duties on the importation of each others goods; by which means the workmen are enabled to tax the home consumer by greater prices, while the higher wages they receive makes them neither happier nor richer, since they only drink more and work less. Therefore the Governments in America do nothing to encourage such projects. The people, by this means, are not imposed on, either by the Merchant or Mechanic: if the Merchant demands too much profit on imported shoes, they buy of the Shoemaker; and if he asks too high a price, they take them of the Merchant: Thus the two professions are checks on each other. The Shoemaker, however, has on the whole, a considerable profit upon his labour in America, beyond what he had in Europe, as he can add to his price a sum nearly equal to all the expences of freight and commission, risque or insurance, etc. necessarily charged by the Merchant. And the case is the same with the workmen in every other mechanic art. Hence it is, that artisans generally live better and more easily in America than in Europe; and such as are good economists, make a comfortable provision for age, and for their children. Such may, therefore, remove with advantage to America.

In the old, long-settled countries of Europe, all arts, trades, professions, farms etc. are so full, that it is difficult for a poor man, who has children, to place them where they may gain, or learn to gain a decent livelihood. The artisans, who fear creating future rivals in business, refuse to take apprentices, but upon conditions of money, maintenance, or the like, which the parents are unable to comply with. Hence the youth are dragged up in ignorance of every gainful art, and obliged to become soldiers or servants, or thieves, for a subsistence. In America, the rapid increase of inhabitants takes away that fear of rivalship, and artisans willingly receive apprentices from the hope of profit by their labour, during the remainder of the time stipulated, after they shall be instructed. Hence it is easy for poor families to get their children

---

* This requires some explanation. England imports all of its raw material for manufacturing silk, and France imports about a third. Both countries get a great deal of wool from Spain because Spanish wool is excellent. Although England has more, the quantity exported by France proves that fine wool manufactures are not unnatural in that country. The amount of silk exported from England is too small to be classed as a commercial enterprise; it is designed to satisfy a few individuals.

instructed; for the artisans are so desirous of apprentices, that many of them will even give money to the parents, to have boys from ten to fifteen years of age bound apprentices to them, till the age of twenty-one; and many poor parents have, by that means, on their arrival in the country, raised money enough to buy land sufficient to establish themselves, and to subsist the rest of their family by agriculture. These contracts for apprentices are made before a Magistrate, who regulates the agreement according to reason and justice; and having in view the formation of a future useful Citizen, obliges the Master to engage by a written indenture, not only that during the time of service stipulated, the apprentice shall be duly provided with meat, drink, apparel, washing, and lodging, and at its expiration with a compleat new suit of clothes, but also that he shall be taught to read, write, and cast accompts; and that he shall be well instructed in the art or profession of his Master, or some other, by which he may afterwards gain a livelihood, and be able in his turn to raise a family. A copy of this indenture is given to the apprentice or his friends, and the Magistrate keeps a record of it, to which recourse may be had, in case of failure by the Master in any point of performance. This desire among the Masters to have more hands employed in working for them, induces them to pay the passages of young persons of both sexes, who on their arrival agree to serve them one, two, three, or four years; those who have already learned a trade, agreeing for a shorter term, in proportion to their skill, and the consequent immediate value of their service; and those who have none, agreeing for a longer term, in consideration of being taught an art their poverty would not permit them to acquire in their own country.

From the almost general mediocrity of fortune that prevails in America, obliging its people to follow some business for subsistence, those vices that arise usually from idleness, are in a great measure prevented. Industry and constant employment are great preservatives of the morals and virtue of a Nation. Hence bad examples to youth are more rare in America, which must be a comfortable consideration to parents. To this may be truly added, that serious Religion, under its various denominations, is not only tolerated, but respected and practiced. Atheism is unknown there; Infidelity [9] rare and secret; so that persons may live to a great age in that country without having their piety shocked by meeting with either an Atheist or an Infidel. And the Divine Being seems to have manifested his approbation of the mutual forbearance and kindness with which the different sects treat each other, by the remarkable prosperity with which he has been pleased to favour the whole country.[10]

[9] Mazzei has "incredulity."

[10] Benjamin Franklin, *Two Tracts:* Information to Those Who Would Remove to America and Remarks concerning the Savages of North America (London, 1784).

Although you can purchase land on frontiers for less than the figure quoted by Dr. Franklin, the following facts may serve as a useful deterrent to prevent imprudent investments.

A European who selects remote areas because they are cheap will not find anyone to work or lease them, since every freeman can be a landowner himself. If he buys slaves, they will be expensive; he runs the risk of losing them, and owning slaves makes people unhappy. If he brings families of peasants from Europe, he will have to pay for their transportation and support them until the new lands can be cleared. If he brings unmarried men, they may leave him to cultivate their own property in some distant spot where it would be difficult to find them.

There is also the risk of illness and death, in addition to the capital he must lay out for buildings, cattle, agricultural implements, and furniture. If he buys just the bare necessities, he will be obliged to send a long way to replace any item that gets broken, and this will involve both money and a loss of time. Every purchase will be more expensive because he is in a remote area, and the profit from his crops will be reduced by the cost of shipping them to the nearest market.

Any European who had the courage to give up the small luxuries to which he was accustomed and who decided to live in an isolated area without farming himself would need a considerable amount of money, patience to put up with the vexations that are part of any new settlement, and a decided taste for agriculture, hunting, and solitude. This kind of life would be suitable for a wealthy patriarch who brought several peasant families and men skilled as carpenters, blacksmiths, tailors, and cobblers. He should also be very certain that he could get used to this mode of life. It is doubtless a happy one if you are accustomed to it from childhood, but a man who wearies of the petty annoyances of a large city may become melancholy, forget his former bitterness, and remember only the little pleasures which his imagination embellishes as they are difficult to obtain.

The law of supply and demand is the same everywhere; so any object in abundance is cheap, while the price rises in proportion to its rarity. Land in the United States is cheaper than in the most cultivated areas of Europe, and the price falls as you go farther away from the sea, navigable rivers, and cities.

Dr. Franklin explains why any European who does not wish to have a useful profession should not become a citizen of the United States. A man can be a farmer without working himself, but he must be intelligent and observant. It is foolish to believe that one can enjoy profit from American lands in Europe. Everyone knows it is a great disadvantage to be unable to keep an eye on one's property, even where labor is cheap and the accounts of managers can be checked. Imagine the situation on the other side of the ocean, where labor is very expensive and it is difficult to find anyone who wants to work for someone else. The chief benefit a man obtains from property in America is that it will support his family, and he loses this if he lives elsewhere.

A wealthy individual who did not need to draw interest on his property could speculate in land, for in many places it doubles in value within a few years; but if he were not a citizen, he would have to make some arrangement to ensure his ownership, for I know no state which permits a foreigner to possess property.*

As it is easy to imagine that everything is perfect in a strange country, I am adding a few reflections to Dr. Franklin's notice. The only men who should emigrate from Europe to America are those who cannot earn enough to support their families, and philosophers who prize equality of citizenship more than small luxuries.

If one of them wanted to buy land without cultivating it himself, I think he would do well to purchase a small amount. Part of this would be farmed and provided with dwellings in a fairly settled district where he could get assistance in case of need. Later, if he wished to sell and move elsewhere, he could make a profit because property values are always enhanced by increased population. Before immigrating, he would be wise to seek advice from an inhabitant of the state where he wishes to live, as farming methods are not the same everywhere. I have no wish to discourage Europeans who would like to become American citizens, but I want to keep them from making a foolish decision. It is cruel to exaggerate the advantages and equally wrong to hide the disadvantages. Disappointed immigrants would have the alternative of returning to Europe, which would be expensive, or of resigning themselves to spending their lives in America, and no country has ever profited from acquiring unhappy citizens.

Those who read the *Letters from an American Farmer* [11] must not imagine these customs to be typical. The writer has only de-

* The Georgia assembly gave the comte d'Estaing 20,000 acres of land as a reward for his services to the state. A year ago they made him a citizen so that he could maintain his rights *in absentia*. All the states did the same for the marquis de Lafayette and his children.

[11] J. Hector St. John [Michel Guillaume Jean de Crèvecoeur], *Letters from an American Farmer* (Dublin, 1782).

scribed the life of frontiersmen who appreciate the kindness extended to them on their arrival and are equally generous when they are wealthy. Some of these practices remain here and there in the interior, but in inhabited areas the mode of life resembles that of Europe. Moreover, what applies to one part of the United States does not apply to other areas. A European who expected to find in Philadelphia or other urban sections of Pennsylvania the customs described in *The American Farmer* would be sadly mistaken, but anyone who has traveled in Europe and seen the difference between cities and villages, the open countryside, and sparsely inhabited mountain areas will understand that customs differ.

I was surprised to discover how many readers got ridiculous ideas from this book, although it is easy to see that the author pretends to be a simple Pennsylvania frontiersman who is amazed at what he sees in Philadelphia, has little information about other parts of America, knows nothing of Europe, and judges without any basis for comparison.

As the writer had never heard of any botanist other than Mr. [John] Bartram, he considers him the greatest in America. The father of Colonel [John] Banister of Virginia preceded Mr. Bartram and was in no way inferior to him, but neither can be compared to the famous Dr. Clayton, who died shortly before the Revolution.[12] He made so many additions to the botanical dictionary that he is known in Europe as the Virginia Linnaeus. It is likely that there have been and still are other botanists in America on a par with or superior to Mr. Bartram who have not become famous. It is also quite likely that some insane asylums were built before the one in Pennsylvania. As a matter of fact, the Virginia asylum is older. The good Pennsylvanian assumes his was the first in America, but these details are not worth verifying. While it is true that the fishermen on little Nantucket Island are the best whalers in the world, the method is the same everywhere. The author seems to think they have a different procedure or that they are the only ones in existence.

His simplicity made him believe the dreadful tale about the Carolina Negro.* Although I made a thorough investigation, I was

---

* This slave had killed the overseer of the plantation. He was suspended in a cage which was hung from the branch of a tree and left there to expire: "I shudder when I recollect that the birds had already picked out his eyes" (Letters of an American Farmer [1782, p. 189]). This story did not appear in the new edition.

[12] The *Flora Virginica* of Dr. John Clayton, a native of Virginia, was published by Gronovius at Leyden in 1762.

unable to find a single inhabitant of the state who did not regard the story as pure poppycock. The author is also very partial to Quakers, but this may be because there were few of them in his area. Any information to be derived from this book relates to the customs of frontiersmen; they are not to be confused with a few wretches who occasionally stir up the Indians against us and cause wars in which we have to defend ourselves.

# Chapter 8

# The Society of the Cincinnati

The founding of the Society of the Cincinnati frightened all friends of liberty who realized what the consequences might be. In Europe, where the evils of aristocracy are omnipresent, it made more of an impression than in America. The society is so out of keeping with the basic principles of the state governments one might believe someone was plotting to overthrow them. Members of this society are subject to very definite obligations, and if Americans were not afraid, it was because the character of almost all the members was opposed to the spirit of aristocracy.

The establishment of this society is a striking example of the mistakes men can make under the power of violent emotion. We must remember the American army was like a great family, in which the officers were deeply attached to one another and devoted to their chief. When the war ended, they were distressed at the probability they would never see each other again; so they founded the society, whose principal functions were to have meetings at set times, to organize a fund to help the needy, to aid their widows, etc. It was then proposed that they accept some honorary members, have a medal, make membership hereditary, and assume certain political responsibilities, the results of which were not foreseen. It would be difficult to ascertain who suggested these various propositions and even harder to learn their true intentions. Everyone was too upset to discuss the terms, which were all accepted without any thought of danger.

Every citizen had as a neighbor some officer of whom he was fond, and everyone was certain his friend would be incapable of establishing an organization that might endanger liberty. But the distinction conferred by the medal and hereditary membership was completely contrary to the fundamental principle of universal equality, and soon the gazettes were full of articles on this subject.

Mr. Aedanus Burke of South Carolina states in his *Considerations on the Order of the Cincinnati* that the principles of this society are aristocratic and injurious to liberty. Several legislative bodies meeting at the time published a resolution declaring the society to be dangerous; the members then realized that they had been blinded by emotion, and General Washington,* the president general, went to the meeting of the Philadelphia society in the spring of 1784 determined to abolish the new institution. He found the officers who had been appointed by the various state assemblies ready to second him, but M. L'Enfant, a French officer who had served as a major in the American army, had brought the medals and ribbons back from France and announced that the king had given permission to his subjects to wear them.[13] The Society of the Cincinnati owes its preservation to this event, for everyone was afraid to displease our great and good ally at the very moment when he had just agreed to this new bond between us and his subjects.

One of the chief purposes of the society was to perpetuate the memory of the sufferings French and American officers had endured together and to strengthen the ties between the two nations; this led to the selection of a blue and white ribbon, the colors of the alliance. After some discussion, the assembly decided to abolish the hereditary character of the medal and the society's political responsibilities, to submit the selection of honorary members to new regulations, and to propose that the funds be entrusted to the legislative bodies in the several states, so that their use might be made known to the public. These changes were addressed to the various state societies in a circular letter signed by General Washington as president general of the society in May 1784. The letter reads:

To the State Society of the Cincinnati in [each state]
 We have retained . . . those devices [the medals] which recognize the manner of our returning to our Citizenship; not as ostentatious marks of discrimination, but as pledges of our friendship, and emblems, whose appearance will never permit us to deviate from the path of virtue.† [14]

Although the intention was praiseworthy, such a decoration will always offend a true republican; so no one wears the medal in America and some officers (Colonel Smith, for example) do not even wear it in Europe. Public opinion was so strong on this sub-

---

* The general assembly consists of representatives appointed by associates of all the states. The president is called president general to distinguish him from the presidents of the state assemblies.

† Cincinnatus returns to his plow.

[13] Washington had commissioned Major Pierre Charles L'Enfant to order the eagles for the Society of the Cincinnati in Paris.

[14] *General Washington's Correspondence concerning the Society of the Cincinnati*, ed. E. E. Hume (Baltimore: Johns Hopkins Press, 1941), p. 173.

ject that the rest of General Washington's letter is a kind of apology.

And, we presume, in this place it may not be inexpedient to inform you that these are considered as the most endearing tokens of Friendship, and held in the highest estimation by such of our allies as have become entitled to them, by having contributed their personal services to the establishment of our Independence; that these gentlemen, who are among the first in rank and reputation, have been permitted by their Sovereign to hold this grateful memorial of our reciprocal affections; and that this fraternal intercourse is viewed by that illustrious Monarch and other distinguished characters, as no small additional cement to that harmony and reciprocation of good offices, which so happily prevail between the two Nations.[15]

The comte de Mirabeau,[16] in his *Considerations on the Order of the Cincinnati*,* seems to think the changes will have little effect. He believes that if the organization is not abolished, its members will constitute a group of prominent families that will keep the medal as a symbol of their glory.

I should have the same fears if public opinion were not so definite. But the medals probably will not last very long, and they can do little harm so long as people keep them at home. If the children of members showed them off someday, they would only hurt themselves. There is no reason to believe that ambition or vanity can remain unpunished in our country, and the examples the comte de Mirabeau used to frighten us do not apply either to the circumstances or to Americans.

The order of Roman patricians (if we can believe Greek and Roman historians) was established under the first king.† When the Tarquins lost the crown, patricians were already set apart by their wealth and influence. Later, when northern conquerors set up distinctions in rank, the same cleavage occurred in Europe, but there are too few members of the Society of the Cincinnati ever to form a large percentage of those distinguished by talent, wealth, and public esteem.

---

* The society was called an order in Europe, but an order usually requires governmental sanction. The legislative bodies which referred to the society criticized it, and if the others did not mention the institution, it was because they thought it was soon to be abolished.

† See Note P for comments by Titus Livius, Denys of Halicarnassus, and Plutarch.

[15] Ibid.

[16] Gabriel Riqueti, comte de Mirabeau favored a constitutional monarchy.

Mr. Burke was right to criticize this society. At that time it had not been reformed, but the reforms were in effect when the comte de Mirabeau published his book. He speaks as a persuasive orator, while I am writing as a historian. The historian must paint with precision, and if his colors are too bright, they betray truth. There is no law to prevent a citizen from wearing a medal attached to a ribbon, and if it was considered dangerous, the best remedy might be for the legislative bodies to invite everyone to wear one.*

I find it difficult to understand writers who, while claiming to be in favor of liberty, occasionally are scornful of the people, even in their zeal to maintain equality. Because they have never lived in a free state, they do not realize one cannot force public opinion. It is by setting an example of intelligence and prudence that the representatives of a free people may hope to direct or reform it.

---

* There were no bishops in America before the Revolution. Later the Anglicans wanted some so that they would not have to send their ministers to Europe to be ordained. These bishops have no jurisdiction, and as their income is derived from voluntary and uncertain contributions, there is no fear that they may display a scandalous luxury. Nevertheless, when the first bishop arrived in Connecticut, anti-Anglicans took the wise precaution of giving all their ministers the title of priest or bishop, which were used indiscriminately.

Chapter 9

# General Washington
# and the Marquis de Lafayette
# and the Society of the Cincinnati

Although the Society of the Cincinnati cast a few clouds in Europe on the character of General Washington, no one who knew him shared these suspicions. It was said that he should not have accepted the presidency if he had opposed the institution, and the comte de Mirabeau accused him of vanity, if not of trickery.* Such accusations are in complete contradiction to a character whose only faults are excessive modesty and lack of self-confidence.

When General Washington finally consented, after much resistance, to take command of the army, he proposed that Congress pay the expenses of his table but refused to accept any salary; he would not even take his share of the lands which were to be distributed according to rank among the officers.‡

Before the Revolution, Washington's income enabled him to receive his friends and acquaintances and to offer decent hospitality

* "So General Washington, the man of the people and of the army, is already an honorary member of the order † that is now seeking recruits in all European monarchies to put itself beyond the range of attack. Natural circumspection, which seems the distinctive trait of this celebrated man, kept him neutral until the association was established. On the day when it was decided to adopt honorary members, Washington, who was so great when he wanted to become an ordinary citizen, Washington the benefactor of a people he set free, wanted to be distinguished from them. Why did he not feel his name was above distinction? Why did the hero of the Revolution which broke the chains of half the world accept the guilty, dangerous and vulgar honor of being a party hero!" (*Considerations on the Order of the Cincinnati*, p. 7).

† "We saw in the introduction that Washington was president of the order; Baron von Steuben was only a figurehead" (*Considerations on the Order of the Cincinnati*, p. 7).

Baron von Steuben was never a president or a figurehead of the society. The comte de Mirabeau's mistake is evidently due to the fact that the baron once signed a letter as senior officer of a committee. Mirabeau is also misinformed when he calls General Washington an honorary member, for this title is applied only to men who, not being army officers, were not eligible for membership. The adoption of honorary members was one of the new ideas which aroused wrath, for it seemed designed to attract leading citizens in every state. This led to the change I discussed in the last chapter.

‡ The marquis de Lafayette, who seems to have followed General Washington in every respect, also declined the offer.

to others, but now it is feared he can no longer do so. On the entire continent there is not a single officer who can deny himself the consolation of going occasionally to spend a few days with his general, and every European traveler wants to see General Washington. His home is therefore constantly filled with strangers, who bring an even larger number of servants and horses, and since there are no villages or inns in the vicinity, the general has to furnish everything.

At the close of the war Congress felt a sum should be provided for this purpose, but the deputies who knew the general best said he was determined not to accept a reward. Early in 1785 members of the General Assembly of Virginia flattered themselves that they could make him accept a present. It had been decided to open navigation up to the falls of the James and Potomac rivers. Stock in these two enterprises cost $300; the assembly ordered the treasurer to purchase fifty of each and told the governor to offer them to the general as a token of gratitude from the state that was honored by being his birthplace.

I called on Mr. [George] Mason a few days after he had received a visit from the general and before the assembly's decree had been officially communicated. The two men had been fellow students, they have always been close friends, and Mr. Mason's opinion carries great weight with General Washington. Mr. Mason tried in vain to prove that this was not so much a present as partial payment of a debt. His arguments were sound, but the general defended himself, saying that he had no children and that if his income was insufficient, he would prefer to sell some of his land, since he had no relatives who would need the estate. He said he simply could not bring himself to accept anything and added: "I hope it is not vanity." *

Another anecdote reveals General Washington's remarkable control over his pride. During the early part of the war some citizens maliciously compared him to Fabius Cunctator.[17] They preferred General Lee and later General Gates, whose reputation was enhanced by the Saratoga affair, although several subordinate officers, such as [Benjamin] Lincoln, [Daniel] Morgan, and the traitor Arnold, should have shared the glory. The opposition consisted of men with talent and means to make themselves appreciated; although they did not declare war openly, everyone knew who they

* See Note Q, the reply of General Washington to the governor's letter.
[17] Fabius Cunctator, or the Delayer, was the Roman general who opposed Hannibal in 210 B.C. with harassing operations rather than decisive battles.

were. After their protests against the commander had continued for a year, Congress sent him a delegation of three men, one of whom was my friend and neighbor, Mr. John Harvie.[18] The deputation soon realized the complete falsity of all this gossip, and when Mr. Harvie was alone with Washington, he said: "My dear general, if you had been willing to explain your position, all this talk would have stopped long ago." "Could I justify myself without risk to the common cause?" replied this great man, whose nobility in this instance cannot be put into words.

Personal anecdotes are the best key to a man's true character. It would take a volume to relate all the remarks that reveal Washington's unselfishness and patriotism. If the general had believed the Society of the Cincinnati might eventually be harmful to liberty, he would certainly have tried to abolish it. But how could he have been more detached than the other officers? Each man was to him a friend, a disciple, a son; most of them, perhaps all of them, were ready to risk their lives for him, and he knew it. General Washington is a man, and that is why we love him. Our feeling would be totally different if he resembled those cold divinities whose felicity consists in being untouched by human passions.

The general's hair turned white during the war, and he developed eye trouble. When the army was about to disband, he received a letter which he had to communicate to the officers. For the first time he was obliged to put on glasses, and he apologized for the brief delay. This unexpected frailty and the sight of his white hair made such an impression that several officers told me later they had never been so deeply moved.

I told these anecdotes to show that at the time when the Society of the Cincinnati was being established, General Washington could not have realized all the evils it might produce. Furthermore, as he had never been in Europe, he did not know how harsh aristocratic pride can be.

The marquis de Lafayette has also been reproached, although he was in Europe when the society was founded. The French officers who had contributed to maintaining our liberty then took the medal to him. Could the marquis have refused it without being criticized even by the men most anxious to abolish the institution? Would it have been proper for him to have declined the medal without the consent of the officers who accepted it?

The somewhat critical remarks about General Washington's be-

18 Colonel Harvie had an estate about six miles from Colle.

havior cast no shadow on his virtue, but in Europe he was exposed to accusations as false as they were ridiculous. The anonymous author of the *Impartial History* (1:185), introduces a certain widow Gibbon into a plot against the general. He says she was his mistress, knew about all his papers, and reported her findings to the British general, so that his best plans were ruined. I defy this writer to produce a single witness to such a horrid lie.*

The character of the marquis de Lafayette rests on such a solid pedestal in America that no malicious gossip can shake it. His courage, which never failed, was less striking than his wisdom. The only question we might ask is whether he was wiser or more human. Among proofs of his humanity let us not forget his release of the English captain [Walter] Butler. This story also illustrates the pitiful falsity of Arnold, who, after his treason, liked to say that for a long time he had hated to spill English blood. At the close of 1777 or early in 1778 the marquis arrived at the Albany camp just as Arnold was about to send Butler to the scaffold. There was no doubt of his guilt, but the marquis thought the trial had not been just; he took advantage of this pretext, and his release of Butler was the first act of his command.

A propensity to find fault with great men is fortunately unknown in America. General Washington and the marquis de Lafayette have nothing to fear, for when a man has performed a long series of virtuous acts, we require definite facts before entertaining any doubts about him.

* The same writer states (p. 118) that at the first Congress, where the state of Georgia was not represented, the president, Peyton Randolph, broke a crown in twelve pieces and gave one to the deputies from each state. Anyone who reads the request to the king, the remonstrance to Parliament, and the appeal to the English people will realize that these men were incapable of anything so childish. Furthermore, those same documents prove that Americans still hoped and believed they could remain united to the mother country.

# Chapter 10

# Slavery

Men who love justice and humanity are naturally surprised to learn that although the principles embodied in the new state governments proclaim liberty and equality, slavery still exists in the United States. We have already said that there are less than 50,000 slaves in the eight northern states and more than 650,000 in the five southern ones.

Little evils are easy to correct; great ones require time and prudence, for haste often makes the remedy worse than the disease. There is no doubt that slavery in the five southern states is the worst, the most humiliating, and the most difficult evil to correct. Every just man will agree the situation should be remedied as soon as possible, but the methods which have been proposed are very ticklish. The most important thing is to teach the Negroes how to value liberty and use it wisely. As they are brought up in ignorance and consider work synonymous with slavery, several who were set free were lazy, became public charges, and died in poverty.

Some wise inhabitants have suggested establishing public schools for children of slaves (both boys and girls) and setting a date to end slavery. Several years ago others recommended that everyone born after promulgation of a law be free. This plan was recently adopted in Pennsylvania. No new laws were necessary in Massachusetts; although there were, and still are, some slaves there, we can call them voluntary, for slavery has never been legally authorized and any slave who demands his liberty receives it.*

At the present time slaves can be brought only to the two Carolinas and to Georgia, and we have reason to hope these states will soon follow the example set by the other ten. Although there are excellent reasons for postponing the liberation of large numbers of slaves, there is no excuse for importing more.

Among those who want to deliver their country from the opprobrium of slavery there is a diversity of opinion about what measures should be taken. Some thought slaves should be sold in the islands in order to provide a partial indemnity for the masters.

---

* Europe has been misinformed about this.

This would be cruel, and I believe that at least 95 out of 100 masters in Virginia would prefer to take a total loss. The only men sent to the islands should be criminals condemned to death. The sentence would be less severe, but in their opinion worse than death; so it would help to prevent crimes.*

Others have suggested the slaves be returned to Africa, but America has become their country; they love our soil, climate, and customs and would have trouble becoming readjusted. Liberty in Africa would be much worse than their ancestors found slavery in America. The author of the *Notes on Virginia* thinks they should be given land to establish a separate colony. After being educated at public expense, young men would be sent there at the age of twenty-one and girls at eighteen. This new colony should be equipped with all the essentials, protected, and made our ally when it was strong enough.

The humanity of this plan does honor to the man who proposed it, and the sacrifice entailed might be regarded as a tribute paid to the ancestors of these unfortunates to expiate the cruelty of ours. But such a project could not be executed until our finances are in a flourishing state and the white population has become much larger. The author also suggests sending ships to another part of the world to get substitutes for the Negroes who went to the new colony. But it would be difficult to find enough men, more money would be needed, and the plan would require far more time than humanity and justice can devote to the abolishment of slavery.

His reasons for wishing to keep the Negroes separate are valid, but he believes, with justice, that if the new colony cannot be established, slaves should be given their liberty and rights as citizens. This is in accordance with the sacred principle in Article 1 of our Declaration of Rights, which states that "all Men are by Nature equally free and independent." It is sound philosophy to make no distinction as soon as a natural right is involved.

Although it would be pleasant to preserve the beauty of color, what is pleasing should never be considered more important than what is just. Moreover, taste is largely a matter of habit. The white skin of the inhabitants of the Far North does not contribute to their happiness any more than a swarthy hue creates misery for those born in a torrid climate. One can never discuss these matters, but there will be no cause for complaint, as white men will never

---

* Our slaves know how their fellows are treated on the islands, and that is why they consider this verdict so terrible.

be required to marry Negroes or mulattoes. The essential thing is that laws must not forbid it.

The right of citizenship cannot be denied to one group without rousing them against those who have it; if they are sufficiently numerous to ask for an explanation, we may presume they will never accept such injustice unless they are crushed by a tyrant.

Those who think that Negroes will never possess the attributes of free citizens are judging by what they see, instead of imagining what they would be had they been reared by free parents and breathed the air of liberty from childhood. They should also realize that if white men became slaves, after several generations their descendants would be what Negroes are today. Their manner of thinking has changed markedly since the Revolution, as they are constantly hearing speeches about the probability of their emancipation. The humanity of their masters has been an important factor in this development, and I have heard several say to them: "If you are not happy, you may leave; I have no right to keep you."

This principle does not have enough adherents. When the marquis de Lafayette made his last trip to America, he was met by a delegation of welcome from the Virginia General Assembly, which was charged to express the sentiments of esteem, respect, and admiration which the entire nation owed him. In his reply he expressed the wish that the state of Virginia, after fighting so bravely for humanity, should seize every opportunity in its power to promote the rights that all men without exception have to liberty.[19]

I shall close by begging my compatriots to read Mr. Schwartz's book, *Reflections on Negro Slavery*,[20] from which I took the following passage to emphasize what I said before, that while there may be excellent reasons for postponing the liberation of slaves there is no excuse for importing more.

[Summary] It is a crime to tolerate an unjust law, but there are times when precautionary measures necessitate delays. It is a crime to deprive a man of his natural rights, but the Negro, like a child or an idiot, must be protected by society until he is capable of exercising them without

[19] The marquis de Lafayette said: "May she [the Commonwealth], in her wisdom and the enjoyment of prosperity, continue to give the world unquestionable proofs of her philanthropy, and her regard to the liberties of all mankind" (*Journal of the House of Delegates of the Commonwealth of Virginia, 1781–86* [Richmond, 1828], p. 30, Friday, 19 Nov. 1784).

[20] Joachim J. Schwartz [pseud. of marquis de Condorcet], *Réflexions sur l'esclavage des nègres* (Neufchâtel, 1781).

doing harm to others or to himself. These are the only motives which can permit a legislator to postpone depriving a man of his rights; neither commercial prosperity nor national wealth can be weighed against justice,* but slavery is quite as contrary to the interests of commerce as to those of justice.

This book will convince anyone who does not put personal gain before humanity and justice.

* This principle is contrary to the ordinary political doctrines, but the majority of men writing on these matters want to get jobs or to be paid by those who have them.

# Chapter 11

# Savages

The aborigines of North America, generally called Indians or savages, are divided into a great many tribes, each of which is independent. History does not describe any people which has ever preserved so much individual freedom in its social fabric. They do not know what it means to command, the power of the chiefs is based on moral supremacy, hereditary rights are unknown, and family prestige is perpetuated by public esteem.

Indians live in villages, each of which has a council house, where the wise men discuss village business. For matters pertaining to the tribe they gather at the home of the chief. Wise men are those who have acquired a reputation for wisdom, and the honorable title of warrior must also be earned. Because public opinion governs everything, failure to conform is dishonorable, so the opinion of the wise men is more respected than laws among nations with police.

Crimes are rare among the savages, and they have no punishment other than scorn. The miscreant, ostracized, is forced to seek exile to escape the bitterness of his solitude, the vengeance of the man he offended or of his relatives and friends. Savages are faithful and generous friends, very hospitable, but exceedingly cruel to prisoners if they do not adopt them. Their adopted prisoners enjoy the same freedom they have, for slavery does not exist.

Our first historians did not state the facts about the treatment of prisoners accurately, and several modern writers have copied them. Hutchinson, speaking of the incursion of Canadian savages into Massachusetts in April 1706, writes (2:164) that Samuel Butterfield of Groton was taken prisoner after he had slain a chief. Some of the Indians wanted to burn him alive, and others suggested beating him to death. As they were unable to agree, they decided to leave the decision to the widow. She told them that "if killing the prisoner would bring her husband back to life, she cared not what kind of death he suffered, but, if not, she desired to have him for a slave, and her request was granted." The story may be true except for the word "slave," which several writers used through ignorance and which Hutchinson copied carelessly.

Prisoners are put to death or adopted as citizens. A father who has lost his son adopts a young prisoner in his place; an orphan takes a father or mother; a widow a husband; one man takes a sister and another a brother. This makes it difficult to rescue prisoners because the savages feel that returning them after adoption is like giving up their own flesh and blood. Many prisoners do not want to leave the savages, especially if they were captured as children. By the peace treaty of 1763 the Indians were ordered to return all their prisoners, and the sorrow of all the savages, and of several prisoners, affected everyone present. Some of the former captives later went back to live with the savages.

Marriage ceremonies consist in the voluntary consent of both parties; infidelity is as rare as divorce is common. It is not unusual for a girl to go to a young man, spend several days with him, and then go to another; people do not marry unless they are perfectly suited to each other.

An Indian who had anything to do with a female prisoner would be dishonored. If he used violence, he would never be forgiven. When I asked one of them what the consequences of such a crime would be, his reply was, "That never happens." But Abbé Raynal, in describing the Natchez (8:19) declares that "French women prisoners were exposed to the brutality of the men who had assassinated their fathers and husbands."

War and hunting are the chief male occupations and bravery and eloquence their prize virtues; there is some fishing, although this is less important than hunting. I have already said that the little farming is done by women, as men consider it beneath their dignity.*

As Indians are not acquainted with the arts and sciences, or even with writing, their ideas and languages are limited. They often aspirate final syllables strongly and gesticulate and raise their voices in proportion to the importance of the subject. Very deliberate, their questions and answers are always to the point. Their language is full of allegories and metaphors, which frequently open a well-rounded sentence as they closed the preceding one.

Since their food supply depends on hunting, they require a vast territory. Nations are usually separated by mountain chains or rivers; so frontiers are always exact except in the vicinity of river sources, where there are often disputes. Wars are frequent because

* See Part III, p. 211.

an insult paid to any individual becomes a national matter. Population growth is handicapped by lack of culture and, to an even greater extent, by the constant fighting.

As they pride themselves on bravery, which always wins female approbation, young blades are almost always in favor of war, and their enthusiasm often triumphs over the wise moderation of the elders. Women do not have a voice in the council unless they are involved in such matters as the transfer of territory. Occasionally, however, the tears and pleading of mothers, joined to the counsel of older men, have prevailed over impetuous youth and prevented war.

Although Indians live in poorly built cabins, they are unimpressed by palaces. They appreciate moral virtues but are indifferent to display. When the hostages of the Shawnee were in Williamsburg in 1774 and 1775, they could dine at the best tables but spent days eating blackberries in the brush. Such indifference is the result of education and habit; it cannot be explained by a lack of discernment or taste. One day at the governor's table the youngest Indian put nearly half of the food in a serving dish on his plate. The oldest looked at him so severely that the boy blushed. Although the explanation was not hard to find, I asked Wolf (the elder) * about it, and he replied that his companion should have counted the guests.

As facts are more revealing of national character than general description, I shall tell several stories about the hostages. On the night he fled to the frigate, Lord Dunmore, the last English governor, summoned the savages to his palace. He told them that he and his family would be murdered if they did not flee and that the Indians would also be victims of the Virginians if they remained in Williamsburg until daybreak. One of the four savages had received the governor's permission to return home several weeks before; the remaining three decided to escape through the woods, walking at night and hiding during the day. Wolf and the youngest stayed together, but the other, known as Judge, lost them in the darkness.

Soon Wolf began to question the governor's sincerity, and at dawn he persuaded his companion to turn around. The arrival of the Indians pleased everyone in Williamsburg, but the inhabitants were alarmed about Judge, who, unknown and a fugitive, might be

---

* As it is customary for Indians to take the names of their friends, several have European names. The two sons of the sachem Massasoit, who is said to have sold land to the founders of the little Plymouth Colony, asked the court to give them English names; Metacomet became Philip and the other Alexander.

killed on the frontiers or perish for lack of food. They were afraid his death might cause a war, or if he returned to his homeland with a false report, the savages would be aroused. Wolf declared he would not starve because blackberries were plentiful everywhere. He could hide securely, and his stories would make no impression, because he was known to be rather timid, although both good and honest.

Indians never get lost, however far they may be from home. They often travel at night and watch during the day. If there is no sun, they study the bark of trees, which differs in color depending on whether it is on the north or south side.

One day while Lord Dunmore was still on board the frigate in the York River, Wolf ran into the assembly, interrupted the meeting, and made the members understand he wanted to explain why he was so upset. The interpreter assigned to the Indians by Lord Dunmore was an Irishman whom people were beginning to suspect. When they got another man, Wolf said the Irishman had never ceased to tell him and his companion that Lord Dunmore was so fond of them both he wanted to see them again before leaving. The interpreter was so insistent about taking them on board that very day he feared some violence. If the hostages had gone home with the ideas Lord Dunmore had endeavored to instill, or if he had taken them away in the frigate, war with the Indians would have been inevitable, and this was doubtless what he had in mind.

Everything Wolf predicted about Judge came true. He arrived home safe and sound, but no one believed the story Lord Dunmore had told him about the Virginians. Not long after this the son of the famous Chief Cornstalk came to Virginia with two companions and heard that people had teased Judge because he was afraid. When the hostages received permission to leave, Wolf, Cornstalk's son, and his two companions stopped at my home for two days. I talked to them with the aid of an interpreter as much as politeness permitted. I say politeness, because although they speak readily and answer all questions good-naturedly, they like to spend several hours alone every day. They practice meditation from childhood until it becomes one of their basic needs.

While the Indians were at my home, the neighbors gathered to see them. Whenever a dozen or more were present, one of the men would get up to make a speech. This custom, which teaches them how to speak logically and eloquently, is intended to show their respect for strangers. On each occasion they spoke with pleasure of the good treatment they had received, promised to tell their nation about it, and expressed the hope that we should always live on terms of peace and friendship.

Indians are surprisingly intelligent. They learn everything easily, doubtless because their mothers make them train their memories. Furthermore, they have the habit of reflection and only a few ideas based on personal experience. Several have done good work in our colleges, but none have remained among us. Their insurmountable aversion to work will probably always prevent them from adopting our customs. As they are taught from childhood that hunting and war are the only occupations worthy of a man, they dislike any other tasks. All the tribes that for the past century and a half have been surrounded by our settlements have gradually declined, and some have vanished. Although they enjoyed complete independence, there was not enough land for hunting, and the men could not bring themselves to do anything else.

Indians are so trained never to show fear that a prisoner will insult the man torturing him. You must never be surprised by the courage of the conquered or the inflexibility of the victors, for vengeance is a sacred duty. Despite the remarks of certain famous writers who believed the tall tales of ignorant travelers, Indians are humane and sensitive on all other occasions. Fathers show greater tenderness to their children than children to their parents. As this is true among civilized nations as well, one may surmise it does not come from a childish desire for liberty, because Indian children are independent.

Indians carry prisoners' children very carefully but kill them if they are pursued and fear the children may slow their march or lead to discovery. Adolescents and women suffer the same fate. Self-preservation and slaughter of the enemy, like vengeance and courage, are considered an obligation. Skill is of primary importance in battle. A warrior must surprise the enemy by a stratagem or stand up to him when they meet. If you compare a savage with a civilized man, he stands up very well indeed, but here I am speaking purely of character, not of the advantages or evils of civilization.

In his *Notes on Virginia* Mr. Jefferson tells a story about Logan, one of the Mingo chiefs, which reveals Indian character. In the spring of 1774 two Indians of the Shawnee * tribe killed a Vir-

* The Indians say Sawanahaac. Our ancestors carelessly wrote Shawnee, and this has been perpetuated. In the first part of my book I wrote Sciuaneese, and that too is wrong.

ginian, and the whites in the area undertook to avenge him. Colonel Cresap, who had already murdered several of these unfortunate savages, assembled a party and went down the Kanawha.[21] Unfortunately a canoe filled with women and children and carrying just one man was crossing the river from the opposite bank. Cresap and his party hid. When the canoe landed, every man chose his victim, and all the Indians were killed. These were relatives of Logan, known for his friendship to the whites. The ingratitude of the white man roused his anger, and he fought valiantly in the war that followed. That fall a decisive battle was waged at the mouth of the Kanawha between the Mingos, the Shawnees, and the Delawares on one side and a detachment of Virginia militia on the other. When the Indians were forced to sue for peace, Logan alone refused to appear among the suppliants. Lest his absence cast doubt on the sincerity of the Indians, he sent this message to Lord Dunmore:

I appeal to any white man to say, if ever he entered Logan's cabin hungry, and he gave him not meat; if ever he came cold and naked, and he cloathed him not. During the course of the last long and bloody war Logan remained idle in his cabin, an advocate for peace. Such was my love for the whites, that my countrymen pointed as they passed, and said, "Logan is the friend of white men." I had even thought to have lived with you, but for the injuries of one man. Colonel Cresap, the last spring, in cold blood, and unprovoked, murdered all the relations of Logan, not even sparing my women and children. There runs not a drop of my blood in the veins of any living creature. This called on me for revenge. I have sought it: I have killed many: I have fully glutted my vengeance; for my country I rejoice at the beams of peace. But do not harbour a thought that mine is the joy of fear. Logan never felt fear. He will not turn on his heel to save his life. Who is there to mourn for Logan? – Not one.[22]

Shegenaba's harangue to the Virginia deputies in the fall of 1778 also reveals one of the finest men nature ever produced. His father, the famous Ottawa chief Pontiac, had been invited on several occasions by our deputies to conferences designed to strengthen the bonds of friendship between the nations. He was always prevented from attending by the English governor of Fort Detroit (the Hamilton who was made prisoner by Colonel Clark in Illinois early in 1779). When war broke out, Pontiac was slain, together with

---

[21] Jefferson, *Notes*, ed. Peden, p. 228. Michael Cresap was a captain, not a colonel, and Logan's family was murdered on the Ohio River, not the Kanawha.

[22] Ibid., pp. 253–54.

several chiefs of his tribe. His son Shegenaba, although still very young, was named to succeed his father. A man of extraordinary ability, he defeated and killed most of the Kaskaskias. Hamilton kept him from coming to see us for some time by the same tactics he had used with Chief Pontiac, but he finally appeared, although with some trepidation. As a boy, Shegenaba had been hospitable to a young Virginian named Field who was lost. He had protected him, helped him, and put him back on his path. The deputies took this opportunity to thank him, gave him a gun, expressed their regrets about the death of his father and the other chiefs, and congratulated him on his vengeance.

Fathers,*
From the information I had of the commandant of Detroit, with distrust, I accepted your invitation, and measured my way to this *council fire* † with trembling feet. Your reception of me convinces me of his falsehood and the groundlessness of my fears. Truth and he have long been enemies. My father, and many of my chiefs, have lately tasted of death. The remembrance of that misfortune almost unmans me, and fills my eyes with tears. Your kind condolence has lightened my heart of its heavy burthen, and shall be transmitted to my latest posterity.
A STRING [Here he presented a string of wampum.]
Fathers,
I rejoice to hear what I this day have heard, and do assure you it shall be faithfully delivered to my nation. Should you want to speak to me in future, I shall joyfully attend, and thank you for the present invitation. The particular favour shewed me, and the gun you have given me for the kindness I shewed your brother, young Field, claims my warmest acknowledgment. I am conscious I did but my duty. He who barely does his duty merits no praise. If any of your people hereafter visit mine, whether through curiosity or business, or if unwillingly compelled by the strong hand of the victor, they shall find the entertainment your brother found. You informed me, if my people visits yours they shall meet an hospitable welcome: My fears are done away; I have not one doubt remaining; I will recommend it to my young men to visit and get acquainted with yours.
Fathers,
What has passed this day is too deeply engraven on my heart for

* "Brothers" is the common expression, but Shegenaba said "fathers" because of his youth.

† At these meetings there is always a fire, even in summer, so that the men can light their pipes and smoke together in friendship. This seems to be the etymology of the expression *council fire*, which is used for an assembly of several nations.

time itself ever to erase. I foretell that the sunny rays of this day's peace shall warm and protect our children's children from the storms of misfortune. To confirm it, I present you my right hand, that hand which never yet was given but the heart consented, which never shed human blood in peace, nor ever spared an enemy in war; and I assure you of my friendship with a tongue which has never mocked at truth since I was at age to know falsehood was a crime.—A BELT [Here he presented a wampum belt.] [23]

During these conferences gifts are exchanged between nations. Formerly they were necklaces and belts of conch shells stitched together. These were greatly prized, as they were difficult to make and required a great deal of labor. The savages who trade with us today use necklaces which are more valuable to them and which they can get for several skins. At every conference a man wears all the gifts he has received to show he remembers his friends. On one occasion when the Indians observed that our deputies did not have a present they had given us fifty years before, they were skeptical about the explanation provided. They offer their presents while they are speaking or at the end of the discourse. Shegenaba presented one string at the close of the first part of his speech and a belt when he had finished.

Occasionally they send a belt to express their state of mind, which is revealed by the colors and design used in making it. Before Lord Dunmore waged an unjust war on the Shawnees, they sent him a belt threatening war if he did not give them satisfaction.

American Indians did not know the use of iron until they traded with our ancestors. They had stone implements rather like axes and scissors, with which they felled trees and hollowed them out to make little boats. As the cutting edge was dull and this weak implement had no handle, the task must have required a vast amount of time. Fish scales were used to plane and polish wood. They made very strong ropes, thirty or forty feet in length, of several materials, chiefly wild hemp. They also made fishing nets, although bone fishhooks were more commonly used, especially for sturgeon. Several kinds of traps were devised to capture birds and quadrupeds. Some writers say they built double walls of brushwood about two miles long; the entrance was nearly a mile in width, but the sides came together gradually until, at the opposite end, the opening was only six or seven feet wide. The Indians placed a trap of shrubbery there and then waited for a deer.

[23] *Journal of the House of Delegates of Virginia, 1781–86*, p. 239.

As they are imbued with a desire for glory and believe that patience in enduring cold and hunger will contribute to their reputation as brave warriors, they harden themselves in early youth by going without food for several days or making a very small amount of corn last a whole week. One species opens when it is fairly warm, becomes mealy, and tastes like bread. They also crush it to form a kind of cake. Meat is boiled in pottery kettles or roasted on a spit. When it has been roasted and dried, it may be kept for a considerable period. Wooden kettles and poorly baked pottery have been used for a long time.

Our ancestors found that Indians played a kind of football, with matches between different villages, as in Europe. They also wrestle and engage in running and swimming matches. This mode of life makes them supple but not very robust.

In former days they drank nothing but water, but they have learned to like alcohol, especially rum and brandy. Occasionally they ruin their health, go mad, and then blame us for introducing them to these dangerous beverages. This has often served as a pretext for war against the whites.

Indians tattoo their skin, using designs of animals and other motifs; years ago corrosive saps were employed for this purpose, but today they do it with our paint. Even their faces are tattooed, and when they fight, they make themselves as hideous as possible. It is not surprising that they expect to frighten their adversaries in this manner, because Europeans have preserved the use of large bonnets and moustaches for the same reason. Noses and ears are pierced and decorated with inserted feathers or other ornaments, shiny objects being preferred. Our ancestors found the Indians practically naked; animal skins, when they had them, were used for beds more frequently than for clothing. Indians like clothes and every kind of adornment but do not relish the work required to obtain them. All Indians pull out their hair, even the down on their faces, and this has led some unobservant travelers to think they are beardless.

They have great veneration for the bones of their dead. When a member of the tribe is buried in a distant country, a frequent occurrence during wartime, they later collect the bones and unite them with those of their own family.

At all their feasts and games an orator harangues them about their victories and defeats. In olden days the principal Indian weapon was a marble or stone arrow, and these are still found occasionally, but today all savages use firearms.

Every writer uses the word *sachem* or *sagamore*; several Indians

have assured me, however, that *loyanelh* was the only name by
which they designated a chief. As they have several dialects, our
ancestors may have found the names *sachem* and *sagamore* in some
tribe which no longer exists. It is also possible that the word has
another meaning but that the Indians imitated us out of politeness,
thinking they were using a word in our tongue. At all events, they
use it when speaking to us, while among themselves they say
*loyanelh*. This is written just as it is pronounced with the final *h*
indicating aspiration.

Our ancestors made several rather unsuccessful attempts to convert the Indians to Christianity. Savages seldom contradict; they do
not deny what they cannot understand but never accept anything
contrary to reason, so that it is futile to discuss miracles, mysteries,
or articles of faith with them. According to our most intelligent
missionaries, they never thought of a divine cult, and only a few
have a confused idea of two invisible beings, one good, the other
evil; they invoke them rarely, the evil being more frequently,
doubtless because they are more afraid of suffering than hopeful of
any blessings. Their superstitions are curious but not so absurd as
those of certain ignorant inhabitants of civilized countries. They
never quarrel about them, and in general, beliefs are considered an
individual matter.

Some of the more intelligent men are known as *powowers* because they have a reputation for special knowledge. It would be
wrong to term them priests, for Indians do not have priests. Powowers acquire their reputation through their medical lore, which
consists of using a few herbs, making the patient sweat, and giving
him a cold bath. They induce perspiration by closing themselves
up in wigwams heated with red-hot stones. They purge themselves
with herbs, use touchwood as a caustic, and draw blood by making
little incisions similar to those obtained with a cupping glass.*

Before the Indians heard about Christianity they had no idea of
another life. Those who have been led to reflect about it imagined
it would satisfy all their desires. They cannot imagine spiritual felicity and refuse to accept the resurrection of the body. R[oger]
Williams, one of the first missionaries, wrote the Society for the
Propagation of the Gospel in Foreign Parts in London that the Indians welcomed what he told them about religion, but when he
spoke of the resurrection of the body, they all cried: "We shall
never believe that."

* The jaws of the garfish, *Acus maxima*, which has needlelike teeth, are used
for this purpose.

New England settlers did not begin to discuss religion with the Indians until 1650, as their own affairs had kept them busy until that time. When they talked about eternal damnation and how one cannot be saved without being baptized, the Indians asked how they could have waited twenty-six years to mention this matter, if it was really so important. The settlers did not have a very good answer, and this gave the Indians a poor opinion both of the missionaries and of the mission.

Colonel Goffe,[24] who was one of the judges of Charles I, spent thirteen or fourteen years preaching to the savages; in his journal he records some of the observations they made to him. 1. "In your text are the words 'Save yourselves from this untoward generation' [Acts 2:40]. And elsewhere: 'I do nothing of myself' [John 8:28]. How do you make these statements agree?" 2. "You say 'The sword of the spirit is the word of God [Ephesians 6:17] by which their hearts are struck.' How shall I use the spirit's sword to strike my heart?" 3. "What was Judas's crime, or how did he sin in betraying Jesus Christ, when God had already decided it should be so?" They asked other missionaries: "Can Jesus Christ, the mediator or interpreter, understand prayers in an Indian tongue?" "How can one be the image of God when images are forbidden by the second commandment?" "If the father is evil and the son is good, why is God angry with his son in the second commandment?" "How is it that the Indians and the English had such different ideas about God and Jesus Christ, since, at the beginning, everyone had the same father?"

The missionaries were most successful with the Oneidas and Delawares; they let themselves be baptized and call themselves Christians, but their religious ideas are both superficial and confused.

On the occasion of a treaty with several nations, a Swedish missionary preached to the Indians at Conestoga, Pennsylvania, in 1710. He talked to them zealously for a long time about the Creation, the sin of Adam, and ended with the eternal damnation of those who were not baptized. That same day one of the chiefs refuted his sermon with so much precision, force, and vehemence that the missionary did not know what to say. The Indian declared the revelation in the Bible could only apply to people who knew the book, and that the All-Powerful Being would not have hidden

[24] Colonel William Goffe was concealed by Captain Joseph Bull and his sons in New England under the name of Mr. Cooke. Both Hutchinson and Ezra Stiles saw Goffe's diaries, but they are no longer extant.

it from so many men if it had been as important as the missionary claimed. If anyone said that God could make this revelation to men only through the aid of this book, it would be contradicting His omnipotence, and it would be inconceivably unjust and barbaric on His part not to communicate it if He could do so. He ended by protesting against the injustice of making the human race suffer for a fault it had not committed and by affirming that Christians were no better than Indians. The latter, he said, should judge the doctrine of the white man by their behavior.

There is no reason to believe that American Indians are anthropophagous. If they practiced anthropophagy, they would not hide it any more than they hide the far more cruel, although less revolting, tortures they inflict on prisoners. Some of our neighbors have heard that the Flat-Heads,* who live very far from us, eat their prisoners, but the Indians themselves do not believe this story. One whom I questioned told me, "White men would be more likely to eat human flesh, because we can find food easily in the forest."

It is probable that Europeans told these stories about cannibalism to justify their own cruelties. Strange tales are readily repeated, and travelers often say they have witnessed the curious things told about faraway lands. They may end by believing these stories themselves. It would not be a proof of cannibalism if one saw savages holding the bones of their enemies, making menacing gestures, and grinding their teeth. If an Indian had seen starving passengers on a European vessel draw lots to see which one should be slain to keep the others alive, he could also report that Europeans eat one another. I do not say that cannibalism does not exist, but I doubt it, and before deciding, I think we need more convincing proof than any we have received so far.

What I have just said about the Indians applies to all of them, with the exception of minor differences peculiar to each nation. The following observations, which Mr. Franklin sent to a European, may provide the reader with what I have omitted.

### Remarks concerning the Savages of North America

Savages we call them, because their manners differ from ours, which we think the perfection of civility; they think the same of theirs.

---

* I have heard people say their foreheads are actually flattened. It is believed they press the children's heads down with a plank, while the Round-Heads, who live east of Lake Superior, make their children's heads round at the moment of birth.

Perhaps if we could examine the manners of different nations with impartiality, we should find no people so rude as to be without any rules of politeness; nor any so polite as not to have some remains of rudeness.

The Indian men, when young, are hunters and warriors; when old, counsellors; for all their government is by the counsel or advice of the sages; there is no force, there are no prisons, no officers to compel obedience, or inflict punishment. Hence they generally study oratory; the best speaker having the most influence. The Indian women till the ground, dress the food, nurse and bring up the children, and preserve and hand down to posterity the memory of public transactions. These employments of men and women are accounted natural and honourable. Having few artificial wants, they have abundance of leisure for improvement by conversation. Our laborious manner of life compared with theirs, they esteem slavish and base; and the learning on which we value ourselves, they regard as frivolous and useless. An instance of this occurred at the Treaty of Lancaster in Pennsylvania, anno 1744, between the Government of Virginia and the Six Nations. After the principal business was settled, the Commissioners from Virginia acquainted the Indians by a speech, that there was at Williamsburg a college with a fund, for educating Indian youth; and that if the Chiefs of the Six Nations would send down half a dozen of their sons to that college, the Government would take care that they should be well provided for, and instructed in all the learning of the white people. It is one of the Indian rules of politeness not to answer a public proposition the same day that it is made; they think it would be treating it as a light matter; and that they shew it respect by taking time to consider it, as of a matter important. They therefore deferred their answer till the day following; when their Speaker began, by expressing their deep sense of the kindness of the Virginia Government, in making them that offer; "for we know" says he, "that you highly esteem the kind of learning taught in those colleges, and that the maintenance of our young men, while with you, would be very expensive to you. We are convinced, therefore, that you mean to do us good by your proposal, and we thank you heartily. But you who are wise must know, that different nations have different conceptions of things; and you will therefore not take it amiss if our ideas of this kind of education happen not to be the same with yours. We have had some experience of it: Several of our young people were formerly brought up at the colleges of the Northern Provinces; they were instructed in all your sciences; but when they came back to us, they were bad runners; ignorant of every means of living in the woods; unable to bear either cold or hunger; knew neither how to build a cabin, take a deer, or kill an enemy; spoke our language imperfectly; were therefore neither fit for hunters, warriors, or counsellors; they were totally good for nothing. We are however not the less obliged by your kind offer, though we decline accepting it: And to show our grateful sense of it, if the Gentlemen of Virginia will send us a dozen of their sons, we will take great care of their education, instruct them in all we know, and make *men* of them."

Having frequent occasions to hold public Councils, they have acquired great order and decency in conducting them. The Old Men sit in the foremost ranks, the Warriors in the next, and the Women and Children in the hindmost. The business of the Women is to take exact notice of what passes, imprint it in their memories, for they have no writing, and communicate it to their Children. They are the Records of the Council, and they preserve tradition of the stipulations in Treaties a hundred years back; which, when we compare with our writings, we always find exact. He that would speak, rises. The rest observe a profound silence. When he has finished, and sits down, they leave him five or six minutes to recollect, that if he has omitted any thing he intended to say, or has any thing to add, he may rise again, and deliver it. To interrupt another, even in common conversation, is reckoned highly indecent. How different this is from the conduct of a polite British House of Commons, where scarce a day passes without some confusion, that makes the Speaker hoarse in calling *to order;* and how different from the mode of conversation in many polite companies of Europe, where, if you do not deliver your sentence with great rapidity, you are cut off in the middle of it by the impatient loquacity of those you converse with, and never suffered to finish it.

The politeness of these Savages in conversation, is, indeed, carried to excess; since it does not permit them to contradict, or deny the truth of what is asserted in their presence. By this means they indeed avoid disputes; but then it becomes difficult to know their minds, or what impression you make upon them. The Missionaries who have attempted to convert them to Christianity, all complain of this as one of the great difficulties of their Mission. The Indians hear with patience the Truths of the Gospel explained to them, and give their usual tokens of assent and approbation: You would think they were convinced. No such matter. It is mere civility.

A Swedish Minister having assembled the Chiefs of the Sasquehanah Indians, made a Sermon to them, acquainting them with the principal historical facts on which our Religion is founded; such as the Fall of our First Parents by eating an Apple; the coming of Christ to repair the mischief; his miracles and suffering, etc.—When he had finished, an Indian Orator stood up to thank him. "What you have told us," says he, "is all very good. It is indeed bad to eat apples. It is better to make them all into cyder. We are much obliged by your kindness in coming so far, to tell us those things which you have heard from your Mothers. In return, I will tell you some of those we have heard from ours.

"In the beginning, our Fathers had only the flesh of animals to subsist on; and if their hunting was unsuccessful, they were starving. Two of our young hunters having killed a deer, made a fire in the woods to broil some parts of it. When they were about to satisfy their hunger, they beheld a beautiful young woman descend from the clouds, and seat herself on that hill which you see yonder among the Blue Mountains. They said to each other, it is a Spirit that perhaps has smelt our broiling venison, and wishes to eat of it: Let us offer some to her. They presented her with the tongue: She was pleased with the taste of it, and said, your kindness shall be rewarded. Come to this place after thirteen moons, and you shall find something that will be of great benefit in nourishing you and your children to the latest generations. They did so, and to their surprise, found plants they had never seen before; but which, from that ancient time, have been constantly cultivated among us, to our great advantage. Where her right hand had touched the ground, they found maize; where her left hand had touched it, they found kidney-beans; and where her backside had sat * on it, they found tobacco." The good Missionary, disgusted with this idle tale, said, "What I delivered to you were sacred truths; but what you tell me is mere fable, fiction, and falsehood." The Indian, offended, replied, "My Brother, it seems your friends have not done you justice in your education; they have not well instructed you in the rules of common civility. You saw, that we who understand and practice those rules, believed all your stories, why do you refuse to believe ours?"

When any of them come into our towns, our people are apt to croud round them, gaze upon them, and incommode them where they desire to be private; this they esteem great rudeness, and the effect of the want of instruction in the rules of civility and good manners. "We have," say they, "as much curiosity as you, and when you come into our towns, we wish for opportunities of looking at you; but for this purpose we hide ourselves behind bushes where you are to pass, and never intrude ourselves into your company."

Their manner of entering one anothers villages has likewise its rules. It is reckoned uncivil in traveling strangers to enter a village abrubtly, without giving notice of their approach. Therefore, as soon as they arrive within hearing, they stop and hollow [holler], remaining there till invited to enter. Two old men usually come out to them, and lead them in. There is in every village a vacant dwelling, called the strangershouse. Here they are placed, while the old men go round from hut to hut, acquainting the inhabitants that strangers are arrived, who are probably hungry and weary; and every one sends them what he can spare of victuals and skins to repose on. When the strangers are refreshed, pipes and tobacco are brought; and then, but not before, conversation begins, with enquiries who they are, whither bound, what news, etc. and it usually ends with offers of service; if the strangers

---

* Mazzei has: "where she had sat."

have occasion of guides, or any necessaries for continuing their journey; and nothing is exacted for the entertainment.

The same hospitality, esteemed among them as a principal virtue, is practiced by private persons; of which *Conrad Weiser*, our Interpreter, gave me the following instance. He had been naturalized among the Six Nations, and spoke well the Mohock [Mohawk] language. In going through the Indian Country, to carry a message from our Governor to the Council at *Onondaga*, he called at the habitation of *Canassetego*, an old acquaintance, who embraced him, spread furs for him to sit on, placed before him some boiled beans and venison, and mixed some rum and water for his drink. When he was well refreshed, and had lit his pipe, Canassetego began to converse with him: Asked how he had fared the many years since they had seen each other, whence he then came, what occasioned the journey, etc. Conrad answered all his questions; and when the discourse began to flag, the Indian, to continue it, said, "Conrad, you have lived long among the White People, and know something of their customs; I have been sometimes at Albany, and have observed, that once in seven days they shut up their shops, and assemble all in the great house; tell me, what it is for? What do they do there?" "They meet there," says Conrad, "to hear and learn *good things.*" "I do not doubt," says the Indian, "that they tell you so; they have told me the same; But I doubt the truth of what they say, and I will tell you my reasons. I went lately to Albany to sell my skins, and buy blankets, knives, powder, rum, etc. You know I used generally to deal with Hans Hanson; but I was a little inclined this time to try some other Merchants. However, I called first upon Hans, and asked him what he would give for beaver. He said he could not give more than four shillings a pound: 'But,' says he, 'I cannot talk on business now; this is the day when we meet together to learn *good things*, and I am going to the meeting.' So I thought to myself, since I cannot do any business to-day, I may as well go to the meeting too, and I went with him. There stood up a man in black, and began to talk to the people very angrily. I did not understand what he said; but perceiving that he looked much at me, and at Hanson, I imagined he was angry at seeing me there; so I went out, sat down near the house, struck fire, and lit my pipe, waiting till the meeting should break up. I thought too, that the man had mentioned something of Beaver, and I suspected it might be the subject of their meeting. So when they came out I accosted my Merchant. 'Well, Hans,' says I, 'I hope you have agreed to give more than four shillings a pound.' 'No,' says he, 'I cannot give so much. I cannot give more than three shillings and sixpence.' I then spoke to several other dealers, but they all sung the same song, three and sixpence. This made it clear to me that my suspicion was right; and that whatever they pretended of meeting to learn *good things*, the real purpose was to consult how to cheat Indians in the price of Beaver. Consider but a little, Conrad, and you must be of my opinion. If they met so often to learn *good things*, they would certainly have learned some before this time. But they are still ignorant. You know our practice. If a white man in travelling through our country, enters one of our cabins, we all treat him as I treat you; we dry him if he is wet, we warm him if he is cold, and give him meat and drink, that he may allay his thirst and hunger; and we spread soft furs for him to rest and sleep on: We demand nothing in return. But if I go into a white man's house at Albany, and ask for victuals and drink, they say, where is your money; and if I have none they say, get out, you Indian Dog. You see they have not yet learned those little *good things*, that we need no meetings to be instructed in, because our mothers taught them to us when we were children; and therefore it is impossible their meetings should be, as they say, for any such purpose, or have any such effect; they are only to contrive *the cheating of Indians in the price of Beaver.*" [25]

[25] Franklin, *Two Tracts . . . and Remarks concerning the Savages of North America.*

# Chapter 12

# Some Recent Books
# about the United States of America
# and Maps of This Country

Dr. Ramsay, a resident of South Carolina, has given us proof of his knowledge in his book on the Revolution.[26] This excellent writer was busy throughout the war in Congress, with the administration of public affairs in his home state, or as an army doctor. As he had an opportunity to examine congressional records, he could have undertaken a general history, but this would have required several years and a trip to Europe. Anyone who wants to write a good general history of the Revolution must visit France, England, and each of the thirteen states or wait for the publication of a history written in France, another in England, a third in the northern states, and a fourth in the southern ones. Since Dr. Ramsay was well informed about the latter, he wrote a complete history of this area, referred to the others only occasionally, and enriched his work with information which conveys a clear idea of the chain of events produced by the Revolution.

An anonymous writer recently published a one-volume history *in*-4° which discusses France in detail.[27] It is believed the author is a naval officer; he seems well informed about maritime matters, and I have heard favorable reports about it from several men qualified to judge.

The only history of the Revolution to come out of England is in the *Annual Register*. It is biased.

Our northern states have not as yet produced a history worth reading.

The marquis de Chastellux described his travels with great care.[28] Those familiar with the country admire the exactitude of his topographical descriptions, especially those of interest to the army. His philosophical letter to Mr. Madison contains comments on

---

[26] See Part II, n. 35 above.

[27] Possibly Stanislas Foace, *Réflexions sur le commerce, la navigation, et les colonies* (Paris, 1787).

[28] François Jean, marquis de Chastellux, *Travels in North America, in the Years 1780–1781, and 1782*, ed. Howard C. Rice, Jr., 2 vols. (Chapel Hill: University of North Carolina Press for the Institute of Early American History and Culture, Williamsburg, 1963).

legislation and administration which have been read with pleasure by a number of well-informed Americans. His observations on the mode of life of the inhabitants, including the Quakers, are usually extremely accurate, although in certain areas he seems to have been misinformed. He is afraid, for example, that the aristocracy will become powerful in Virginia.* It was powerful before the Revolution, when English governors encouraged it, but today the little that remains is in the vicinity of Williamsburg, where the marquis stayed. It is incorrect to say that Virginia has ever shown less zeal for our glorious cause than any other state.† He would have heard the same complaint in the other twelve. He claims that Virginians do not consider literacy important.‡ There is no more ignorance in Virginia than elsewhere in America or Europe. Our representatives in Congress have always been as well educated as those from other states.

The following details also need to be revised. "Because their lands and their Negroes [are] supplying them with the products and labor they need, this renowned hospitality is no burden to them." § "If they sometimes dissipate their fortunes, this is through gaming, hunting and horse races." ** "They are strongly attached to their interests, and their great wealth, joined to their pretensions, further distorts this vice." ||

The character of the Virginians, which is totally unlike this, is well described in the *Philosophical History of the Two Indies*, as I said, in chapter 7 of Part III. It is most unusual for anyone to be ruined by gambling, hunting costs nothing, and family indebtedness is almost always due to excessive hospitality. When the troops of our allies were in Virginia, the destruction of furniture and the total lack of luxuries made many people, especially women, embarrassed to welcome foreigners. One of my friends,¶ whose furniture had been seriously damaged, said to his neighbors: "Shall we permit our country, famous for its hospitality, to lose its reputation when our friends are here? If we have no chairs, we will take tree trunks, saw them up, and make footstools out of them;

* [Rice ed., p. 435.]
† [Ibid., p. 438.]
‡ [Ibid., p. 443.]
§ [Ibid., p. 441.]
** [Ibid.]
|| [*Ibid.*, p. 442].
¶ Mr. David Meade, brother of the two colonels I have mentioned.

if we cannot offer choice viands, they will see we are giving what we have."

Virginians are apt to say that what they get from their plantations costs nothing, since they do not have to purchase it. But imagine a European whose fortune is in land. If strangers consume most of his harvests, will he say that hospitality involves no expense? The provisions given to strangers, their servants, and horses cannot be sold to buy the linen, wines, coffee, sugar, and other items which the guests also enjoy. The labor of the slaves who served them should also be counted a loss.

It is quite possible someone gave the marquis reason to believe the inhabitants are deeply attached to business, for this was a period of disaster. Like every other state, Virginia is free from the curse of beggary, but as the marquis was known to be exceedingly generous, a vagabond may have taken advantage of him.

Every parish has twelve men authorized to levy a tax for the poor. Two of the men are chosen to act, in an emergency, as administrators, to call a meeting when necessary, and to provide funds themselves so that the poor do not suffer. A majority of the twelve is required for the meeting and a majority of those present to determine the amount to be levied. During wartime it was difficult to get the requisite number, and funds were often lacking. I was one of the administrators in my parish in 1778, and more than once I was obliged to give scrip with which the poor could get what they needed. The entire parish was responsible for payment.

In Virginia poor people are those who, having neither slaves nor servants, are obliged to farm the land themselves. The marquis did not understand this, and he was equally mistaken about why some families remain poor. He says: "Among these rich plantations where the Negro alone is wretched, one often finds miserable huts inhabited by whites, whose wane looks and ragged garments bespeak poverty. At first I found it difficult to understand how, in a country where there is still so much land to clear, men who do not refuse to work could remain in misery." *

If they were willing to work they would not be poor. Their trouble comes from laziness, for they think that since they are not black, they do not have to work. They are quite content to wear rags so long as they can eat, and they often get food from their neighbors' slaves, with whom they are in cahoots. If they would

* [Ibid., p. 438.]

work and their little plot was inadequate to support them, they could sell it for a much larger property near the frontier. Or, if they preferred not to move away, they could rent from a neighbor or work for others at a salary which would permit them to live comfortably. According to the marquis, this poverty is caused by the objection of large landowners to selling part of their lands. If anyone thinks he would harm his property by selling a piece of it, he is naturally averse to the proposal.

If we now examine what the writer says about the quality of the soil, we shall see he does not do justice to its fertility. Speaking of New England, he says: "The soil, naturally barren affording but scanty resources, they resorted to fishing and navigation." * "But as land is not generally good in America, especially in Virginia, it takes a good deal of it to make cultivation profitable." † We know what an immense amount of tobacco is grown in Virginia, and the marquis must be aware that soil which produces it would be considered excellent anywhere. On several occasions he refers to the wealth of Virginia; this can only come from its soil, since the state has no factories or precious metals, no fishing or navigation, and most of the commerce is handled by foreigners. It is apparent that this traveler relied on inaccurate reports. Furthermore, some local expressions are misleading. Virginians say, for example, that land is poor if it will not grow tobacco; yet it might produce fine wheat or barley.

Elsewhere the marquis states, "Beauty here serves only to find husbands; for the wealthiest among them give but a trifling dowry to their daughters and it is in general the young ladies' faces that determine their fortunes. The consequence of this is that they are often coquettish and prudish before marriage, and dull and tiresome afterwards." ‡ He is correct in calling dowries rather modest but mistaken in his comments. Young people are together all day and do not marry unless well suited to one another. A girl's beauty has never seemed to exert a special attraction on wealthy young men, and it is not unusual for a girl to refuse a suitor whose only attributes are his good looks and his fortune.

The slightest trace of coquetry can hurt a girl's reputation; customs differ, however; so any European who has not lived for a long time in America might easily misunderstand them. It is in-

* [Ibid., p. 436.]
† [*Ibid.*, p. 438.]
‡ [Ibid., pp. 441–42.]

decent, for example, for a woman to show two or three inches of leg above her ankle, while on some of the Aegean islands she would be laughed at if her skirt came below her knee.*

In certain European countries girls must be very reserved with men, especially young men. In America they flirt; married women are reserved, and their husbands no longer so familiar with girls as when they were bachelors. If a young man did not want his sweetheart to see other young blades he would be called jealous and would find it hard to get a wife. City customs have lost some of their innocence and simplicity, but I hope with all my heart that our Virginia girls will keep their liberty. Married women are too busy with housekeeping to spend a great deal of time with men, but they are pleasant conversationalists and more or less communicative, depending on how well they know you.

Girls with little or nothing to do have parties, ride horseback, and go from one house to another, crossing woods and rivers and stopping for various periods of time to make visits, so that their journey may last for several months and cover 250 miles. They take along daughters from the houses where they have been staying. Since they dance as much as possible, no absent lover should imagine his mistress is pining; however, no one has the right to criticize another country about its customs.

The marquis claims Virginia does not grant the right of suffrage to ministers, and he adds that judges and lawyers are also unable to vote. Theoretically he believes this offers certain advantages, but at the present time he finds it means that administration is entrusted to men who are not properly qualified.

Judging by his letter to Mr. Madison, the marquis has examined American constitutions carefully; so I should like to think the mistake in this passage is a typographical error. Ministers have the right of suffrage like other citizens, and lawyers are not excluded from public office; no member of the judiciary or of the legislative and executive bodies may hold other offices. Some men in the executive branch, which is doubtless what the marquis means by "the administration," have been lawyers; he knows several of them well, including Mr. Short,[29] of whom he speaks nicely.†

---

* On the island called Argentiera [Cimolus, an island in the southwest Cyclades] skirts were so heavy the wind could not lift them.

† [Ibid. pp. 443–44].

[29] William Short, a diplomat, graduated from the College of William and Mary, where he helped found Phi Beta Kappa. He arranged a commercial treaty between Prussia and the United States and served as Jefferson's private secretary.

I have already mentioned some curious peculiarities falsely attributed to this country. "This Mr. Lambert," said the marquis, "is something of a phenomenon in America, where longevity is not common; he is eighty-three years old but appears to be scarcely more than fifty-five." * The marquis next came to the home of Captain Muller, where he found an eighty-year-old man who had stopped there after being bitten by a dog. The following day he visited an old man of seventy-two, named Hodnett, who had been in America for forty years. As this idea of unusual longevity cannot be the result of his own observations, he probably got it from the inhabitants and other writers.

A European who had spent several years in Virginia heard the climate was unhealthy and life very short in the places where the marquis stayed a long time. He felt it was only thanks to a salubrious climate that the inhabitants could survive more than a couple of years. At lat. 37° or lat. 38° they eat more meat than the English, even in summer, put quantities of butter in almost all their dishes, call Port and Bordeaux light wines, and banish water from their tables. Another recently arrived European asked me one day how much water cost, and when I replied it was free, he remarked he thought it must be the most expensive beverage because it was so difficult to get a glass, whereas wine, cider, beer, grog, or toddy † was served at once. In 1774 when I was attending a dinner for thirty-two people in Norfolk, I requested a glass of water. The servants looked embarrassed and the water did not appear. Finally, the master of the house whispered in my ear that this unexpected request had upset the whole establishment and he wondered if I would be willing to drink something else instead.

Americans who live quietly have the same life span as Europeans. A salubrious climate is derived from the same causes in both hemispheres, and the peculiarities ascribed to ours are due to quackery or ignorance.

I have no intention of analyzing the marquis's book but merely of correcting some inaccuracies which could lead to false ideas about the physical character or morale of the country. I shall close with a quotation dealing with social precedence. As he was going from one ballroom to another in Philadelphia, "The Chevalier de La Luzerne offered his hand to Mrs. [Robert] Morris, and gave her the precedence, an honor rather generally bestowed on her, as

---

* [Ibid., p. 412.]

† Grog is made of rum and water; if sugar is added, it is called toddy.

she is the richest woman in the city." * [30] Precedence for men is regulated by their position, and custom decrees that a woman should have her husband's rank. An American reading this description will conclude correctly that the wives of the president of Congress, of the president of Pennsylvania, and of the Speaker of the General Assembly did not attend this party.

The marquis is right when he says: "One must be in the country itself, one must be acquainted with the language, and enjoy conversing and listening, to be able to arrive, even slowly, at one's own opinion and verdict." † These advantages enabled him to avoid many errors found in travel books, but he did not remain long enough to correct the false impressions he got from conversation. On many matters he was probably led astray by blind confidence in men whose judgment he trusted. Those who have not traveled are poorly equipped to describe their country, since they have no basis for comparison. The more you desire what is right, the more you involuntarily exaggerate the wrongs. We must remember the marquis visited America at a very unhappy time, but whatever caused his mistakes, everyone respects and admires him.

A publication called *Essay on the United States* with eighty-nine pages *in*-4° of double columns in small print deals with the political and diplomatic economy. It will appear in the *Encyclopédie Méthodique*.[31]

At the close of the introduction the author says: "And we can assure the reader he will find accurate facts and sound reflections." After such a declaration we must conclude the writer is thinking of the *Philosophical History of the Two Indies*. In the first section he promises an abstract of the political history of the English colonies of North America up to the period of the Revolution. Then he begins: "The English, who were persecuted at home for their civil and religious opinions, took refuge on the shores of North America, but this first emigration could not establish flourishing colonies. The inhabitants of the British Isles like to travel but are so attached to their native soil that it takes civil wars and revolutions to make men with property or a business leave the country."

* [Ibid., p. 164.]

† [Ibid., p. 430.]

[30] Anne-César de la Luzerne was sent to replace M. Gérard as French minister to the United States in 1779.

[31] Jean Nicolas Démeunier, *Essai sur les Etats-Unis* (Paris, 1786). This essay also appeared in the *Encyclopédie Méthodique* (Paris, 1786).

The author did not find it necessary to make many changes, even in the style of the *Philosophical History*, for Raynal writes (9:171): "The English who were persecuted at home for their civil and religious opinions were the first to come to this savage and deserted region. The inhabitants of Great Britain are so attached to their native soil that it takes civil wars or revolutions to make anyone with property or a business leave his home."

The only original remark in this passage is that the inhabitants of Great Britain like to travel. The author might have given the reader more pleasure had he explained why.*

The author of the *Essay* refutes what he himself had written about miscreants. "A man well informed about history and current conditions in the Union believes the colonies never received more than two thousand criminals. The majority were ill; few married and bore children; so they and their descendants probably number less than four thousand or scarcely a thousandth of the total population."

The well-informed man to whom he refers realized mistakes in the *Encyclopédie* would be handed down to posterity; so he took the trouble to collect some interesting observations on the United States. The author of the *Essay* scatters them throughout his work, but as he failed to indicate their source, the uninformed have trouble recognizing them, and these are the only readers to whom they would be useful.

It would also be difficult to identify all the passages from the *Philosophical History*, as he neglected to mark sentences he had changed in any way. Among passages credited to Abbé Raynal, and which he approves, is a statement about England: "Since 1764 its harbors have not shipped any merchandise to foreign countries or accepted any item without charging heavy duty." † When were the English ever so foolish as to tax merchandise for export? Everyone knows they return fees levied on goods brought into the coun-

---

* It is said that the wealthy in Great Britain are more inclined to travel than citizens of other nations because they are looking for a better climate and various advantages they do not have at home. These are only secondary causes. Lapps do not leave their homeland unless forced to do so and the Swiss travel only to seek their fortune. The main reason for travel is the government. In Great Britain, as taxes fall chiefly on luxuries, the wealthy save money by traveling and the poor are not tempted to leave. When taxes are levied on necessities and industry, the indigent emigrate to relieve their misery, while the rich, who can satisfy every wish, become accustomed to spending their entire income and cannot travel without spending the principal.

† P. 7, col. 1, l. 32.

try in order to encourage shipments abroad. How easy it is for mistakes to be perpetuated by carelessness! *

Anyone who has read the English constitutions must have observed that there is not enough distinction between the legislative, executive, and judiciary branches. The king, who has all the executive power, can annul any resolutions of the legislative body. The House of Lords, one of the branches of the legislative power, is also the supreme court of justice; the other branch, the House of Commons, often assumes an indefinite authority which stems from the other two powers.

When the American states formed their new governments, they established the principle that these three powers were to be absolutely separate and distinct, but this has not always been respected. The legislative power, like the English Parliament, has occasionally followed old customs. See Letter E in the Notes to Part II, where Virginia proved this. Although the three powers are much more distinct in all the states than in England, and although departures from the established principle have been minor, zealous citizens want the lines more clearly drawn. In all probability the writer of the *Essay* erred because he misinterpreted their zeal, for he seems not to have examined either the English constitutions or those of the various American governments. "The article on Virginia proves that if Americans were wise in imitating the English constitution to a certain degree, they should also have set fixed barriers between the legislative, executive, and judiciary powers; the best feature of the British constitution is the perfect counterbalance of these three branches of government." †

I should say no more about this *Essay* if a friend of Mr. Turgot had not asked me to add the following observations:

When the author of this *Essay* refers to the letter to Dr. Price,[32] he accuses Mr. Turgot (p. 20, col. 1, l. 30) of being the dupe of "too ardent a zeal for the happiness of men; his opinions may have been visionary because he attempted too much." But he does not want to

---

* The first authors of the *Maison rustique* said that horned animals shed their horns every three years. Count Buffon put this in his book, and the editors of the old edition of the *Encyclopédie* quoted it. The statement is refuted in an article on the ox in the new edition. But this error, which the most ignorant French peasant would have caught, may be perpetuated among writers and philosophers who read only Count Buffon's *Natural History* or the old edition of the *Encyclopédie*.

† P. 20, col. 2, l. 8.

[32] Richard Price, *Observations on the Importance of the American Revolution and the Means of Making It a Benefit to the World* (London, 1785).

"mention the mistakes of a statesman" because it would seem as if he were "putting his opinions above those of this statesman."

We shall call his attention to the fact that the more respectable a man is, the more dangerous his mistakes are. We should have liked an explanation of this doctrine of counterbalances which Mr. Turgot should apparently have taken more seriously. We wish he had made us see the visionary character of Mr. Turgot's ideas about the injustice of prohibitions and certain kinds of taxes, and the absurdity of Mr. Turgot's extension of man's natural rights. This luminous idea takes the yoke of commerce and finance from politics and submits it to morals.

The author should also have told us how American character could oppose the establishment of a representative constitution based on equality and liberty. It seems that love of liberty and equality has been their dominant characteristic up to the present time. Is it not possible that in these particular forms of government, where the author thinks you have to yield to the character of a people and to local conditions, there might often be institutions opposed to these invariable human rights which may be greater than he realizes? On the other hand, is it not possible to find a constitution which would be best for all peoples, since justice and reason are the same for all men? This is the idea shared by Mr. Turgot and several philosophers. Should the author have merely told them that a statesman scorns such opinions? Have these statesmen been so superior to Mr. Turgot? Is he so sure that the scorn of a statesman should disconcert a philosopher? Would it not be possible for these philosophers to scorn the statesmen whose votes seem so important to the author? What would he say if anyone showed him that their opinions were taken from books scorned by contemporary statesmen? So the scorn, with which the author hopes to crush political writers, merely proves that the statesmen of whom he speaks have not kept up with progress.

I should not ignore a little book called *Influence of the American Revolution on Europe*, whose only fault is its brevity.[33] You cannot make extracts; you can only comment on it. Since the book is not for sale, I hope my readers will be glad to find it at the end of the notes on this last volume.*

Mr. John Adams's book, *A Defence of the Constitutions of the United States of America*, has just been printed [1787] in London. The author aims to prove, contrary to Mr. Turgot, Abbé Mably, and Dr. Price, that the various state constitutions thus far established were wise to set up different bodies in order to balance the

---

* See Note R [omitted].

[33] [Marquis de Condorcet], *Influence of the American Revolution on Europe* (Amsterdam, 1786).

three powers insofar as possible. The first volume contains a suc-
cinct analysis of the constitutions of the best-known republics,
ancient as well as modern, together with the opinions of outstanding legislators since Plato about the organization of republican
governments. The second volume, soon to appear, will show that
the form recommended by these authors actually has fewer advantages and much less solidity than the one of which he has
undertaken an apology.

Among the best descriptions of America is that of my com-
patriot, Mr. Jefferson. His studies in natural history have interested
even those who could not share all his other opinions. Geographical details, pictures of the population, both European and Indian,
his plan to free the Negroes, his reflections on customs, laws, public
establishments—everything bears the stamp of truth, reason, and
love for humanity. You can disagree with some of his ideas, but
you must read his book if you wish to have a general knowledge of
America and a good background on Virginia. He deals only with
this state, for in our country we limit our discussion to matters with
which we are familiar. We have not yet developed a talent for
writing big volumes about countries we have never seen, and the
portrait of us in most European books is such that we do not care
to acquire it.

*The American Atlas*, published in London by Jeffreys (I refer
only to the one corrected after the Revolution) has a collection of
the best maps which have been made of this part of the world.* [34]
You should add the map of the Western world by Mr. Hutchins,
which came out later.[35] Several French officers have recently
drawn some very good maps, but they deal only with information
useful to navigators. Mr. Jefferson has an excellent map of Virginia, Pennsylvania, and the adjacent parts of the bordering states
in his *Notes on the State of Virginia*.† Old maps of these areas are
usually based on conjecture rather than experience.

* This collection costs two guineas.

† The original and a translation are now in Paris, together with Dr. Ramsay's
*History*.

[34] Thomas Jeffreys died in 1771; *The American Atlas* was issued posthumously
by Sayer and Bennett in 1776. Another English edition appeared in 1778, and a
French edition by Major Holland, Evans, et al. appeared the same year.

[35] Thomas Hutchins, *A New Map of the Western Parts of Virginia, Pennsylvania, Maryland and North Carolina* . . . (London, 1778).

# Notes N-R

## Note N (see page 323)

Whether motivated by vanity or ambition, man is eager to be distinguished and respected. This passion can be extremely useful if it is well directed; otherwise it leads to disaster. Happy is the nation where public esteem is guided toward activity and virtue, while vice and idleness are regarded with scorn and shame. Although nothing is easier to achieve, abuses dating from a period of barbaric ignorance retain their hold. In this enlightened century no one doubts that national prosperity consists in having an abundance of all the necessities of life and enjoying a few luxuries. This requires an intelligent effort to get as much from the soil and industry as possible. Those who contribute most by ingenious discoveries or fine workmanship are our true benefactors. Open to such men the road to honors and they will multiply. Unfortunately, when you speak of a man of merit, your listeners seem to be conferring a favor by doing him justice; if, on the other hand, you mention an idler who does nothing, everyone expresses a kind of veneration, varying in degree according to his wealth and ancestral titles.*

A desire to be distinguished is natural, but methods of attaining distinction are prescribed by usage, and usage is the result of ancient laws. When these are changed the result will change, but not until then. Men are opposed to innovations, which always require some sacrifice, and private interest often conflicts with public welfare.

In speaking of the idleness of the wealthy, I had no intention of approving the sad and ridiculous philosophy that advises us to embrace poverty. One of the greatest reproaches we can make to legislators is that they opposed natural inclinations instead of directing them. They thus made their systems seem odious. I should like to make wealth useful, for the wealthy can serve the state much more easily than the poor. If their services are rewarded, they will turn their attention to the protection and encouragement

* In France a commoner who lives on his income without working is said to live nobly. What nobility!

of agriculture, the arts, commerce, and the sciences. How many useful discoveries and improvements could be made by those with the leisure and means to make the necessary experiments! Wealth, which now serves to feed corruption and idleness, would then be devoted to making work more pleasant.

It is not enough to draw everything possible from the soil and industry; it is also essential to make worthwhile exchanges. Differences in soil, climate, and other conditions produce the great variety found in plants and manufactured products. Exchanges are even more necessary to diminish losses caused by bad harvests. They would be immensely useful if they had not been fettered by ignorance.

Exchanges are usually made through merchants and negotiants, as they are called in some countries. To be successful in these enterprises, a man needs intelligence, experience, and capital and is happy to use all three when his profession is respected. In France, however, he acquires a title by filling various positions, some of which are superfluous, but it is lost if he becomes a merchant. There is only one province in this vast kingdom * where a title is merely suspended while a man engages in commercial transactions.

It is easy to see what a stigma is attached to this profession, and it is natural that a tradesman should think of getting out of business as soon as he has become rich. This is the very moment when he could be useful because of his experience and his fortune. It is also natural that men should prefer a quick killing to more modest and stable returns. These dishonorable actions are falsely attributed to our national character.

## Note O (see page 324)

If all the products of the soil and works of art could be freely exchanged, without customs duties, every country would gain from this happy revolution. Wars would be very rare, if they occurred; government expenditures would be greatly reduced; men would no longer take advantage of each other by trickery; idleness would decrease tremendously; industry would flourish; and, in a word, the world would be a much better place.

If only one powerful nation had the wisdom to adopt this system, the obstacles produced by other countries could not prevent a considerable growth of its wealth, population, and strength.

* Brittany.

The absurdity of complicated systems, the advantages of a single direct tax, and the impossibility of enjoying real prosperity without complete freedom of commerce and industry are truths brought to light by French writers, truths which are finally beginning to triumph over childish jokes,* and intrigues directed undercover by self-interest.† French writers were the first to develop these truths, which were expressed with admirable clarity by one of the greatest men who ever lived.‡

People say that England prospers despite its complicated fiscal system. A bad system may seem good in comparison to others which are worse, and a very mediocre prosperity may appear remarkable if measured by the same criterion. It is also true that well-established taxes do less harm to national prosperity.

France is much more fortunate than Great Britain both in the variety and wealth of its products and in its geographical location. Its territory is approximately double that of Great Britain and Ireland, and its population more than twice as great. The national debt of Great Britain is larger than that of France; yet British taxes pay the interest, provide for the ordinary expenses of government, and, according to a recent report by the chancellor of the exchequer, leave a balance in the treasury.**

Although French revenue from taxation is considerably larger, it does not pay for normal government expenses and interest on the debt; taxes are proportionately two-fifths smaller than in England but constitute a much greater burden. One reason lies in the fact that the English system lacks the endless subdivisions and hindrances which undermine French industry. Their agriculture is not fettered by prohibitions. Taxes fall chiefly on the wealthy and idle; insofar as possible they spare the poor man and the artisan. I have already said that English taxes are levied on luxuries; in other European countries they are levied on necessities. A

---

* These estimable men were called the economists, to make them resemble a sect, by someone who was jealous of them or a punster. When you think how many truths have been scorned, it seems incredible that men should continue to poke fun at what they do not understand.

† Two powerful groups are interested in continuing this complicated and underhanded system. Although opposed to each other, they are united in their resistance to reforms in abuses which perpetuate their existence.

‡ Mr. Turgot.

** Some unprejudiced individuals claim there is an annual deficit of more than £1 million. However that may be, their taxation is preferable to the French system, although natural resources in France are more than twice those of Great Britain.

careful examination might prove that England enjoys a kind of prosperity because the system is efficiently directed. The opposite is true in France where, for example, taxes on all kinds of carriages are paid by individuals who cannot afford them; in England only the rich pay these taxes.

Among the nuisances unknown in England are internal taxes * and a great variety of provincial taxes. These unfair and harmful privileges were devised in emergency situations, and France is riddled with them. It has been said that if France made the most of its natural advantages it would be formidable. I think its example would be useful.

In a country where the best principles of administration are better known than elsewhere, it is not my place to mention the chain of disorders whose ramifications embrace every part of the state. I refer to the tobacco monopoly. The interests of a company are often opposed to those of the nation, and the merit of the men forming it cannot remedy the vices of the establishment. Let me repeat what I said in chapter 6. It will be useless for the government to request the Farmers General to buy all their tobacco in France at the conclusion of the arrangement with Mr. Morris. The evil may diminish, but it will continue.

The seller will always be hurt if there is only one buyer, and the reverse is equally true. There are many ways of getting the better of a salesman when there is no competition. If the salesmen join forces (and this is difficult) to oppose the monopoly, the purchaser can get tobacco in England, as he has done before. Moreover, he can get it cheaply by taking leftovers, and because he has no competitors, he need not fear about the quality of his merchandise. If the government ordered all tobacco purchased in France, who could prevent a powerful company from importing what it wanted, especially if it had bribed the inspectors who should prohibit smuggling?

Although it is true that French merchants can ship tobacco to other countries, the loss of time and the expenses involved will discourage the practice. Moreover, once commerce has been diverted it is difficult to build it up again. Excise taxes should be paid at the frontiers and internal commerce kept free of other tariffs. After tobacco has been taxed at English ports, where it provides a good sum for the treasury, it is no longer subject to fines. It thus en-

* Without paying a cent, the rich man imports produce from his land into cities where the working man and the poor do not have a slice of bread which has not been taxed.

courages commerce and industry because competition obliges every manufacturer to produce the best articles he can. It has been claimed this system is impossible in France, since it is more difficult to prevent smuggling on the continent. If that is true, how can agents of the Farmers General be prevented from bringing tobacco from England?

The new law would enable the state to receive more from the farmers; yet individuals would have better tobacco for less money. The country would export about £50 million more in merchandise annually to America and would also derive a large profit from the sales of manufactured tobacco to foreigners.

Among all the enemies which ignorance and malice have spawned, the worst is the legal monopoly. As long as this curse exists, neither commerce nor industry can flourish.

## Note P (see page 338)

Romulus established a council to share the administrative duties and appointed a hundred senators. They were called Fathers and their descendants Patricians (Titus Livius, bk. 1).

He separated those distinguished by their merits, birth, or wealth from the Plebeians, who had none of these attributes. The Fathers were given this title because of their age, because they had children, or because of their family. Romulus ordered the Patricians to take charge of the sacred ceremonies, serve as magistrates, govern the republic with him, and fulfill all municipal responsibilities. He decreed that Plebeians should have no part in these affairs, as they were not well educated; their task was to cultivate the soil and tend the animals. Lest the poor be envious, he authorized every Plebeian to select a Patrician as his patron (Denys of Halicarnassus, *Antiquities of Rome*, bk. 2).

He established a council of a hundred outstanding men selected from the Patricians to govern the republic with him; this council was named the Senate. Some say the men were called Fathers because they had legitimate children, others claim it was because they could name their fathers, which was not easy among these early inhabitants. It seems most likely that Romulus chose this name because he realized the duty of the great is to watch over the people with paternal solicitude; moreover, he wanted the people to be fond of their superiors and to consider them as their fathers (Plutarch, *Life of Romulus*).

One can scarcely find the source of the Roman aristocracy which caused so many ravages. A group of men who lived very simply chose several elderly members as magistrates. As they had no distinction other than age, experience, and the affection they presumably had for the common people, they were called Fathers. Soon the descendants of these simple, rustic men considered themselves different from their fellow citizens, claimed prerogatives, etc. (comte de Mirabeau, *Considerations on the Order of the Cincinnati*).

The ideas in this passage are so different from those in Titus Livius, Denys of Halicarnassus, and Plutarch that we are sorry we do not know where the comte de Mirabeau got his information.

### Note Q (see page 341)

#### George Washington to Governor Patrick Henry

October 29, 1785
Mount Vernon

Sir:

Your Excellency having been pleased to transmit to me a copy of the Act appropriating to my benefit certain shares in the companies for opening the navigation of James and Potomac rivers; I take the liberty of returning to the General Assembly, thro' your hands, the profound and grateful acknowledgments inspired by so signal a mark of their beneficent intentions towards me. I beg you Sir, to assure them, that I am filled on this occasion with every sentiment, which can flow from a heart warm with love for my Country, sensible to every token of its approbation and affection, and solicitous to testify in every instance a respectful submission to its wishes.

With these sentiments in my bosom, I need not dwell on the anxiety I feel in being obliged in this instance to decline a favor which is rendered no less flattering by the manner in which it is conveyed, than it is affectionate in itself. In explaining this observation I pass over a comparison of my endeavors in the public service with the many honorable testimonies of approbation which have already so far over rated and over paid them; reciting one consideration only which supersedes the necessity of recurring to every other.

When I was first called to the station with which I was honored during the late conflict for our liberties, to the diffidence which I had so many reasons to feel in accepting it, I thought it my duty to join a firm resolution to shut my hand against every pecuniary recompense. To this resolution I have invariably adhered, and from it (if I had the inclination) I do not consider myself at liberty now to depart.

Whilst I repeat therefore my fervent acknowledgments to the legislature for their very kind sentiments and intentions in my favor, and at the same time beg them to be persuaded that a remembrance of this singular proof of their goodness towards me, will never cease to cherish returns of the warmest affection and gratitude, I must pray that their Act, so far as it has for its object my personal emolument, may not have its effect; but if it should please the General Assembly to permit me to turn the destination of the fund vested in me, from my private emolument, to objects of a public nature, it will be my study in selecting these to prove the sincerity of my gratitude for the honor conferred on me, by preferring such as may appear most subservient to the enlightened and patriotic views of the Legislature.[36]

### Note R (see page 374)

#### Influence of the American Revolution on Europe

To the marquis de Lafayette, who, at the age when ordinary men are scarcely known, earned the title of benefactor of both worlds. By an obscure inhabitant of the Old World [the marquis de Condorcet]

### [Omitted]

[36] Washington, *Writings of George Washington*, ed. John C. Fitzpatrick, 39 vols. (Washington, D.C., 1931–44), 28:303–4.

# Supplement

Recent reports from the United States require a supplement. We hope this will please those eager to learn about affairs in this country so that they can predict what may happen in the future.

Europe gets news about the United States from English gazettes, and well-informed Americans have said many times that if you believe the opposite of what is published, you will have accurate information. It is, however, impossible to hide the truth forever. For several years gazetteers have entertained their readers with accounts of imaginary riots, and they finally announced a real one; only the details are inexact.

In the fourth chapter of Part IV, I said there was dissatisfaction in the state of Massachusetts because many citizens could not pay their taxes and debts without going bankrupt. The prodigious amount of foreign merchandise which flooded the country right after the war and the vast number of payments made to English creditors for debts contracted before the Revolution used up all the hard money. As unpaid taxes had accumulated for several years, the government was forced to clamp down, and in several counties a group of desperate men tried to revolt. Their leader was a former army sergeant-major named Shays.[1]

The wisest men did not attend a meeting of citizens convoked by the rebels. The rebels decided to close the tribunals, stop levying taxes, circulate paper money, and make some changes in the government. All these proposals seemed popular. If the tribunals were closed, debtors would not be prosecuted. Paper money offered a prospect of paying debts easily, and the changes in the government were designed to reduce expenses, which were very small anyway.

As Shays and his followers had no hope of getting enough votes to act legally, they paraded in large numbers, bearing guns, and interrupted sessions in several county courts. The governor at once convoked the General Court with the intention of raising fifteen

---

[1] Daniel Shays, a former army captain, led Shays's Rebellion, 1786–87, the outstanding manifestation of discontent during the economic depression following the Revolution.

hundred men under command of General Lincoln and then reinforcing them with as many militiamen as necessary to restore order.

In the meantime General Shepard had assembled about 800 militiamen to defend the Springfield arsenal. Shays, with 1,200, ordered him to surrender, but he replied with a volley of artillery which killed 4 men, wounded several more, and scattered the rest. They reassembled some distance away, but General Lincoln, who had made a forced march, ended the affair in a moment.* A tall hill made it impossible for him to surprise them, but he took 150 prisoners and got rid of the others without shedding a drop of blood. Shays escaped with 17 ringleaders, some of whom are now believed to be in Canada. A company of volunteers from Boston captured 3 and took them to prison. The Massachusetts government offered a reward to anyone who would arrest the others, and the governments of New Hampshire and Vermont † followed suit.

When the tumult died down, the General Court set up a commission to examine the affair and pardon the innocent. These men had not perpetrated the slightest crime against any individual, and the majority had good intentions. According to the latest reports, 790 men have already been pardoned; only a small number of the leaders were found guilty, and they have been jailed in their respective counties, where they will be examined and judged. It is believed that several of those condemned to death will be pardoned and only three or four executed. A general amnesty was considered unwise, since it might inculcate the opinion that the affair was insignificant or the government weak.

The Massachusetts uprising gave rise in Europe to bombastic attacks against popular governments. I say bombastic, since any reasoning would have shown the popular governments were kind. During the eleven years since the American governments were founded, this has been the only uprising. If the same thing should occur in the other twelve states at equal intervals, 143 years would elapse before the final one. In what other governments have uprisings been so rare? If you examine the history of Asiatic kingdoms, you find that no despotism could prevent them. If you reflect on what has happened during the past eleven years in Constantinople, France, and England, you will see we have enjoyed

---

* He had covered 30 miles between 8:00 P.M. and 9:00 A.M. over roads covered with deep snow.

† This action on the part of the state of Vermont should be compared to what was published in the gazettes.

relative peace. Let us now examine the causes and results of these disorders.

The Massachusetts rebellion was due to a series of unfortunate events which came to a head with large tax levies. As this crisis has passed, we may hope the catastrophe will not be repeated.

The uprising caused a temporary suspension of several tribunals and an encounter in which four men were killed and several wounded; it will end with the punishment of three or four others. What is this in comparison to rebellions in England, such as Lord Gordon's riot, and recent troubles in Glasgow? The Massachusetts rebels did not insult anyone and paid for their equipment. Where else would you find companies of volunteers running to defend the government? This uprising, which has been laughed at in Europe, is one of the most convincing proofs that to keep good order you need to entrust the task to the nation. A country where equal rights prevail will uphold a government believed to be good. As there are no odious or unjust social distinctions, national dissensions cannot have deep roots, and when happiness and safety depend on good order, everyone will be interested in preserving it.

In Part II, I spoke of the progress being made in every state in favor of liberty of conscience. The Virginia General Assembly has now passed a law establishing it on the best possible basis. This resulted from a complaint of the inhabitants, inserted as Note G above.

The comte de Mirabeau was right when he said: "You speak of tolerance! And there is not a single country on earth, including the new American republic, where a man can enjoy all the advantages of society if he practices the social virtues." * He will now have to make an exception, at least for Virginia, where religion is distinct from the rights and responsibilities of citizenship. It is hoped the other American republics will pass similar legislation.

In Virginia there is no longer any partiality in favor of primogeniture or sex. The same reforms are gradually being made throughout the country, and if Europe were aware of what was happening, it would realize that the dire prophecies of so-called legislators have no foundation.

Recently we heard the consoling news that the South Carolina General Assembly has prohibited the importation of slaves for three years. Friends of liberty did not dare insist on a permanent prohibition, but it is hoped such a law will be passed before the

* Letter from the comte de Mirabeau to . . . about Messrs. de Cagliostro and Lavater, Berlin, 1786.

present one expires, and North Carolina and Georgia, the only states where slaves can still be imported, will probably approve it too.

The peace treaty between the United States and Great Britain has not been fully executed on either side, but Europe is no better informed about this than other matters. When the treaty was signed, there were in New York some four thousand slaves, most of whom belonged to the inhabitants of Virginia. They were to be returned to their owners before the English troops left. When questioned about this, Sir Guy Carleton, commander in chief, replied that he was familiar with the terms of the treaty but did not want to break his word to the slaves, whom he had promised to set free. He therefore took them and left to the British government the task of reimbursing the owners. It is unfortunate that the first point of the treaty that Great Britain failed to observe stems from an honorable act on the commander's part.

During the war courts were closed in several states and English creditors forbidden to pursue their debtors. An article of the treaty states that all claims of English creditors shall be set aside. When General Carleton refused to agree, the Virginia General Assembly permitted claims to remain. Congress complained, and the assembly then passed the law mentioned in chapter 5 by which English creditors could demand what was due to them in seven equal yearly payments bearing interest since the close of the war. This law was to the advantage of both sides, because many debtors were going bankrupt without being able to satisfy their creditors. The body of creditors met in London with our ministers to the courts of France and England, but the British secretary of state,[2] who had at first been in favor of negotiations, refused to participate at the final moment.

In the western territory which, according to the treaty, belongs to the United States, the English are keeping several forts that should have been evacuated. They find these very useful for trading with the savages.

Virginia did not have the right to close its courts to English creditors or to authorize them to demand payment in seven equal installments, for the peace treaty states that its tribunals are to be open. The English were the first to err, since they did not return or pay for the slaves, but Virginia should have appealed to Congress, which alone has the right to deal with matters pertaining to the Confederation.

[2] Francis Osborne, marquis of Carmarthen and later fifth duke of Leeds.

The result of the discussions between Congress and the British government appears in a letter from Lord Carmarthen, secretary of state of Great Britain, to Mr. Adams, minister plenipotentiary of the United States at the Court of Saint James's. Lord Carmarthen makes it clear that Great Britain will not fulfill the conditions of the treaty until we have done so ourselves, and he refers to certain states that have been negligent in this respect. On 22 September 1786 a letter was published in Philadelphia concerning Pennsylvania's role in this affair. It states that English creditors have never found the tribunals closed except in the case of internal debts. "British merchants since the peace have had full scope in Pennsylvania, against the lands as well as goods of their debtors, which is not so in England, in like cases, lands there not being liable to sale for debts." [3] The apology goes back to court minutes for the proof of cases heard since the peace, debts to the state only excepted. Cases have been tried since the war ended, and actions are brought daily to institute proceedings against English creditors, for the law specifies an exception of debts due by citizens of Pennsylvania to British subjects.

Congress was chiefly concerned with the execution of our part of the peace treaty. The following letter was sent to the leading magistrate in each of the thirteen states.

SIR:

Our Secretary for Foreign Affairs has transmitted to you copies of a letter to him from our Minister at the Court of London of the 4th day of March, 1786, and of the papers mentioned to have been enclosed with it.

We have deliberately and dispassionately examined and considered the several facts and matters urged by Britain as infractions of the treaty of peace on the part of America, and we regret that in some of the States too little attention appears to have been paid to the public faith pledged by that treaty. Not only the obvious dictates of religion, morality, and national honor, but also the first principles of good policy, demand a candid and punctual compliance with engagements constitutionally and fairly made. Our national constitution having committed to us the management of the national concerns with foreign States and powers, it is our duty to take care that all the rights which they ought to enjoy within our jurisdiction by the laws of nations and the faith of treaties remain inviolate. And it is also our duty to provide that the essential interests and peace of the whole confederacy be not

[3] *Pennsylvania Mercury and Universal Advertiser* (Philadelphia), no. 110 (Friday, 22 Sept. 1786).

impaired or endangered by deviations from the line of public faith into which any of its members may from whatever cause be unadviseedly drawn. Let it be remembered that the thirteen Independent Sovereign States have by express delegation of power, formed and vested in us a general though limited Sovereignty for the general and national purposes specified in the Confederation. In this Sovereignty they cannot severally participate (except by their Delegates) nor with it have concurrent Jurisdiction, for the 9th Article of the confederation most expressly conveys to us the sole and exclusive right and power of determining on war and peace, and of entering into treaties and alliances etc. When therefore a treaty is constitutionally made ratified and published by us, it immediately becomes binding on the whole nation and superadded to the laws of the land, without the intervention of State Legislatures. Treaties derive their obligation from being compacts between the Sovereign of this, and the Sovereign of another Nation, whereas laws or statutes derive their force from being the Acts of a Legislature competent to the passing of them. Hence it is clear that Treaties must be implicitly received and observed by every Member of the Nation; for as State Legislatures are not competent to the making of such compacts or treaties, so neither are they competent in that capacity, authoritatively to decide on, or ascertain the construction and sense of them. When doubts arise respecting the construction of State laws, it is not unusual nor improper for the State Legislatures by explanatory or declaratory Acts to remove those doubts; but the case between laws and compacts or treaties is in this widely different; for when doubts arise respecting the sense and meaning of a treaty they are so far from being cognizable by a State Legislature that the United States in Congress Assembled have no authority to settle and determine them; For as the Legislature only which constitutionally passes a law has power to revise and amend it, so the sovereigns only who are parties to the treaty have power, by mutual consent and posterior Articles to correct or explain it.

In cases between Individuals, all doubts respecting the meaning of a treaty, like all doubts respecting the meaning of a law, are in the first instance mere judicial questions, and are to be heard and decided in the Courts of Justice having cognizance of the causes in which they arise; and whose duty it is to determine them according to the rules and maxims established by the laws of Nations for the interpretation of treaties. From these principles it follows of necessary consequence, that no individual State has a right by legislative Acts to decide and point out the sense in which their particular Citizens and Courts shall understand this or that Article of a treaty.

It is evident that a contrary doctrine would not only militate against the common and established maxims and Ideas relative to this subject, but would prove no less inconvenient in practice, than it is irrational in theory; for in that case the same Article of the same treaty might by law be made to mean one thing in New Hampshire, another thing in New York, and neither the one nor the other of them in Georgia.

How far such legislative Acts would be valid and obligatory even within the limits of the State passing them, is a question which we hope never to have occasion to discuss. Certain however it is that such Acts cannot bind either of the contracting Sovereigns, and consequently cannot be obligatory on their respective Nations.

But if treaties and every Article in them be (as they are and ought to be) binding on the whole Nation, if individual States have no right to accept some Articles and reject others, and if the impropriety of State Acts to interpret and decide the sense and construction of them be apparent; still more manifest must be the impropriety of State Acts to controul, delay or modify the operation and execution of these national compacts.

When it is considered that the several States Assembled by their Delegates in Congress have express power to form treaties, surely the treaties so formed are not afterwards to be subject to such alterations as this or that State Legislature may think expedient to make, and that too without the consent of either of the parties to it—that is, in the present case, without the consent of all the United States, who collectively are parties to this treaty on the one side, and his britannic Majesty on the other. Were the Legislatures to possess and to exercise such power, we should soon be involved as a Nation in Anarchy and confusion at home, and in disputes which would probably terminate in hostilities and War with the Nations with whom we may have formed treaties. Instances would then be frequent of treaties fully executed in one State, and only partly executed in another and of the same Article being executed in one manner in one State, and in a different manner, or not at all in another State. History furnishes no precedent of such liberties taken with treaties under form of Law in any nation. Contracts between Nations, like contracts between Individuals, should be faithfully executed even though the sword in the one case, and the law in the other did not compel it, honest nations like honest Men require no constraint to do Justice; and tho impunity and the necessity of Affairs may sometimes afford temptations to pare down contracts to the Measure of convenience, yet it is never done but at the expense of that esteem, and confidence, and credit which are of infinitely more worth than all the momentary advantages which such expedients can extort.

But although contracting Nations cannot like individuals avail themselves of Courts of Justice to compel performance of contracts, yet an appeal to Heaven and to Arms, is always in their power and often in their Inclination.

But it is their duty to take care that they never lead their people to make and support such Appeals, unless the sincerity and propriety of their conduct affords them good reason to rely with confidence on the Justice and protection of Heaven.

Thus much we think it useful to observe in order to explain the principles on which we have unanimously come to the following resolution, (viz) "*Resolved*, That the Legislatures of the several States cannot of right pass any Act or Acts for interpreting, explaining or construing a national treaty or any part or clause of it, nor for restraining, limiting or in any manner impeding, retarding, or counteracting the operation and execution of the same; for that on being constitutionally made, ratified and published they become in virtue of the confederation part of the Law of the Land, and are not only independent of the will and power of such Legislatures, but also binding and obligatory on them."

As the treaty of peace so far as it respects the matters and things provided for in it, is a Law to the United States, which cannot by all or any of them be altered or changed, all State Acts establishing provisions relative to the same objects, which are incompatible with it, must in every point of view be improper. Such Acts do nevertheless exist, but we do not think it necessary either to enumerate them particularly, or to make them severally the subjects of discussion. It appears to us sufficient to observe and insist, that the treaty ought to have free course in its operation and execution, and that all obstacles interposed by State Acts be removed. We mean to act with the most scrupulous regard to Justice and candour towards Great Britain, and with an equal degree of delicacy, moderation and decision towards the States who have given occasion to these discussions.

For these reasons we have in general terms

*Resolved*, That all such acts or parts of Acts, as may be now existing in any of the States repugnant to the treaty of peace ought to be forthwith repealed, as well to prevent their continuing to be regarded as violations of that treaty as to avoid the disagreeable necessity there might otherwise be of raising and discussing questions touching their validity and obligation.

Although this resolution applies strictly only to such of the States as have passed the exceptionable Acts alluded to, yet to obviate all future disputes and questions as well as to remove those which now exist, we think it best that every State without exception should pass a law on the Subject. We have therefore "*Resolved*, That it be recommended to the several States to make such repeal rather by describing than reciting the said Acts, and for that purpose to pass an Act, declaring in general terms, that all such Acts and parts of Acts repugnant to the treaty of peace between the United States, and his Britannic Majesty, or any Article thereof, shall be and thereby are repealed; And that the Courts of Law and Equity in all causes and Questions cognizable by them respectively, and arising from or touching the said Treaty, shall decide and adjudge according to the true intent and meaning of the same, any thing in the said Acts or parts of Acts to the contrary thereof in any wise notwithstanding.

Such Laws would answer every purpose and be easily formed, the more they were of the like tenor throughout the States the better. They might each recite that, Whereas certain Laws or Statutes made and passed in some of the United States, are regarded and complained of as repugnant to the Treaty of peace with Great Britain, by reason whereof not only the good faith of the United States, pledged by that treaty has been drawn into Question, but their essential Interests under that treaty greatly affected. And Whereas Justice to Great Britain as well as regard to the honor and Interests of the United States require, that the said treaty be faithfully executed, and that all obstacles thereto, and particularly such as do or may be construed to proceed from the Laws of this State, be effectually removed, therefore,

Be it enacted by         and it is hereby enacted by the Authority of the same, that such of the Acts or parts of Acts of the Legislature of this State, as are repugnant to the treaty of peace between the United States, and his Britannic Majesty, or any Article thereof, shall be and hereby are repealed. And further that the Courts of Law and Equity within this State be and they hereby are directed and required, in all causes and questions cognizable by them respectively, and arising from or touching the said treaty, to decide and adjudge according to the tenor, true intent and meaning of the same anything in the said Acts or parts of Acts to the contrary thereof in any wise notwithstanding.

Such a general Law would we think be preferable to one that should minutely enumerate the Acts and clauses intended to be repealed; because omissions might accidentally be made in the enumeration, or Questions might arise and perhaps not be satisfactorily determined respecting particular Acts or clauses, about which contrary opinions may be entertained. By repealing in general terms all Acts and clauses repugnant to the treaty, the business will be turned over to its proper Department, viz, the Judicial, and the Courts of Law will find no difficulty in deciding whether any particular Act or clause is or is not contrary to the treaty. Besides when it is considered that the Judges in general are Men of Character and Learning, and feel as well as know the obligations of Office and the value of reputation, there is no reason to doubt that their conduct and Judgments relative to these as well as other Judicial matters will be wise and upright.

Be please, Sir, to lay this letter before the Legislature of Your State without delay. We flatter ourselves they will concur with us in opinion, that candour and Justice are as necessary to true policy, as they are to sound Morality, and that the most honorable way of delivering ourselves from the embarrassment of mistakes is fairly to correct them. It certainly is time that all doubts respecting the public faith be removed, and that all questions and differences between us and Great Britain be amicably and finally settled. The States are informed of the reasons why his britannic Majesty still continues to occupy the frontier Posts, which by the treaty he agreed to evacuate; and we have the strongest assurances that an exact compliance with the treaty on our part, shall be followed by a punctual performance of it on the part of Great Britain.

It is important that the several Legislatures should as soon as possible take these matters into consideration; and we request the favor of You to transmit to us an authenticated copy of such Acts and proceedings of the Legislature of Your State, as may take place on the Subject, and in pursuance of this letter.

By order of Congress,

(Signed)  Arthur Saint-Clair, President.[4]

Several states have already passed the law recommended by Congress, and the others will doubtless follow their example as soon as their legislative bodies assemble. When this is done, British intentions cannot remain much longer in the shadow.

In chapter 5 of Part IV I said the various states were going to send deputies to a convention where they would deliberate about how to give the Confederation more stability. The convention met in Philadelphia, lasted four months, and ended by proposing to the states the plan for a new federal constitution which I shall give, together with the letter of the president addressed to the president of Congress.

The chief cause of the delay in the meeting of the assembly was Article 13 of the Confederation, which declares "nor shall any alteration at any time hereafter be made in any of them [these articles]; unless such alteration be agreed to in a congress of the United States, and be afterwards confirmed by the legislature of every state." Several states said that because Congress had the right to deliberate on the necessary reforms, it was useless to convoke a special convention, but they finally agreed to join the others. Any citizen was eligible to be a member of the convention, even if he had a governmental post. Virginia sent Mr. Edmund Randolph, the current governor; Dr. McClurg, member of the state council; Mr. James Madison, member of Congress; and Mr. George Wythe and Mr. John Blair, judges of the Court of Chancery.[5] General Washington and Mr. George Mason also accepted the invitation to serve, although they have retired from public office.

---

[4] *Journals of Continental Congress* 32:176–84, 13 April 1787.

[5] The Virginia delegates were Edmund Randolph, governor of Virginia 1786–88; Dr. James McClurg, the leading physician in Williamsburg; James Madison, who had already served in the Continental Congress 1780–83 and the Virginia House of Delegates 1784–86; George Wythe, signer of the Declaration of Independence and chancellor of Virginia; and John Blair, a judge of the Virginia Court of Appeals.

Letter of the President of the Convention to the President of Congress
September 17, 1787

Sir,

We have now the honor to submit to the consideration of the United States in Congress assembled, that Constitution which has appeared to us the most advisable.

The friends of our country have long seen and desired, that the power of making war, peace, and treaties; that of levying money and regulating commerce, and the correspondent executive and judicial authorities, should be fully and effectually vested in the general government of the Union. But the impropriety of delegating such extensive trust to one body of men is evident—Hence results the necessity of a different organization.

It is obviously impracticable in the federal government of these States, to secure all rights of independent sovereignty to each, and yet provide for the interest and safety of all: Individuals entering into society, must give up a share of liberty to preserve the rest. The magnitude of the sacrifice must depend as well on situation and circumstance, as on the object to be obtained. It is at all times difficult to draw with precision the line between those rights which must be surrendered, and those which may be reserved; and on the present occasion, this difficulty was increased by a difference among the several States as to their situation, extent, habits, and particular interests.

In all our deliberations on this subject, we kept steadily in our view, that which appears to us the greatest interest of every true American, the consolidation of our Union, in which is involved our prosperity, felicity, safety, perhaps our national existence. This important consideration, seriously and deeply impressed on our minds, led each State in the Convention to be less rigid on points of inferior magnitude, than might have been otherwise expected; and thus the Constitution, which we now present, is the result of a spirit of amity, and of that mutual deference and concession which the peculiarity of our political situation rendered indispensable.

That it will meet the full and entire approbation of every State, is not perhaps to be expected; but each will doubtless consider, that had her interest been alone consulted, the consequences might have been particularly disagreeable or injurious to others; that it is liable to as few exceptions as could reasonably have been expected, we hope and believe; that it may promote the lasting welfare of that country, so dear to us all, and secure her freedom and happiness is our most ardent wish.

With great respect,

We have the honor to be, Sir, your Excellency's most obedient and humble servants.

George Washington, President
By unanimous Order of the Convention [6]

[6] *The Records of the Federal Convention of 1787*, ed. Max Farrand, 4 vols. (New Haven: Yale University Press, 1911–37), 2:666–67.

The first federative constitution, called the Articles of Confederation, is so worded that any group of wise and virtuous men could feel honored to have written it. The few faults are due to the precautions of its authors and are easily corrected. I think it should have been preserved as the fundamental basis for our Union with whatever supplements were necessary to make it as perfect as it could be, but the proposed constitution ignores it completely so that anyone unfamiliar with the document could get an altogether false impression of it.

In the first constitution the power of Congress is not sufficiently broad in some instances or clearly defined in others. The proposed constitution gives it, in some circumstances, power exceeding that of a purely federal government. The first puts the legislative and executive branches in a single body; the second subdivides the legislative branch. To correct and improve the first constitution, it was necessary only to change Article 8, as Congress proposed on 18 April 1783, by separating the legislative and executive powers and by granting Congress the right to levy sums of money, to regulate commerce, to prevent any state from coining money or giving legal value to paper or any other kind of fictitious money, and to determine how many states will be required to form a plurality so that the absent cannot influence deliberations.

The corrections and additions necessary to perfect the first constitution are included in the second but along with several others to which I hope my fellow citizens will pay the attention they deserve.

Article 1, Section 1. "All legislative Powers herein granted shall be vested in a Congress of the United States, which shall consist of a Senate and House of Representatives." Even if you admitted the usefulness of dividing the legislative power in the constitution of a single state, it would not follow that this should be done in a federal constitution. The letter I have just mentioned tries to justify this by saying it is improper to confide so much power to a single body. It would be as difficult to prove that a complication of the system ensured an adequate restraint as it is simple to demonstrate that the necessary legislative power can safely be given to one legislative body. The fear of a single body, which may seem significant in the case of a real legislative body, cannot be seriously alleged here (1) because the power of a federative congress is by its nature much more limited than that of a legislative body which reduces the danger and (2) because it is easier for all the parts of this Congress to meet as it forms a much more distinct group from the citizenry. This makes the remedy less efficacious.

The reader will discover here, as elsewhere, various reasons which are either not expressed or are simply indicated; a discussion of them would make this supplement too long.

Section 2. "The House of Representatives shall be composed of Members chosen . . . by the People of the several States." In most states the inhabitants believe their representatives are the men best suited to select candidates for certain positions in the republic; so they have left the choice to them. These same inhabitants will doubtless not consider themselves capable of making a better selection of men to administer the affairs of the Union or to deal with foreign powers. Furthermore, we do not see why Congress should determine the method of election. Each state should give the Confederation any power which might hurt its allies if it acted separately, but there is no reason why the method of election in one state should influence that of another. Uniformity on this point would be absurd, since the inhabitants of small states vote directly, whereas others feel obliged to have representatives. This law should only prevent certain conditions, such as electing a family forever, a deputy for life, etc., because a state can require another to outlaw anything which might be harmful to the general liberty.

Section 3. "The Senate of the United States shall be composed of two Senators from each State, chosen by the Legislature thereof, for six Years; and each Senator shall have one Vote." Here I have several comments: (1) Six years is too long a term, for a three-year absence alienates the people's confidence and that is a great problem in our government. (2) There is not a single plausible reason for emphasizing the difference between the election of senators and representatives. Every complication in the system and every distinction is fundamentally bad and can be justified only by necessity. The other distinction, pertaining to the influence of the states, will cause trouble. We have already seen the number of representatives must be proportionate to the number of inhabitants and that each representative must have a vote, as each senator does. Now let us see why there is equality in one case and not in the other.

Some men think the influence of a state in national affairs should depend on the taxes it pays; others believe there should be perfect equality, without regard for either size or population. Up to the present every state has had one vote; the proposed constitution follows the same system for the Senate but another for the House of Representatives. Virginia will therefore have ten times as much influence as Rhode Island and Delaware in the House of Representatives, but they will be equal in the Senate. However, because the resolutions of one house must be approved by the other, the smaller states, if defeated in the House of Representatives, will carry their resolutions to the Senate.

It is a mistake to think opposing principles can be reconciled. Such expedients may serve for a time, but they will never form the basis of a solid edifice. A choice between sides must be made. The principles must be firm and everything must be planned to uphold them. It would be desirable to have the states equal or nearly so, but since that is not the case, the disadvantages should not be increased. The question is a difficult one. The arguments advanced on both sides left the wisest and least prejudiced members of Congress undecided. A need for unanimity influenced these great men to decide in favor of equality, and the convention adopted this expedient. I am afraid of the consequences. If anyone could find a real solution and could present it clearly and decisively, he would render a great service both to America and to Europe, where the progress of philosophy makes one hope that eventually there will be a confederation, which could greatly decrease the suffering of humanity.

Section 6. "The Senators and Representatives shall receive a Compensation for their Services, to be ascertained by Law, and paid out of the Treasury of the United States." The laws of the Union are made by Congress. I hope it will never be permitted to determine its own salary. This could lead to a dangerous abuse, whereas excessive zeal might produce too much unselfishness. Both extremes should be avoided. It might also be unsatisfactory to let each state determine its payment; but uniformity in salaries should be determined by a convention, not by Congress itself.

Section 9. "The Privilege of the Writ of Habeas Corpus shall not be suspended, unless when in Cases of Rebellion or Invasion the public safety may require it." In every state the declaration of rights states that this privilege must never be suspended. If they wanted to mention it in the federative constitution, they should have spoken of it only to show to what extent everyone is determined that it shall always be held sacred. At one period during the Revolution (toward the end of 1776) the instability of the governments and various other circumstances demanded its suspension, but this was denied, although we were in a critical state. These conditions will never recur. It is never very embarrassing or dangerous to give the citizen who is being arrested judges and means to defend himself immediately.

"No Tax or Duty shall be laid on Articles exported from any State." Congress should neither have this power nor be authorized to forbid a state to exercise it. The state alone would bear the brunt of this. Similarly the Union should not share the product of such a tax, as proposed in Section 10.

"No money shall be drawn from the Treasury, but in Consequence of Appropriations made by Law; and a regular Statement and Account of the Receipts and Expenditures of all public Money shall be published from time to time." These accountings should be at fixed intervals, such as once a year. That would give the nation an opportunity to check the facts and verify the good behavior of its administrators. If Congress can render an accounting whenever it wishes, as indicated in the vague "from time to time" and levy taxes at what it deems a suitable moment, you might as well grant it unlimited power because nothing could resist these men authorized to dispose of the states' wealth.

As for Article 2 dealing with the election, functions, emoluments, etc. of the president, we should observe that: (1) the method of election tends to prefer the most conspicuous man to the one with the best qualities, and everyone knows that true merit usually attracts less attention than charlatanism; (2) he is authorized to command the army and navy in person, whereas he should only be given the task of selecting the commanders and forbidden to command in person; (3) the executive power is entrusted to him alone without the assistance of a council; this is dangerous for public welfare, and a judicious president would never want it; he would run many risks if he were deprived of the resource of a council on delicate matters, and their opinion would justify his conduct; (4) it would set a very bad example to have the president serve as long as the inhabitants wanted him; it would be better to renounce having him than to accustom the people to seeing the same individual in the post; one more step and you would have a hereditary ruler.

Article 3, Section 2. The method proposed to solve differences between two or several states is capable of producing a systematic cabal, whereas the one outlined in the Articles of Confederation is the best that could be devised (see Note I above). Cases between citizens of different states, or between a citizen of the Union and a foreigner, should be judged in the tribunals of the state where it is easiest to check the facts, and not in federal tribunals as proposed here. It also appears that jurors can be excluded from civil cases, and this must be corrected.

I do not see any explanation for the arithmetical proportion according to which age for the different posts is determined.* This is

---

* The proposed federal constitution requires that a representative be 25, a senator 30, and a president 35 years old.

detrimental to both youth and experience. Think how young men have been exemplary in their conduct. Among the Ancients I shall mention only Scipio the African, who at twenty-two astonished the world by his virtue, wisdom, and moderation, as well as by his courage and ability to command. The conduct of a young hero who at nineteen crossed the ocean to offer us his aid at the most critical time of the Revolution is enough to make us blush at our hesitation to admit young men to positions in the republic. I could name a number of young Americans who justify my opinion. Prejudice, characteristic of old age, is only too apt to prefer mediocre men to talented young ones. No one is inclined to prefer a young man unless he is outstanding; so why pass an unjust and useless law, which can be harmful to public welfare? Fear of the young may come from pride or from a decline of the courage and nobility of spirit characteristic of the young. If you want to regulate the age of public servants, it would be preferable to exclude those whose feebleness of body almost always affects their mind. The precautions about the required years of residence are useless, unjust, and indicative of a shamefully limited intelligence.

The privilege of absolving criminals condemned for certain crimes, which is granted to the president in Section 2 of Article 2, will open the door to abusive credit and intrigue. Just as Congress should never judge a trial, the president should never be permitted to pardon; this right could, at the most, be granted to Congress in case of treason to the Confederation or for military crimes. It would be better not to grant it at all.

Article 7. "The Ratification of the Conventions of nine States, shall be sufficient for the Establishment of this Constitution." It would be better to require three-quarters as in Article 5 for future changes to avoid possible secession by the four with the largest populations. The proportion of the populations of four states such as Virginia, Massachusetts, Pennsylvania, and New York or Maryland compared to the sum of the other nine is almost 32 to 23. If you take out Massachusetts but include the four others, the proportion is 30 to 35; however, they enclose New Jersey and Delaware and separate the remaining seven, so that four are in the north and three in the south.

I have not attempted to examine all the points which deserve discussion, such as the question of whether the power granted to Congress does not reduce the governments of the respective states to figureheads. I am sure, however, that the wise and zealous men who proposed the constitution must have had powerful reasons for their decisions. During the four months they devoted to this discussion they must have examined the constitution from every angle, and anyone who was not present is scarcely capable of determining why they endorsed it unanimously, although everyone doubtless saw its faults.

At a distance it is difficult to perceive the specific causes opposing general principles. A reader familiar with the true principles of legislation and government will blame me for not objecting to the power granted Congress to regulate commerce and raise sums of money in the respective states. There is no doubt that commerce should be free of taxes. It is also certain that Congress should set the amount of the taxes and demand payment, according to forms previously determined by law, but present circumstances are such that Congress needs the right to levy a direct tax and one on foreign merchandise. This should be permitted for only a definite period because the causes for disregarding general principles cannot last forever unless they are produced by an absolute need, such as the location of the country.

As long as cheap land discourages the establishment of factories and as long as there are public and private foreign debts, it will be wise to have a small tax on foreign products as well as a direct tax. This is designed to increase public revenue and to oblige the consumer to make the smallest possible use of imports. Without exercising a great deal of economy, our exports cannot match the cost of our imports and we cannot pay the existing debt. We are thus obliged to make a few exceptions to the general principles, but it would be advisable to have the preamble of each of these laws explain the reasons to the people and say how long the situation will last. This will naturally expedite matters.

The letter from the president of the convention to the president of Congress clearly implies that these judicious men believe they are offering the states not the most perfect system of legislation but the best they can devise at the present time. The reader will find a more positive proof in the remarks Dr. Franklin made to his colleagues on the final day of the session, when nothing remained save to sign the constitution.

Mr. President,

I confess that there are several parts of this constitution which I do not at present approve, but I am not sure I shall never approve them; for having lived long, I have experienced many instances of being obliged by better information or fuller consideration, to change opinions even on important subjects, which I once thought right, but found to be otherwise. It is therefore that the older I grow, the more apt I am to doubt my own judgment, and to pay more respect to the judgment of others. Most men indeed as well as most sects in Religion, think themselves in possession of all truth, and that whereever others differ from them it is so far error. . . . But though many private persons think almost as highly of their own infallibility as of that of their sect, few express it so naturally as a certain french lady, who in a dispute with her sister, said "I don't know how it happens, Sister but I meet with no body but myself, that's always in the right"—*Il n'y a que moi qui a toujours raison.*" *

In these sentiments, Sir, I agree to this Constitution with all its faults, if they are such; because I think a general Government necessary for us, and there is no form of Government but what may be a blessing to the people if well administered. . . . I doubt too whether any other Convention we can obtain may be able to make a better Constitution. For when you assemble a number of men to have the advantage of their joint wisdom, you inevitably assemble with those men, all their prejudices, their passions, their errors of opinion, their local interests, and their selfish views. From such an Assembly can a perfect production be expected? . . . Thus I consent, Sir, to this Constitution because I expect no better, and because I am not sure, that it is not the best. The opinions I have had of its errors, I sacrifice to the public good— I have never whispered a syllable of them abroad— Within these walls they were born, and here they shall die— . . .

On the whole, Sir, I cannot help expressing a wish that every member of the Convention who may still have objections to it, would with me, on this occasion doubt a little of his own infallibility—and to make manifest our unanimity, put his name to this instrument." † ⁷

The fear of granting too much power to Congress produced the weakness we found in the first federative constitution, and this doubtless explains why the authors of the second went too far in the other direction. They doubtless hoped that when the legislative assemblies of the states adopted it, this power would be reduced. They themselves will be the first to propose suitable changes.

---

* The duchess de la Ferté remarked one day to mademoiselle de Launay, who later became madame de Staël: "The truth is, my dear daughter, that I am the only one who is always right."

† Three deputies, two from Virginia and one from New York, left the assembly so that the decision would be unanimous. The state of Rhode Island took no part in any of the proceedings, and I shall not discuss the motives ascribed to this performance. It is obvious, since it has only about 60,000 inhabitants, that its existence depends on union with the other republics, and it is likely its more level-headed citizens will soon have a majority.

⁷ Ibid., pp. 641–43.

The most dangerous article is the power granted to the president of Congress to command the armies in person and to remain in office for an indefinite period. If this is not changed, our grandchildren would be justified in complaining about us. The president's power would become so great that we might have reason to fear interference with our elections by European courts, as has been the case for a long time in Poland. As such an important matter cannot be due to carelessness, we shall examine the motives that led to this decision and see if these same motives can make us wish to defer the modifications.

Lack of vigor has produced an unfortunate inactivity. To remedy it we need an extraordinary man with more than normal vigor, and we are blessed in having General Washington, who is strong, robust, and only fifty-five years old. Although he has indicated he wishes to retire to private life, the voice of the country will tell him he is needed. Those who know him well foresee the day when he will call for a convention to complete the federative constitution and reduce to reasonable limits the duties of this position which they will let him leave in order to avoid setting a dangerous precedent. No prophet is needed to predict this; an average intelligence, combined with a knowledge of American character is sufficient.

We need strong action to deal with the schemes of Great Britain for they are trying to harm us everywhere in Europe. Our minister at the Court of Saint James's is being treated with an affected negligence and His Majesty's government has not sent any representative to the United States. Men in key positions in England claim we want to go back under British rule and say they would refuse to grant such a request; this statement is denied by British subjects in America. The general opinion in Massachusetts is that these maneuvers had much to do with Shay's Rebellion. British dealings with the Indians do not bode us any good, and their troops are still holding frontier posts they should have evacuated four years ago; but a change in matters relative to the Confederation might solve this problem because for some time they have been venerating whatever is expedient.

Europe has seen all the efforts which have been made to prejudice the continent against us. It was said two groups took part in a heated presidential election and General Washington defeated Dr. Franklin by one vote. The facts are that Dr. Franklin himself proposed General Washington and accompanied him to his chair after our modest hero had acceded to the wishes of his colleagues.

I shall now report the latest news from America. Last May the internal debt of the Confederation was reduced $11 million, thanks to taxes imposed by the respective states and paid in national bonds. Meanwhile lands valued at $5 million were sold, thus reducing the internal debt to $12 million. As payment is made in bonds, which are sold at a loss in private contracts, there is reason to believe this will soon pay the internal debt. Then land can be sold at a lower price for cash, and these sales will discharge the foreign debt.

We have just heard that no one was executed as a result of Shay's Rebellion; two or three ringleaders were led to the scaffold, where to everyone's surprise they heard they were pardoned. The country was pleased with the action of the government and calm has been restored.

At the last report the General Assembly of New York was on the point of consenting to the independence of Vermont, and it was believed North Carolina would follow the same procedure for Franklin. The inhabitants of Kentucky, now estimated at some sixty thousand, decided, however, that it was still too soon for them to think about emancipation. They will remain under a trusteeship for several years more, and the gazetteers will doubtless take advantage of this opportunity to sow rumors of confusion and anarchy.

# Index

# Index

Acadia, 15
Adams, Abigail, 181
Adams, John, 135, 177, 183, 374, 387
Adams, Samuel, 191
Adams, Thomas, xii
Albany, fur trading in, 353, 363-64
Albemarle, George Monck, first duke of, 43-44
Albemarle County, 180
Albemarle Sound, 6
Allegheny Mountains, 304
*Alliance*, 186
Altamaha River, 287
American colonies, 5-64; Raynal on, 207-12
American Revolution, causes of, 60-62, 108-10
Amphictyonic Council, 168
Anabaptists, 22, 43, 212
Anderson, Adam, 58
André, Major John, 186-87
Andros, Sir Edmund, 32, 65
Anglican church, 15, 18, 23, 43, 48, 50-52, 157, 160-61, 339
Annapolis, 189
Anne, queen of England, 52-53, 197
*Annual Register*, 365
Anson, George, Baron Anson, 255
Antinomians, 22
Antoni, Antonia, xvi
Appleton, Thomas, xvi
Apprentices, 121, 330-31
Aquidneck Island (Rhode Island), 23
*Arabella*, 19
Archdale, John, 52
Argall, Sir Samuel, 29
Argentiera [Cimolus in southwest Cyclades], 369
Arnold, Benedict, 188-89, 341, 343
Articles of Confederation, 79, 119, 204, 329, 394, 397

Arundel, Thomas Howard, second earl of, 18
Auberteuil, Michel René Hilliard de, 2

Bacon, Francis, 152
Bahama Islands, 49
Bailey, John, 225
Baltimore, Cecilius Calvert, second Baron, 27-28, 38, 65
Baltimore, George Calvert, first Baron, 27
Baltimore, 189, 318
Bancroft, George, 183
Banister, John, 334
Barbados, 27
Barrington, Admiral Samuel, 268
Bartram, John, 334
Beaumarchais, Caron de, 318
Belknap, Jeremy, 25-26
Berkeley, John, first Baron Berkeley of Stratton, 30, 32, 43
Berkeley, Sir William, 13, 43
Bermuda, 10
Bernard, Sir Francis, 59-60
Billingsport, 195
Blackdon (possibly Blagden), Major Samuel, 187
Blackstone, Sir William, 154, 197
Blackwell, John, 39
Blair, John, 392
Bland, Colonel Richard, 8-9
Blue Ridge Mountains, 180
Boston, 26, 62, 67, 141, 181, 186, 193, 304, 306, 384
Bradford, William, 17
Brandywine, battle of, 195, 262-63
Brazil, 29-30
Breda, treaty of, 31
Brest, 290
Bristol, Eng., 15, 70
Brittany, 194, 377
Brownists, 22

Buckingham, George Villiers, first duke of, 18
Buffon, comte de, 242, 373
Bull, Captain Joseph, 358
Burgh, James, 251
Burgoyne, General John, 264-65, 279
Burke, Aedanus, 336
Burke, Edmund, 70-71, 258
Butler, Captain Walter, 343
Butterfield, Samuel, 348
Byron, Admiral John, 268

Caluélan, chevalier de, 287
Calvert, Cecilius, *see* Baltimore, second Baron
Calvert, George, *see* Baltimore, first Baron
Calvert, Leonard, 27
Campbell, Captain Colin, 182, 267
Canada, 384
Canassetego, 363
Cape Breton Island, 306
Cape Charles, 9
Cape Cod, 14, 16-17
Cape Hatteras, 6-7
Cape Henry, 9
Caraman, Victor Maurice Riquet, chevalier de, 185
Carleton, General Guy, 270, 272, 386
Carmigniani, Giovanni, xvi
Carr, Dabney, 67
Carteret, Sir George, 30, 32-33, 43
Carteret, John, first earl of Granville, 52, 54
Carteret, Captain Philip, 32
Carver, John, 17
Catherine II, empress of Russia, xiv
Catholics, 22, 24, 27-28, 31, 43, 156, 163
Census, estimated 1775 and 1783, 284-85
Chadds Ford, 263
Charles I, king of England, 12-13, 25, 58, 60, 174, 358
Charles II, king of England, 13, 22, 24, 30-31, 33, 50, 59, 60, 65, 108, 214, 225
Charleston, xiv, 49, 54, 187-88, 239, 274
Charter of Privileges (of Penn), 95-96
Chastellux, François Jean, marquis de, 365
Chesapeake Bay, 6, 9, 180, 189

Chester, 38
Christianity, 199-200, 357, 361
Christina Creek, 263
Cincinnati, Society of the, xv, 336-43
Clarendon, Edward Hyde, first earl of, 43-44
Clark, General George Rogers, 183-84, 353
Clark, Captain Oliver, 194-95
Clayton, Dr. John, 334
Clergy, privilege of, 196-97
Climate, *see* United States
Clinton, General Sir Henry, 188, 190, 259, 263-64, 267, 292
Coligny, Admiral Gaspard de, 44
Colle, xiii, xvi, 342
Colleton, James, 51
Colleton, Sir John, 44
Colonial governments: relations with king and British government, 59; relations with Indians, 214
Commager, Henry S., 17
Commerce, freedom shackled by monopoly of Farmers General in France, 380
Commercial relations with Great Britain, 71; with France, 318-24
Committee of Safety, 68
Committee of Six, 112-13
Concord, British raid on, 181
Condorcet, Marie Jean Antoine Nicolas de Caritat, marquis de, xv, 110, 374, 382
Condorcet, marquise de, xv
Conestoga, Pa., 358
Confederation, 169, 300-301, 312, 386, 392, 398, 401-2
Congregationalists, 22-23, 43
Congress, 143, 163, 168-71, 184, 186-88, 191-93, 203, 299, 300, 302, 304, 308-9, 311, 314-15, 317, 329, 340-42, 365-66, 371, 386-87, 392, 396-99, 400-401
Connecticut, 21, 65, 182, 186, 188, 339; founding, 24; charter, 24; coming of Revolution in, 67-70; suffrage and election requirements, 81; composition of legislature, 86; elections, 88; courts, 92; election of secretary and treasurer, 94
Connecticut River, 24

Cononicut, 224, 292
Constantinople, 384
Constitution, U.S., *see* United States
Cooke, Mr., *see* Goffe, Colonel William
Corbin, Margaret, 186
Cornstalk, Chief, 351
Cornwallis, Charles, 189-90, 193, 259, 265, 319
Cornwallis, Thomas, 27
Council for New England, 16
Counterfeiting, 309
Cowes, 27
Cradock, Matthew, 19
Craven, William Craven, earl of, 43-44
Cresap, Captain Michael, 353
Crèvecoeur, Michel Guillaume Jean de, 333
Cromwell, 12-13, 26, 28, 60, 174
Crowninshield, Elizabeth, 181
Culpeper, Thomas Culpeper, second Baron, 108

Danville, 302
Darby, 263
Deane, Silas, 215, 249
Declaration of Independence, xvii, 76, 157
Declaration of Rights, Virginia, 73-77, 80, 83, 87, 93, 133, 144, 149, 160, 164, 175, 196, 198-99, 202, 301, 345
Delaware, 29, 33, 398; founding, 38; lack of aristocracy, 65; suffrage, 78-85; legislative, executive, and judicial power, 86-92; chief magistrate, 89; religion in, 166; influence of, 395
Delaware Bay, 28-29
Delaware Indians, 353, 358
Delaware River (South River), 30, 183, 261-62, 264
De la Warr, Thomas West, third Baron, 10, 30
Démeunier, Jean Nicolas, 371
Denmark, 26
Denton, Daniel, 225
Denys of Halicarnassus, 338, 380-81
De Pauw, Cornelius, 243
Derby, Elias Hasket, 181
Descartes, René, 164

Destouches, Charles-René-Dominique Sochet, chevalier, 189
Detroit, 183, 353-54
Deux Ponts, Christian de Forbach, marquis de, 279
Dinwiddie, Governor Robert, 62
*Dolphin*, 291
Donop, Colonel Carl Emil Curt von, 194
Dorchester, 24
Douglass, William, 15-17, 29, 212, 225, 228
Drake, Admiral Francis, 6
Dudley, Thomas, 19
Dunkers, 219
Dunmore, John Murray, fourth earl of, 66, 105-7, 350-51, 353, 355
Dutch, 29-32, 51

Eaton, Theophilus, 19
Edict of Nantes, revocation of, 50, 323
Egg Harbor, 216
Elections, 84, 127
El Ferrol, 290
Elizabeth, queen of England, 5, 9
Elkton, 189
Endecott, John, 19
*Endymion*, 256
England, 157, 174, 298, 323, 328, 330, 365, 372, 378, 380, 384-87; debt, 307; colonial imports from, 312; colonial exports to, 313; commercial practices, 321-22; taxes, 378-79
Episcopalians, 31
Estaing, Charles Hector Théodat, comte d', 263, 318, 333
Euclid, 132
Evans, John, 42, 100
Ezechiel (South Carolina boy), 194

Fabius Cunctator, 341
Fairfax, Thomas Fairfax, sixth Baron, 29
Farmers General, tobacco monopoly, 320-21, 324, 379-80
Faure (translator), xv
Fay, Bernard, xv
Federal Convention, 392
Ferté, duchess de la, 400
Field (young Virginian), 354

Finch, Daniel, *see* Nottingham
Flatbush, 259
Flat-head Indians, 359
Fletcher, Colonel, 99-100
Florence, xi, 137-38, 176
Florida, 238
Foace, Stanislas, 365
*Foedera*, 58
Fort Casimir (New Castle), 30
Fothergill, Dr. John, 245
*Fowey*, 105
France, 125, 157, 164, 187, 191, 318, 320, 322, 330, 337, 365, 380, 384, 386; behavior, 247-57; commercial competition with England, 321; commercial practices, 322-23; Farmers General monopoly in, 324; abolishes titles of those becoming merchants, 377; taxes, 378-79
Franklin, Benjamin: Polly Baker story, 215; at French court, 248, 273; on immigration, 325-33; on the savages, 359-64; letter on Constitution, 399-401
Franklin, state of, 304, 402
Freehold, 264
French navy, 252, 254
Frogs Point, *see* Throgs Neck
Fundamental Constitutions of Carolina, 45-58

Gage, General Thomas, 181
Galileo, 132, 164
Gasden's Wharf, 194
Gates, General Horatio, 265, 341
Gates, Sir Thomas, 9-10
Gee, Joshua, 42
Genesee Country, 187
Geneva, 169, 176
George I, king of England, 53
George II, king of England, 257
George III, king of England, 11, 118, 319
Georgia, 144, 333, 343, 389; founding, 54; denies right of a man with title to hold public office, 79; legislative power, 86; chief magistrate, 89; suffrage, 81-82; and entails, 146; Constitution, 147; exclusion of Catholics, 166; slavery in, 344, 386

Gérard, Conrad-Alexandre, 268
Germain, George Sackville, first viscount Sackville, 190
Germany, 22, 328
Gibbon, Edward, 168, 203
Gibbon, Widow, 343
Gibraltar, 254, 291
Gilbert, Sir John, 14
Glasgow, 385
Glover, Colonel John, 261
Goffe, Thomas, 19
Goffe, Colonel William, 358
Goochland County, 67
Gookin (of Pa.), 104
Gordon, Lord, 385
Gorges, Edward, Lord, 18
Gorges, Sir Ferdinando, 14-16, 18, 25
Gosnold, Captain Bartholomew, 14
Gourgues, Dominique de, 44
Grant, General James, 259
Grasse, Admiral François Joseph Paul de, 274
Great Britain, 13, 107, 110, 150, 173, 298, 312; relations with colonies, 4; Parliament, 12-13, 60, 106, 108-10, 160, 197, 306, 343, 373; colonial exports to, 71; Virigina separates from, 72, 76; colonial trade prohibited elsewhere, 109; chief cause of scarcity of money, 307; change in attitude, 313; and Farmers General, 324; taxes on luxuries, 372; and national debt, 378; peace treaty with United States, 386-87; American law about, 390-92; attempts to harm United States in Europe, 401
Greene, General Nathanael, 183, 187, 189, 264
Grenada, 268
Grenville, Sir Richard, 6
Grimaldi, Don Geronimo, marquis de, 290
Grimball, Paul, 51
Groton, 348
Guy, John, 104

Hale, Captain Nathan, 186-87
Hamilton, Henry, 183, 353-54
Hamilton, James Hamilton, second marquis of, 18, 23

Hampton, 61, 319
Hancock, John, xiii, 69-70
Hanover, 13, 53, 118
Hanson, Hans, 363
Harlem Heights, battle of, 181, 260
Hartford, 24, 65
Harvie, John, 342
Havana, 186
Hawke, David, 154
Hawley, Jerome, 27
Hayley, William, 168, 203
Hazard, Ebenezer, 18, 22
Head-of-Elk (Elkton), 180
Heister, General Leopold Philip von, 259
Henry IV, king of France, 15
Henry, Governor Patrick, 381
Herman, Augustin, 225
Hessians, 259, 262
Hewatt, Alexander, 44, 52-54
Hillsborough, Wills Hill, first earl of, 63
Hogendorp, M. van, xiv
Holland, xiii, 13, 15, 256
Howe, Admiral Richard Howe, first Earl, 180
Howe, General Sir William Howe, fifth Viscount, 180-82, 258-61, 263
Hubbard, William, 20
Hudson, Captain Henry, 15, 29
Hudson River, 15, 29-30
Huguenots, 323
Humphreys, Colonel David, 187, 194
Hunt, Captain, 15
Hutchins, Thomas, 375
Hutchinson, Anne, 26
Hutchinson, Thomas, 16, 20-21, 211-13, 225, 348, 358

Illinois, 183, 353
Immigration, *see* United States
Independents, 22
India Company, 62
Indians, 6, 183, 317, 401; forays in South Carolina, 49; sold in the islands by pirates, 50, 52; chief male occupations, 211; character, 214, 348, 349, 350, 352, 361, 363; purchase of land from, 17, 225; give little assistance during Rev-

olution, 272; independent tribes, 348; council house, 348; treatment of prisoners, 349; and marriage, 349; wampum, 355; implements, 355; food and pottery, 356; and alcohol, 356; adornment, 356; religious beliefs, 357; powwows, 357; record keeping, 361
Ireland, 306, 312, 328, 378
Italy, xii, xiii, xvi

Jackson, Richard, 37
James I, king of England, 8-12, 16, 29-30, 174, 197
James II, king of England (York, duke of), 28, 30, 32, 33, 36, 38, 40, 43, 49, 50, 59, 65, 118, 214, 300, 306
James River, 9-10, 71, 341, 381
Jamestown, 9, 66
Jefferson, Thomas, xi, xii, xiv, 369, 375; comment on *Researches*, xv; friend of Mazzei, xvi; Declaration of Rights, 73; Declaration of Independence, 76; article on education, 145; essay on American court of chancery, 155; on religious freedom, 157-60; *Notes on the State of Virginia*, 164-65; visit to Europe, 244; proposal about slavery, 345; story about Logan, 352
Jeffreys, Thomas, 375
John, king of England, 92
Johnson, Lady Arabella, 20
Johnson, Isaac, 19
Johnson, Governor Robert, 53-54
*Johnston*, xiii
Judge, a Shawnee Indian, 350-51

Kanawha River, 353
Kaskaskia Indians, 354
Keith, William, 104
Kentucky, 242, 301, 302-4, 402
Kingsbridge, 182, 260
Kirkland, Samuel, 272
Kizeing, John, 30
Knox, General Henry, 264

Lacedaemon, 141
Lafayette, Marie Joseph P. Y. R. Gilbert du Motier, marquis de, 184-

Lafayette, marquis de (*cont.*)
    85, 187, 189-93, 264, 333, 340, 342-43,
    382; on slavery, 346
Lancaster, Treaty of, 360
Lane, Ralph, 6
Langdon, Edward, 29
Laudonnière, René de, 44
Launay, mademoiselle de (later
    Madame de Staël), 400
Leavit, Thomas, 25
Lee, General Charles, 71, 182, 263-64,
    266, 341
Leghorn, xi, xii
Legislative power: term and salary, 78;
    no danger to liberty, 78; titles have
    no influence, 79
L'Enfant, Major Pierre Charles, 337
Lennox, Ludovick Stuart, second duke
    of, 18
Leopold, Grand Duke of Tuscany, xiii,
    xvii
*Letter to the Abbé Raynal,* 218
Lexington, battle of, 181
*Lexington,* 291
Leyden, 16, 334
Lincoln, General Benjamin, 341, 384
Lloyd, Thomas, 99
Locke, John, 45-48, 237
Logan, a Mingo chief, 352, 353
London, xi, 28, 34, 36, 38, 42, 62, 138,
    158, 183, 329, 331, 357, 373-75, 386
London Company, 9, 16, 29, 209
Longchamps, Pierre de, *Impartial His-
    tory,* 2, 287, 343
Long Island, 24, 30, 186, 258-59
Louis XVI, king of France, 250, 251,
    253, 292
Low Countries, 312
Ludwell, Philip, 51-52
Luzerne, Anne-César de la, 370

Mably, Gabriel Bonnot de, xiv, 2, 94,
    374; on American laws and English
    sovereignty, 115; on common peo-
    ple's envy of their superiors, 121;
    on virtues of the Ancients, 122; on
    importance of magistrates, 125; crit-
    icizes Pennsylvania Constitution,
    127; criticizes freedom of press, 132-
    34; criticizes freedom of assembly,

135-36; aristocratic principles, 140-
    41; administrative ideas, 143-44; on
    government salaries, 146; disap-
    proves of freedom of conscience,
    156; on unlimited power for Con-
    gress, 168, 170-71; advises special
    privileges for rich, 173
McClurg, James, 392
Macdougall, General Alexander, 261
Madagascar, 52
Madison, Bishop James, 111
Madison, James, 365, 369, 392
Magdalen College, 39
Magna Carta, 92, 160
Maine, 304
Malaga, 15
Mansfield, William Murray, first earl
    of, 154
Mantua, xii
Marmontel, xiv
Marraro, Howard R., xi
Martha's Vineyard, 15
Martin, Joseph, xii
Martin, Mrs. Joseph, *see* Mazzei, Mrs.
    Philip
Maryland, 190, 398; founding, 27; nam-
    ing, 27; growth of population, 28;
    House of Delegates, 86; election of
    Senate, 88; suffrage, 140; removal
    of justices, 148; religion in, 166;
    Raynal's errors about, 235; college,
    326
Mason, George, 86, 286, 341, 392
Mason, John, 15-16, 18, 25-26
Massachusetts, 181, 191, 314, 398; found-
    ing, 14-20; General Court, 20-21,
    90, 383-84; charter, 59, 214, 300;
    coming of Revolution in, 60-65;
    blockade of Boston in, 67; suffrage,
    82; elections, 85, 88-89; power of
    magistrates, 89-90; Constitution,
    135; Mably on, 139-41, 143-44, 146;
    and standing armies, 147; removal
    of justices, 148; favors Protestant-
    ism, 166; divided by New Hamp-
    shire, 304; slavery in, 344; taxes,
    383; Shays's Rebellion, 383-85, 401
Massachusetts Bay, 20
Massachusetts Bay Colony, 25, 306-7
Massasoit, 17, 23, 350

Mauduit Duplessis, Lieutenant Colonel Thomas-Antoine, chevalier de, 194-95, 264
Mauritius, 290
Mayflower Compact, 17
Mazzei, Elisabetta, xvi
Mazzei, Guiseppe, xi
Mazzei, Jacopo, xi
Mazzei, Mrs. Philip, xii, xiii
Meade, David, 366
Meade, Major Everard, 185
Meade, Colonel Richard K., 185-86, 192
Meade, Mrs., 185
Mechunk Creek, 192
Menéndez, Pedro de Avilés, 44
Menonists, 199
*Mercure de France*, xv
Metacomet, a Shawnee Indian, 350
Mingo Indians, 352-53
Minisink Hills, 264
Minorca, 291
Mirabeau, Gabriel Riqueti, comte de, 338-40, 381, 385
Mississippi River, 183, 301
Money, paper, *see* United States
Monmouth, Battle of, 186, 195
Montesquieu, 41
Monticello, xii, xiv, 167
Monts, Pierre du Guast, sieur de, 15
Moore, James, 53-54
Morgan (soldier), 191
Morgan, Daniel, 341
Morgan, Sir Henry, 50
Morris, Robert, 324, 379
Morris, Mrs. Robert, 370
Morton, Governor Joseph, 50
Muggletonians, 22, 231

Nantucket Island, 334
Natchez Indians, 349
Naumkeag (Salem), 224
Neal, Daniel, *The History of New-England*, 209
Nelson, Thomas, 184
New Albion, 29
New Amsterdam, 30
New Belgium, 29-31, 38, 49, 300
New Castle, 40
New England, 32, 33, 316, 358; famine in, 19; and Quakers, 43; commerce and fishing, 109; inheritance law, 146; intolerance, 156-57; Raynal on, 209-15; expedition against Canada, 306; colleges, 326; soil, 368
New Hampshire, 21, 91, 300, 304, 384, 389; founding, 25-26; Upper House, 65; elections, 85; General Court, 86; suffrage, 88; chief magistrate, 89; Constitution revised, 94; removal of justices, 148; favors Protestantism, 166
New Haven, 24
New Jersey, 29-30, 38, 183, 313, 398; founding, 32; division and unification, 33; Legislative Council, 86; magistrate's power, 89, 91; suffrage, 94, 140; Catholics excluded from some positions in, 166; Raynal on, 216-18; college, 326
*New Jersey Gazette*, 191
New Netherlands, 29-30
New Plymouth, *see* Plymouth Colony
Newport, Captain Christopher, 9
Newport, R.I., 24, 189
New Rochelle, 181, 261
Newton, Isaac, 132, 187; Newtonian principle, 164
Newtown, 23-24
New York: founding, 29-30; civil and religious liberty in, 31; relationship with Great Britain, 31; and Andros, 33; shipment of tea not permitted to dock in, 62-63; suffrage, 82, 140; magistrate, 89; Constitution, 90; ballot, 128; Mably on, 144; removal of justices, 148; freedom of worship, except to Catholics, 156; Constitution, 163, 188, 189, 300-301, 306, 309, 326, 389, 398, 400; General Assembly, 402
New York City, 181-82, 300
Nicholson, Sir Francis, 53
Nicolls, Governor Richard, 225
Noailles, Louis-Marie-Antoine, vicomte de, 293
Noailles, Emmanuel-Marie-Louis, marquis de, 292
Norfolk, 66, 370
North, Frederick Lord, 253, 255

North Carolina: legislative, executive, and judicial power, 86-92; and entails, 146; Catholics excluded from some positions in, 166, 185; Constitution, 301, 304; slavery in, 344, 386, 402; *see also* Two Carolinas

Northern Neck, 29

North River (Hudson), 30

Northumberland County, 56

Norton, Francis, 26

Nottingham, Daniel Finch, second earl of, 152

Nova Scotia, 156

Oglethorpe, James, 54

Ohio River, 303, 353

Ohonooraro, Adam, 272

Oldys, William, 7

Oneida Indians, 270, 358

Onondaga, 363

Osborne, Francis, marquis of Carmarthen and later fifth duke of Leeds, 386-87

Paine, Thomas, 218, 251, 255-57, 262, 269-70, 273, 274-75, 276, 282, 318

Palatine Court, 50-51

Paoli, Pasquali, 248

Paris, xiv, 138, 158, 329, 371, 375

Parliament, *see* Great Britain

Pawtucket River, 23

Pelham, 261

Penn, William: charter from Charles II, 33-34; agreement with emigrants, 34; charter for province, 35-36; troubles with followers, 37, 227; refusal to pay taxes, 37-38; 1701 Assembly, 40-41; new system of government, 41; financial difficulties, 42; Charter of Privileges, 95-96; Remonstrances of 1704 and 1707, 97-105; Mably on, 128; and freedom of worship, 156; Raynal on, 224-29

Pennsylvania, 92, 180, 188, 190, 192, 308, 314, 328, 334, 360, 371, 375, 387, 398; founding and charter, 33-35; as refuge for French Protestants, 51; suffrage, 81-82; and Penn family, 65; legislative power, 86; limit to

time of service, 88; chief magistrate, 89; Council of Censors, 113; Mably on, 127-29, 130-33, 135, 137-41, 143-44, 146, 161, 172; religious freedom, 156, 165; term of office, 169; Raynal on, 218-23; college, 326; slavery in, 344

Percy, Hugh, son of earl of Northumberland, 181, 259

Perth Amboy, 216

Philadelphia, 36, 38, 40, 62-63, 69, 100-103, 130, 188, 192, 194, 262-63, 324, 334, 337, 370, 387, 392

Philip V, duke of Anjou and later king of Spain, 253

Phillips, General William, 189-90

Pisa, xvi, 244

Piscataqua, 25

Pitt, William, 63, 109, 255

Plato, 176, 178, 375

Plutarch, 338, 380-81

Plymouth Colony, 23, 350

Plymouth Company, 14-17, 23, 209

Plymouth Council, 18, 25, 210

Poland, xvi, 401

Pontiac, Ottawa chief, 353-54

Popham, George, 14

Popham, Sir John, 14

Portsmouth, R.I., 24

Portsmouth, Va., 189

Potomac River, 27-28, 341, 381

Powhatan County, 184

Powhatan River, 9

Presbyterians, 15, 22, 157

Press, liberty of, *see* United States

Price, Richard, 373-74

Princeton, 262

Prisoners, British treatment of, 267

Protestants, 163

Providence, 23-24

Prussia, 369

Puritans, 15-16

Purry, Jean Pierre, 54

Purrysburg, 54

Putnam, General Israel, 258

Quakers, 22, 36, 43, 82, 100, 104, 157, 199, 212, 229, 308, 335, 366; Raynal's erroneous description, 230;

Quakers (*cont.*)
 Paine's letter to, 232-33; classes of,
  233
Quebec, 108
Quitrent, 28, 32, 37, 236

Raleigh, Sir Walter, 5-9, 14
Raleigh, 6
Rall, Colonel Johann, 262
Ramsay, David, 192, 365, 375
Ramsey, David, 58
Randolph, Anne Meade, 185
Randolph, Edmund, 392
Randolph, Peyton, 343
Randolph, Richard, Jr., 185
Rapidan River, 192
Rappahannock River, 28-29, 192
Raynal, Guillaume-Thomas François,
  xiv, 2, 7, 318-19, 349, 372; on Geor-
  gia, 54-55; on governments, 93; on
  founding of colonies, 206-10; on
  Pennsylvania, 218-23; on Penn,
  225-29; on French aid to Ameri-
  cans, 247-48; sympathy for British
  cause, 255; on battle on Long Is-
  land, 258-61; considers Americans
  cowardly, 268; counsel to France,
  Spain, and United States, 276-78;
  contradictions, 279; errors widely
  believed, 287
Red Bank, 194-95
Religion: intolerance in Massachusetts,
  22; freedom of, 24, 31-32, 36; *see
  also* United States
Remonstrances, 97-104
Representatives, requirements for election, 81
*Reprisal,* 291
Réunion Island, 290
Revel, John, 19
Rhode Island, 186, 189, 193, 395, 400;
  founding, 21; charter, 24; cattle,
  26, 242; tolerance of Quakers, 43;
  governor, 65; suffrage and election
  requirements, 81; religious free-
  dom, except for Catholics, 156
Ribaut, Jean, 44
Rice, Howard C., Jr., 365
Richmond, 69, 72, 190
*Richmond Enquirer,* xvi

Riedesel, Baron von, xiv
Roanoke Island, 6, 9, 54
Roanoke River, 53
Roberts, Colonel Owen, 194
Robertson, William, 203
Robinson, John, 16
Rochambeau, Jean Baptiste Donatien
  de Vimeur, comte de, 189, 191,
  313
Rodney, Vice Admiral George, 274,
  319
Rome, 141, 171
Romulus, 122, 380
Round Head Indians, 359
Roxbury, 24
Rymer, Thomas, 58

Sacy, Claude-Louis Michel de, 193
Sagadahoc, 14
Saint Christopher, 27
Saint-Clair, Arthur, 265, 387-92
St. John, J. Hector, *see* Crèvecoeur
Saint Lawrence, Gulf of, 6
Saint-Simon, Claude-Henri de Rou-
  vroy, comte de, 190, 293
Saint Vincent, 268
Salem, 20, 22, 67, 181
Salinas, Dr., xi
Salisbury, Robert Cecil, earl of, 9
Saltonstall, Sir Richard, 19
Sandwich, John Montague, fourth earl
  of, 253
Santo Domingo, 320-21
Saratoga, battle of, 265, 341
Savages, *see* Indians
Savannah River, 54, 287
Sayle, William, 49
Schuylkill, 263
Schwartz, Joachim J. (pseud. of mar-
  quis de Condorcet), 346
Scotland, 56, 154, 309, 312, 328
Scott, General Charles, 184
Seekonk, 22-23
Separatists, 22
Shaftesbury, Anthony Ashley Cooper,
  first earl of, 44
Shawnee (Sawanahaac) Indians, 72,
  350, 352-53, 355
Shawomet, 23

Shays, Daniel, 383-84

Shays's Rebellion, 401-2

Sheepscot or Nagwasac, 224

Shegenaba, 353-55

Shepard, Colonel (later General) William, 261, 384

Short, William, 369

Simcoe, Colonel John Graves, 191

Slavery, *see* United States

Smith, John, 181

Smith, Captain John, 9, 18

Smith, Mrs. John, 182

Smith, Thomas, 7-8

Smith, Landgrave Thomas, 52

Smith, William, 30

Smith, William S., 181-83, 262, 337

Smyrna, xi, 239

Society of the Cincinnati, *see* Cincinnati, Society of the

Somers, Sir George, 9-10

Southampton, Henry Wriothesley, third earl of, 11

Southampton, 16

South Carolina, 163, 185, 189, 194, 314, 336, 365; and rice, 52, 67; elections, 88; Constitution, 129, 140; favors Protestantism, 166; slavery in, 344, 385; *see also* Two Carolinas

Spain, 330

Spanish Armada, 6

Sparta, 174

Springfield, 24, 384

Staël, Madame de, *see* Launay

Stamp Act, 61

Stanislas, king of Poland, xvi

Staten Island, 268

Steuben, Baron Friedrich Wilhelm von, 187-88, 340

Stiles, Ezra, 358

Stirling, Lord (William Alexander), 264

Stone, William L., 272

Stono Ferry, 194

Stormont, David Murray, seventh Viscount, 253, 291-92

Story (or Storer), Augustine, 25

Stuarts, 26, 118

Stuyvesant, Peter, 30

Suffrage, 83, 128-29

Sullivan, General John, 182-83, 187

Superior, Lake, 359

Susquehanna Indians, 361

Susquehanna River, 187

Sweden, 176

Swedes, 30

Tarbox, Rev. Increase, 5

Tarquins, 122, 174, 338

Taylor, Lieutenant, 187

Taxation: in France and England, 378; in United States, 399

Ternay, Charles Louis d'Arsac, chevalier de, 191

Throgs Neck (Frogs Point), 181, 260

Ticonderoga, 265

Titus Livius, 338, 380-81

Tory, 313

Toulon, 249, 290

Tower of London, 18

Trenton, 183, 262

Trumbull, Governor Jonathan, 94, 270

Turgot, Anne Robert, baron de l'Aulne, 249, 288-93, 373-74, 378

Turnbull, Dr. Andrew, 239

Tuscany, xi, xii, 243

Two Carolinas, 190, 192; founding, 43-45; influence of Locke's system on, 49; problems with governor, 51; religious quarrels, 51; divided into South Carolina and North Carolina, 54; coming of Revolution in, 67-68; suffrage, 78, 85; legislative, executive, and judicial power, 86-92

United Colonies, declared free and independent states, 73

United States, 164, 193, 203, 298-99, 302-3, 372, 383; immigration to, 56-58, 325-35; name adopted, 77; elections and salaries, 84; legislative, executive, and judicial power, 86-92; liberty of the press, 132-34; supreme courts, 148-50; religious liberty, 156-66; Revolutionary period, 167; confederation, 168-71; and English constitution, 174; climate, 240-41; soil, 241-42; paper money, 306-11; taxes, 309-10; national debt, 312-14;

United States (*cont.*)
commercial credit, 315; commerce with France, 320-24; cheap land, 326; manufacturing, 329; slavery in, 344-47; recent books about, 365-75; social distinctions, 385; peace treaty with Great Britain, 386-92; Constitution, 393, 394-401; *see also* individual states

Valley Forge, 264
Vergennes, Charles Gravier, comte de, 288, 291
Vermont, 384; attempt to evict residents, 300; appeal to Congress to be made a separate state, 300; upcoming independence, 402
Vincennes, Fort, 183
Virginia, xii, xiv, xv, 19, 28-30, 32, 45, 94, 125, 143, 154, 180, 184, 185, 189-92, 202, 300-301, 312-14, 316, 334, 351, 353, 360-61, 373, 385; founding, 5-13; division into counties, 66; coming of Revolution in, 72-73; suffrage and government, 79-81, 141; House of Delegates and Senate, 86; legislative, executive, and judicial power, 86-92; Senate cannot propose laws, 88; chief magistrate, 89; courts, 92; justices of peace, 91-92; people retained only right to elect legislative body, 93; education, 145; entails proscribed in, 146; Court of Appeals, 152; religious intolerance, 43, 156-57; freedom after Revolution, 158, 160-61; Raynal on, 235-37; social customs, 237, 366, 368-69; drainage, 240; horses, 242; grapes, 243-45; emancipation of Kentucky, 302-4; Virginia capes, 318; college, 326; slavery in, 345, 386; tax for the poor, 367; tobacco, 308; causes of poverty in, 368; climate, 370; books on, 375; delegates to convention, 392; Constitution, 395, 398, 400; *see also* Declaration of Rights; Virginia General Assembly
Virginia Company patent, 14
Virginia Convention, 72

Virginia General Assembly, 13, 108, 111, 184-85, 191-92, 196, 315, 346, 386; created, 11; Articles of Capitulation, 12; representation in, 66; and separation from Great Britain, 72; and secret ballot, 128; and education, 145; and religion, 158-60; Memorial and Remonstrance to, 197-203; and Kentucky, 301-2; payment of debts, 316; offers stock to Washington, 341, 381-82; and liberty of conscience, 385

Wales, Prince of, 28
Warwick, Sir Robert Dudley, earl of, 18, 24
Warwick, 23
Washington, George, 125, 180, 182, 184-87, 189, 191-92, 194, 264, 266; selected commander-in-chief of troops, 69; retreat across New Jersey, 183, 261; battle on Long Island, 258-59; and Society of Cincinnati, 337-38, 340, 342; declines stock, 341, 381-82; character, 342-43, 401; delegate to convention, 392; letter submitting Constitution, 393
Washington, Fort, 181, 186
Watauga, 304
Watertown, 24
Watson, Luke, 225
Wayne, General Anthony, 188, 264
Weiser, Conrad, 363
Wentworth, William, 25
Wethersfield, 24
Westchester, 181
West Indies, 109
Westminster, treaty of, 31
West Point, 189
Wheelwright, John, 25-26
Wheelwright and Company, 224
Wheelwright Deed, 25
White, John, 6-8
White Plains, 261, 264
Wight, Thomas, 25
William III and Mary, king and queen of England, 28, 33, 59, 197
William and Mary, College of, 111
Williams, Roger, 22-24, 357

Williamsburg, 66, 68, 72, 107, 158, 184-85, 190, 219, 293, 321, 350, 360, 365-66; government moved from, 301
Wilmington Church, 263
Windsor, 28
Windsor Castle, 24, 28, 33
Winslow, Edward, 17
Winthrop, John, 19
Witchcraft in New England, 212
Wolf, a Shawnee Indian, 350-51
Women, American, 235
Woods, William, 180

Wright, Nathaniel, 19
Wyllys, George, 94
Wythe, George, 392

Yoacomaco (St. Mary's), 28
Yoghtanawa, Thomas, 272
York, duke of, *see* James II
York, 106
York County, Virginia, 319
York River, 10, 266, 351
Yorktown, 184, 188, 190, 275, 313
Young, J., 19

# Date Due